Alice in the Country of Joker

~Circus and Liar's Game~

- STORY -

This is a love adventure game based on Lewis Carroll's *Alice in Wonderland* that develops into a completely different storyline. This Wonderland is a fairy tale gone very wrong—or very *right*, if you like a land of gunfights where the "Hatters" are a mafia syndicate.

The main character is far from a romantic. In fact, she's especially sick of love relationships.

In *Alice in the Country of Joker*, Alice can experience the changing seasons that were absent in the other storylines. The Circus comes along with April Season, the season of lies. The Circus's dazzle and glitter hides its terrible purpose, and as Alice tries to wrap her head around the shifting world, she falls deeper and deeper into a nefarious trap.

When this story begins, Alice is already close to the inhabitants of Wonderland but hasn't fallen in love. Each role-holder treasures Alice differently with their own bizarre love—those who want to *protect* Alice from the Joker are competing with those who would rather be jailers. In the Country of Joker, there's more at stake than Alice's romantic affections...

SEVEN SEAS ENTERTAINMENT PRESENTS

Alice IN THE COUNTRY OF Joker

CIRCUS AND LIAR'S GAME

story by QUINROSE / art by MAMENOSUKE FUJIMARU VOLUME 4

TRANSLATION
Angela Liu

ADAPTATION
Lianne Sentar

LETTERING AND LAYOUT
Laura Scoville

LOGO DESIGN
Courtney Williams

COVER DESIGN
Nicky Lim

PROOFREADER
Shanti Whitesides

MANAGING EDITOR
Adam Arnold

PUBLISHER
Jason DeAngelis

Seven Seas books may be purchased in bulk for educational, business, or promotional use. For information on bulk purchases, please contact Macmillan Corporate & Premium Sales Department at 1-800-221-7945 (ext 5442) or write specialmarkets@macmillan.com.

ISBN: 978-1-626920-01-9

Printed in Canada

First Printing: February 2014

10 9 8 7 6 5 4 3 2 1

FOLLOW US ONLINE: ***www.gomanga.com***

READING DIRECTIONS

This book reads from ***right to left***, Japanese style. If this is your first time reading manga, you start reading from the top right panel on each page and take it from there. If you get lost, just follow the numbered diagram here. It may seem backwards at first, but you'll get the hang of it! Have fun!!

1
2
3
4
5
6
7
8
9

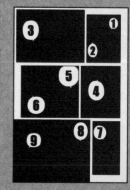

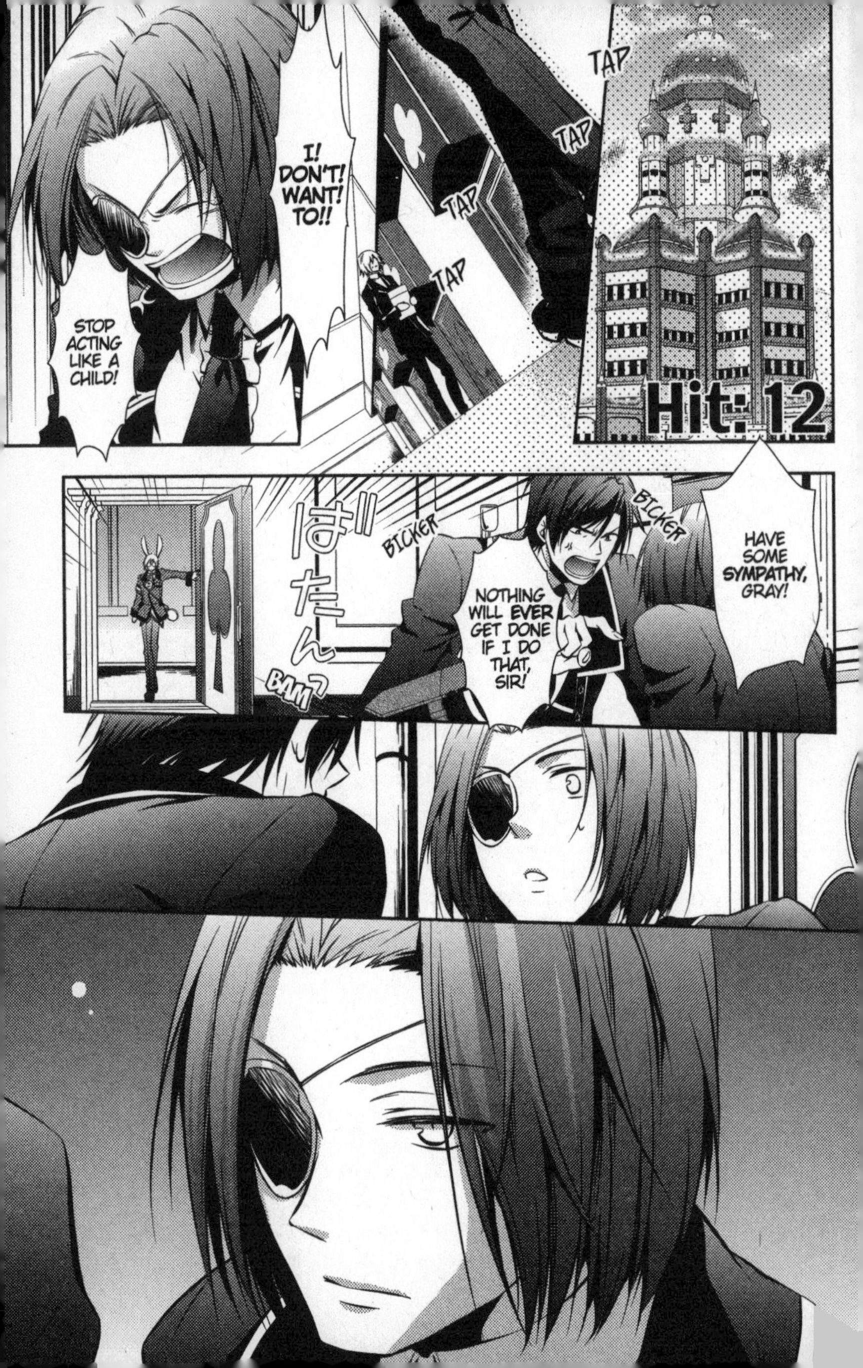
Hit: 12
TAP
TAP
TAP
TAP
I! DON'T! WANT! TO!!
STOP ACTING LIKE A CHILD!
HAVE SOME SYMPATHY, GRAY!
BICKER
BICKER
NOTHING WILL EVER GET DONE IF I DO THAT, SIR!
ばたん
BAM

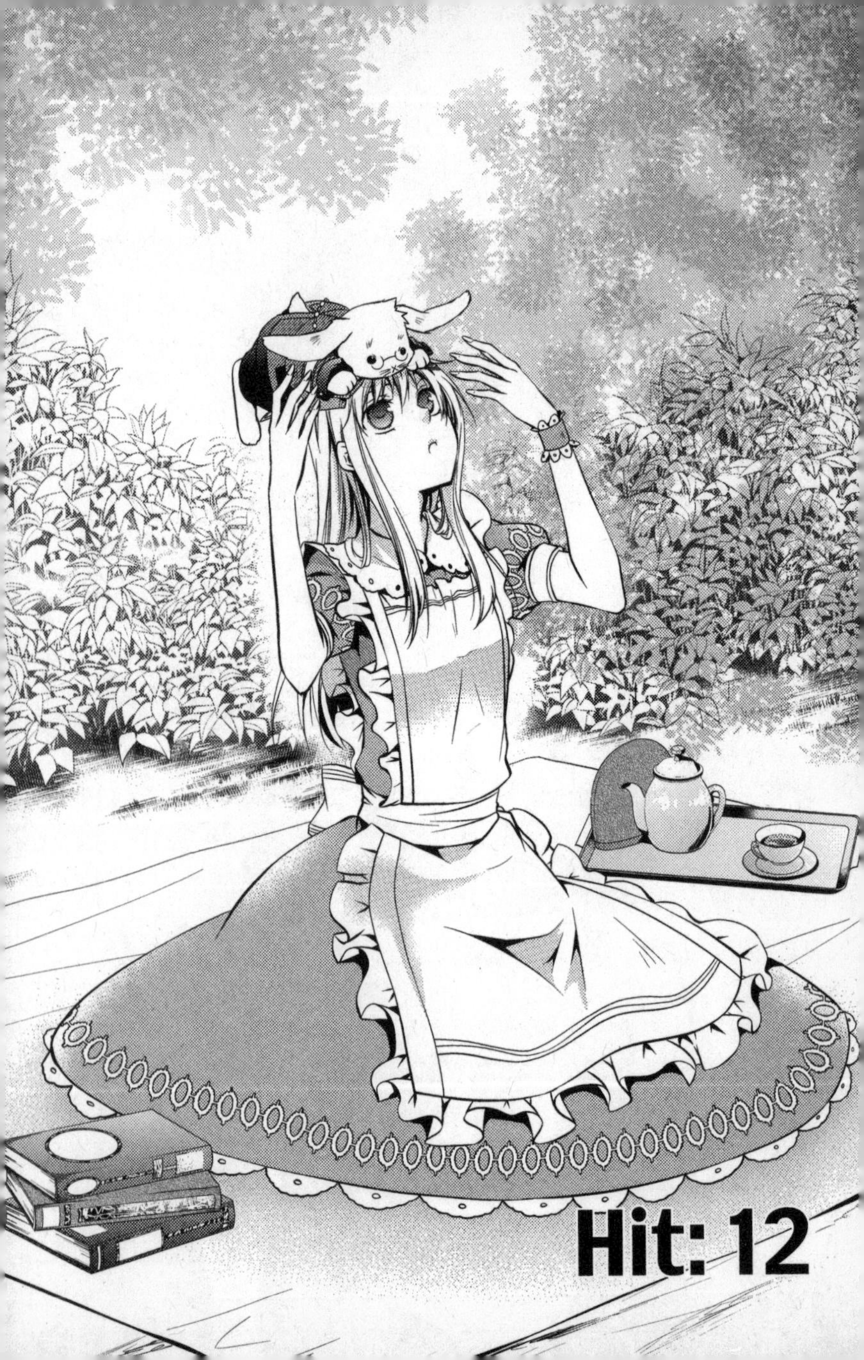
Hit: 12

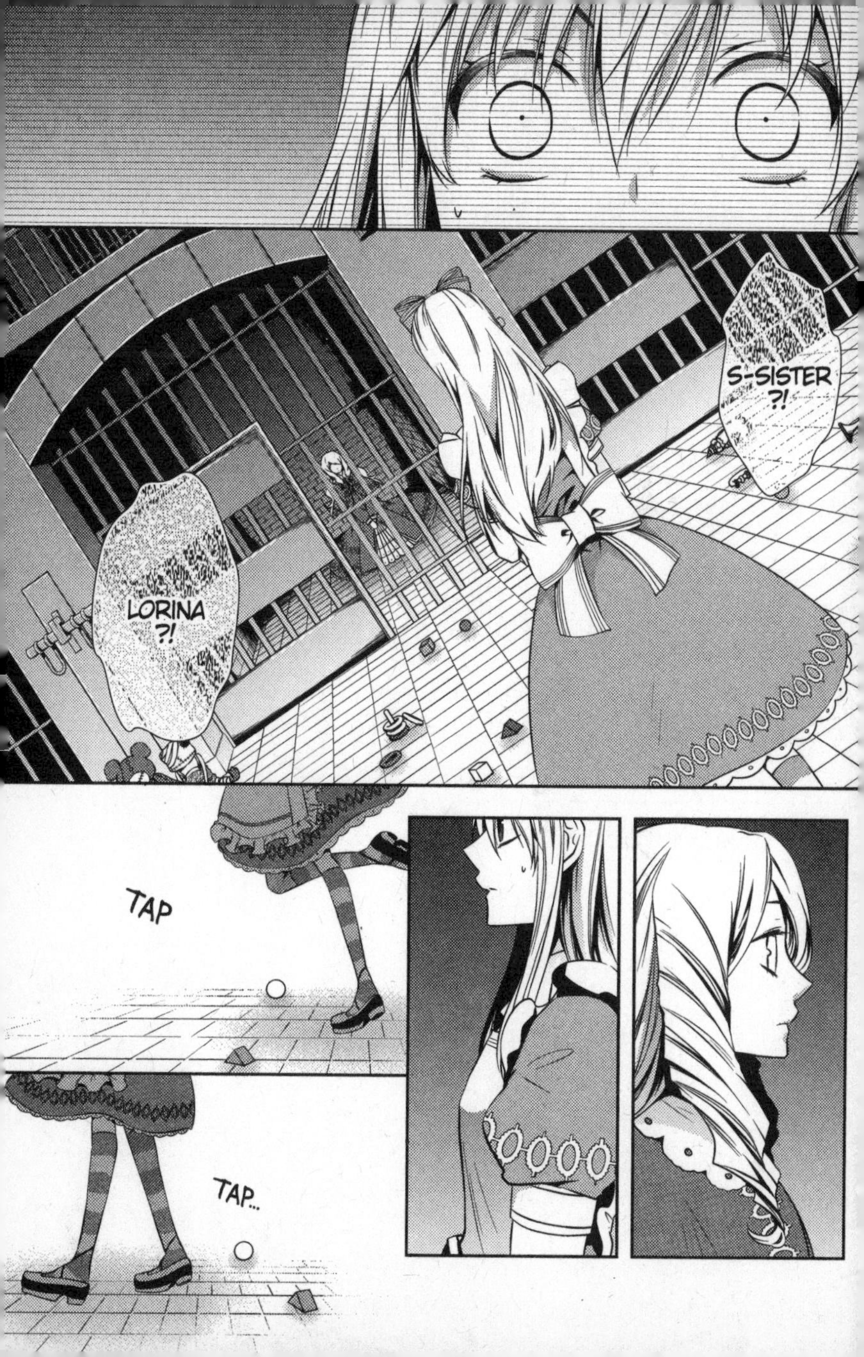
S-SISTER ?!
LORINA ?!
TAP
TAP...

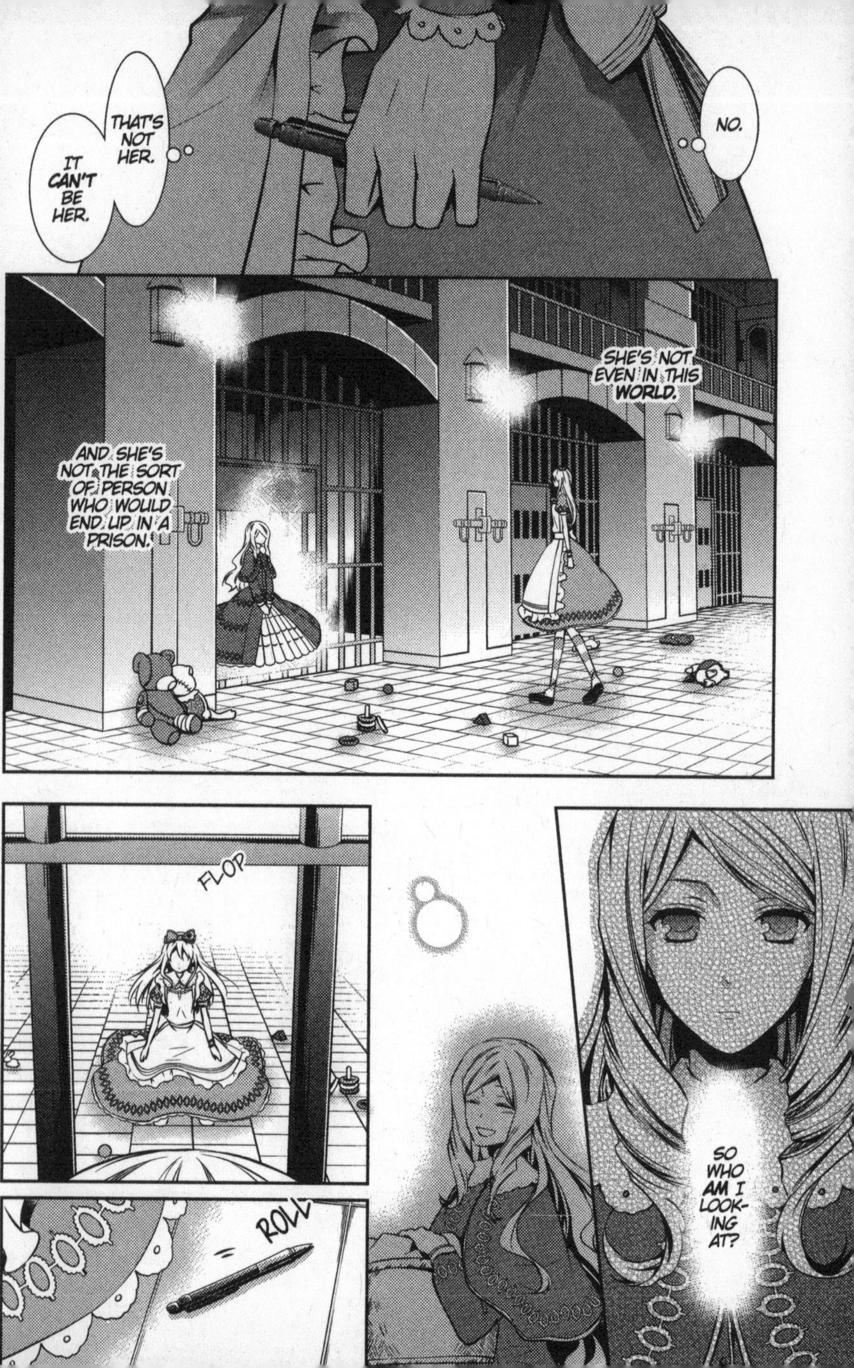
NO.
THAT'S NOT HER.
IT CAN'T BE HER.
SHE'S NOT EVEN IN THIS WORLD.
AND SHE'S NOT THE SORT OF PERSON WHO WOULD END UP IN A PRISON.
SO WHO AM I LOOKING-ING AT?
FLOP
ROLL

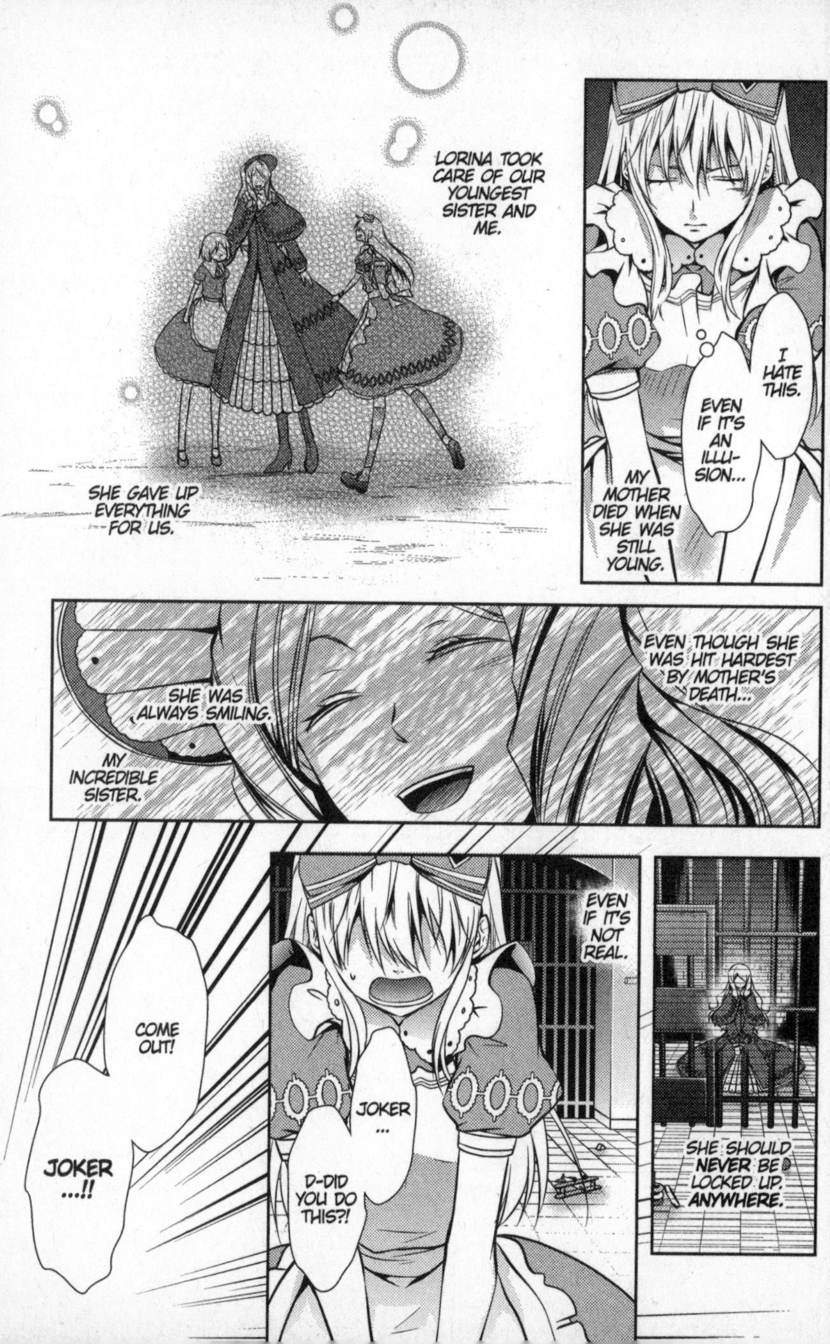
I HATE THIS.
EVEN IF IT'S AN ILLUSION...
MY MOTHER DIED WHEN SHE WAS STILL YOUNG.
LORINA TOOK CARE OF OUR YOUNGEST SISTER AND ME.
SHE GAVE UP EVERYTHING FOR US.
EVEN THOUGH SHE WAS HIT HARDEST BY MOTHER'S DEATH...
SHE WAS ALWAYS SMILING.
MY INCREDIBLE SISTER.
SHE SHOULD NEVER BE LOCKED UP. ANYWHERE.
EVEN IF IT'S NOT REAL.
JOKER ...
D-DID YOU DO THIS?!
COME OUT!
JOKER ...!!

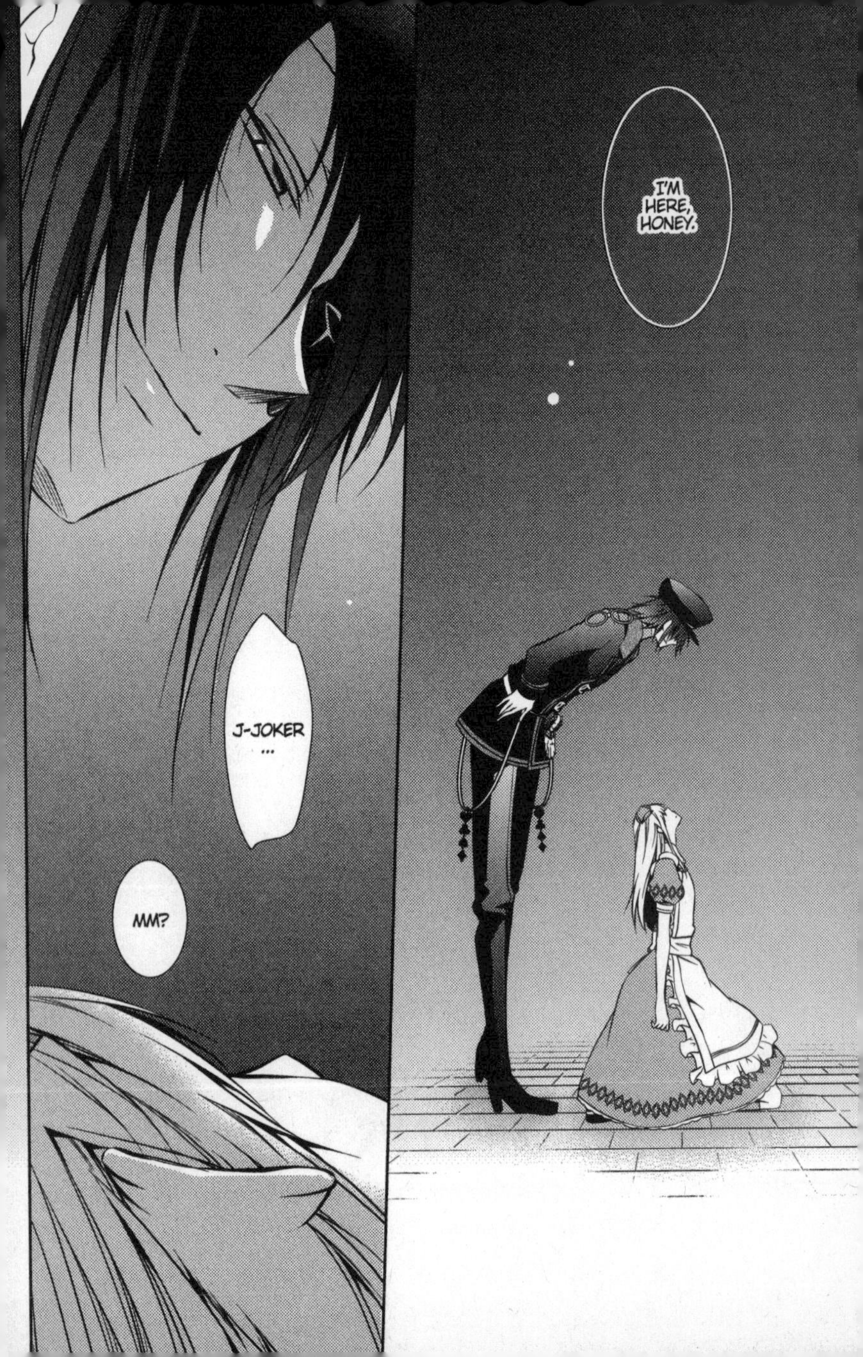
I'M HERE, HONEY.
J-JOKER ...
MM?

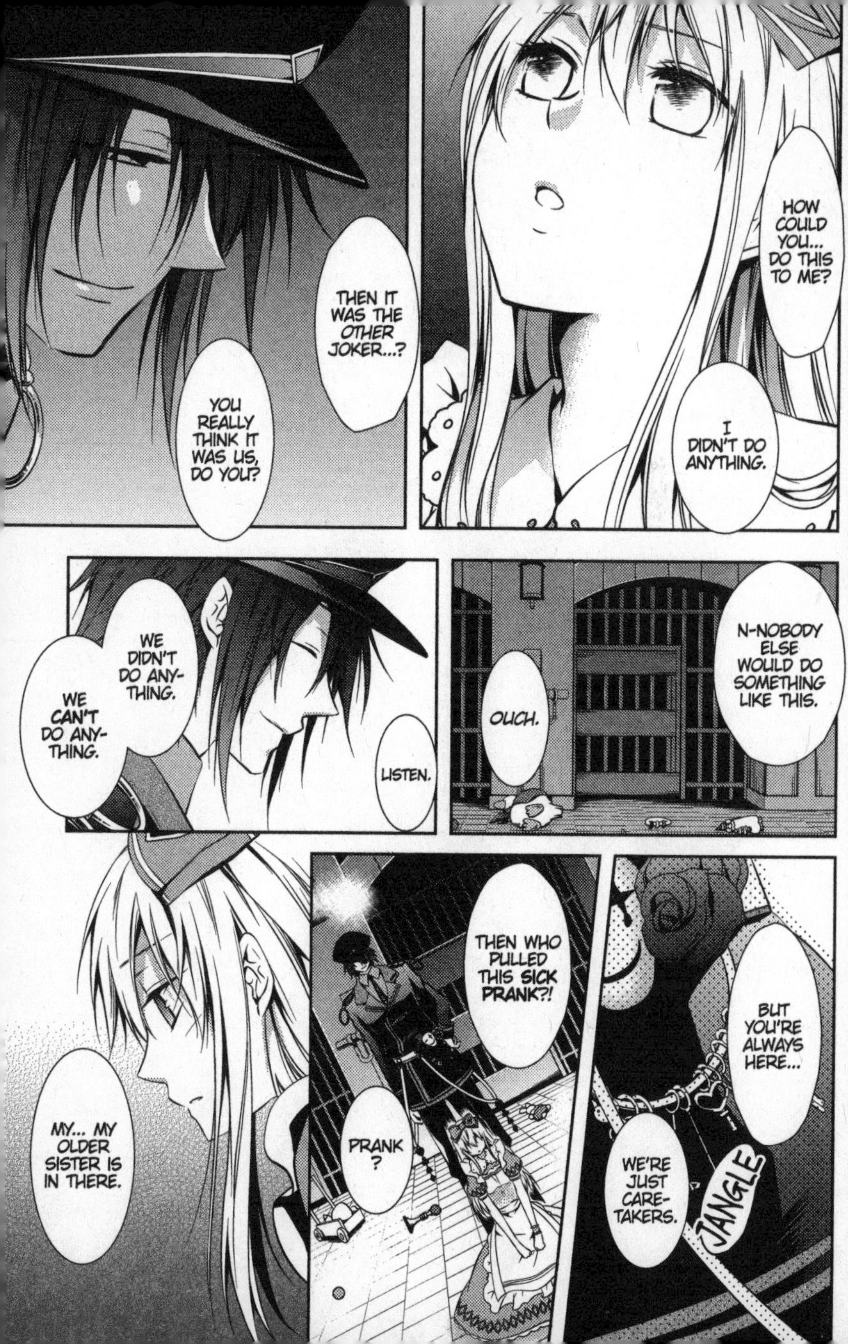
HOW COULD YOU... DO THIS TO ME?
I DIDN'T DO ANYTHING.
THEN IT WAS THE OTHER JOKER...?
YOU REALLY THINK IT WAS US, DO YOU?
N-NOBODY ELSE WOULD DO SOMETHING LIKE THIS.
OUCH.
LISTEN.
WE DIDN'T DO ANY-THING.
WE CAN'T DO ANY-THING.
BUT YOU'RE ALWAYS HERE...
WE'RE JUST CARE-TAKERS.
JANGLE
THEN WHO PULLED THIS SICK PRANK?!
PRANK?
MY... MY OLDER SISTER IS IN THERE.

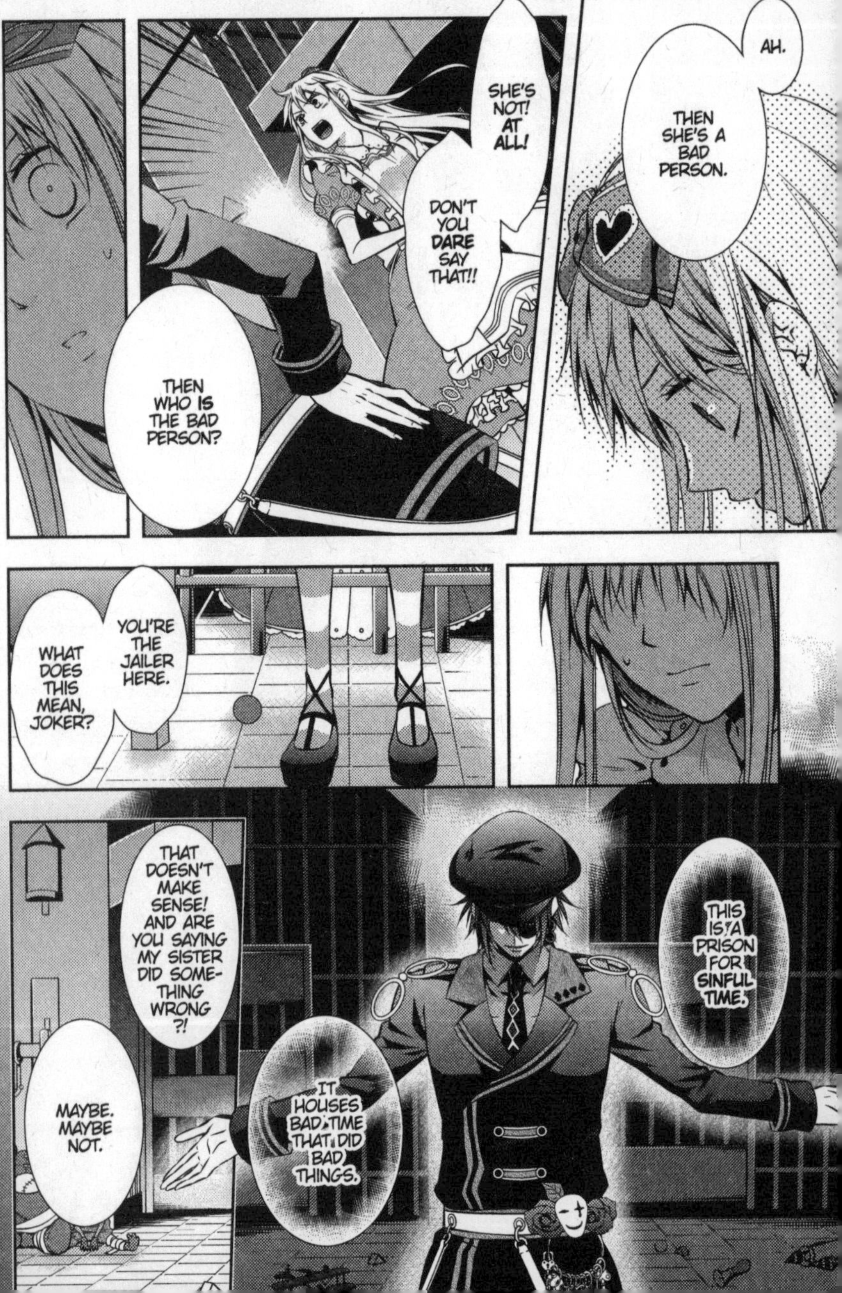
AH.
THEN SHE'S A BAD PERSON.
SHE'S NOT! AT ALL!
DON'T YOU DARE SAY THAT!!
THEN WHO IS THE BAD PERSON?
YOU'RE THE JAILER HERE.
WHAT DOES THIS MEAN, JOKER?
THIS IS A PRISON FOR SINFUL TIME.
IT HOUSES BAD TIME THAT DID BAD THINGS.
THAT DOESN'T MAKE SENSE! AND ARE YOU SAYING MY SISTER DID SOMETHING WRONG?!
MAYBE. MAYBE NOT.

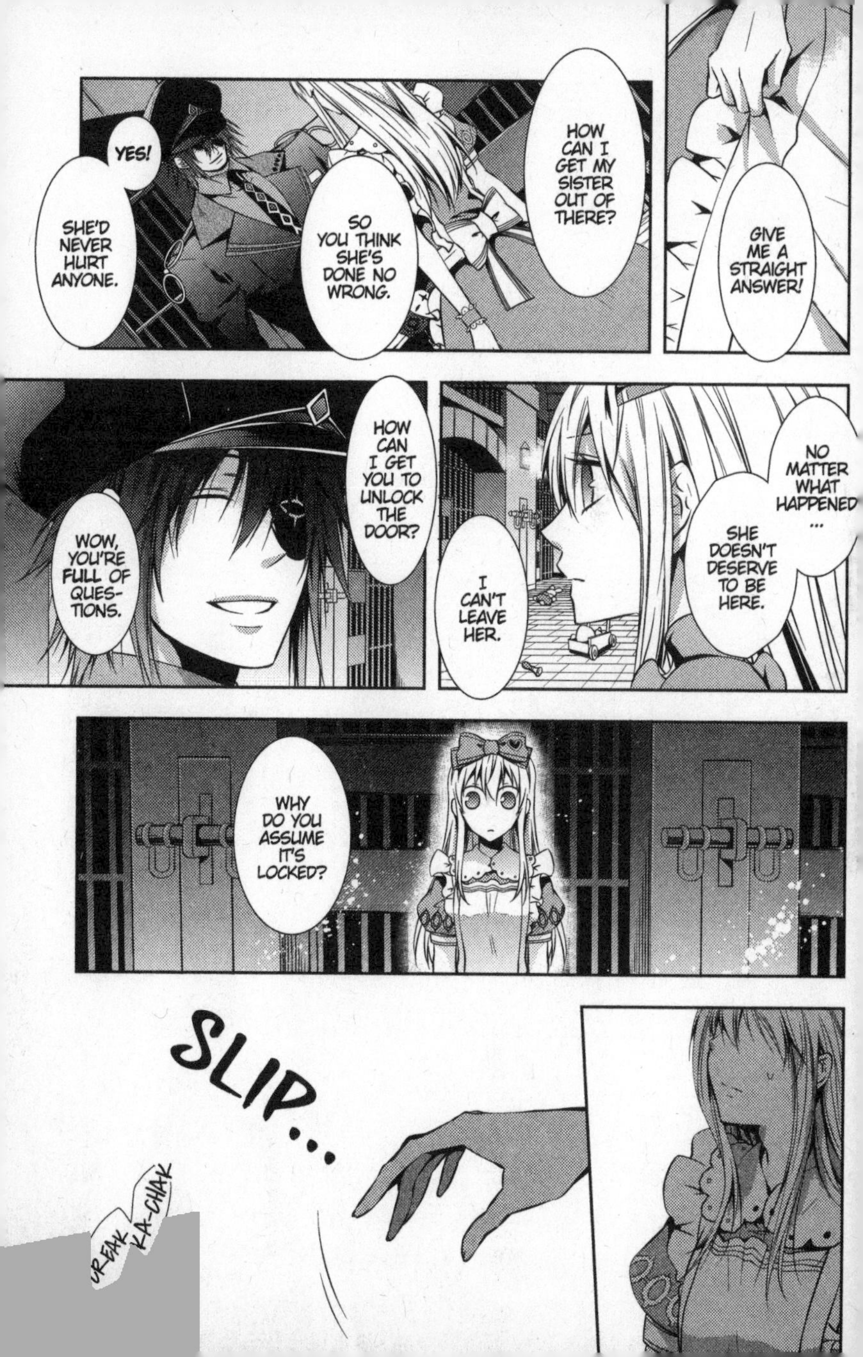
GIVE ME A STRAIGHT ANSWER!
HOW CAN I GET MY SISTER OUT OF THERE?
SO YOU THINK SHE'S DONE NO WRONG.
YES!
SHE'D NEVER HURT ANYONE.
NO MATTER WHAT HAPPENED...
SHE DOESN'T DESERVE TO BE HERE.
I CAN'T LEAVE HER.
HOW CAN I GET YOU TO UNLOCK THE DOOR?
WOW, YOU'RE FULL OF QUES-TIONS.
WHY DO YOU ASSUME IT'S LOCKED?
SLIP...
KA-CHAK

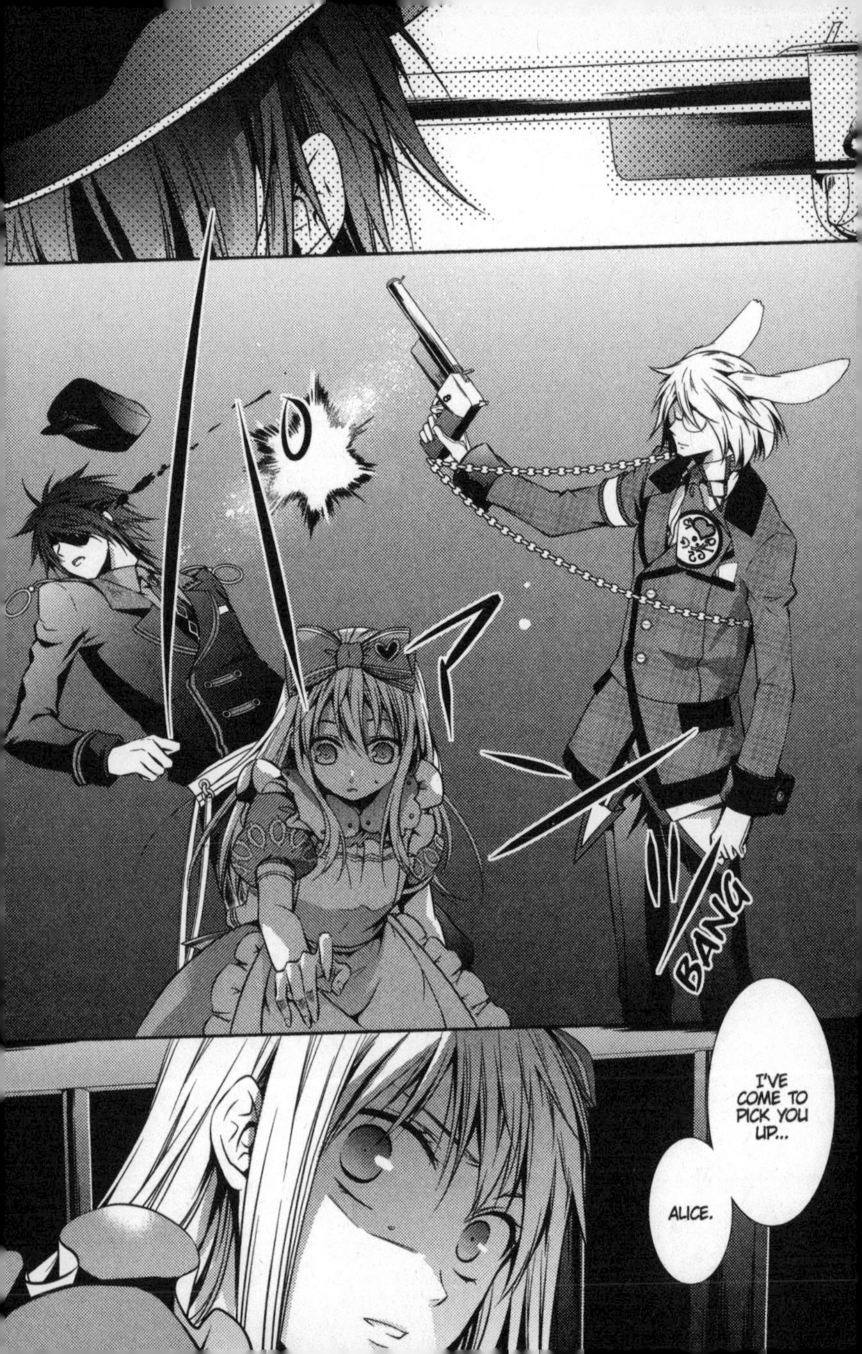
BANG
I'VE COME TO PICK YOU UP...
ALICE.

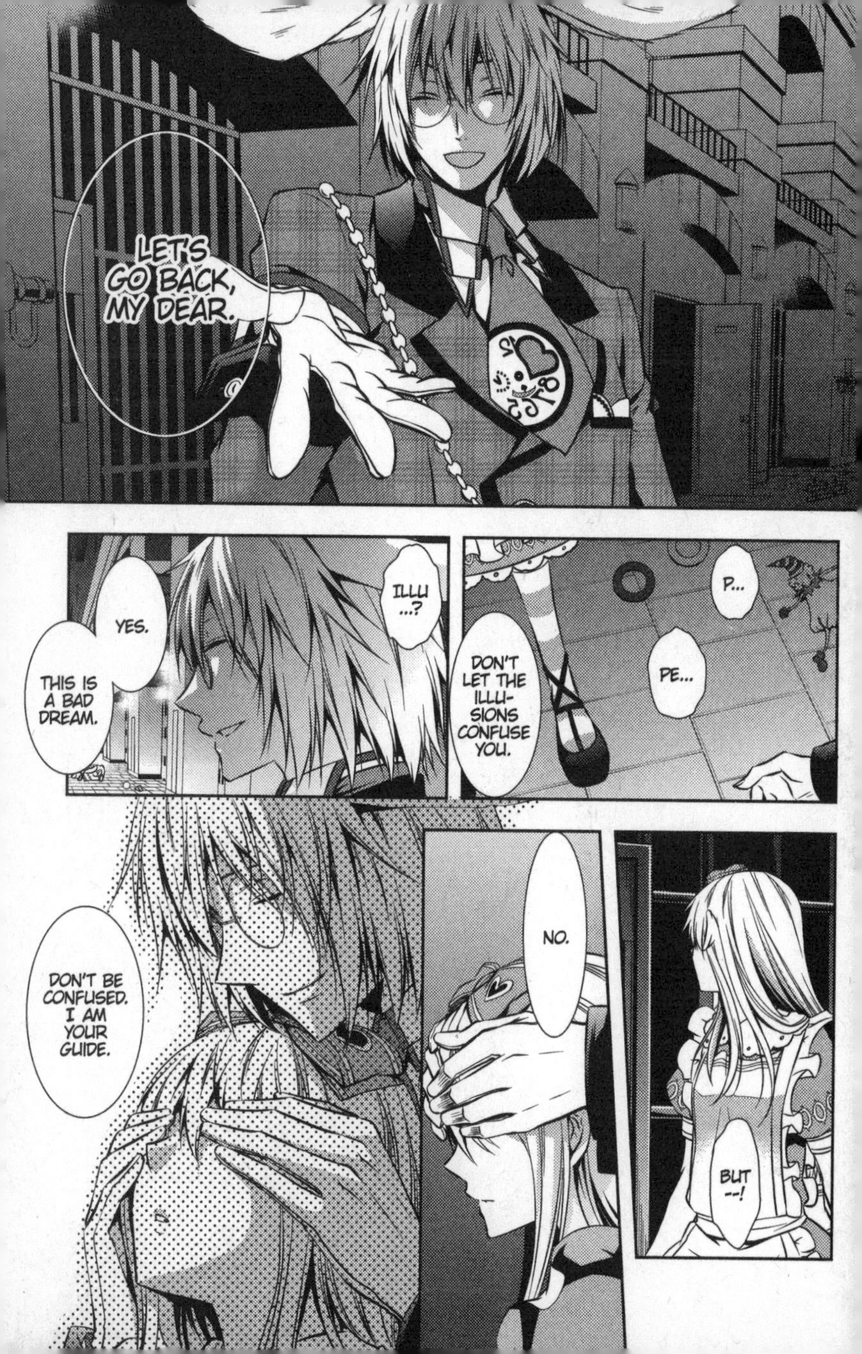
LET'S GO BACK, MY DEAR.
P...
PE...
DON'T LET THE ILLU-SIONS CONFUSE YOU.
ILLU ...?
YES.
THIS IS A BAD DREAM.
BUT --!
NO.
DON'T BE CONFUSED. I AM YOUR GUIDE.

CLACK

JUST LISTEN TO THE SOUND OF MY VOICE...

FORGET ...?

HUH?

NOT AGAIN ...

SWAY

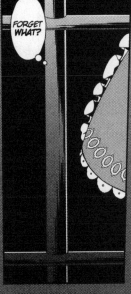

FORGET WHAT?

AND PLEASE.

FORGET.

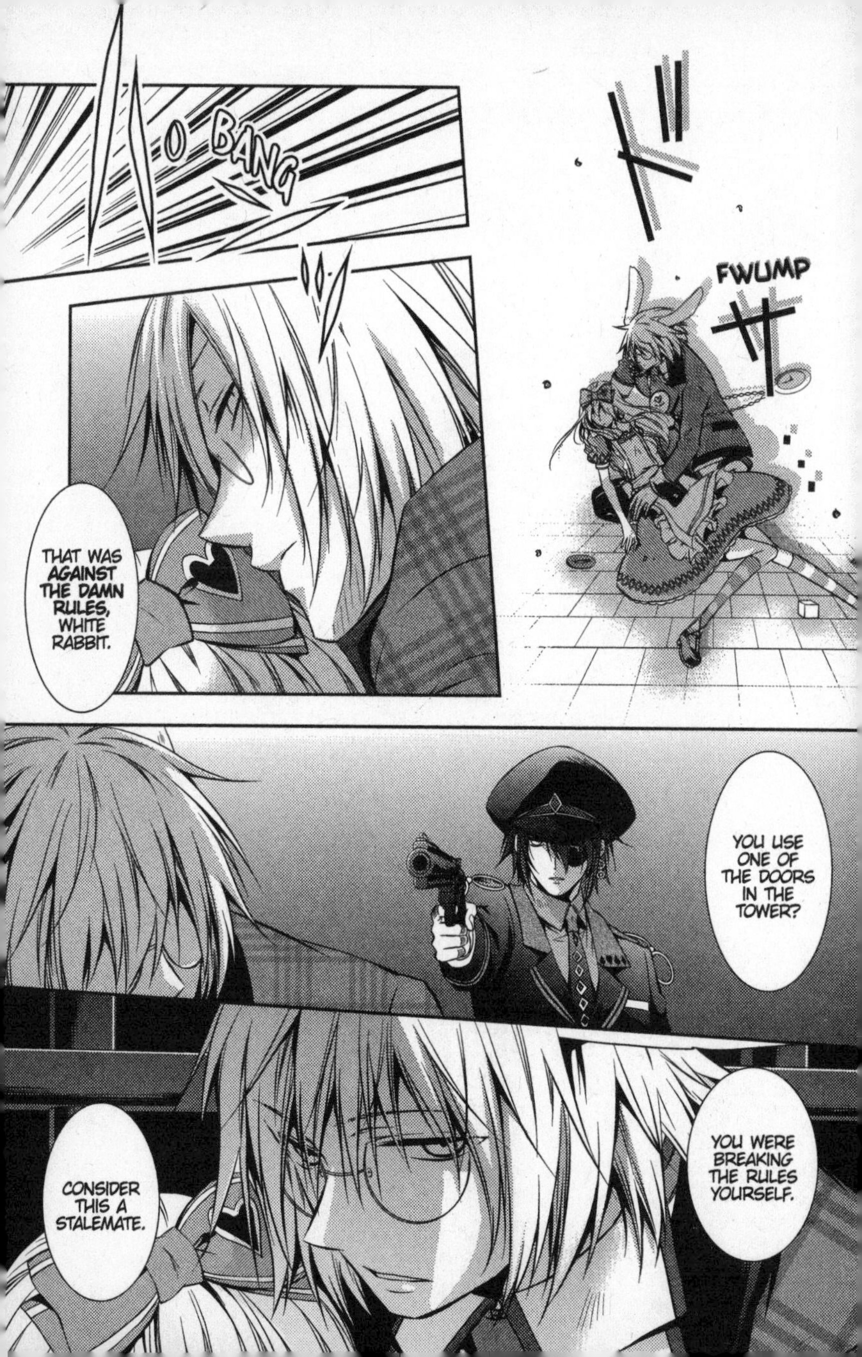
FWUMP
BANG
THAT WAS AGAINST THE DAMN RULES, WHITE RABBIT.
YOU USE ONE OF THE DOORS IN THE TOWER?
YOU WERE BREAKING THE RULES YOURSELF.
CONSIDER THIS A STALEMATE.

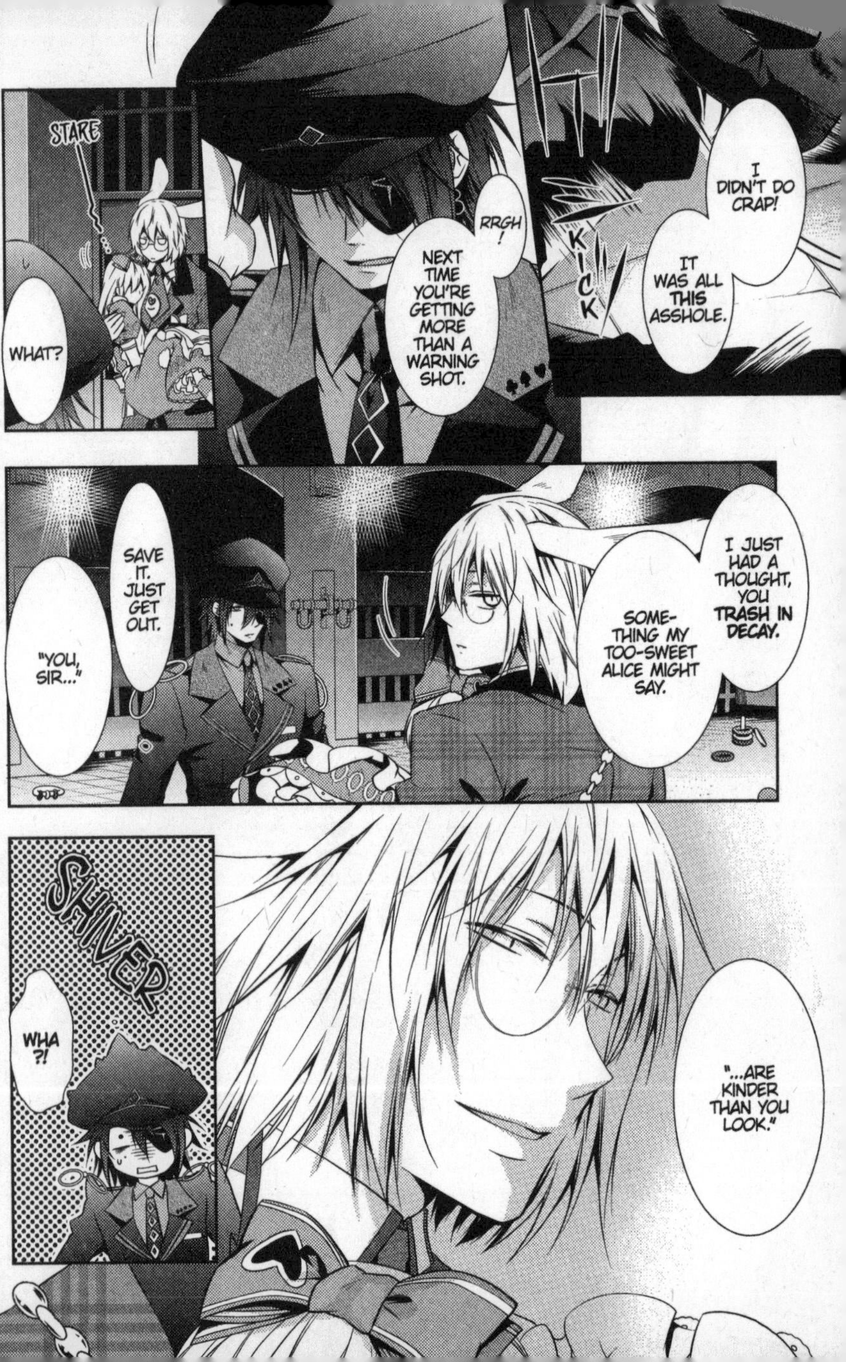
I DIDN'T DO CRAP!
IT WAS ALL THIS ASSHOLE.
KICK
RRGH!
NEXT TIME YOU'RE GETTING MORE THAN A WARNING SHOT.
STARE
WHAT?
I JUST HAD A THOUGHT, YOU TRASH IN DECAY.
SOME-THING MY TOO-SWEET ALICE MIGHT SAY.
SAVE IT. JUST GET OUT.
"YOU, SIR..."
"...ARE KINDER THAN YOU LOOK."
SHIVER
WHA?!

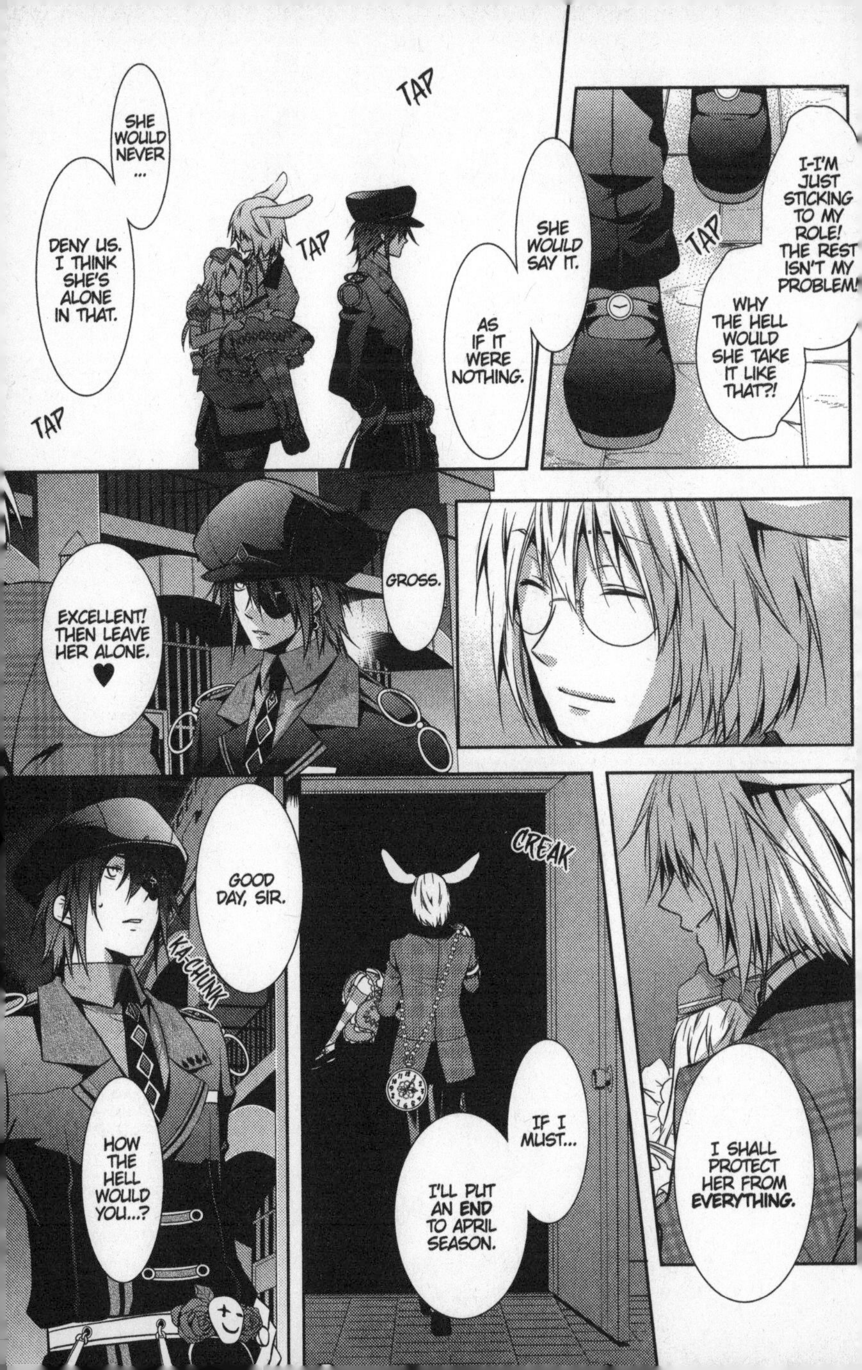
I-I'M JUST STICKING TO MY ROLE! THE REST ISN'T MY PROBLEM!
WHY THE HELL WOULD SHE TAKE IT LIKE THAT?!
TAP
SHE WOULD SAY IT.
AS IF IT WERE NOTHING.
TAP
SHE WOULD NEVER ...
TAP
DENY US. I THINK SHE'S ALONE IN THAT.
TAP
GROSS.
EXCELLENT! THEN LEAVE HER ALONE. ♥
I SHALL PROTECT HER FROM EVERYTHING.
CREAK
IF I MUST...
I'LL PUT AN END TO APRIL SEASON.
GOOD DAY, SIR.
KA-CHUNK
HOW THE HELL WOULD YOU...?

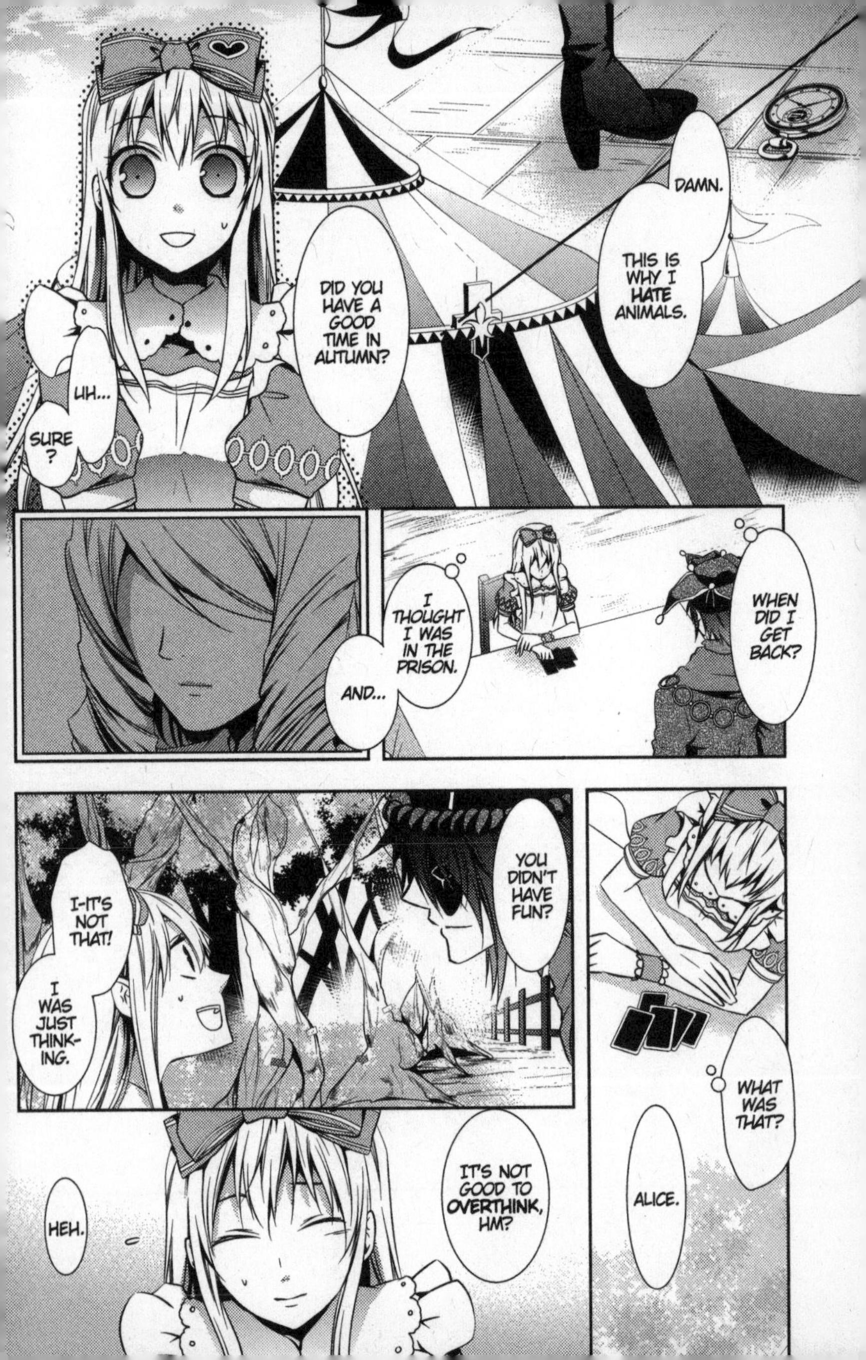
DAMN.
THIS IS WHY I HATE ANIMALS.
DID YOU HAVE A GOOD TIME IN AUTUMN?
UH...
SURE?
WHEN DID I GET BACK?
I THOUGHT I WAS IN THE PRISON.
AND...
YOU DIDN'T HAVE FUN?
I-IT'S NOT THAT!
I WAS JUST THINKING.
WHAT WAS THAT?
ALICE.
IT'S NOT GOOD TO OVERTHINK, HM?
HEH.

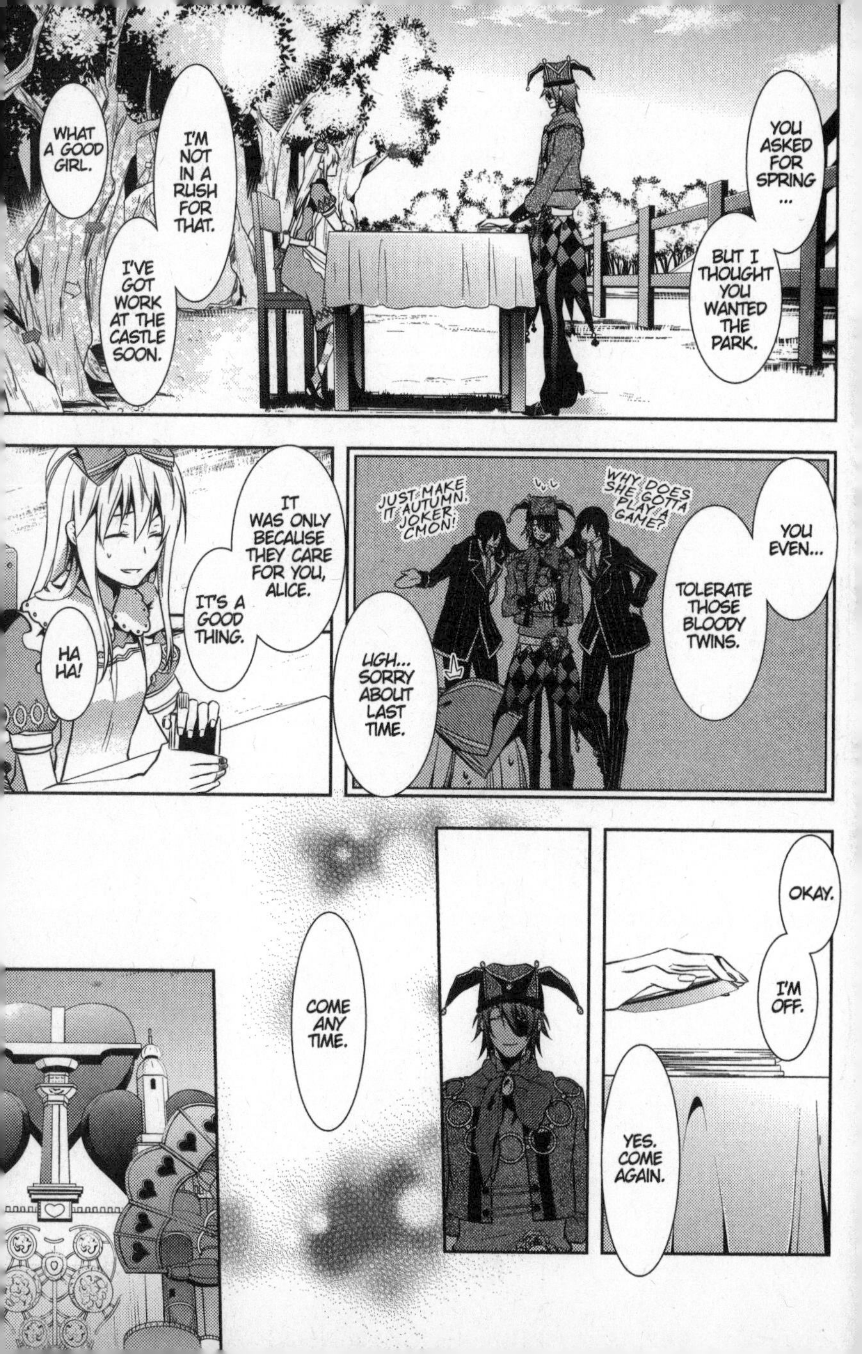
YOU ASKED FOR SPRING...
BUT I THOUGHT YOU WANTED THE PARK.
I'M NOT IN A RUSH FOR THAT.
I'VE GOT WORK AT THE CASTLE SOON.
WHAT A GOOD GIRL.
YOU EVEN...
TOLERATE THOSE BLOODY TWINS.
WHY DOES SHE GOTTA PLAY A GAME?
JUST MAKE IT AUTUMN, JOKER. CMON!
UGH... SORRY ABOUT LAST TIME.
IT WAS ONLY BECAUSE THEY CARE FOR YOU, ALICE.
IT'S A GOOD THING.
HA HA!
OKAY.
I'M OFF.
YES. COME AGAIN.
COME ANY TIME.

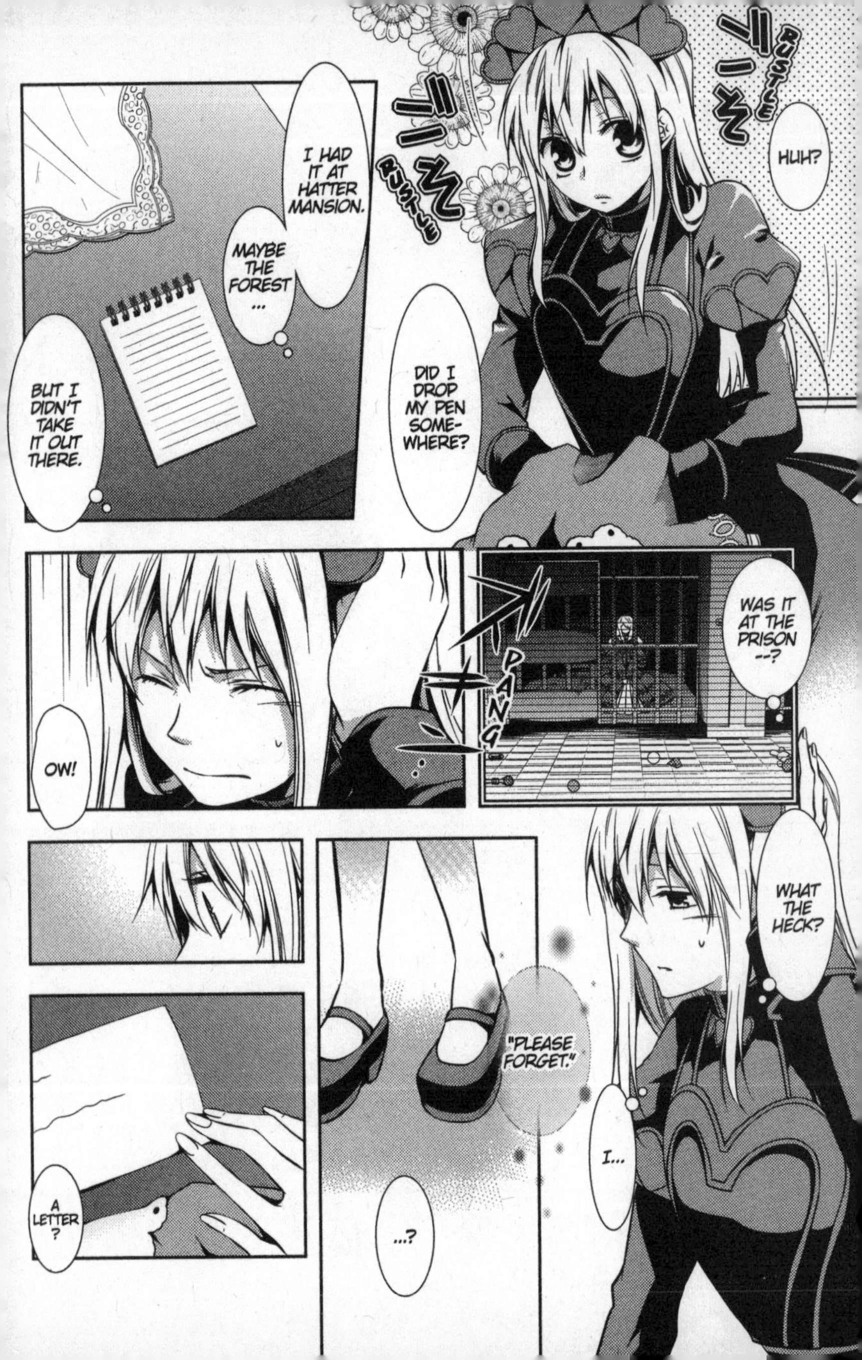
RUSTLE
RUSTLE
HUH?
DID I DROP MY PEN SOME-WHERE?
I HAD IT AT HATTER MANSION.
MAYBE THE FOREST ...
BUT I DIDN'T TAKE IT OUT THERE.
WAS IT AT THE PRISON --?
PANG
OW!
WHAT THE HECK?
"PLEASE FORGET."
I...
...?
A LETTER ?

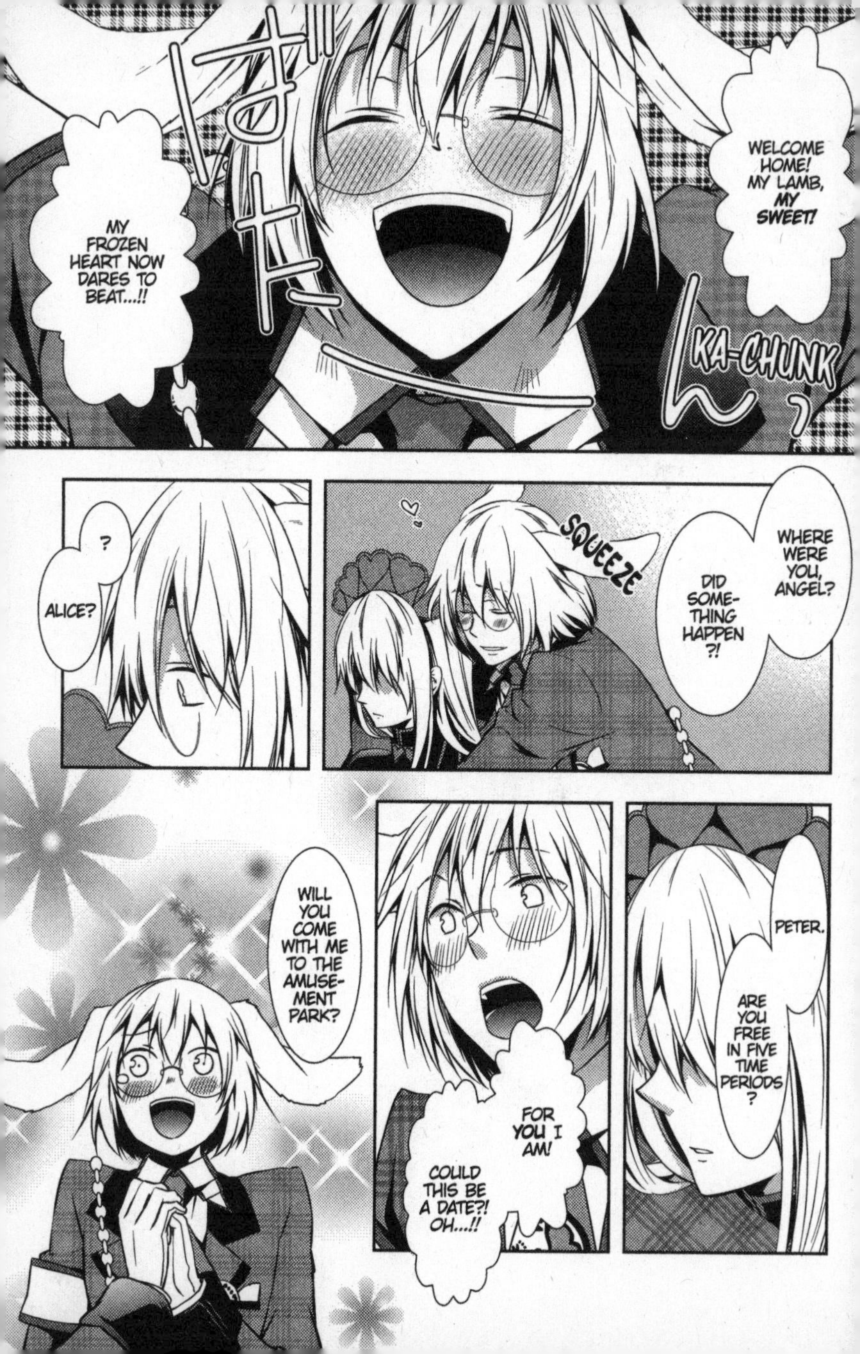
WELCOME HOME! MY LAMB, MY SWEET!
KA-CHUNK
MY FROZEN HEART NOW DARES TO BEAT...!!
WHERE WERE YOU, ANGEL?
SQUEEZE
DID SOMETHING HAPPEN?!
?
ALICE?
PETER.
ARE YOU FREE IN FIVE TIME PERIODS?
FOR YOU I AM!
COULD THIS BE A DATE?! OH...!!
WILL YOU COME WITH ME TO THE AMUSEMENT PARK?

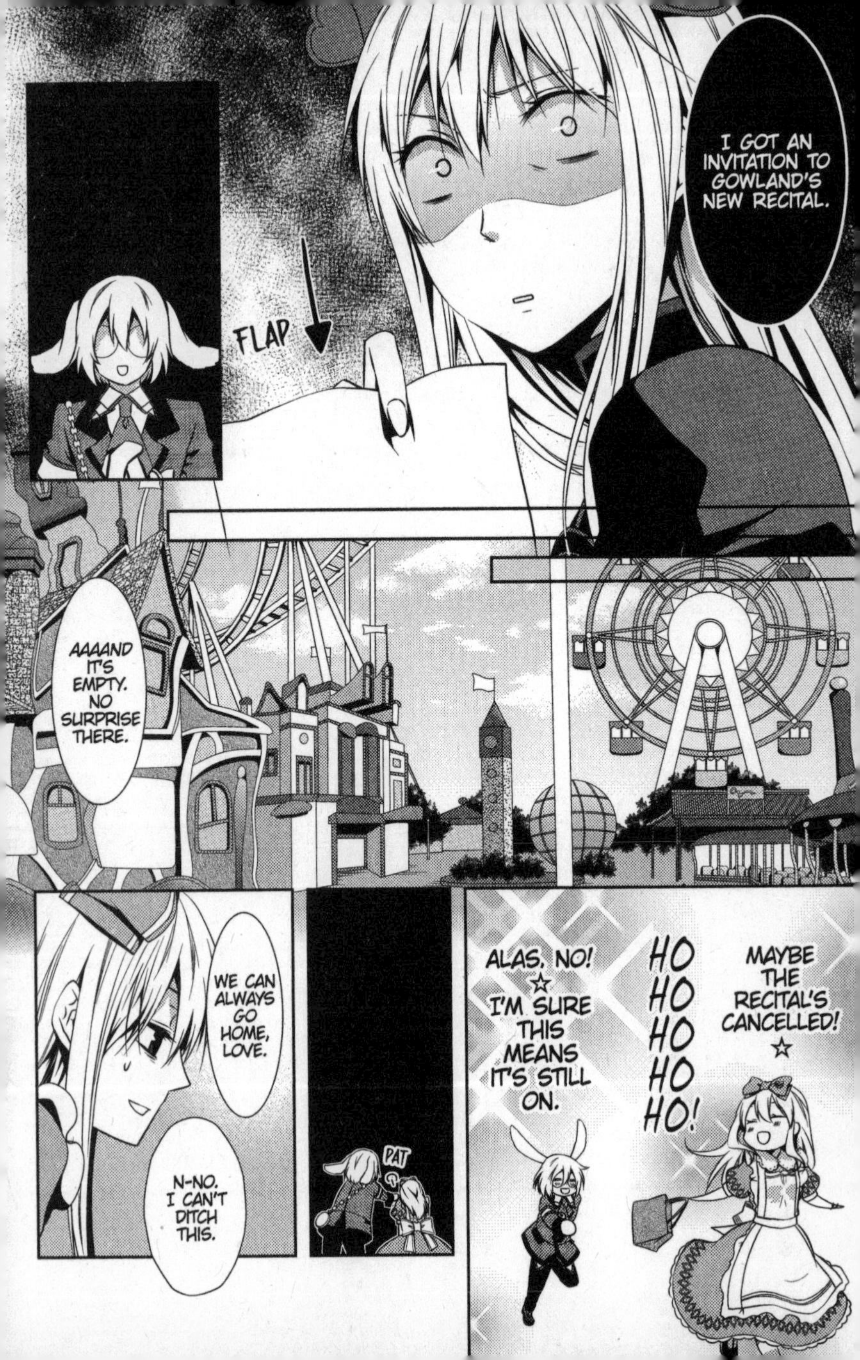
I GOT AN INVITATION TO GOWLAND'S NEW RECITAL.
FLAP
AAAAND IT'S EMPTY. NO SURPRISE THERE.
MAYBE THE RECITAL'S CANCELLED! ☆
HO HO HO HO HO HO!
ALAS. NO! ☆ I'M SURE THIS MEANS IT'S STILL ON.
PAT
WE CAN ALWAYS GO HOME, LOVE.
N-NO. I CAN'T DITCH THIS.

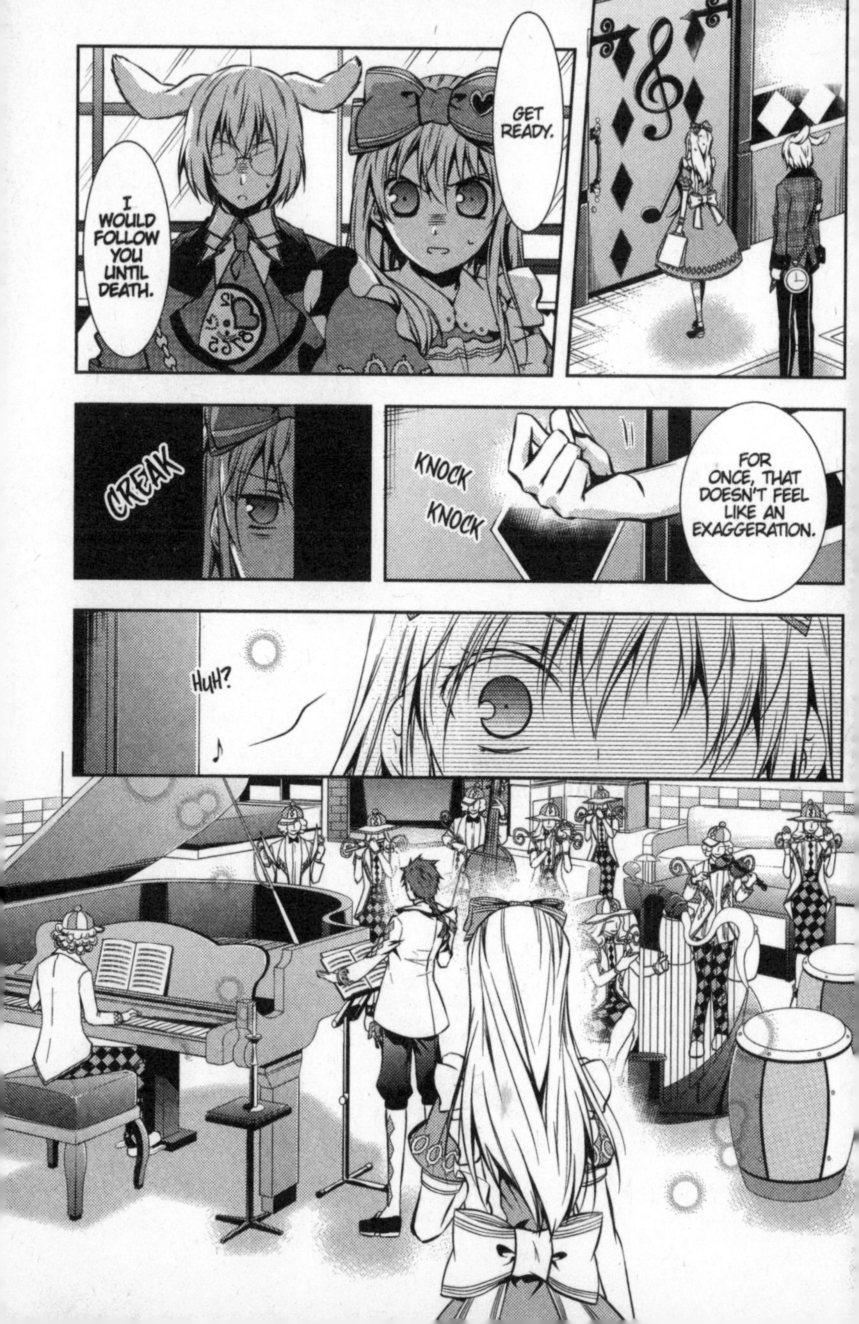
GET READY.
I WOULD FOLLOW YOU UNTIL DEATH.
FOR ONCE, THAT DOESN'T FEEL LIKE AN EXAGGERATION.
KNOCK KNOCK
CREAK
HUH?

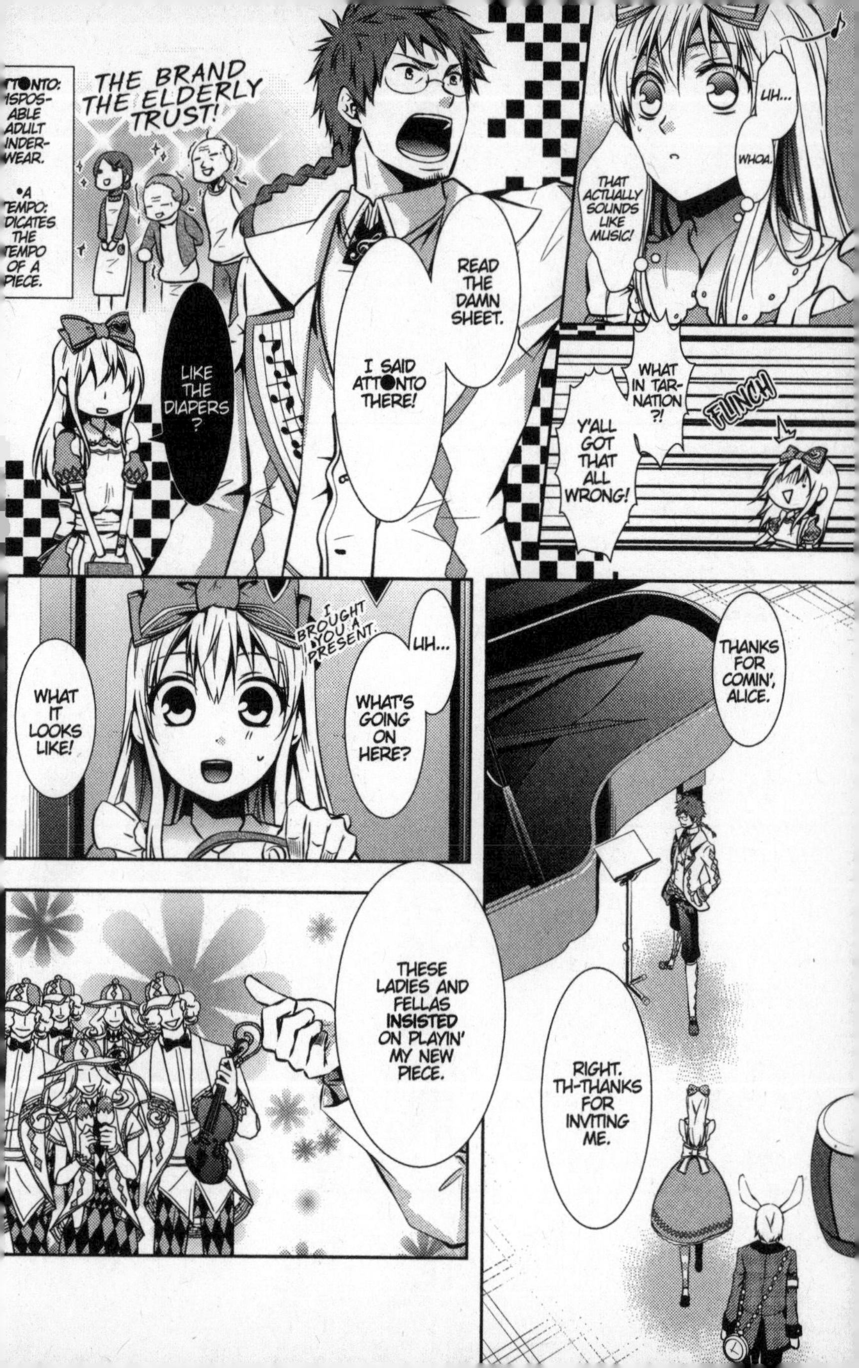
UH...
WHOA.
THAT ACTUALLY SOUNDS LIKE MUSIC!
WHAT IN TARNATION?!
Y'ALL GOT THAT ALL WRONG!
FLINCH
READ THE DAMN SHEET.
I SAID ATTONTO THERE!
THE BRAND THE ELDERLY TRUST!
LIKE THE DIAPERS?
TTONTO: ISPOSABLE ADULT INDERWEAR.
•A TEMPO: DICATES THE TEMPO OF A PIECE.
THANKS FOR COMIN', ALICE.
RIGHT. TH-THANKS FOR INVITING ME.
UH...
WHAT'S GOING ON HERE?
I BROUGHT YOU A PRESENT.
WHAT IT LOOKS LIKE!
THESE LADIES AND FELLAS INSISTED ON PLAYIN' MY NEW PIECE.

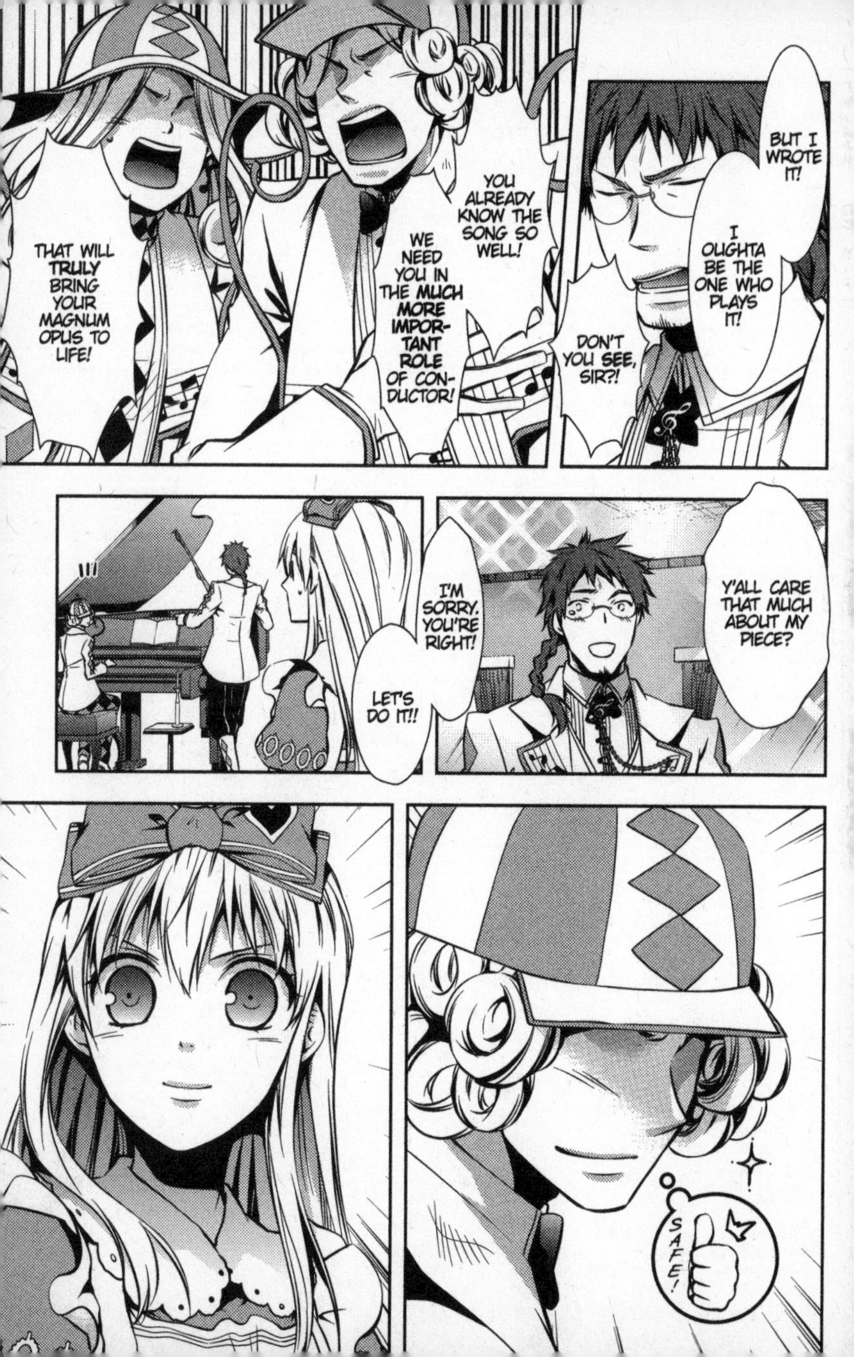
BUT I WROTE IT!
I OUGHTA BE THE ONE WHO PLAYS IT!
DON'T YOU SEE, SIR?!
YOU ALREADY KNOW THE SONG SO WELL!
WE NEED YOU IN THE MUCH MORE IMPORTANT ROLE OF CONDUCTOR!
THAT WILL TRULY BRING YOUR MAGNUM OPUS TO LIFE!
Y'ALL CARE THAT MUCH ABOUT MY PIECE?
I'M SORRY. YOU'RE RIGHT!
LET'S DO IT!!
SAFE!

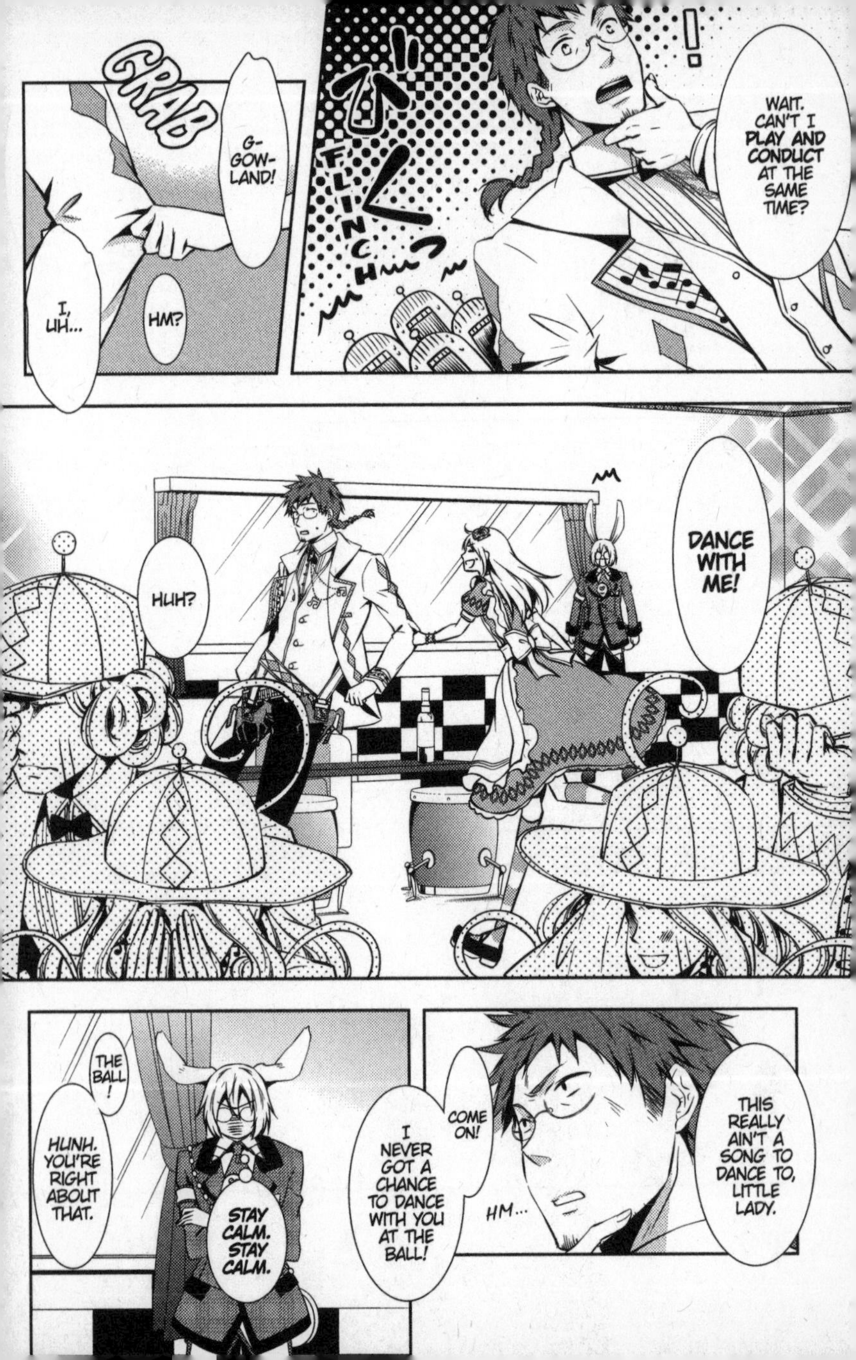
!
WAIT. CAN'T I PLAY AND CONDUCT AT THE SAME TIME?
FLINCH
GRAB
G-GOWLAND!
HM?
I, UH...
DANCE WITH ME!
HUH?
THIS REALLY AIN'T A SONG TO DANCE TO, LITTLE LADY.
HM...
COME ON!
I NEVER GOT A CHANCE TO DANCE WITH YOU AT THE BALL!
THE BALL!
HUNH. YOU'RE RIGHT ABOUT THAT.
STAY CALM. STAY CALM.

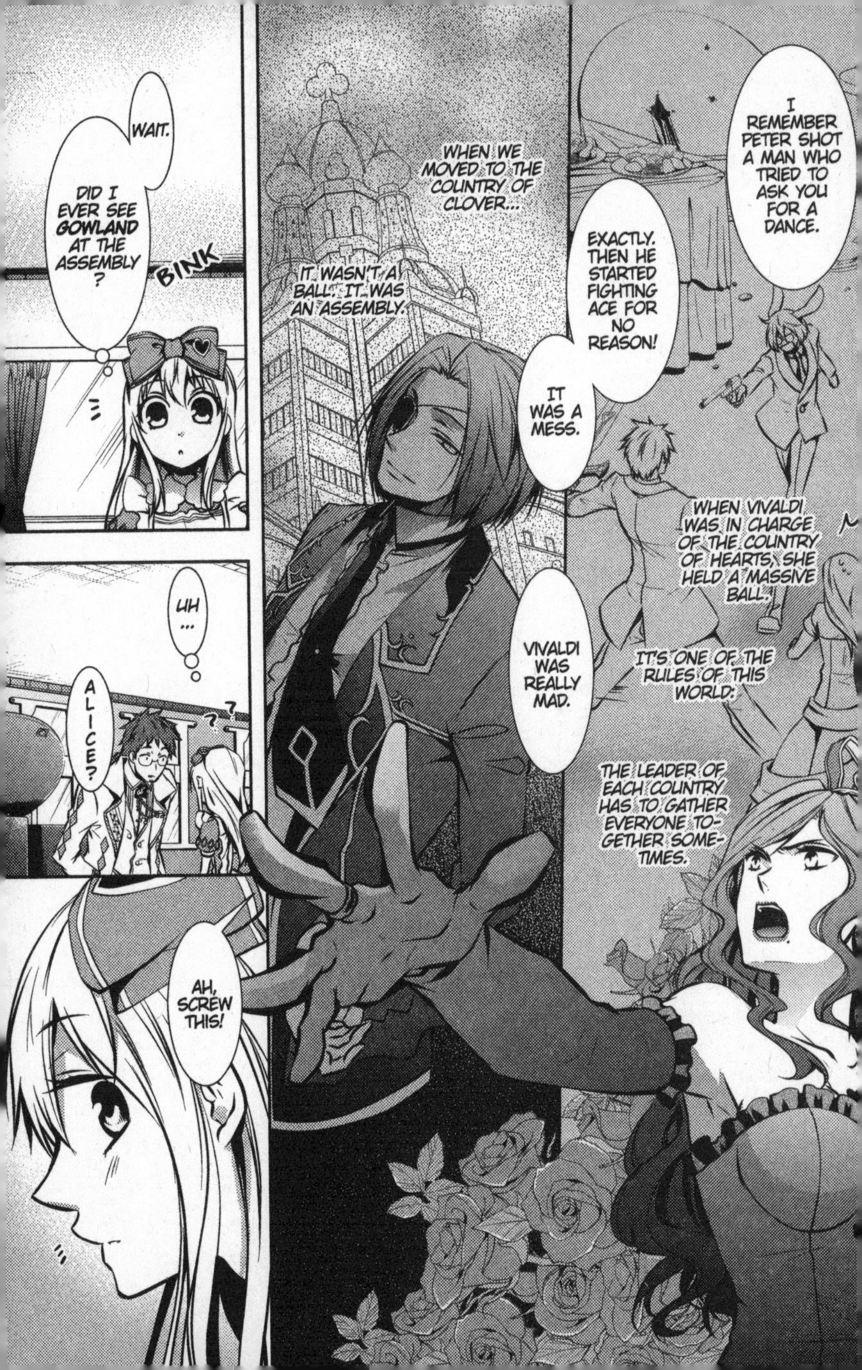
I REMEMBER PETER SHOT A MAN WHO TRIED TO ASK YOU FOR A DANCE.
EXACTLY. THEN HE STARTED FIGHTING ACE FOR NO REASON!
IT WAS A MESS.
WHEN VIVALDI WAS IN CHARGE OF THE COUNTRY OF HEARTS, SHE HELD A MASSIVE BALL.
VIVALDI WAS REALLY MAD.
IT'S ONE OF THE RULES OF THIS WORLD.
THE LEADER OF EACH COUNTRY HAS TO GATHER EVERYONE TOGETHER SOMETIMES.
WHEN WE MOVED TO THE COUNTRY OF CLOVER...
IT WASN'T A BALL. IT WAS AN ASSEMBLY.
WAIT.
DID I EVER SEE GOWLAND AT THE ASSEMBLY?
BINK
UH...
ALICE?
??
AH, SCREW THIS!

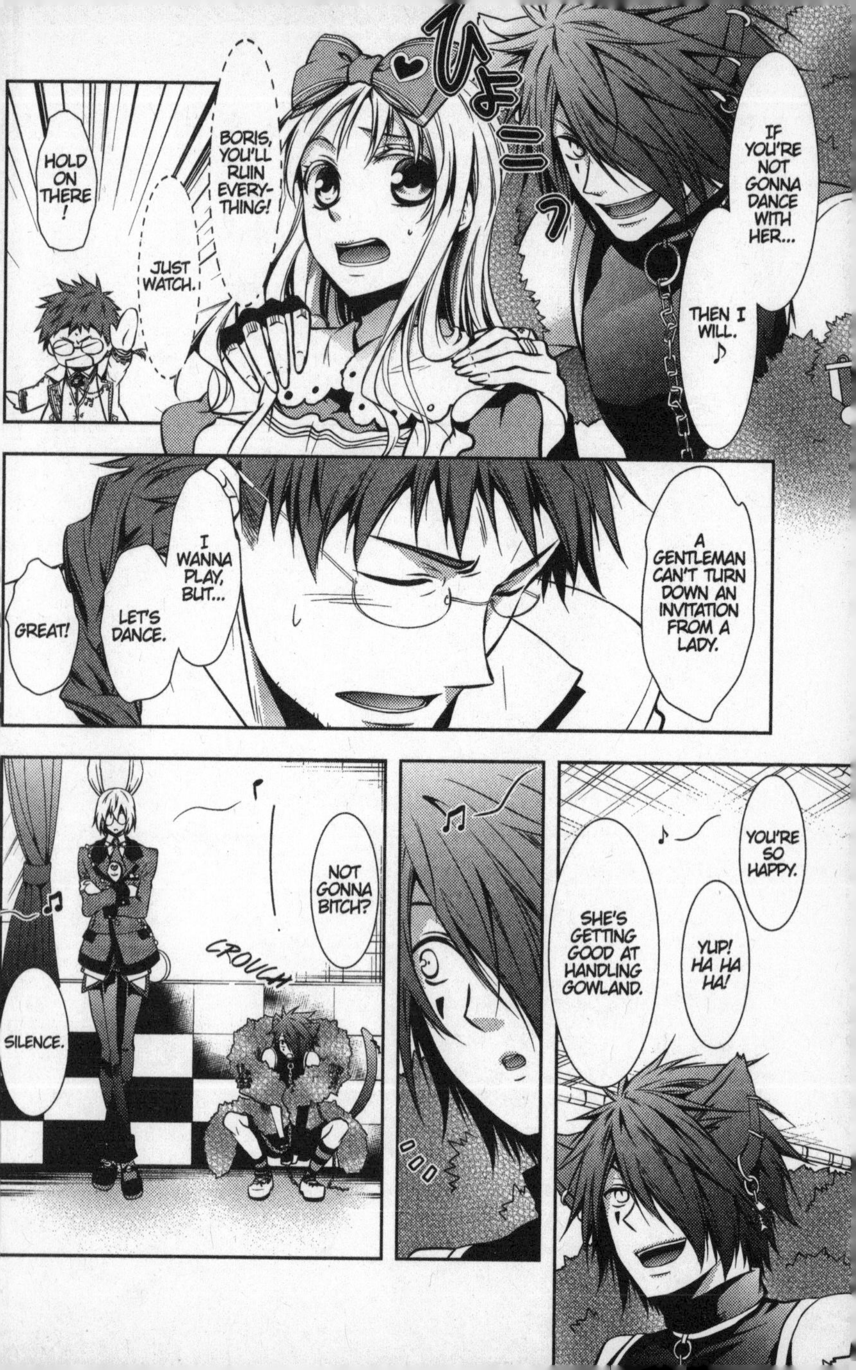
ひょこっ
IF YOU'RE NOT GONNA DANCE WITH HER...
THEN I WILL. ♪
BORIS, YOU'LL RUIN EVERYTHING!
JUST WATCH.
HOLD ON THERE!
A GENTLEMAN CAN'T TURN DOWN AN INVITATION FROM A LADY.
I WANNA PLAY, BUT...
LET'S DANCE.
GREAT!
YOU'RE SO HAPPY.
YUP! HA HA HA!
SHE'S GETTING GOOD AT HANDLING GOWLAND.
NOT GONNA BITCH?
CROUCH
SILENCE.

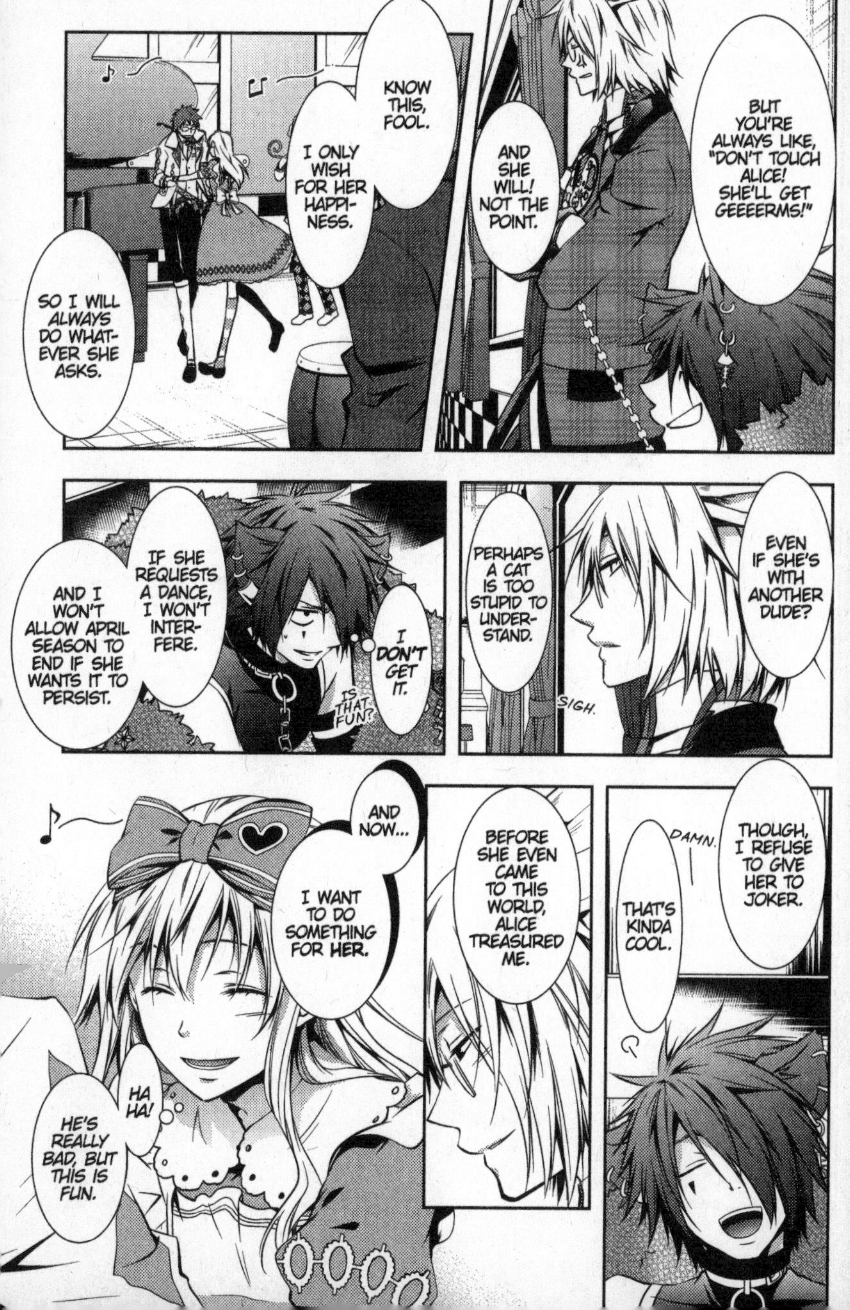
BUT YOU'RE ALWAYS LIKE, "DON'T TOUCH ALICE! SHE'LL GET GEEEERMS!"
AND SHE WILL! NOT THE POINT.
KNOW THIS, FOOL.
I ONLY WISH FOR HER HAPPINESS.
SO I WILL ALWAYS DO WHATEVER SHE ASKS.
EVEN IF SHE'S WITH ANOTHER DUDE?
PERHAPS A CAT IS TOO STUPID TO UNDERSTAND.
SIGH.
I DON'T GET IT.
IS THAT FUN?
IF SHE REQUESTS A DANCE, I WON'T INTERFERE.
AND I WON'T ALLOW APRIL SEASON TO END IF SHE WANTS IT TO PERSIST.
THOUGH, I REFUSE TO GIVE HER TO JOKER.
DAMN.
THAT'S KINDA COOL.
BEFORE SHE EVEN CAME TO THIS WORLD, ALICE TREASURED ME.
AND NOW...
I WANT TO DO SOMETHING FOR HER.
HA HA!
HE'S REALLY BAD, BUT THIS IS FUN.

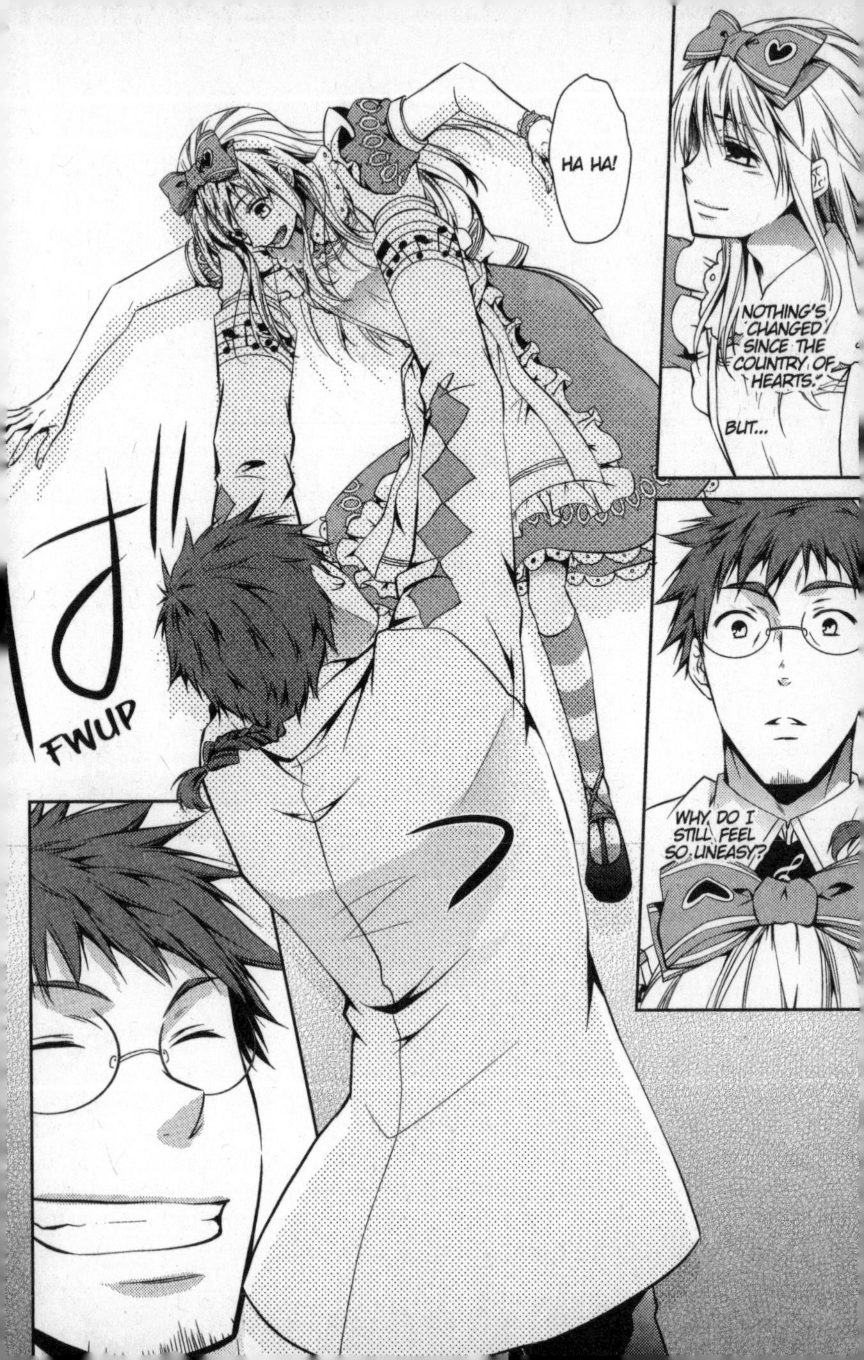
NOTHING'S CHANGED SINCE THE COUNTRY OF HEARTS.
BUT...
WHY DO I STILL FEEL SO UNEASY?
HA HA!
FWUP

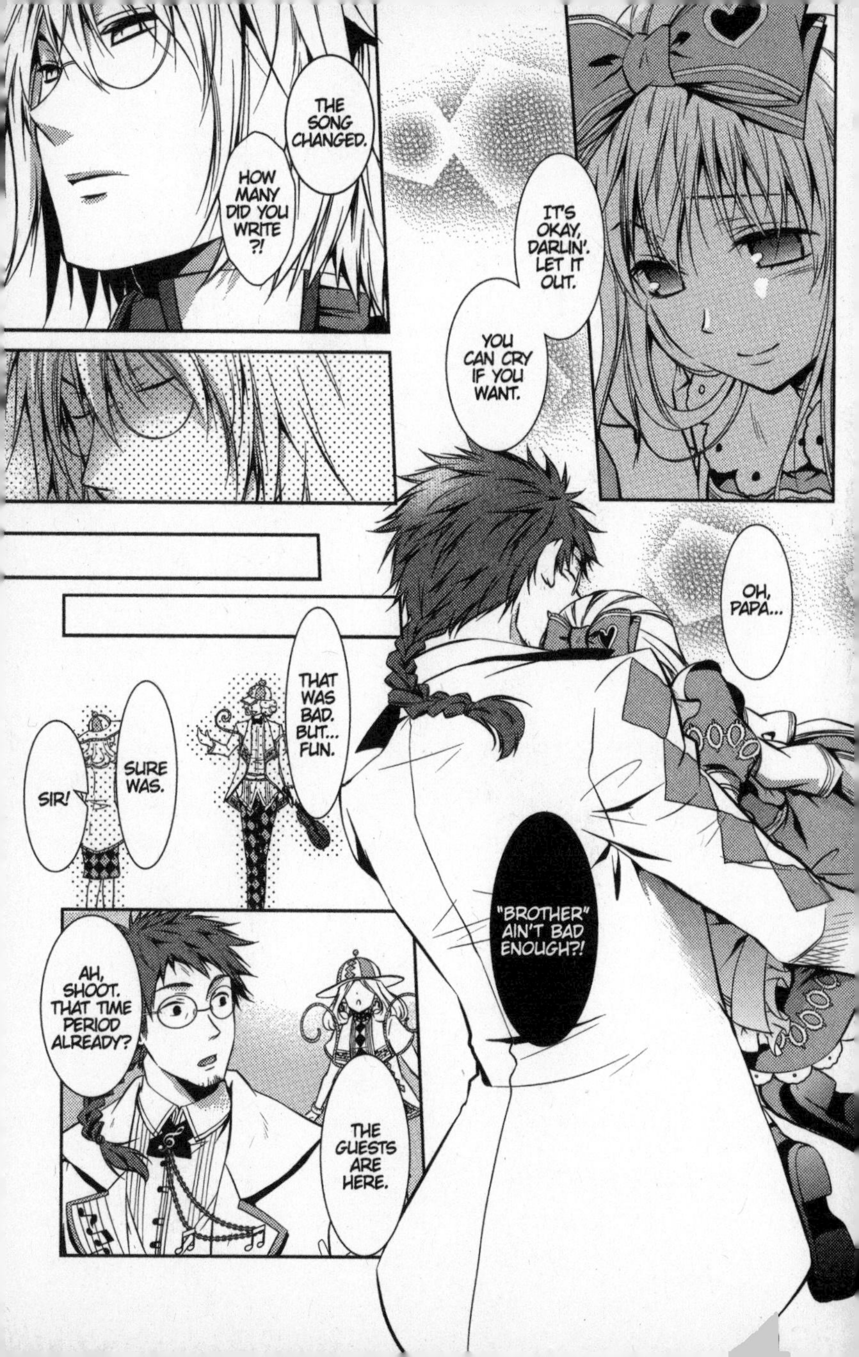
IT'S OKAY, DARLIN'. LET IT OUT.
YOU CAN CRY IF YOU WANT.
THE SONG CHANGED.
HOW MANY DID YOU WRITE ?!
OH, PAPA...
"BROTHER" AIN'T BAD ENOUGH?!
THAT WAS BAD. BUT... FUN.
SURE WAS.
SIR!
AH, SHOOT. THAT TIME PERIOD ALREADY?
THE GUESTS ARE HERE.

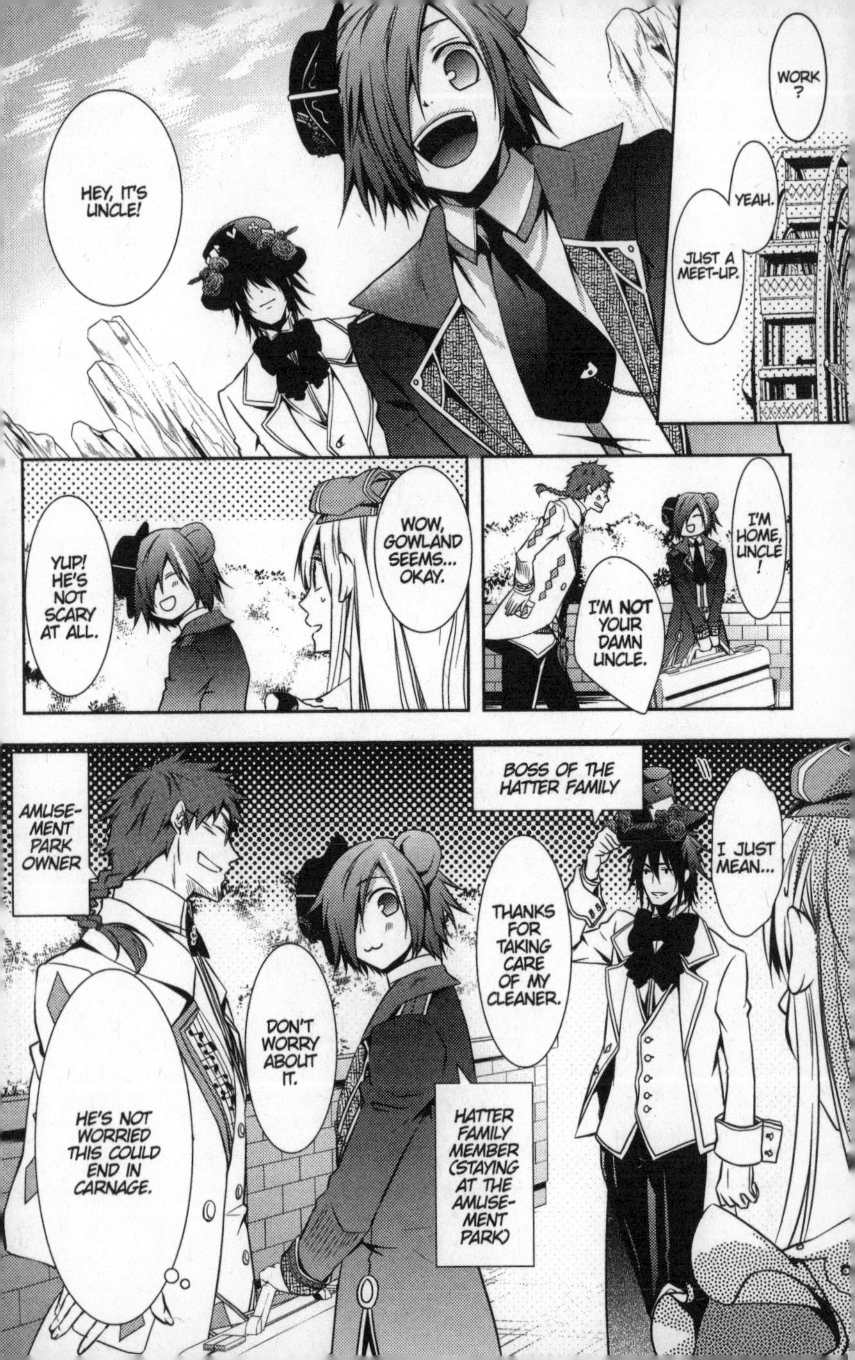
WORK?
YEAH.
JUST A MEET-UP.
HEY, IT'S UNCLE!
I'M HOME, UNCLE!
I'M NOT YOUR DAMN UNCLE.
WOW, GOWLAND SEEMS... OKAY.
YUP! HE'S NOT SCARY AT ALL.
I JUST MEAN...
BOSS OF THE HATTER FAMILY
THANKS FOR TAKING CARE OF MY CLEANER.
AMUSEMENT PARK OWNER
DON'T WORRY ABOUT IT.
HATTER FAMILY MEMBER (STAYING AT THE AMUSEMENT PARK)
HE'S NOT WORRIED THIS COULD END IN CARNAGE.

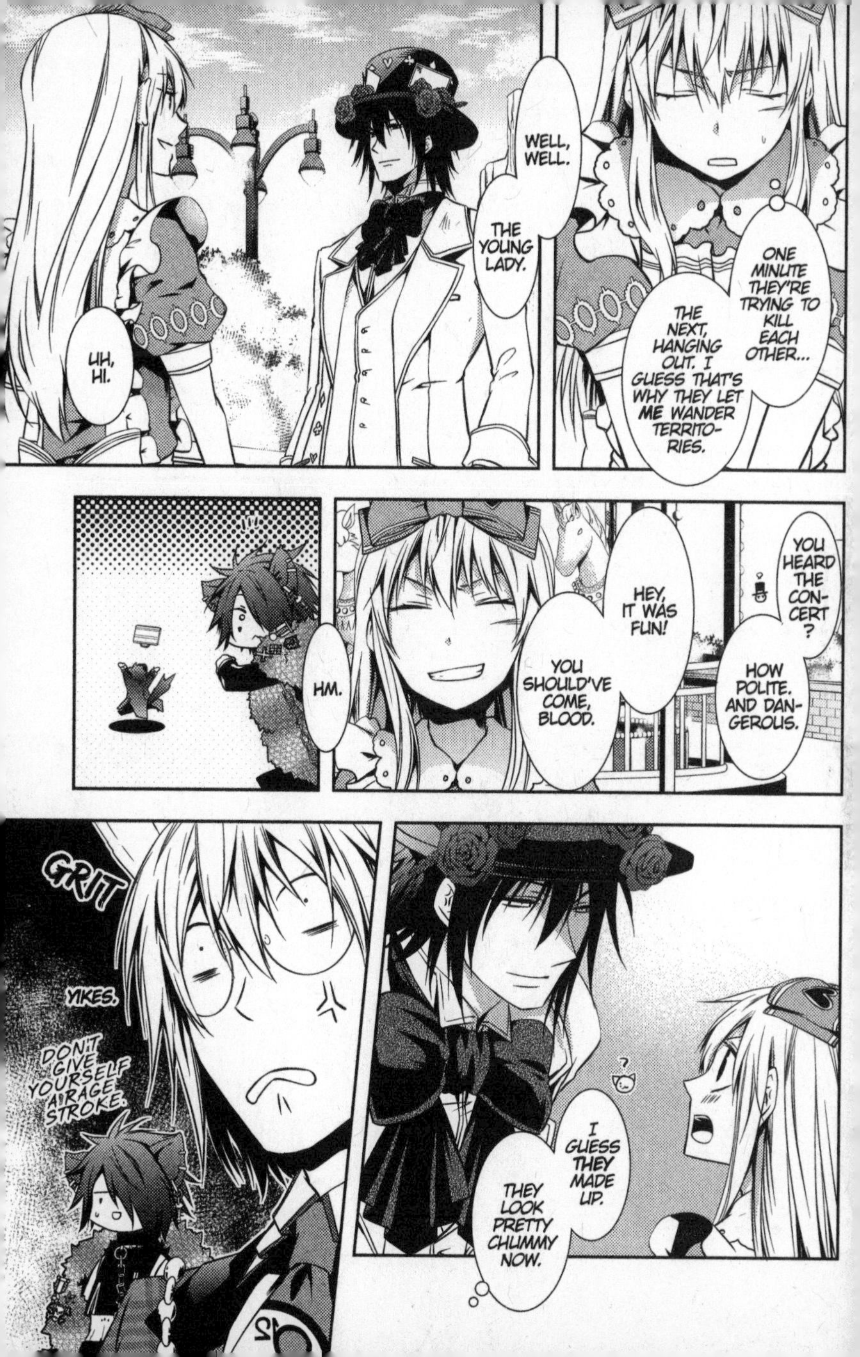
ONE MINUTE THEY'RE TRYING TO KILL EACH OTHER...
THE NEXT, HANGING OUT. I GUESS THAT'S WHY THEY LET ME WANDER TERRITORIES.
WELL, WELL.
THE YOUNG LADY.
UH, HI.
YOU HEARD THE CONCERT?
HOW POLITE. AND DANGEROUS.
HEY, IT WAS FUN!
YOU SHOULD'VE COME, BLOOD.
HM.
I GUESS THEY MADE UP.
THEY LOOK PRETTY CHUMMY NOW.
GRIT
YIKES.
DON'T GIVE YOURSELF A RAGE STROKE.

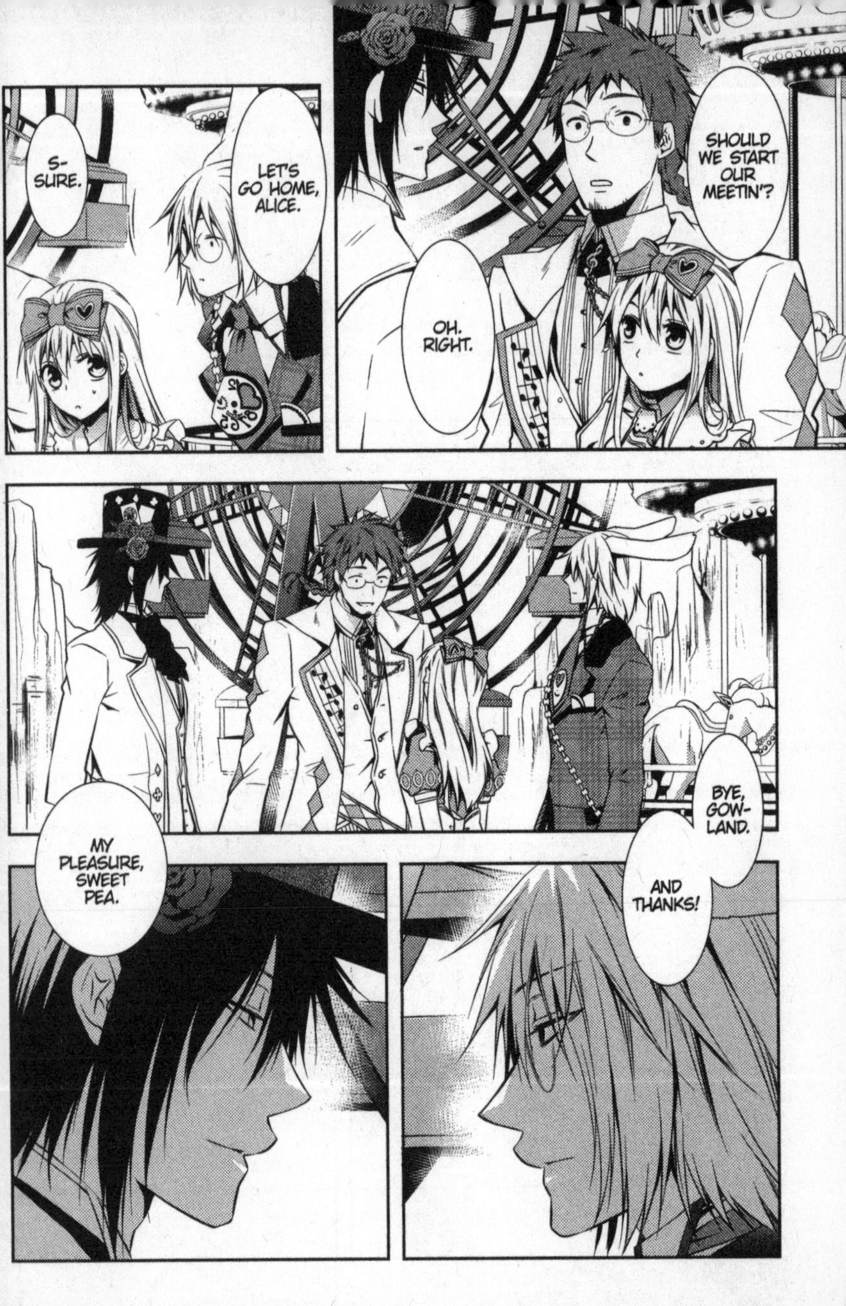
SHOULD WE START OUR MEETIN'?
OH. RIGHT.
LET'S GO HOME, ALICE.
S-SURE.
BYE, GOW-LAND.
AND THANKS!
MY PLEASURE, SWEET PEA.

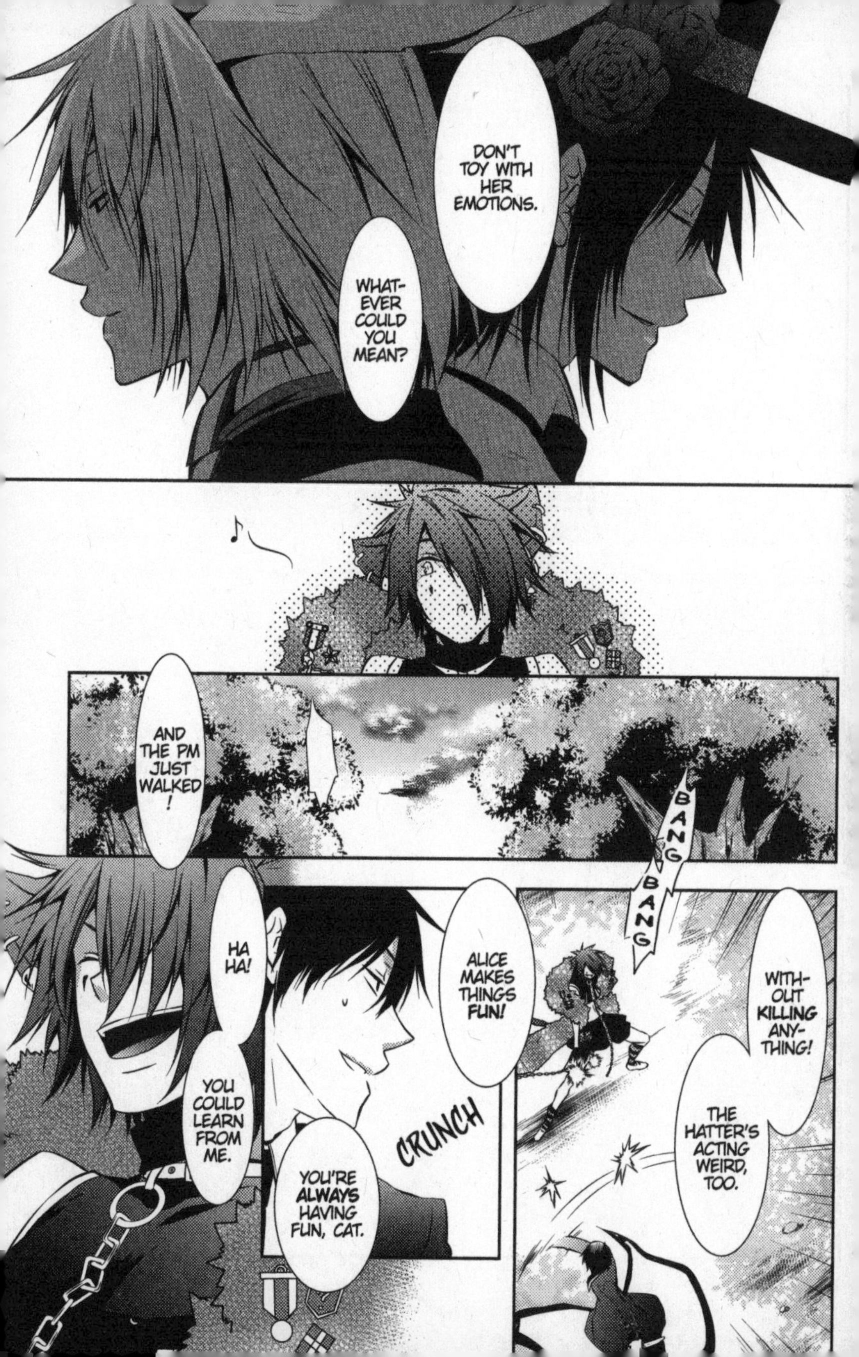
DON'T TOY WITH HER EMOTIONS.
WHAT-EVER COULD YOU MEAN?
BANG BANG
AND THE PM JUST WALKED!
WITH-OUT KILLING ANY-THING!
THE HATTER'S ACTING WEIRD, TOO.
ALICE MAKES THINGS FUN!
CRUNCH
YOU'RE ALWAYS HAVING FUN, CAT.
HA HA!
YOU COULD LEARN FROM ME.

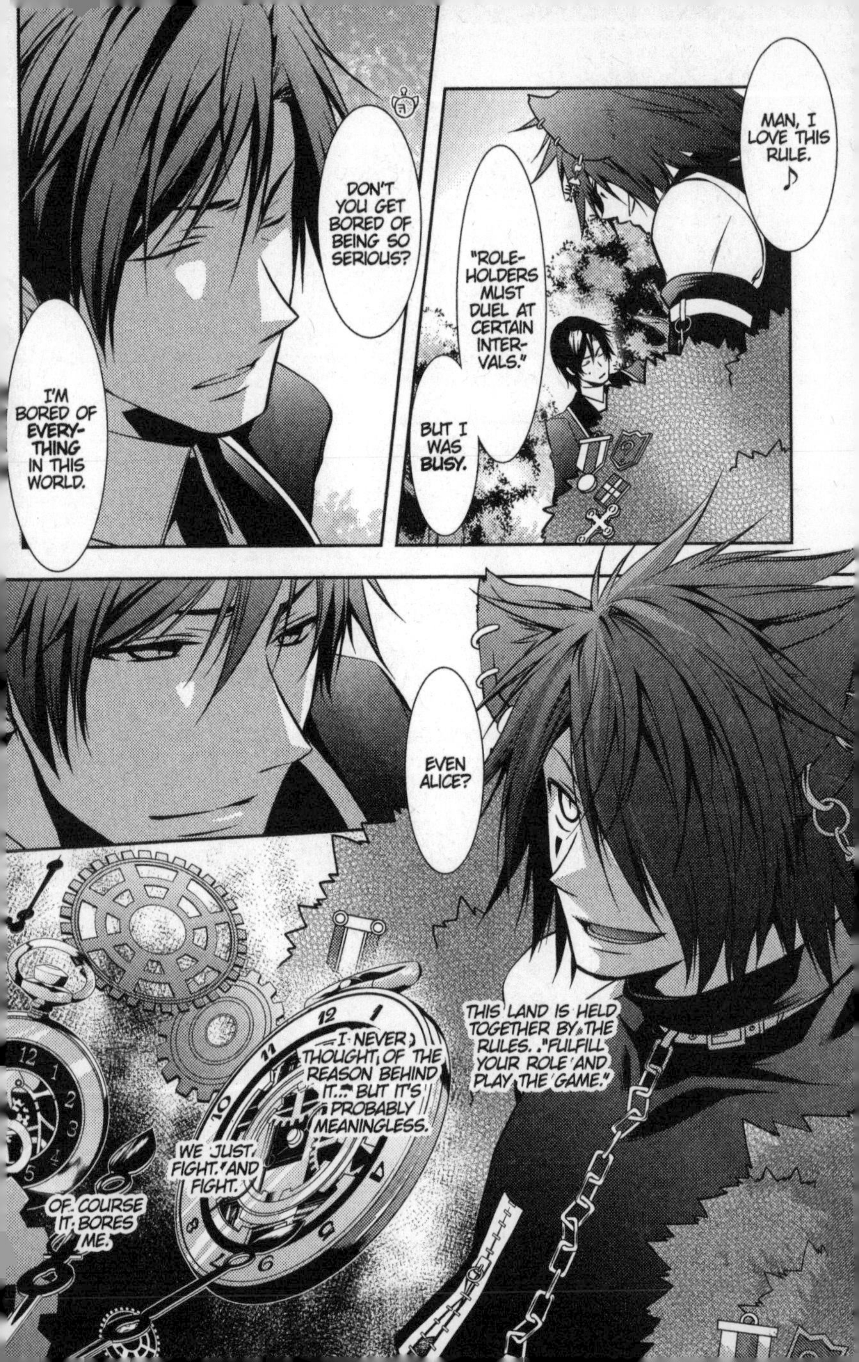
MAN, I LOVE THIS RULE. ♪
"ROLE-HOLDERS MUST DUEL AT CERTAIN INTERVALS."
BUT I WAS BUSY.
DON'T YOU GET BORED OF BEING SO SERIOUS?
I'M BORED OF EVERYTHING IN THIS WORLD.
EVEN ALICE?
THIS LAND IS HELD TOGETHER BY THE RULES. "FULFILL YOUR ROLE AND PLAY THE GAME."
I NEVER THOUGHT OF THE REASON BEHIND IT... BUT IT'S PROBABLY MEANINGLESS.
WE JUST FIGHT AND FIGHT.
OF COURSE IT BORES ME.

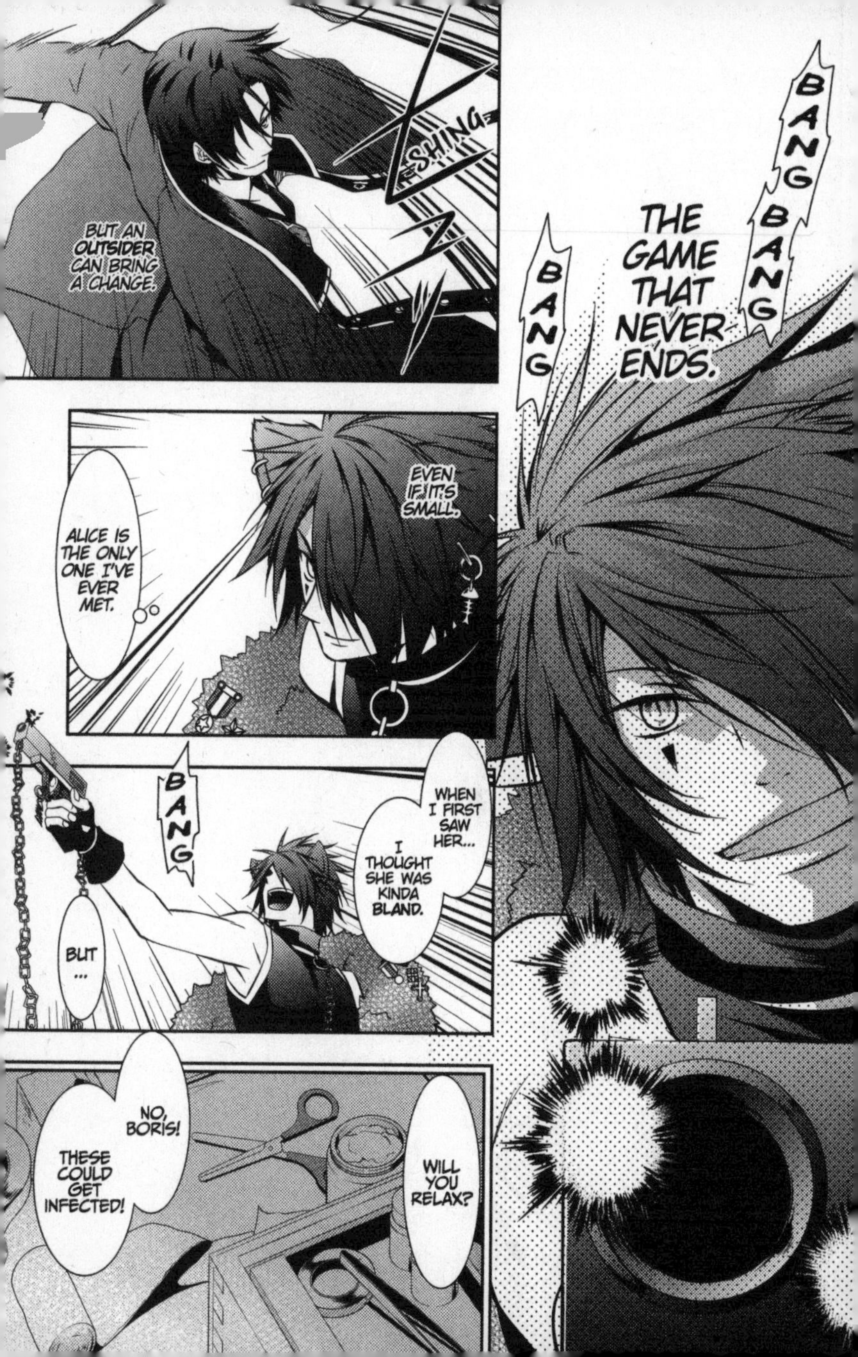
BANG BANG
THE GAME THAT NEVER ENDS.
BANG
SHING
BUT AN OUTSIDER CAN BRING A CHANGE.
EVEN IF IT'S SMALL.
ALICE IS THE ONLY ONE I'VE EVER MET.
WHEN I FIRST SAW HER...
I THOUGHT SHE WAS KINDA BLAND.
BANG
BUT ...
WILL YOU RELAX?
NO, BORIS!
THESE COULD GET INFECTED!

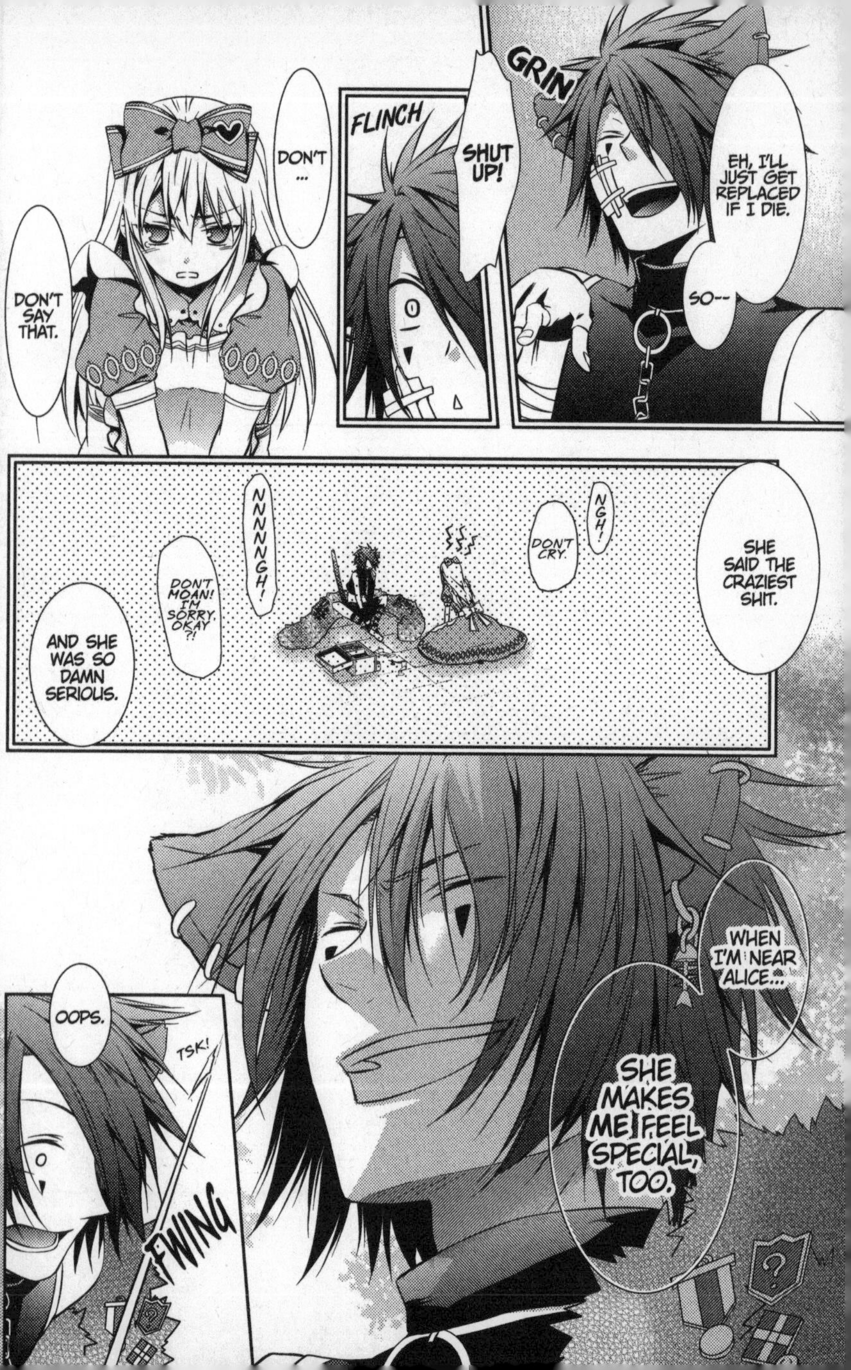
GRIN
EH, I'LL JUST GET REPLACED IF I DIE.
SO--
SHUT UP!
FLINCH
DON'T ...
DON'T SAY THAT.
SHE SAID THE CRAZIEST SHIT.
NGH!
DON'T CRY.
NNNNNGH!
DON'T MOAN! I'M SORRY, OKAY?!
AND SHE WAS SO DAMN SERIOUS.
WHEN I'M NEAR ALICE...
SHE MAKES ME FEEL SPECIAL, TOO.
OOPS.
TSK!
FWING

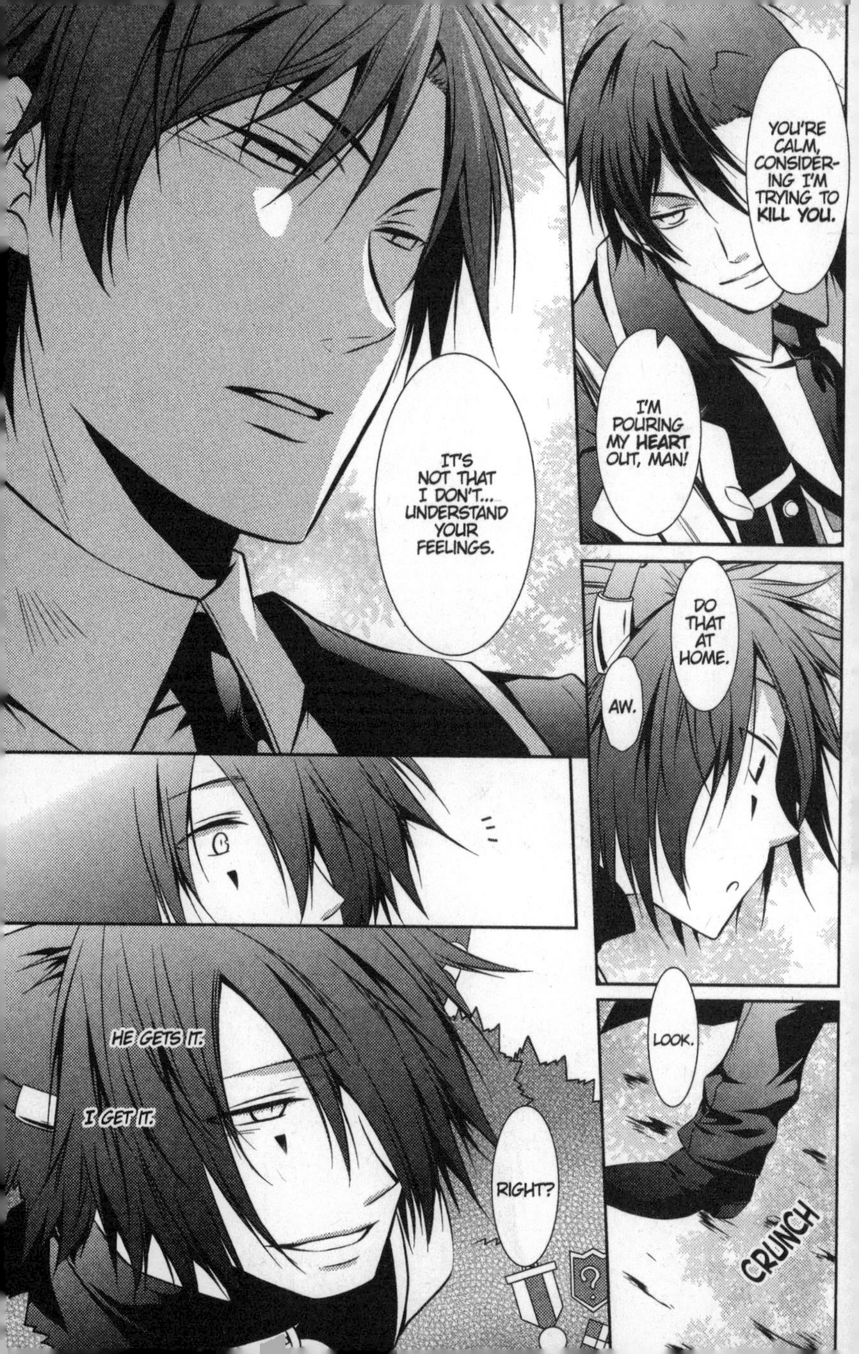
YOU'RE CALM, CONSIDER-ING I'M TRYING TO KILL YOU.
I'M POURING MY HEART OUT, MAN!
IT'S NOT THAT I DON'T... UNDERSTAND YOUR FEELINGS.
DO THAT AT HOME.
AW.
LOOK.
CRUNCH
HE GETS IT.
I GET IT.
RIGHT?

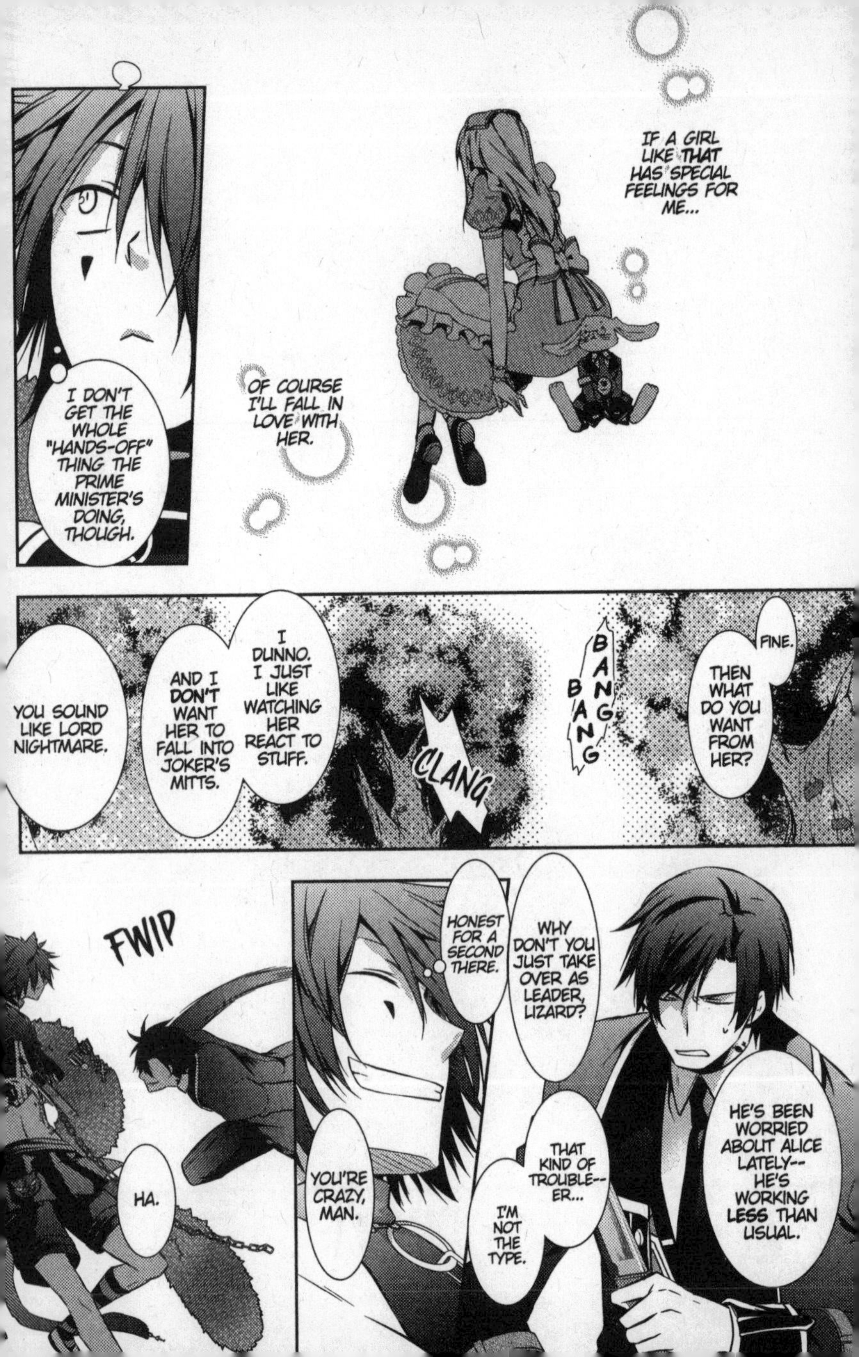
IF A GIRL LIKE THAT HAS SPECIAL FEELINGS FOR ME...
OF COURSE I'LL FALL IN LOVE WITH HER.
I DON'T GET THE WHOLE "HANDS-OFF" THING THE PRIME MINISTER'S DOING, THOUGH.
FINE.
THEN WHAT DO YOU WANT FROM HER?
BANG
BANG
CLANG
I DUNNO. I JUST LIKE WATCHING HER REACT TO STUFF.
AND I DON'T WANT HER TO FALL INTO JOKER'S MITTS.
YOU SOUND LIKE LORD NIGHTMARE.
WHY DON'T YOU JUST TAKE OVER AS LEADER, LIZARD?
HONEST FOR A SECOND THERE.
HE'S BEEN WORRIED ABOUT ALICE LATELY-- HE'S WORKING LESS THAN USUAL.
THAT KIND OF TROUBLE-- ER...
I'M NOT THE TYPE.
YOU'RE CRAZY, MAN.
FWIP
HA.

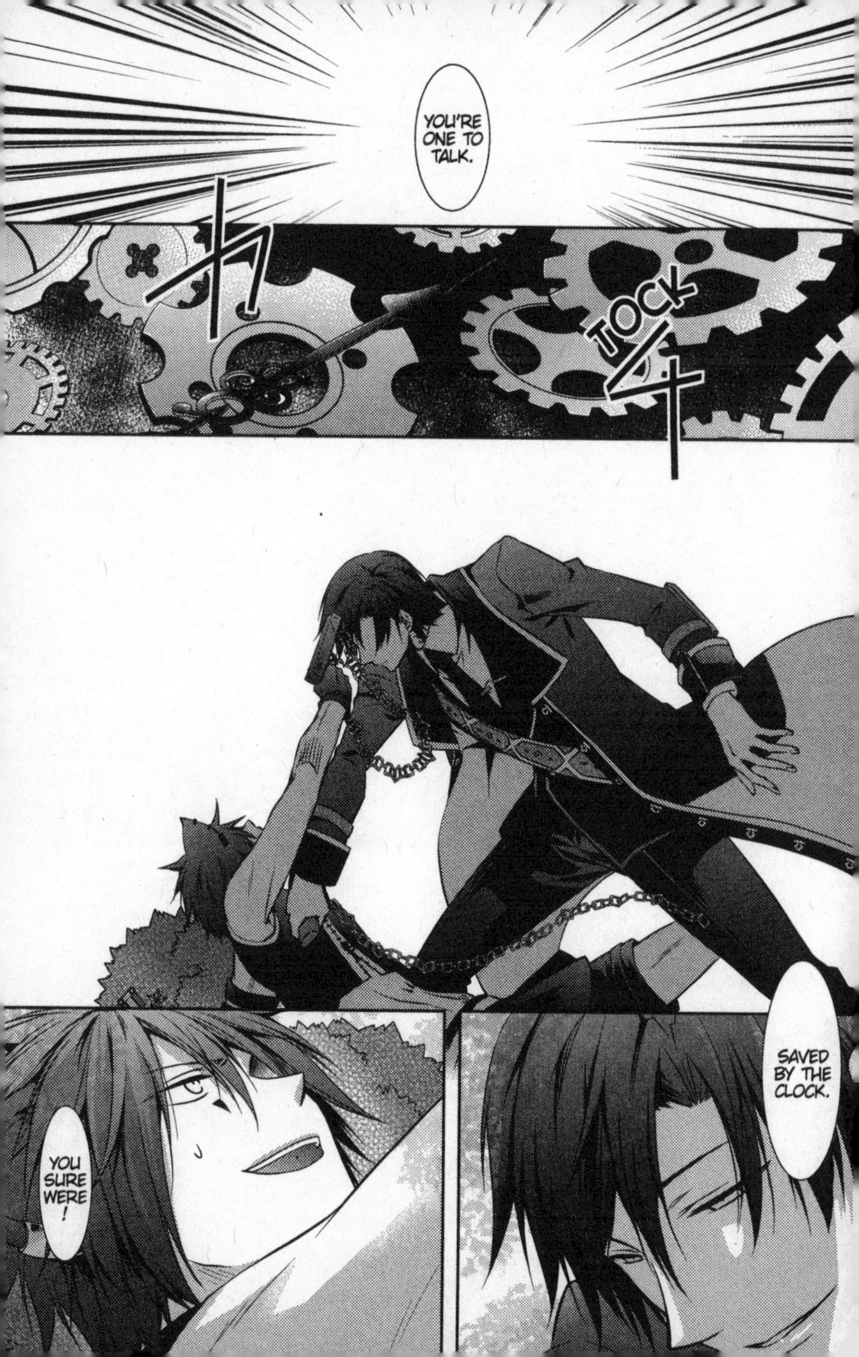
YOU'RE ONE TO TALK.
TOCK
SAVED BY THE CLOCK.
YOU SURE WERE!

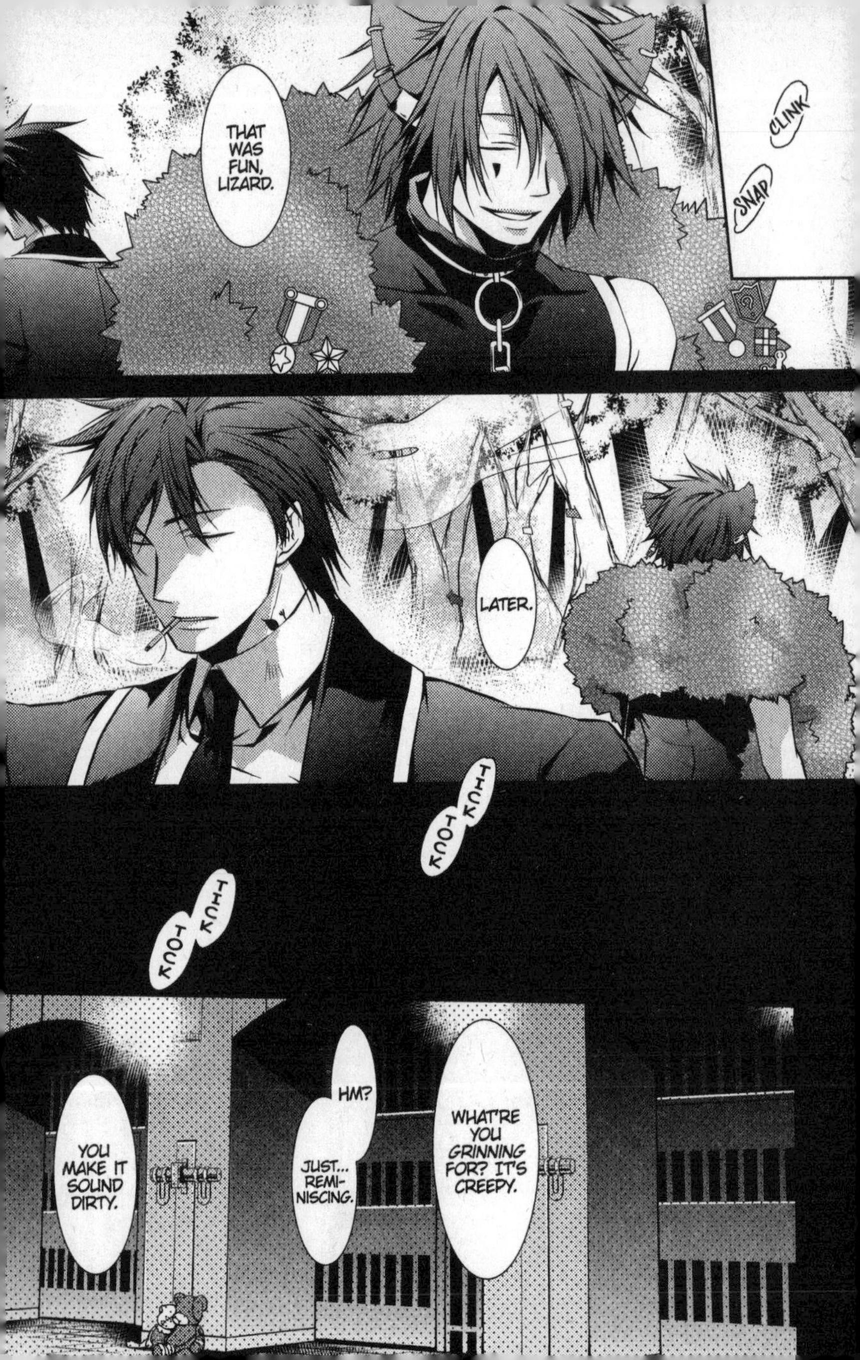
CLINK
SNAP
THAT WAS FUN, LIZARD.
LATER.
TICK TOCK
TICK TOCK
WHAT'RE YOU GRINNING FOR? IT'S CREEPY.
HM?
JUST... REMI-NISCING.
YOU MAKE IT SOUND DIRTY.

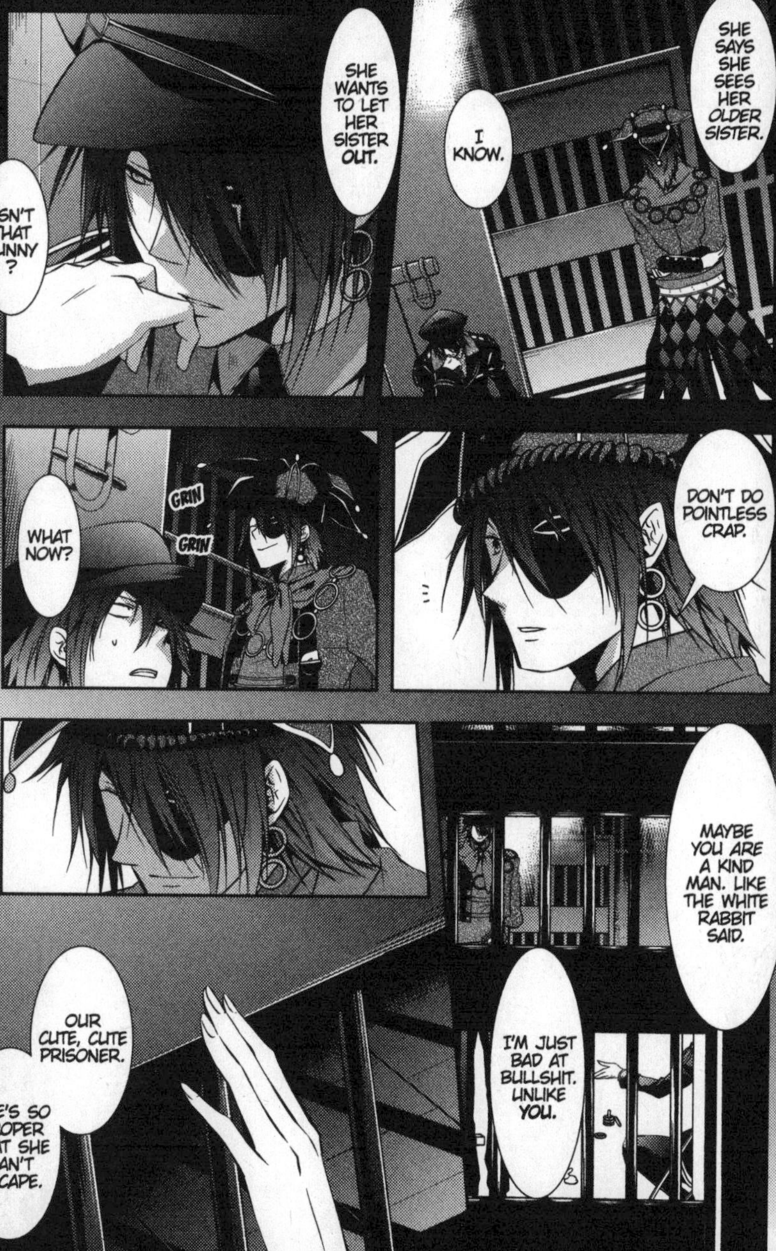
SHE SAYS SHE SEES HER OLDER SISTER.
I KNOW.
SHE WANTS TO LET HER SISTER OUT.
ISN'T THAT FUNNY?
DON'T DO POINTLESS CRAP.
GRIN
GRIN
WHAT NOW?
MAYBE YOU ARE A KIND MAN. LIKE THE WHITE RABBIT SAID.
I'M JUST BAD AT BULLSHIT. UNLIKE YOU.
OUR CUTE, CUTE PRISONER.
SHE'S SO PROPER THAT SHE CAN'T ESCAPE.

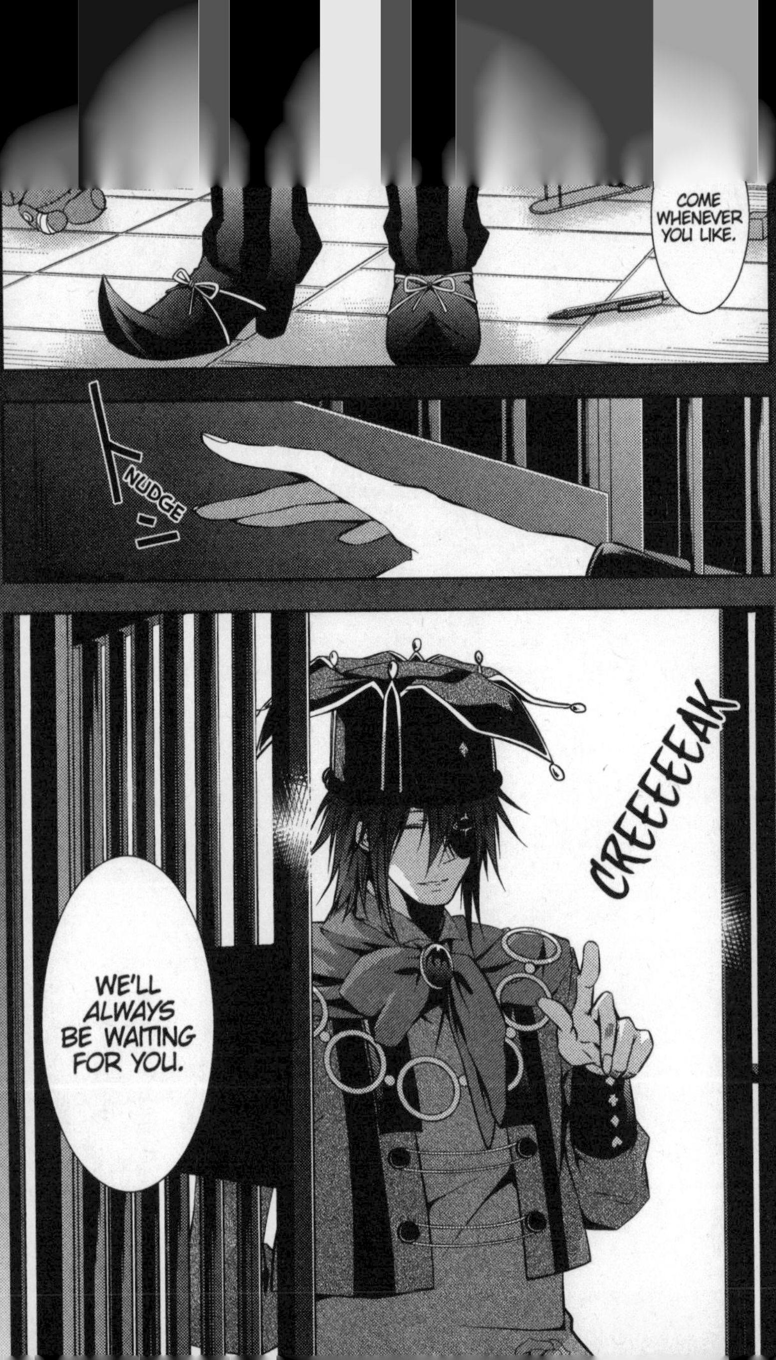
COME WHENEVER YOU LIKE.
NUDGE
CREEEEEAK
WE'LL ALWAYS BE WAITING FOR YOU.

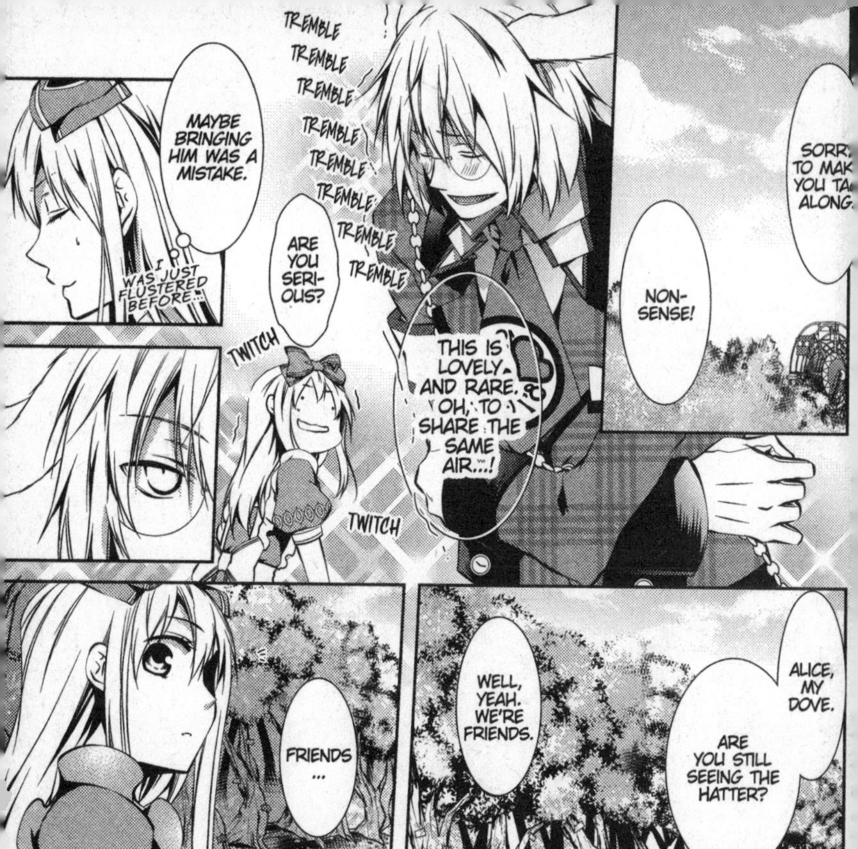
SORR TO MAK YOU TA ALONG.
NON-SENSE!
TREMBLE TREMBLE TREMBLE TREMBLE TREMBLE TREMBLE TREMBLE TREMBLE
THIS IS LOVELY AND RARE. OH, TO SHARE THE SAME AIR...!
ARE YOU SERI-OUS?
TWITCH
TWITCH
MAYBE BRINGING HIM WAS A MISTAKE.
I WAS JUST FLUSTERED BEFORE...
ALICE, MY DOVE.
ARE YOU STILL SEEING THE HATTER?
WELL, YEAH. WE'RE FRIENDS.
FRIENDS...

Hit: 13

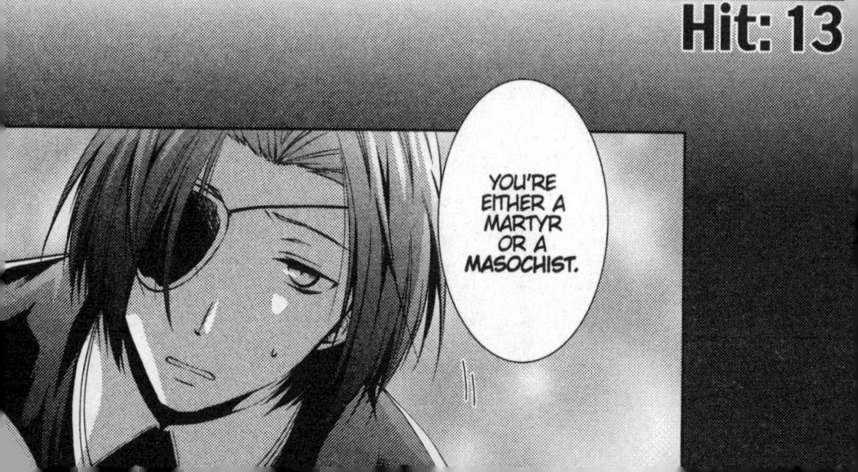
YOU'RE EITHER A MARTYR OR A MASOCHIST.

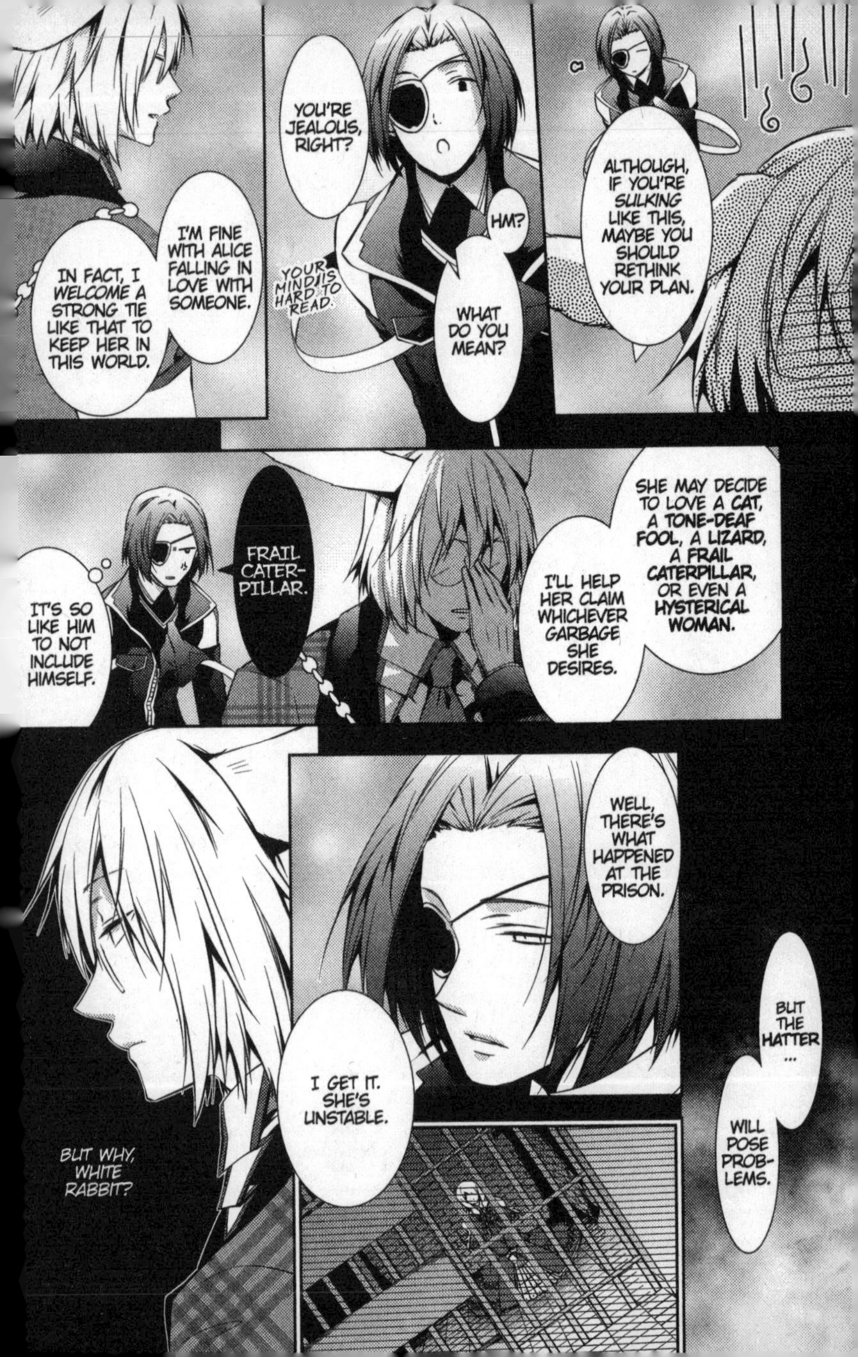
ALTHOUGH, IF YOU'RE SULKING LIKE THIS, MAYBE YOU SHOULD RETHINK YOUR PLAN.
YOU'RE JEALOUS, RIGHT?
HM?
WHAT DO YOU MEAN?
YOUR MIND IS HARD TO READ.
I'M FINE WITH ALICE FALLING IN LOVE WITH SOMEONE.
IN FACT, I WELCOME A STRONG TIE LIKE THAT TO KEEP HER IN THIS WORLD.
SHE MAY DECIDE TO LOVE A CAT, A TONE-DEAF FOOL, A LIZARD, A FRAIL CATERPILLAR, OR EVEN A HYSTERICAL WOMAN.
I'LL HELP HER CLAIM WHICHEVER GARBAGE SHE DESIRES.
FRAIL CATER-PILLAR.
IT'S SO LIKE HIM TO NOT INCLUDE HIMSELF.
BUT THE HATTER...
WILL POSE PROB-LEMS.
WELL, THERE'S WHAT HAPPENED AT THE PRISON.
I GET IT. SHE'S UNSTABLE.
BUT WHY, WHITE RABBIT?

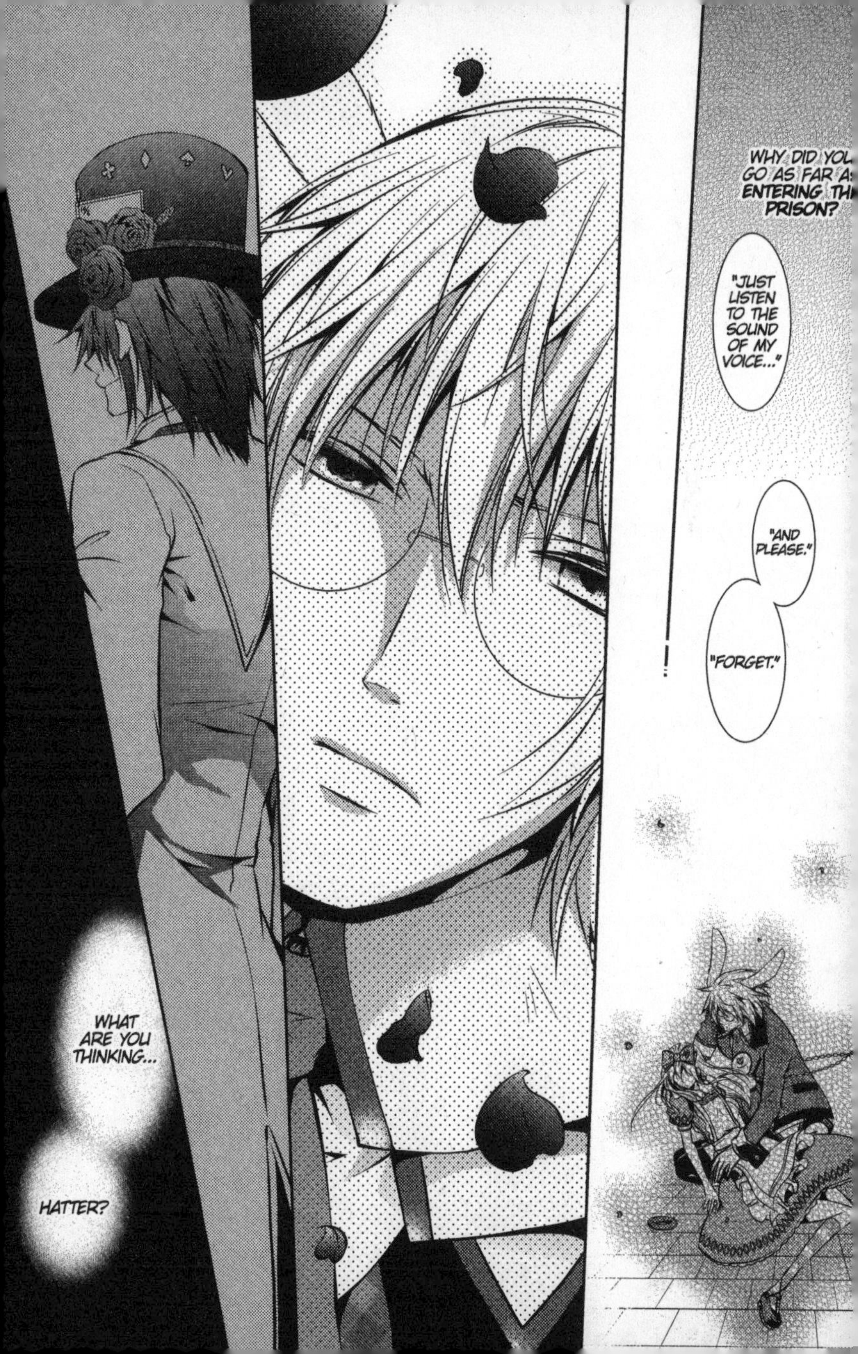
WHY DID YOU GO AS FAR AS ENTERING THE PRISON?
"JUST LISTEN TO THE SOUND OF MY VOICE..."
"AND PLEASE."
"FORGET."
WHAT ARE YOU THINKING...
HATTER?

Hit: 13

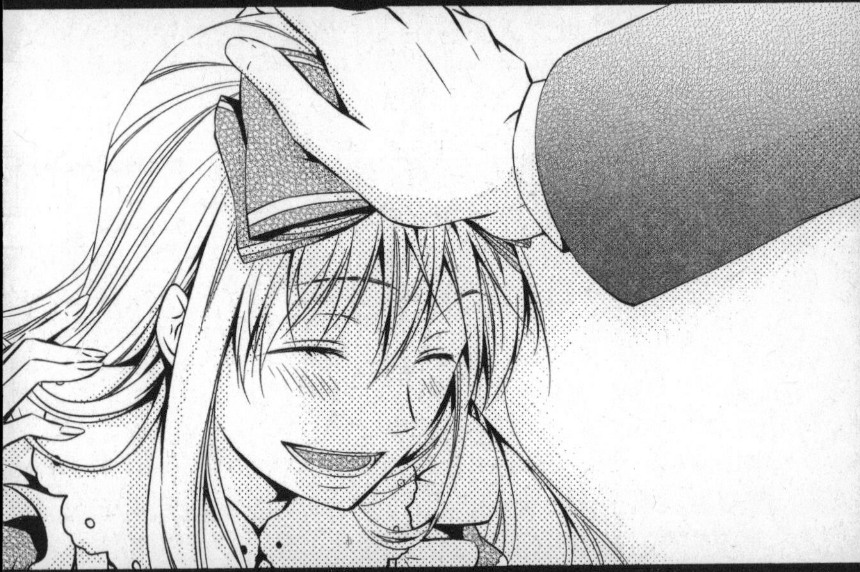

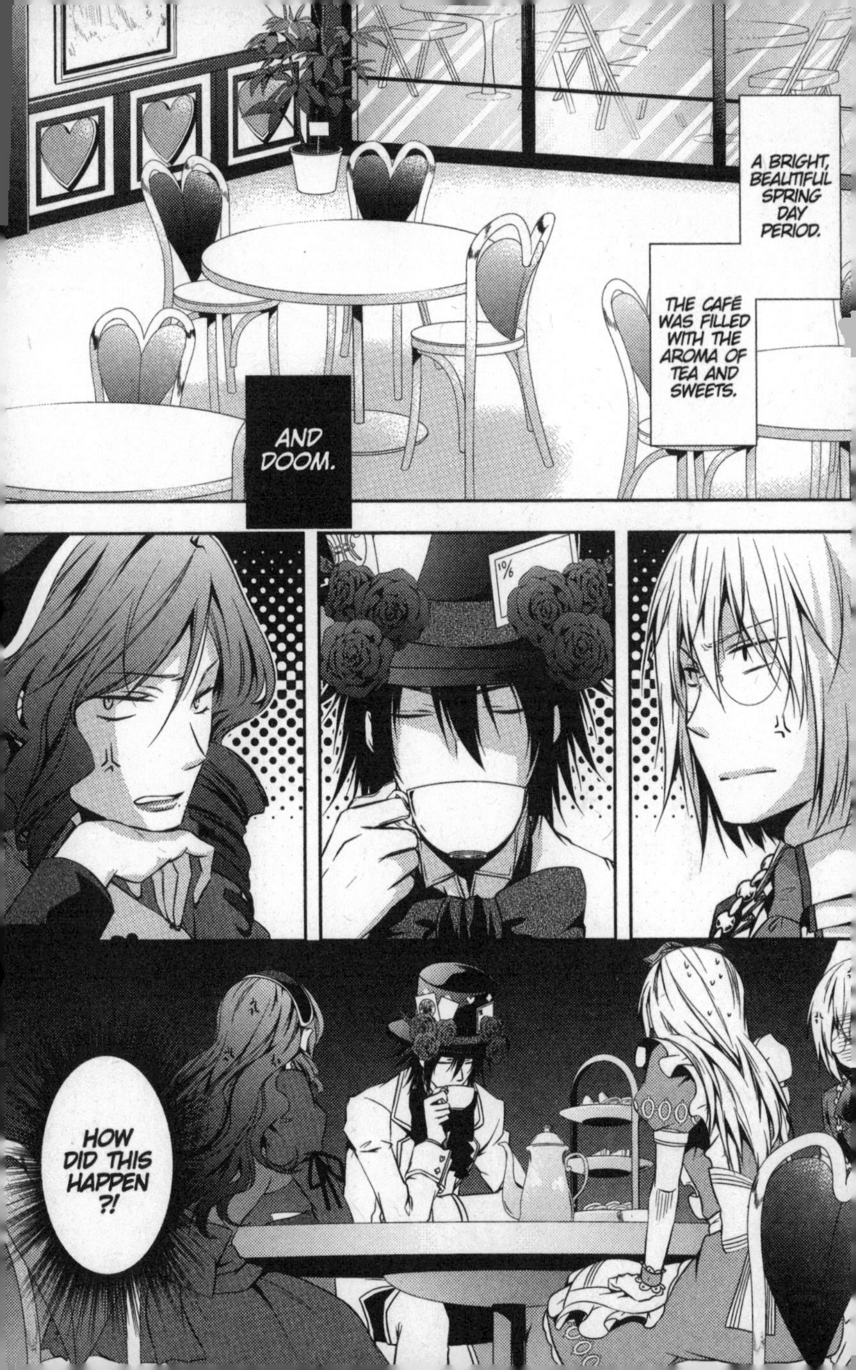
A BRIGHT, BEAUTIFUL SPRING DAY PERIOD.
THE CAFÉ WAS FILLED WITH THE AROMA OF TEA AND SWEETS.
AND DOOM.
HOW DID THIS HAPPEN ?!

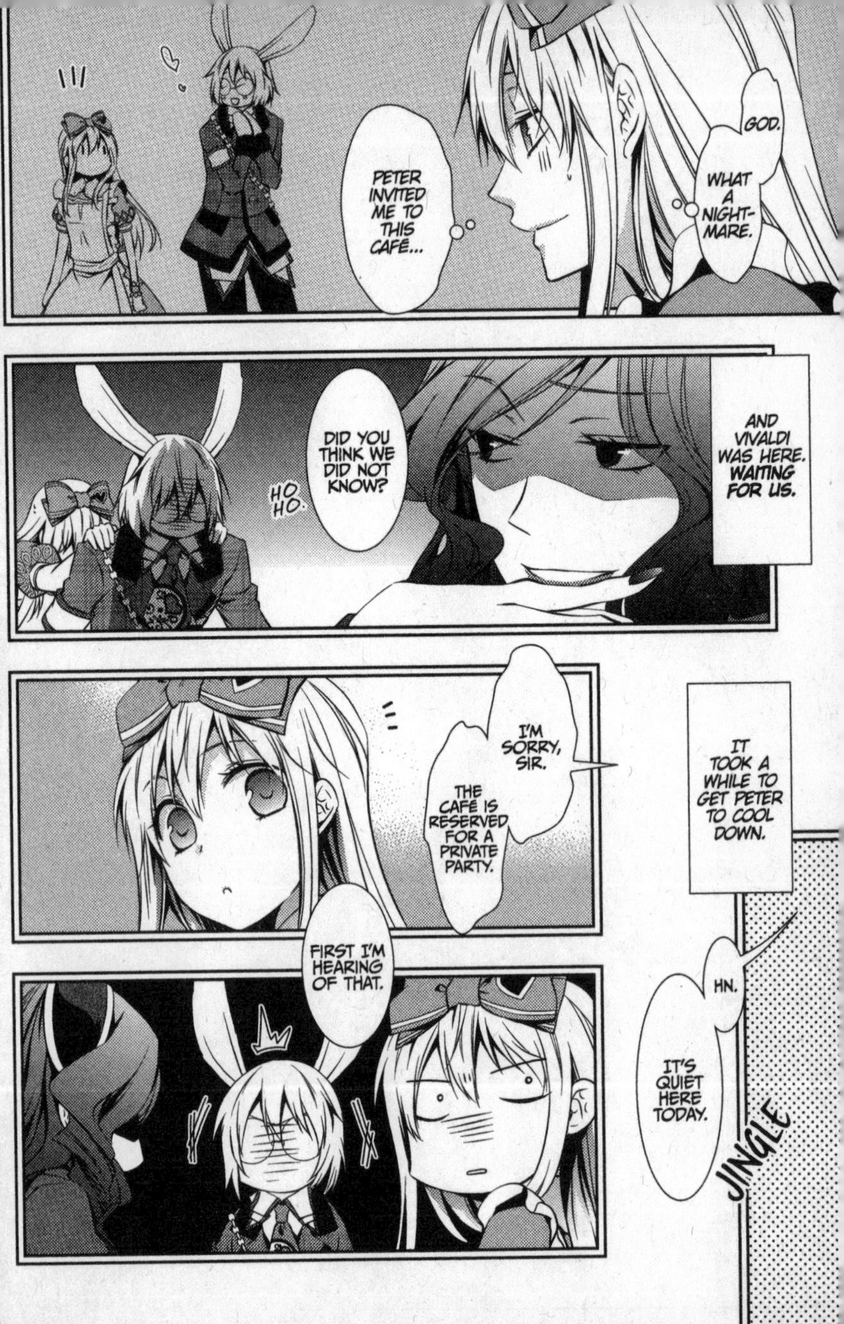
GOD.
WHAT A NIGHT-MARE.
PETER INVITED ME TO THIS CAFÉ...
AND VIVALDI WAS HERE. WAITING FOR US.
DID YOU THINK WE DID NOT KNOW?
HO HO.
IT TOOK A WHILE TO GET PETER TO COOL DOWN.
JINGLE
HN.
IT'S QUIET HERE TODAY.
I'M SORRY, SIR.
THE CAFÉ IS RESERVED FOR A PRIVATE PARTY.
FIRST I'M HEARING OF THAT.

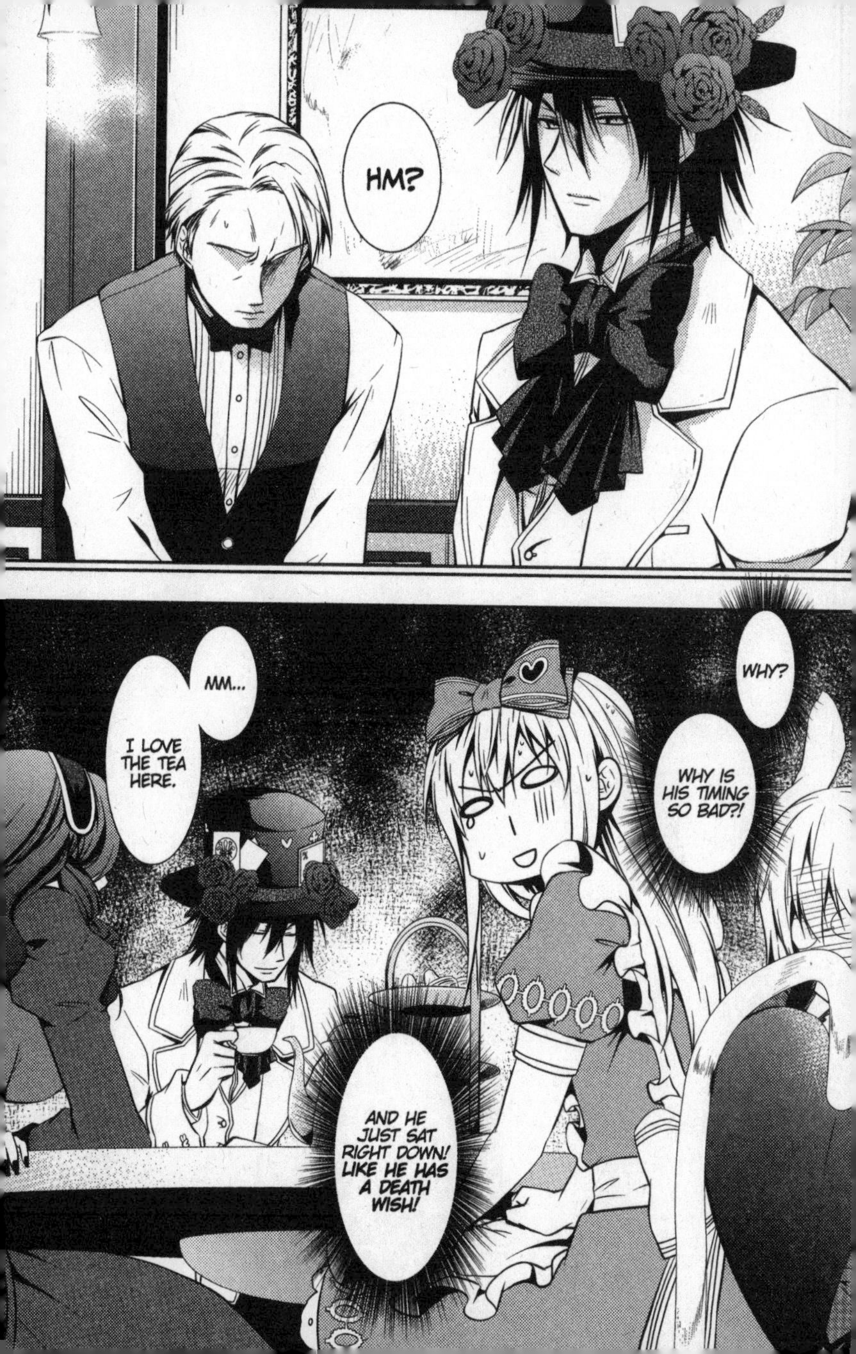
HM?
WHY?
WHY IS HIS TIMING SO BAD?!
MM...
I LOVE THE TEA HERE.
AND HE JUST SAT RIGHT DOWN! LIKE HE HAS A DEATH WISH!

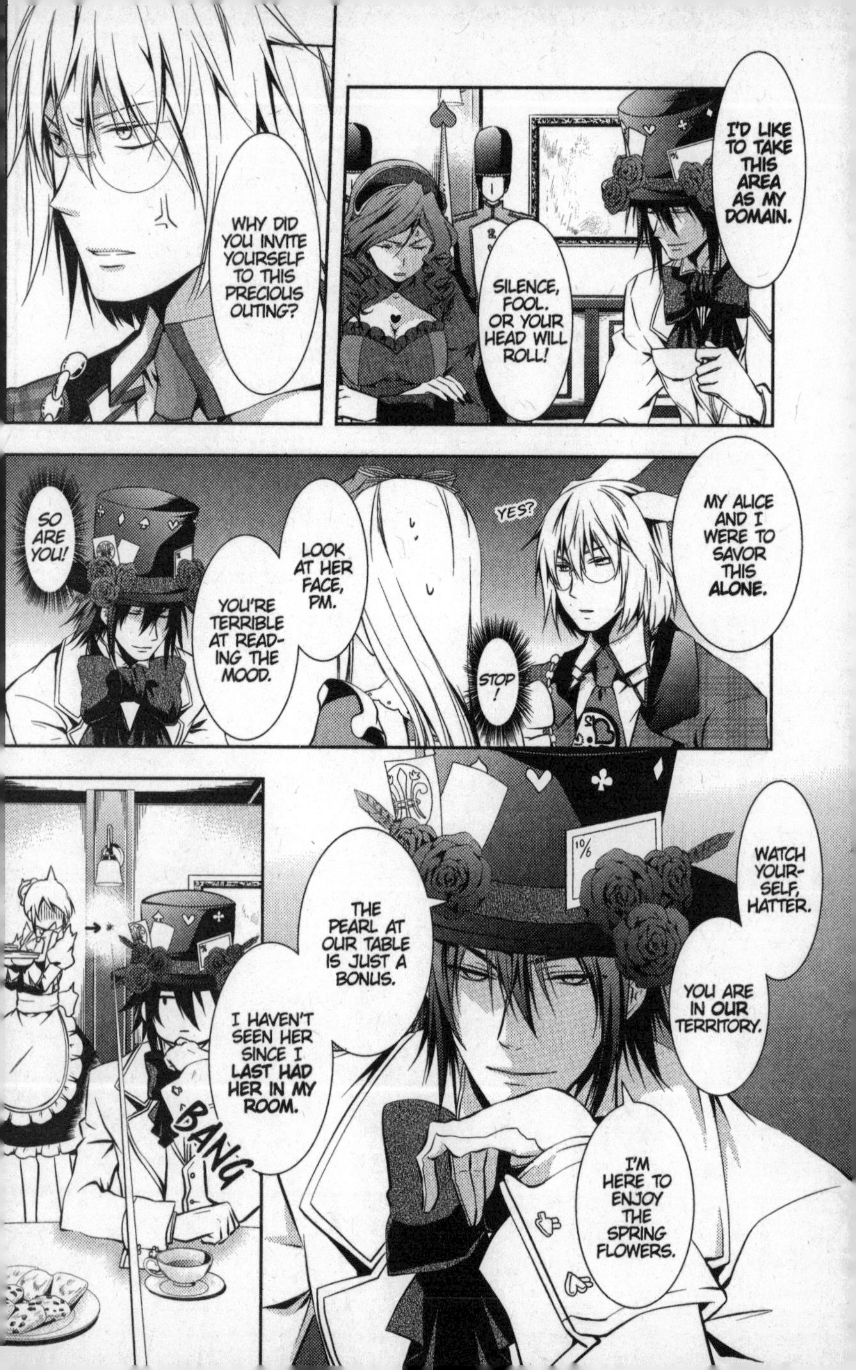
I'D LIKE TO TAKE THIS AREA AS MY DOMAIN.
SILENCE, FOOL. OR YOUR HEAD WILL ROLL!
WHY DID YOU INVITE YOURSELF TO THIS PRECIOUS OUTING?
MY ALICE AND I WERE TO SAVOR THIS ALONE.
YES?
STOP!
LOOK AT HER FACE, PM.
YOU'RE TERRIBLE AT READING THE MOOD.
SO ARE YOU!
WATCH YOURSELF, HATTER.
YOU ARE IN OUR TERRITORY.
I'M HERE TO ENJOY THE SPRING FLOWERS.
THE PEARL AT OUR TABLE IS JUST A BONUS.
I HAVEN'T SEEN HER SINCE I LAST HAD HER IN MY ROOM.
BANG

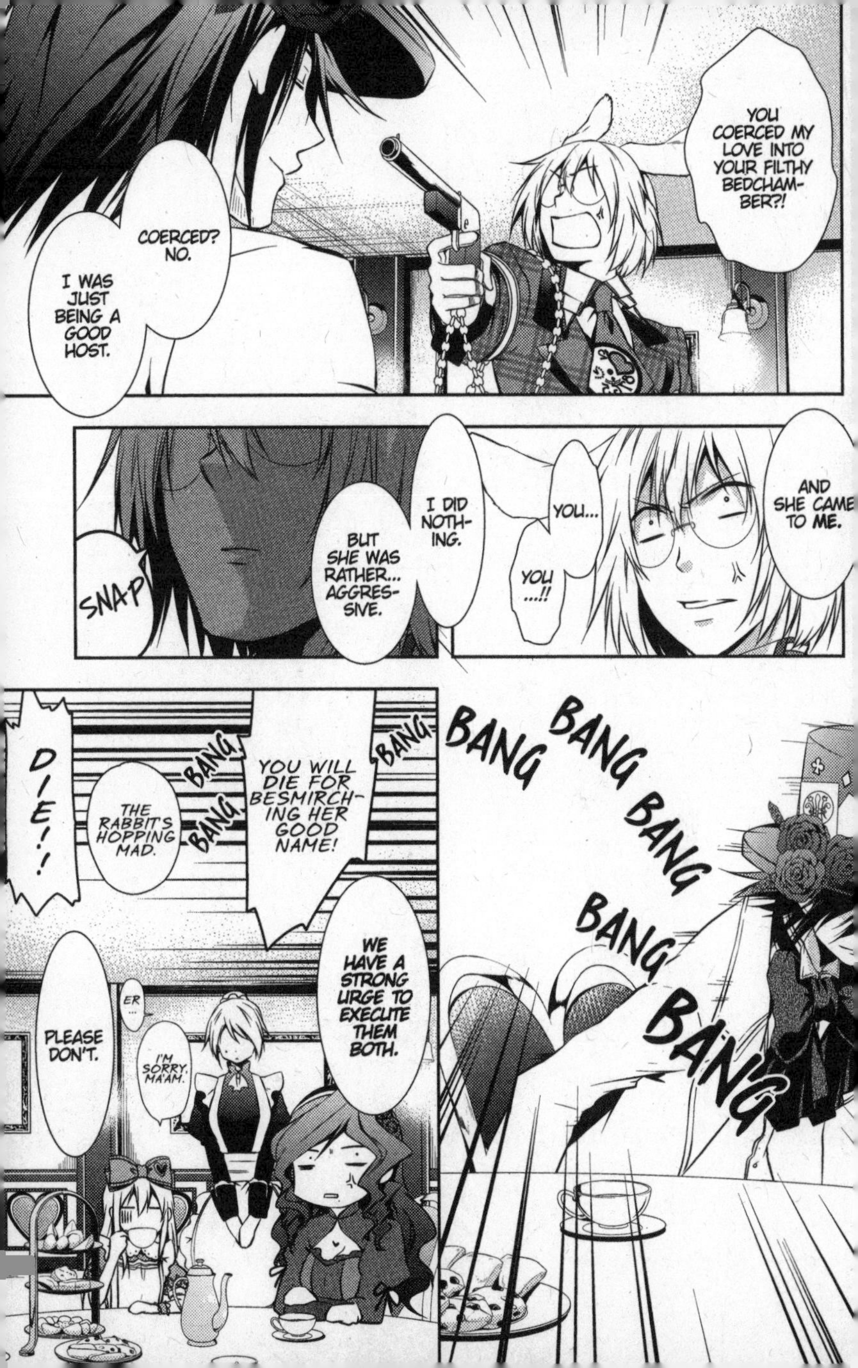
YOU COERCED MY LOVE INTO YOUR FILTHY BEDCHAMBER?!
COERCED? NO.
I WAS JUST BEING A GOOD HOST.
AND SHE CAME TO ME.
YOU...
YOU ...!!
I DID NOTHING.
BUT SHE WAS RATHER... AGGRESSIVE.
SNAP
BANG BANG BANG BANG BANG BANG
BANG
YOU WILL DIE FOR BESMIRCHING HER GOOD NAME!
BANG
BANG
THE RABBIT'S HOPPING MAD.
DIE!!
WE HAVE A STRONG URGE TO EXECUTE THEM BOTH.
ER...
I'M SORRY, MA'AM.
PLEASE DON'T.

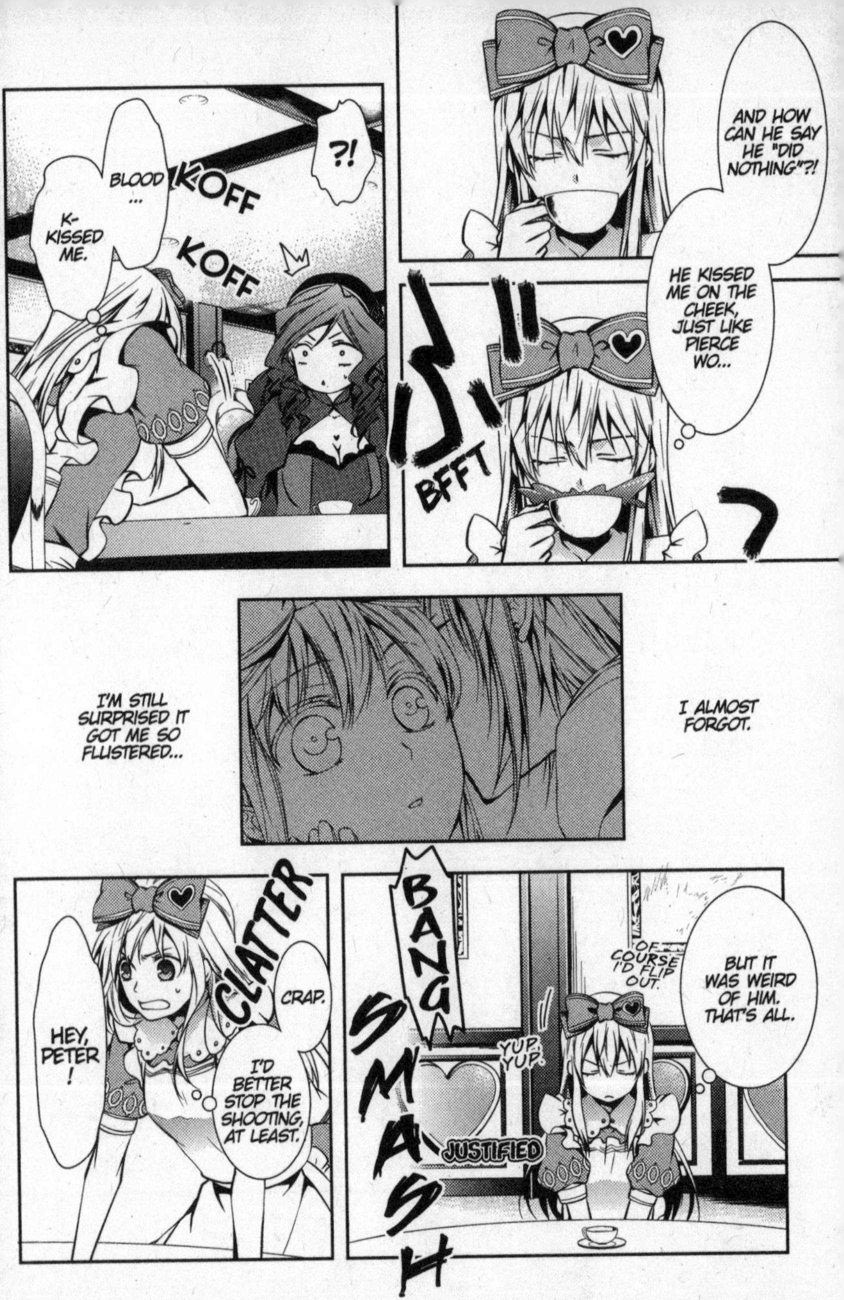
AND HOW CAN HE SAY HE "DID NOTHING"?!
HE KISSED ME ON THE CHEEK, JUST LIKE PIERCE WO...
BFFT
?!
KOFF
KOFF
BLOOD ...
K-KISSED ME.
I ALMOST FORGOT.
I'M STILL SURPRISED IT GOT ME SO FLUSTERED...
BUT IT WAS WEIRD OF HIM. THAT'S ALL.
OF COURSE I'D FLIP OUT.
YUP, YUP.
JUSTIFIED
BANG
SMASH
CLATTER
CRAP.
I'D BETTER STOP THE SHOOTING, AT LEAST.
HEY, PETER!

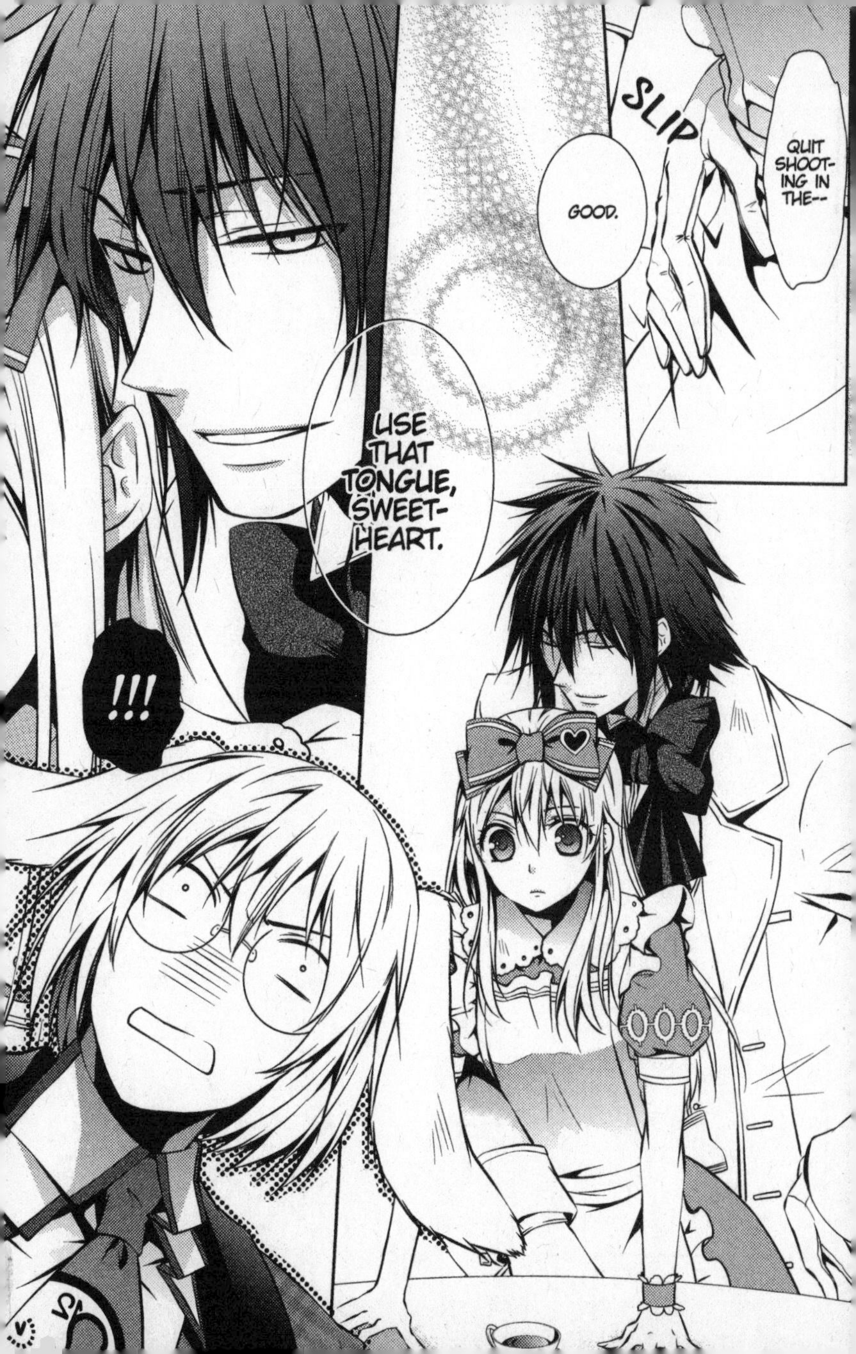

QUIT SHOOTING IN THE--
SLIP
GOOD.
USE THAT TONGUE, SWEET-HEART.
!!!

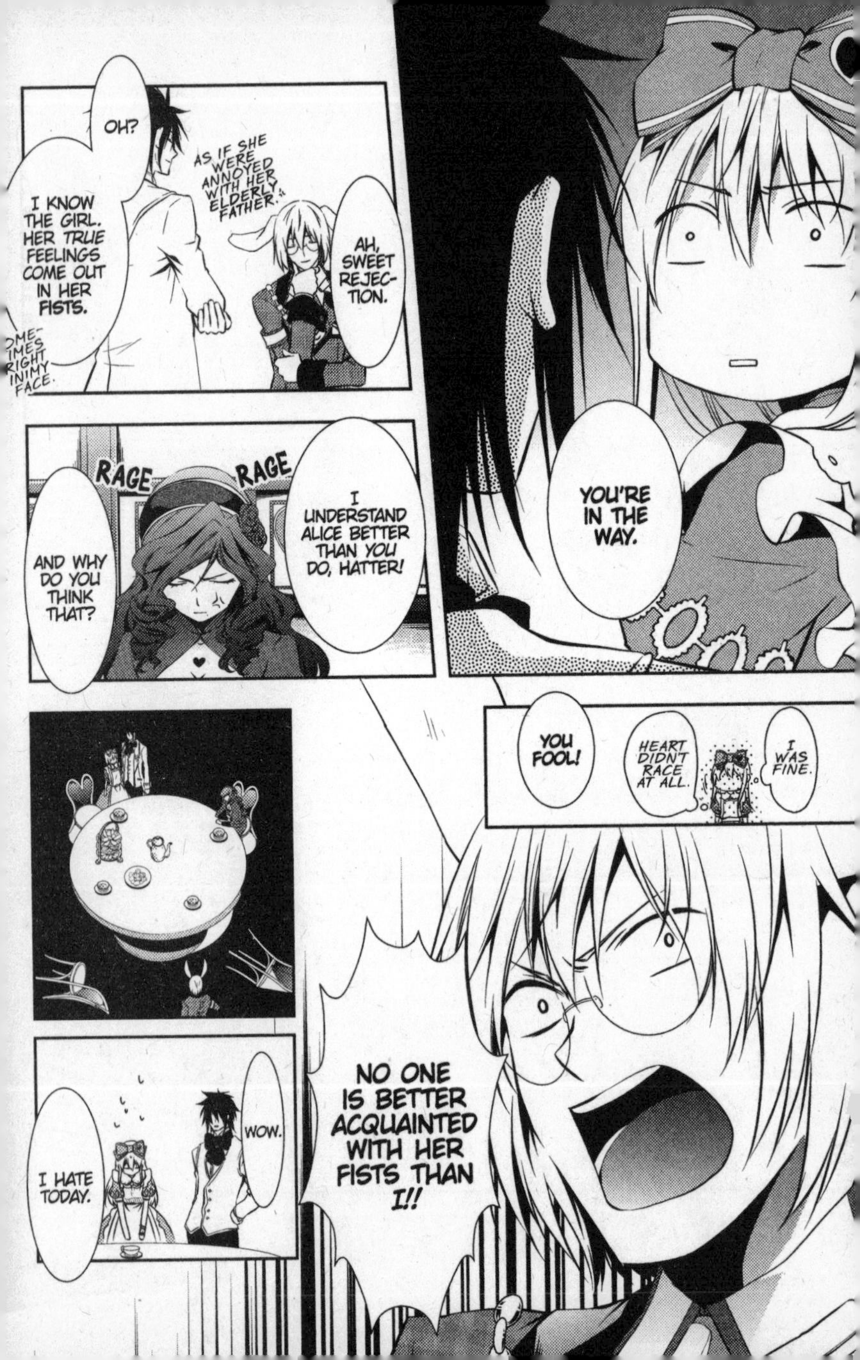
YOU'RE IN THE WAY.
AH, SWEET REJECTION.
AS IF SHE WERE ANNOYED WITH HER ELDERLY FATHER.
OH?
I KNOW THE GIRL. HER TRUE FEELINGS COME OUT IN HER FISTS.
OME- IMES RIGHT IN MY FACE.
I UNDERSTAND ALICE BETTER THAN YOU DO, HATTER!
RAGE
RAGE
AND WHY DO YOU THINK THAT?
I WAS FINE.
HEART DIDN'T RACE AT ALL.
YOU FOOL!
NO ONE IS BETTER ACQUAINTED WITH HER FISTS THAN I!!
WOW.
I HATE TODAY.

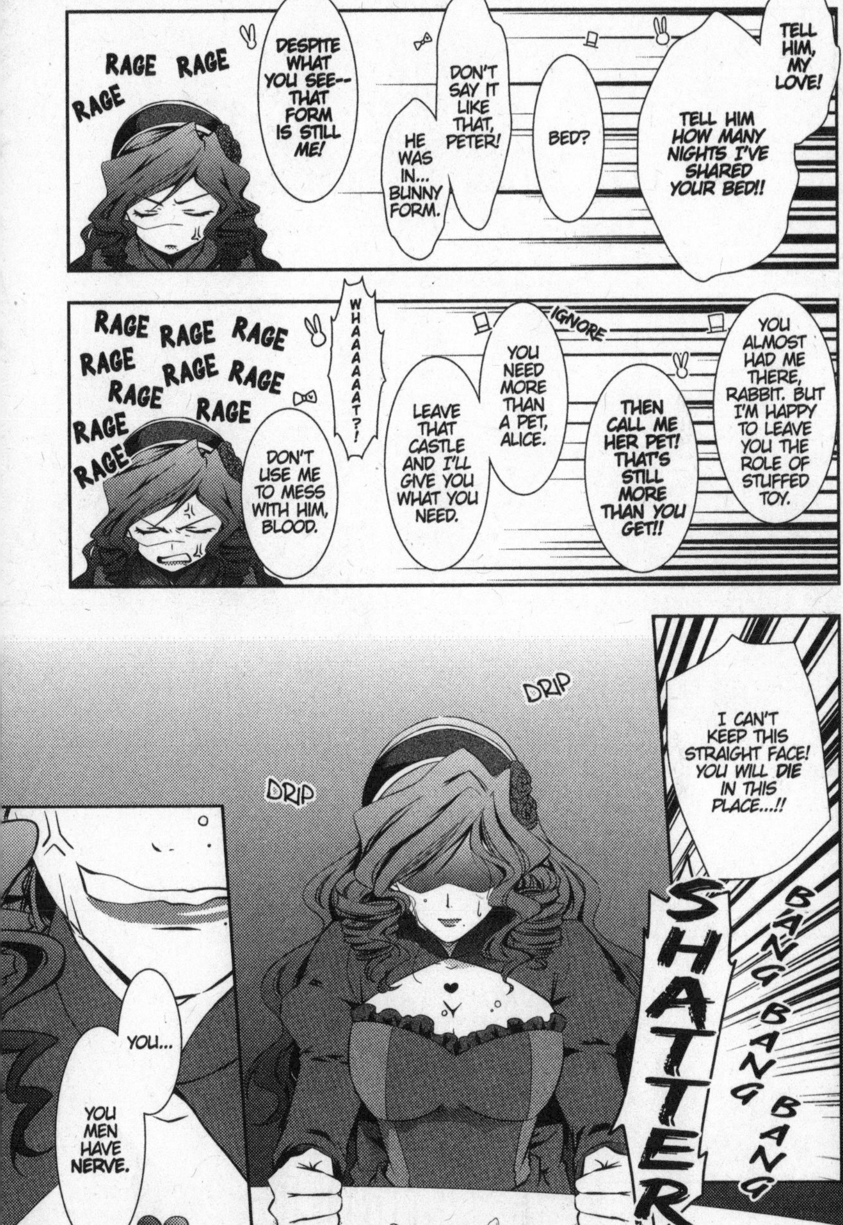
TELL HIM, MY LOVE!
TELL HIM HOW MANY NIGHTS I'VE SHARED YOUR BED!!
BED?
DON'T SAY IT LIKE THAT, PETER!
HE WAS IN... BUNNY FORM.
DESPITE WHAT YOU SEE--THAT FORM IS STILL ME!
RAGE RAGE RAGE
YOU ALMOST HAD ME THERE, RABBIT. BUT I'M HAPPY TO LEAVE YOU THE ROLE OF STUFFED TOY.
THEN CALL ME HER PET! THAT'S STILL MORE THAN YOU GET!!
IGNORE
YOU NEED MORE THAN A PET, ALICE.
LEAVE THAT CASTLE AND I'LL GIVE YOU WHAT YOU NEED.
WHAAAAAAAT?!
DON'T USE ME TO MESS WITH HIM, BLOOD.
RAGE RAGE RAGE RAGE RAGE RAGE RAGE RAGE RAGE RAGE
I CAN'T KEEP THIS STRAIGHT FACE! YOU WILL DIE IN THIS PLACE...!!
BANG BANG BANG
SHATTER
DRIP
DRIP
YOU...
YOU MEN HAVE NERVE.

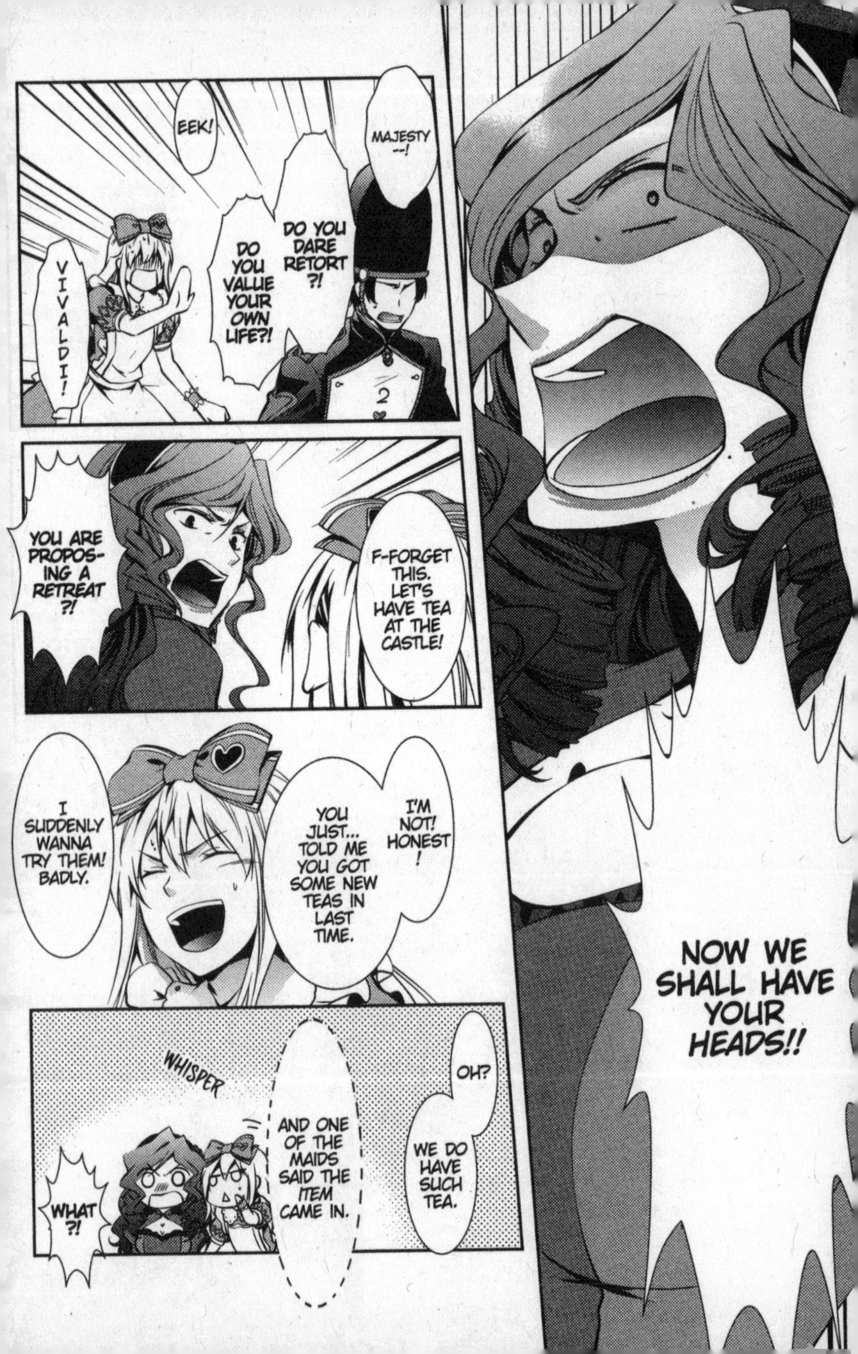
NOW WE SHALL HAVE YOUR HEADS!!
MAJESTY --!
EEK!
DO YOU DARE RETORT ?!
DO YOU VALUE YOUR OWN LIFE?!
VIVALDI!
2
F-FORGET THIS. LET'S HAVE TEA AT THE CASTLE!
YOU ARE PROPOSING A RETREAT ?!
I'M NOT! HONEST !
YOU JUST... TOLD ME YOU GOT SOME NEW TEAS IN LAST TIME.
I SUDDENLY WANNA TRY THEM! BADLY.
OH?
WE DO HAVE SUCH TEA.
AND ONE OF THE MAIDS SAID THE ITEM CAME IN.
WHISPER
WHAT ?!

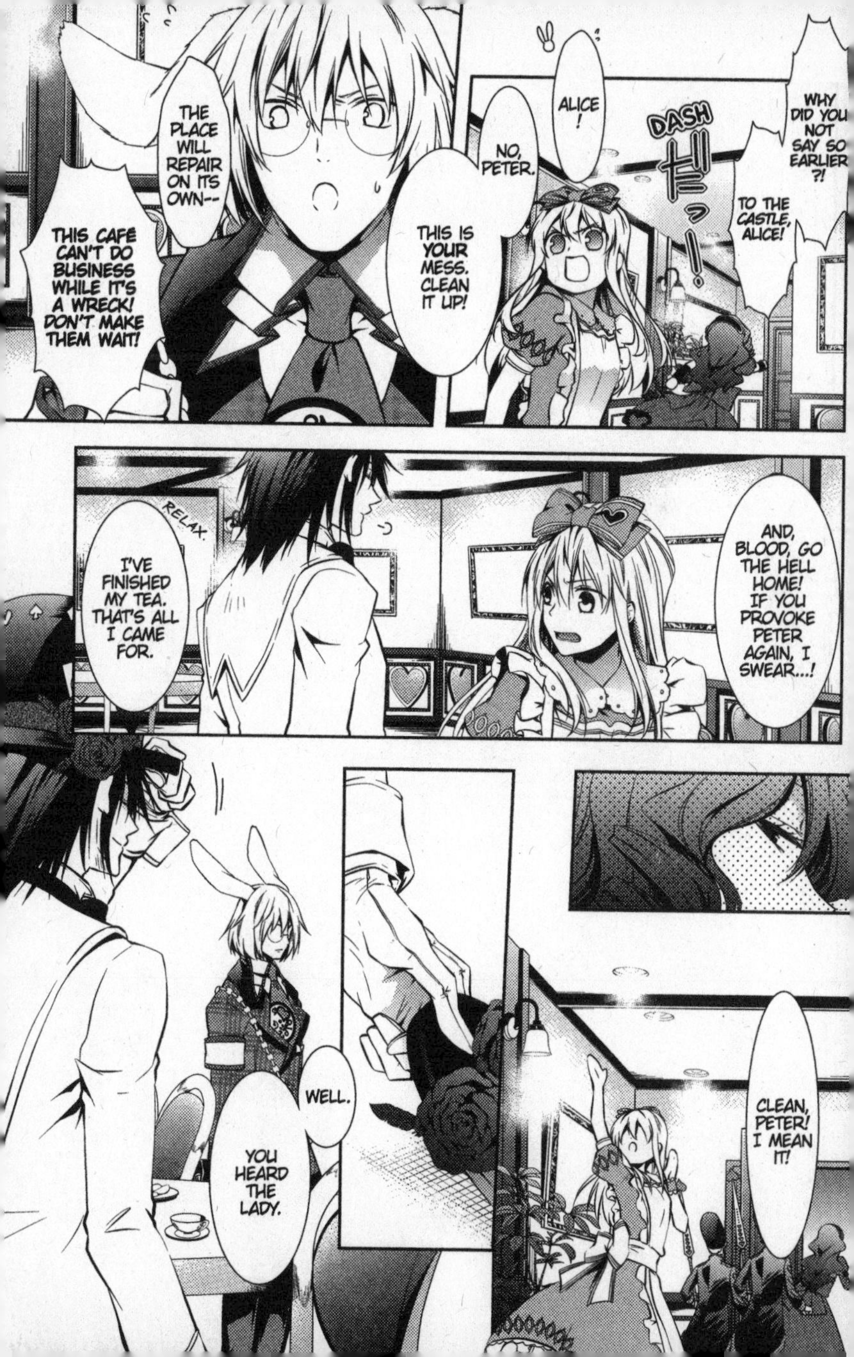
WHY DID YOU NOT SAY SO EARLIER?!
TO THE CASTLE, ALICE!
DASH
ALICE!
NO, PETER.
THE PLACE WILL REPAIR ON ITS OWN--
THIS IS YOUR MESS. CLEAN IT UP!
THIS CAFE CAN'T DO BUSINESS WHILE IT'S A WRECK! DON'T MAKE THEM WAIT!
AND, BLOOD, GO THE HELL HOME! IF YOU PROVOKE PETER AGAIN, I SWEAR...!
RELAX.
I'VE FINISHED MY TEA. THAT'S ALL I CAME FOR.
CLEAN, PETER! I MEAN IT!
WELL.
YOU HEARD THE LADY.

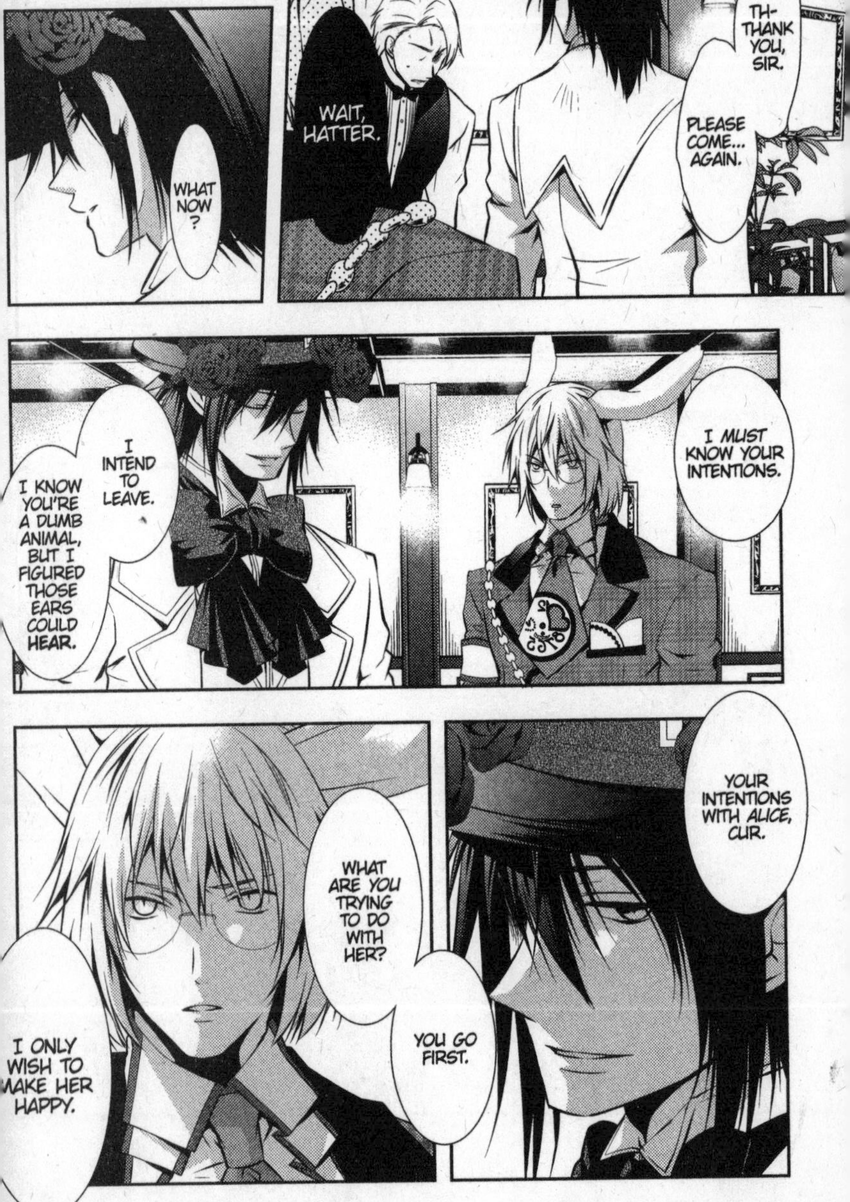
TH-THANK YOU, SIR.
PLEASE COME... AGAIN.
WAIT, HATTER.
WHAT NOW?
I MUST KNOW YOUR INTENTIONS.
I INTEND TO LEAVE.
I KNOW YOU'RE A DUMB ANIMAL, BUT I FIGURED THOSE EARS COULD HEAR.
YOUR INTENTIONS WITH ALICE, CUR.
WHAT ARE YOU TRYING TO DO WITH HER?
YOU GO FIRST.
I ONLY WISH TO MAKE HER HAPPY.

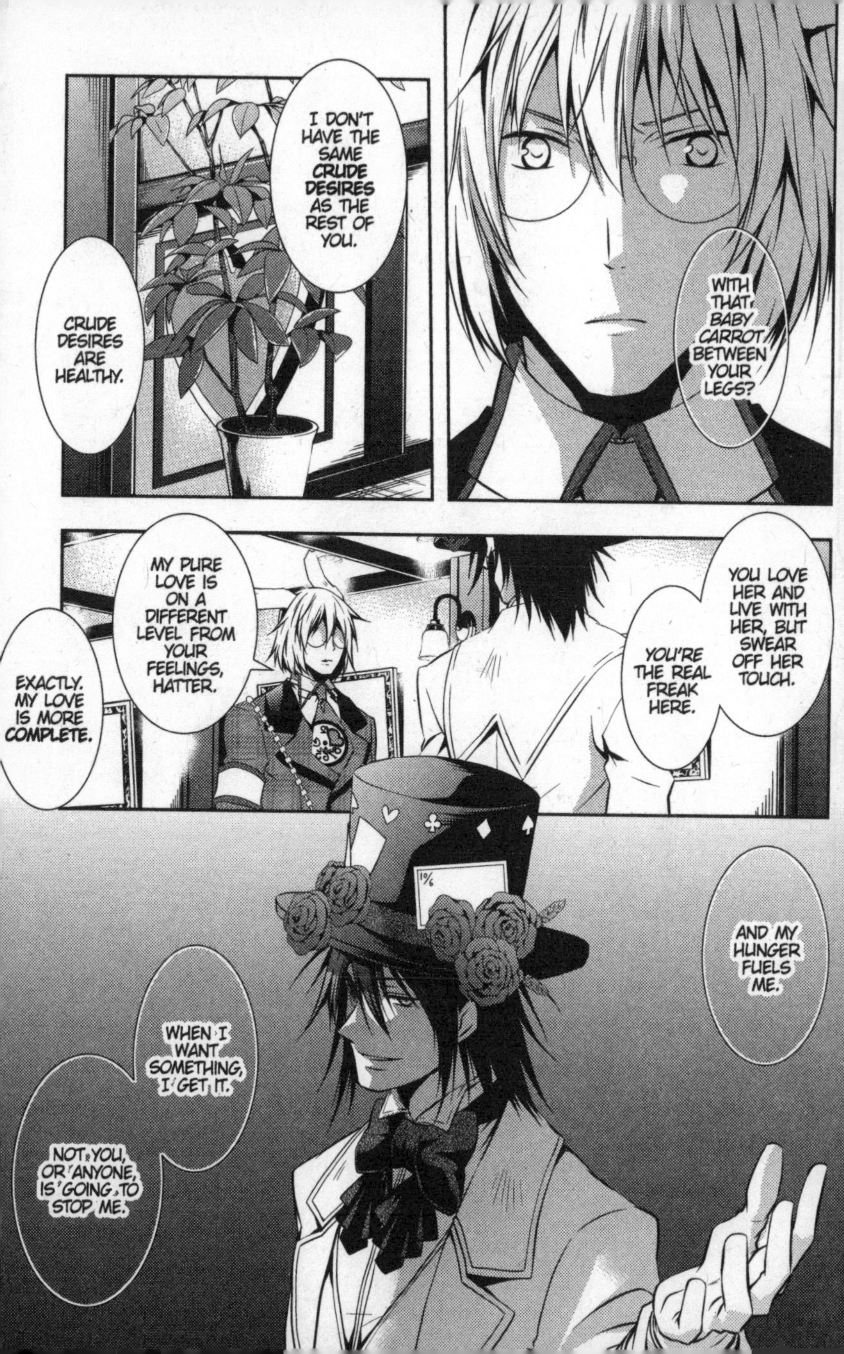
WITH THAT, BABY CARROT BETWEEN YOUR LEGS?
I DON'T HAVE THE SAME CRUDE DESIRES AS THE REST OF YOU.
CRUDE DESIRES ARE HEALTHY.
YOU LOVE HER AND LIVE WITH HER, BUT SWEAR OFF HER TOUCH.
YOU'RE THE REAL FREAK HERE.
MY PURE LOVE IS ON A DIFFERENT LEVEL FROM YOUR FEELINGS, HATTER.
EXACTLY. MY LOVE IS MORE COMPLETE.
AND MY HUNGER FUELS ME.
WHEN I WANT SOMETHING, I GET IT.
NOT YOU, OR ANYONE, IS GOING TO STOP ME.

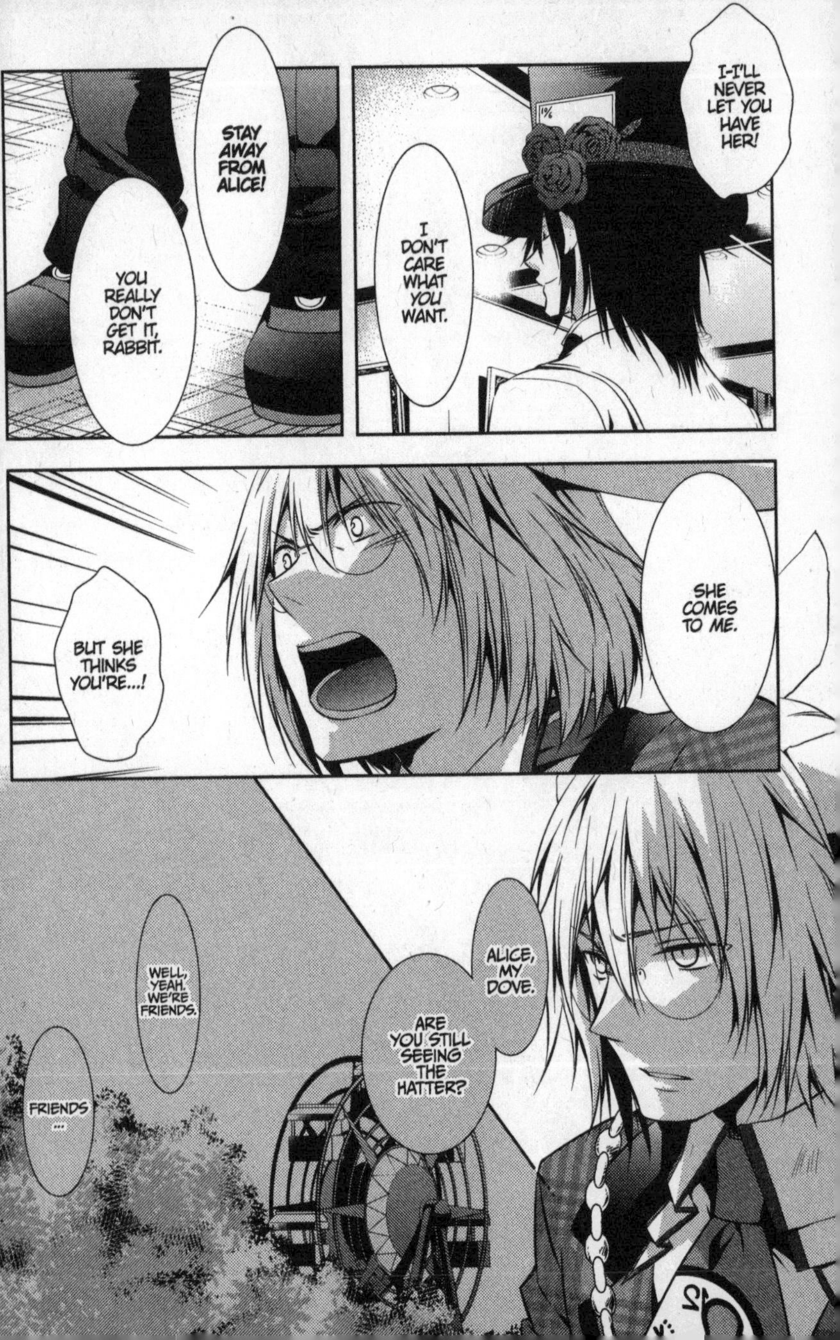
I-I'LL NEVER LET YOU HAVE HER!
I DON'T CARE WHAT YOU WANT.
STAY AWAY FROM ALICE!
YOU REALLY DON'T GET IT, RABBIT.
SHE COMES TO ME.
BUT SHE THINKS YOU'RE...!
ALICE, MY DOVE.
ARE YOU STILL SEEING THE HATTER?
WELL, YEAH. WE'RE FRIENDS.
FRIENDS...

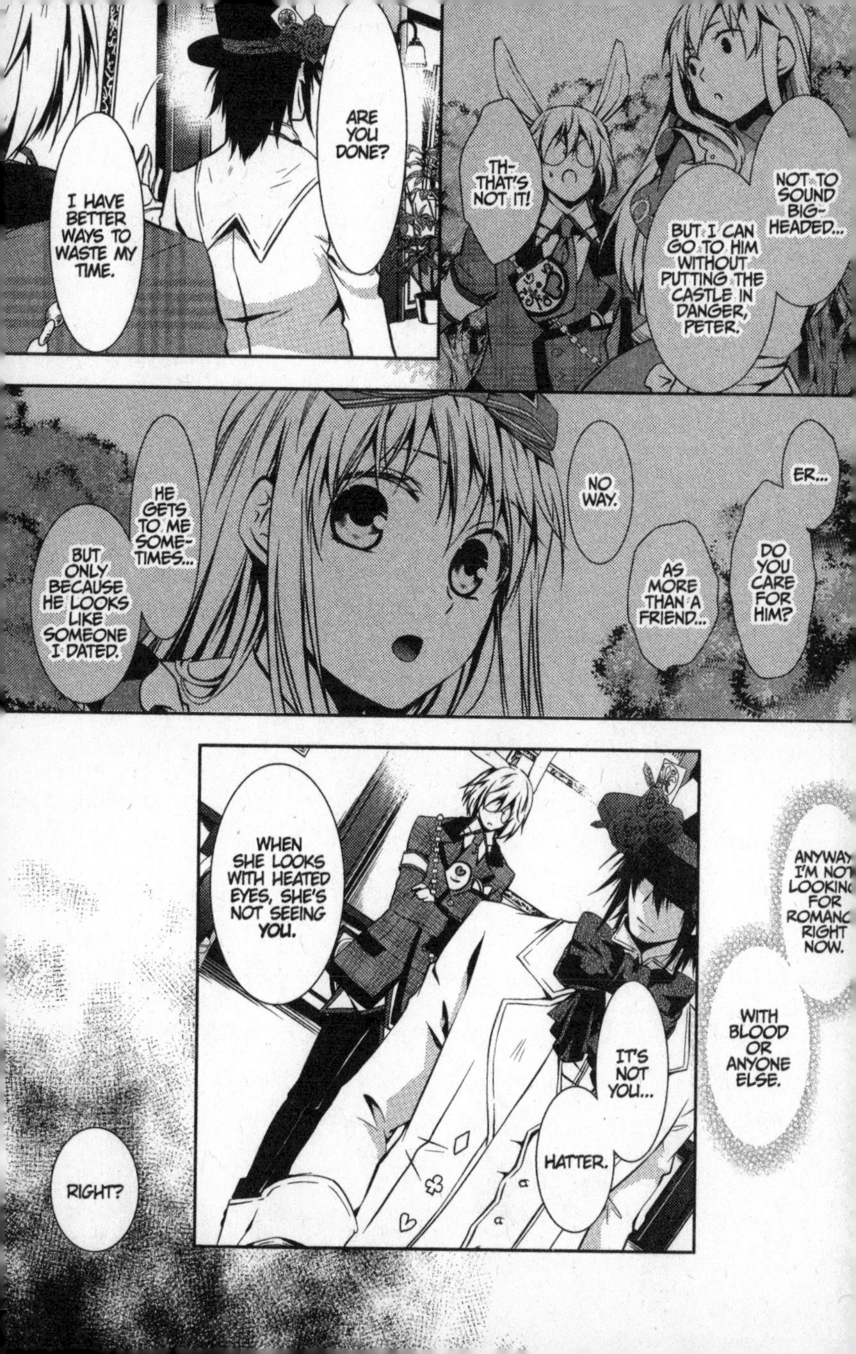
NOT TO SOUND BIG-HEADED...
BUT I CAN GO TO HIM WITHOUT PUTTING THE CASTLE IN DANGER, PETER.
TH-THAT'S NOT IT!
ARE YOU DONE?
I HAVE BETTER WAYS TO WASTE MY TIME.
ER...
DO YOU CARE FOR HIM?
AS MORE THAN A FRIEND...
NO WAY.
HE GETS TO ME SOME-TIMES...
BUT ONLY BECAUSE HE LOOKS LIKE SOMEONE I DATED.
ANYWAY I'M NOT LOOKING FOR ROMANC RIGHT NOW.
WITH BLOOD OR ANYONE ELSE.
WHEN SHE LOOKS WITH HEATED EYES, SHE'S NOT SEEING YOU.
IT'S NOT YOU...
HATTER.
RIGHT?

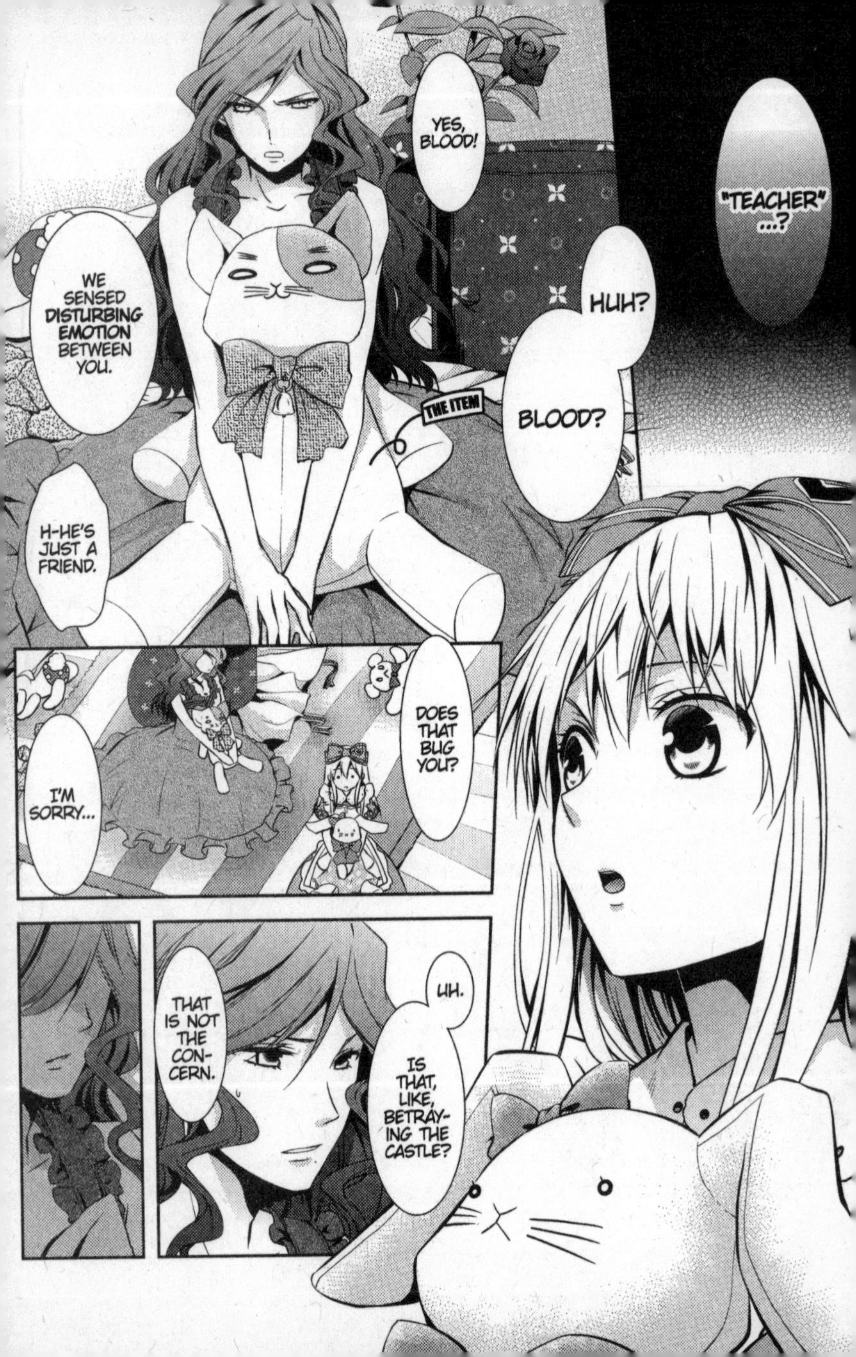
"TEACHER" ...?
YES, BLOOD!
HUH?
BLOOD?
WE SENSED DISTURBING EMOTION BETWEEN YOU.
THE ITEM
H-HE'S JUST A FRIEND.
DOES THAT BUG YOU?
I'M SORRY...
UH.
IS THAT, LIKE, BETRAYING THE CASTLE?
THAT IS NOT THE CON-CERN.

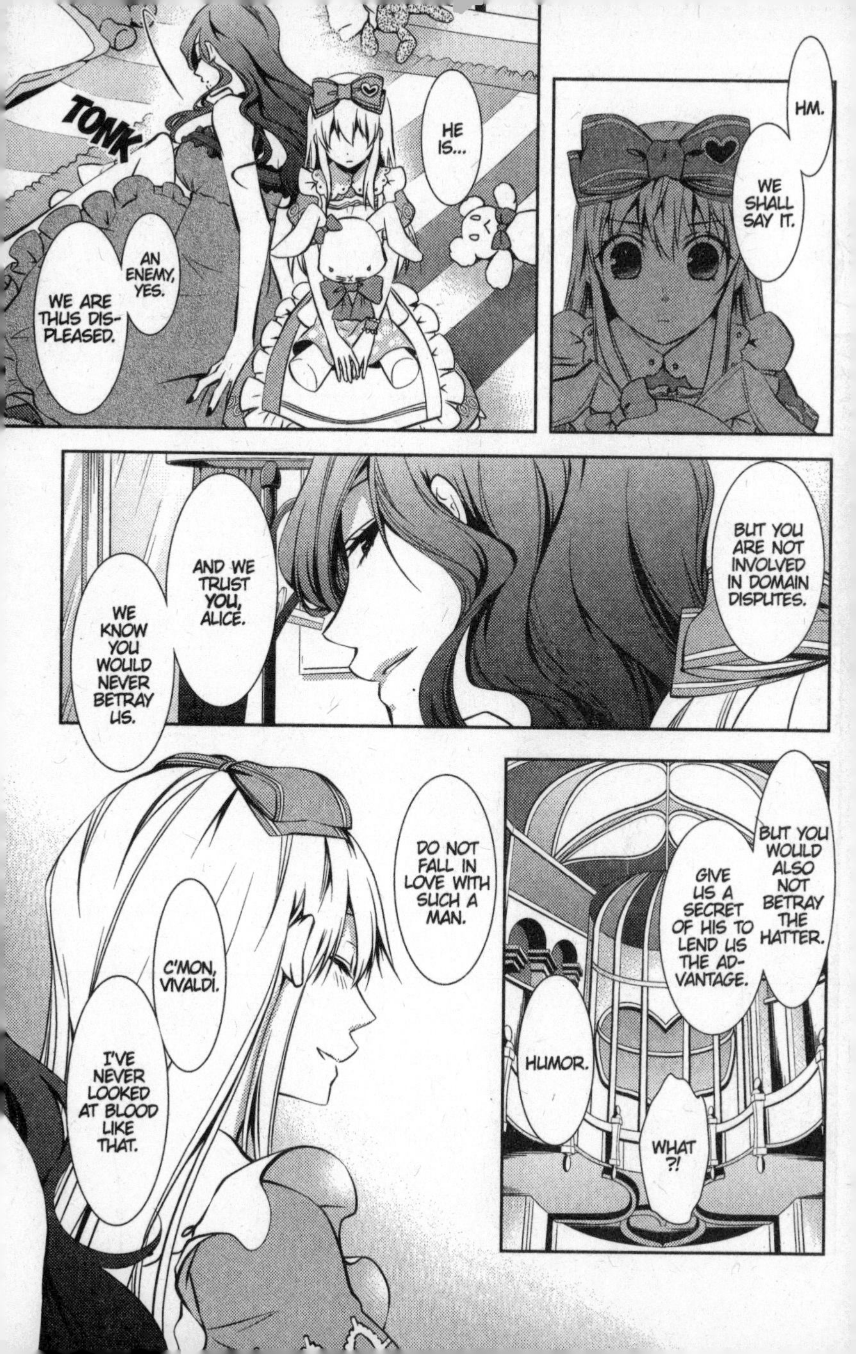
HM.
WE SHALL SAY IT.
HE IS...
TONK
AN ENEMY, YES.
WE ARE THUS DISPLEASED.
BUT YOU ARE NOT INVOLVED IN DOMAIN DISPUTES.
AND WE TRUST YOU, ALICE.
WE KNOW YOU WOULD NEVER BETRAY US.
BUT YOU WOULD ALSO NOT BETRAY THE HATTER.
GIVE US A SECRET OF HIS TO LEND US THE ADVANTAGE.
HUMOR.
WHAT?!
DO NOT FALL IN LOVE WITH SUCH A MAN.
C'MON, VIVALDI.
I'VE NEVER LOOKED AT BLOOD LIKE THAT.

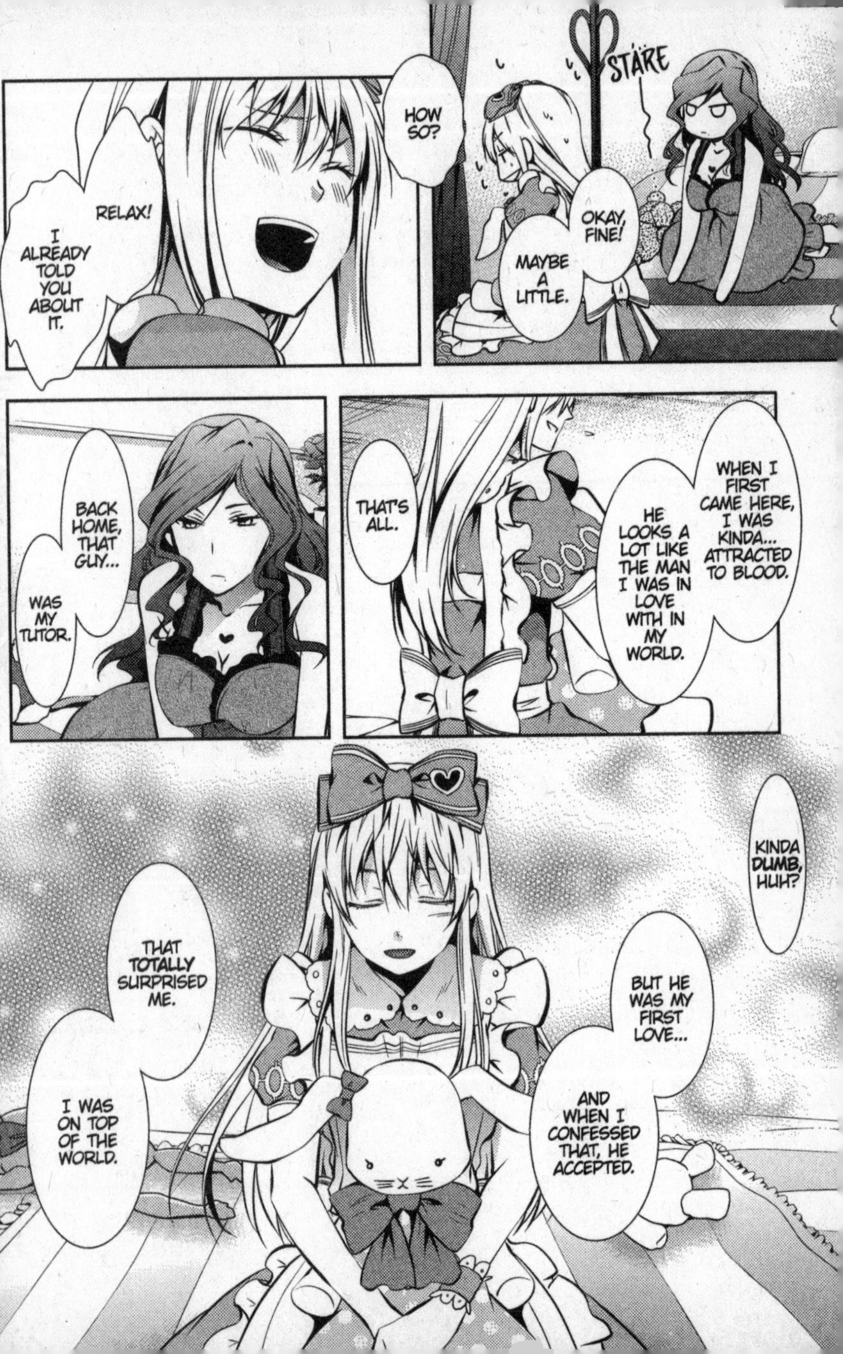
STARE
OKAY, FINE!
MAYBE A LITTLE.
HOW SO?
RELAX!
I ALREADY TOLD YOU ABOUT IT.
WHEN I FIRST CAME HERE, I WAS KINDA... ATTRACTED TO BLOOD.
HE LOOKS A LOT LIKE THE MAN I WAS IN LOVE WITH IN MY WORLD.
THAT'S ALL.
BACK HOME, THAT GUY...
WAS MY TUTOR.
KINDA DUMB, HUH?
BUT HE WAS MY FIRST LOVE...
AND WHEN I CONFESSED THAT, HE ACCEPTED.
THAT TOTALLY SURPRISED ME.
I WAS ON TOP OF THE WORLD.

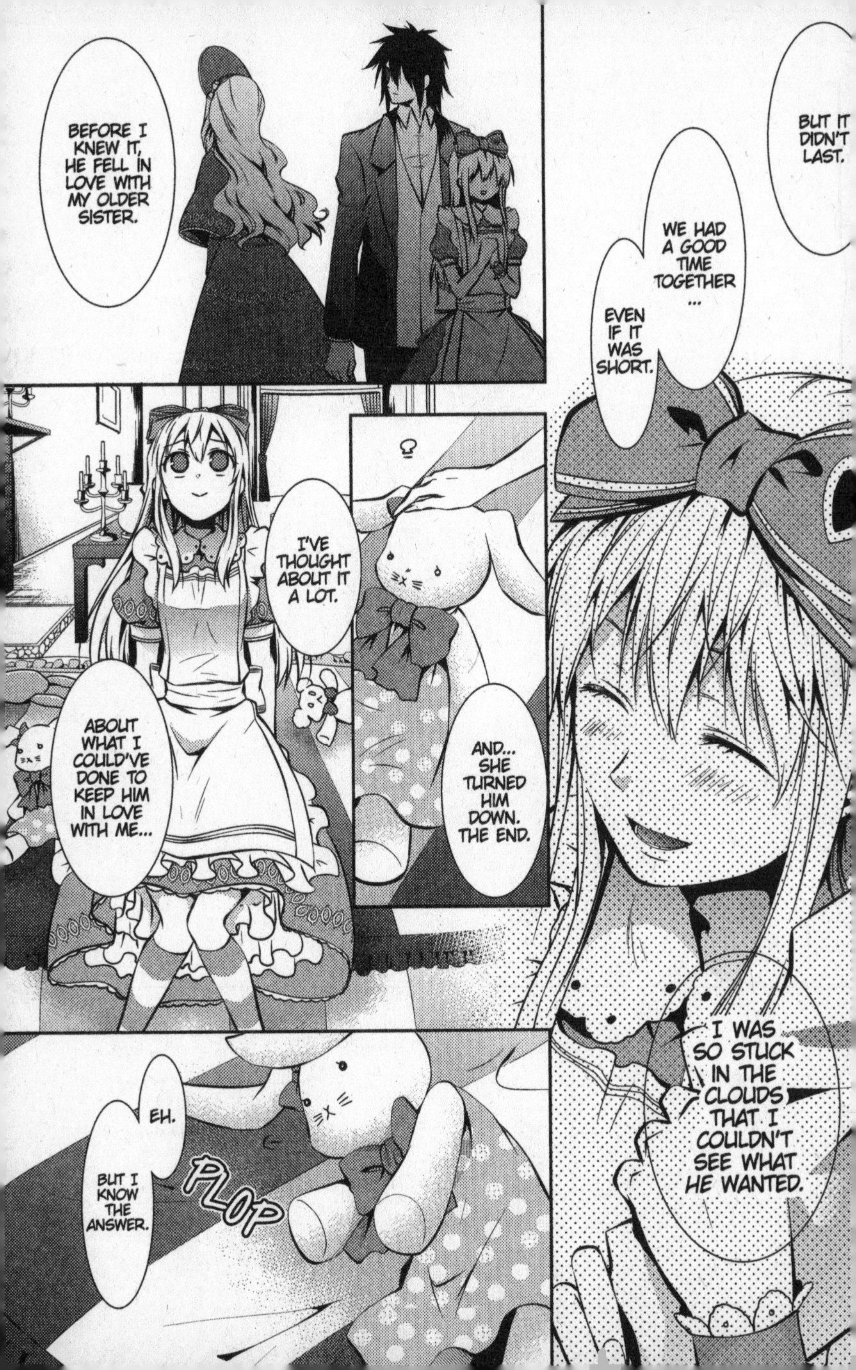
BUT IT DIDN'T LAST.
WE HAD A GOOD TIME TOGETHER ...
EVEN IF IT WAS SHORT.
BEFORE I KNEW IT, HE FELL IN LOVE WITH MY OLDER SISTER.
AND... SHE TURNED HIM DOWN. THE END.
I'VE THOUGHT ABOUT IT A LOT.
ABOUT WHAT I COULD'VE DONE TO KEEP HIM IN LOVE WITH ME...
I WAS SO STUCK IN THE CLOUDS THAT I COULDN'T SEE WHAT HE WANTED.
EH.
BUT I KNOW THE ANSWER.
PLOP

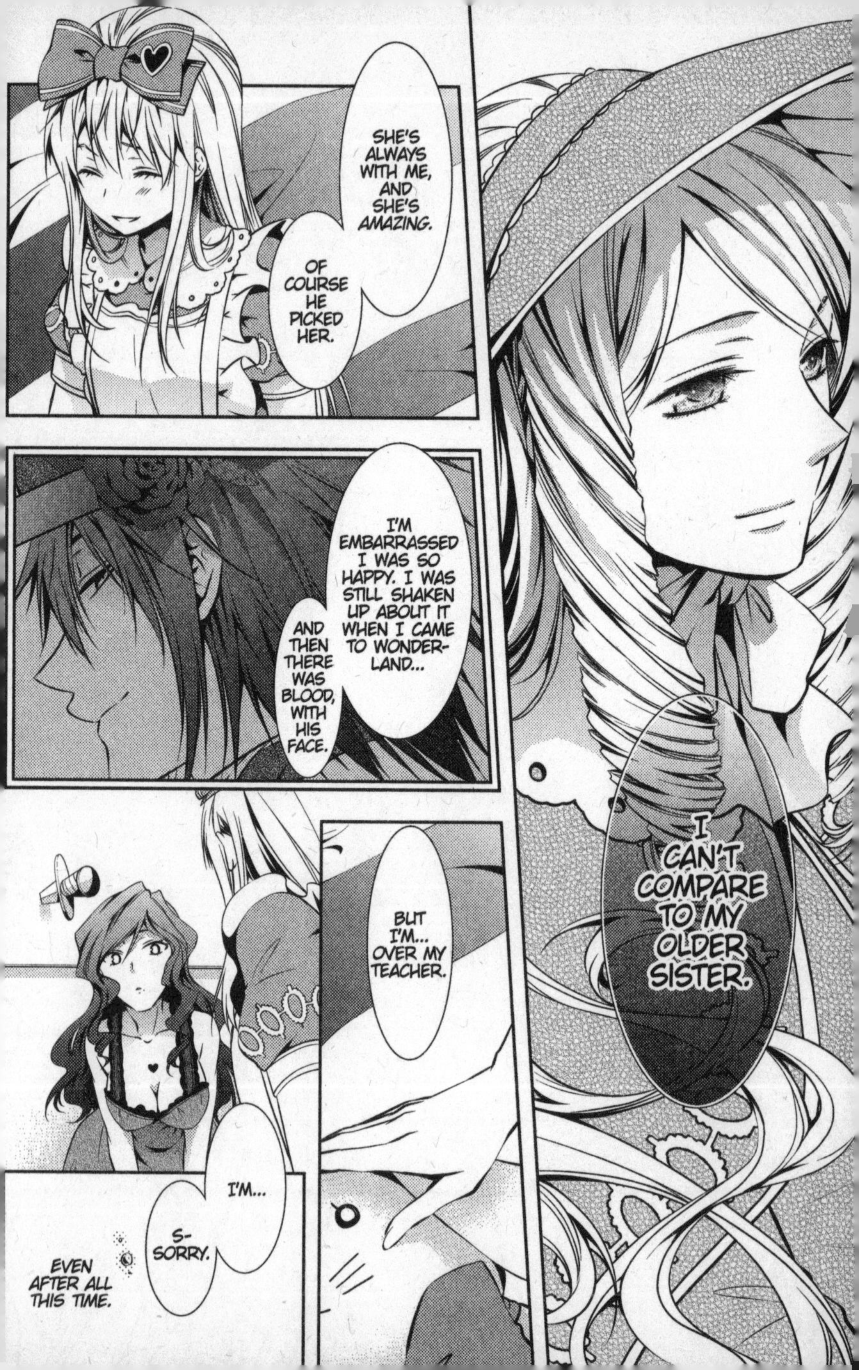
I CAN'T COMPARE TO MY OLDER SISTER.
SHE'S ALWAYS WITH ME, AND SHE'S AMAZING.
OF COURSE HE PICKED HER.
I'M EMBARRASSED I WAS SO HAPPY. I WAS STILL SHAKEN UP ABOUT IT WHEN I CAME TO WONDER-LAND...
AND THEN THERE WAS BLOOD, WITH HIS FACE.
BUT I'M... OVER MY TEACHER.
I'M...
S-SORRY.
EVEN AFTER ALL THIS TIME.

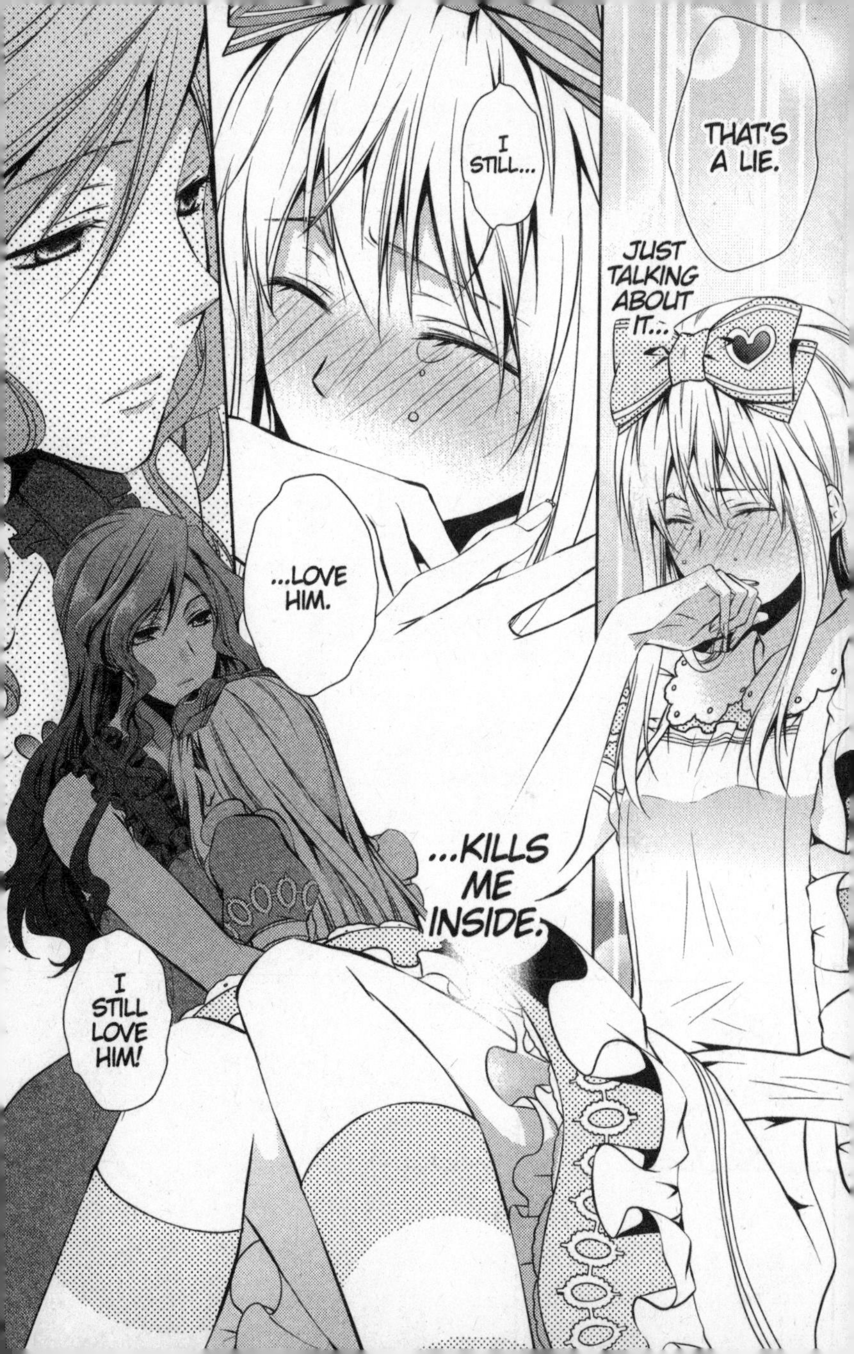
THAT'S A LIE.
JUST TALKING ABOUT IT...
I STILL...
...LOVE HIM.
...KILLS ME INSIDE.
I STILL LOVE HIM!

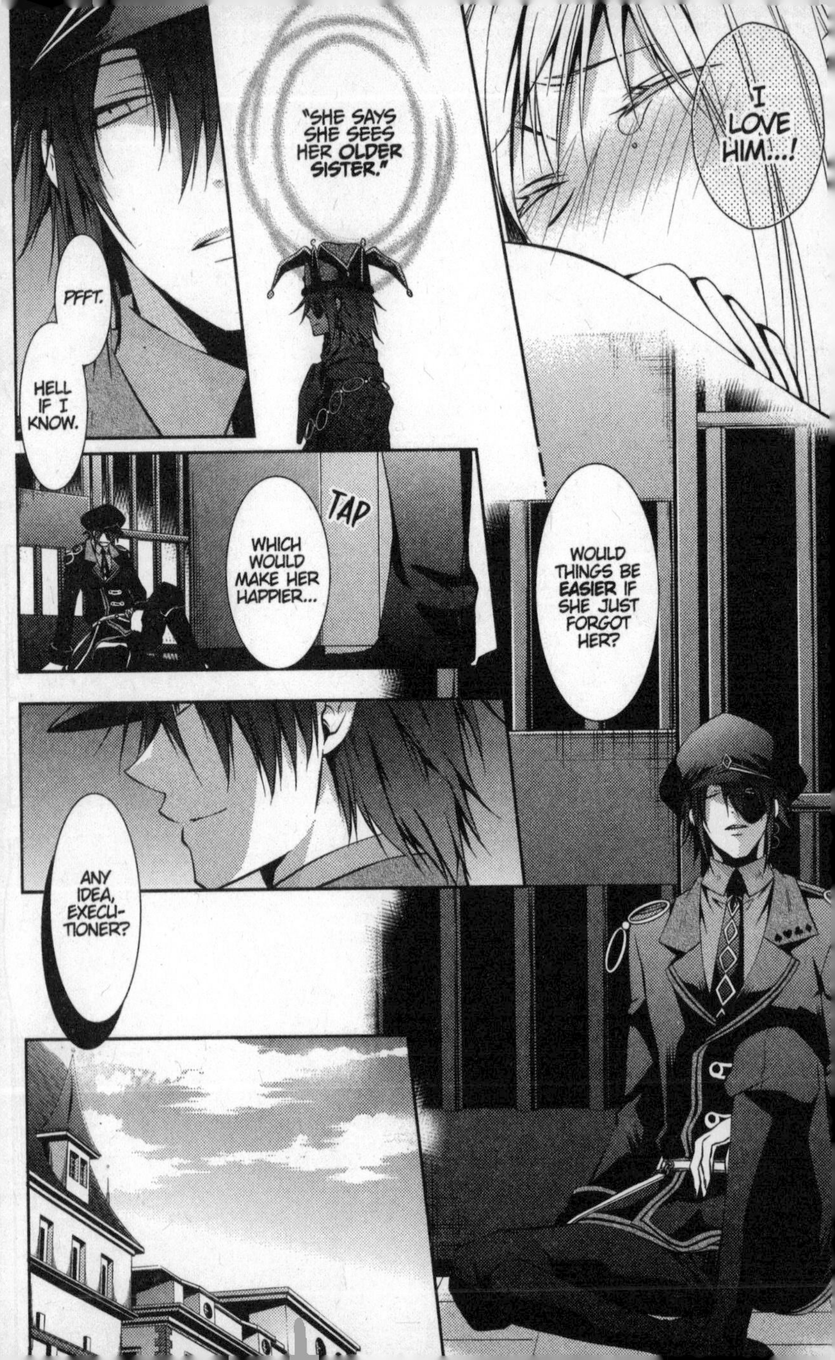
I LOVE HIM...!
"SHE SAYS SHE SEES HER OLDER SISTER."
PFFT.
HELL IF I KNOW.
WOULD THINGS BE EASIER IF SHE JUST FORGOT HER?
TAP
WHICH WOULD MAKE HER HAPPIER...
ANY IDEA, EXECUTIONER?

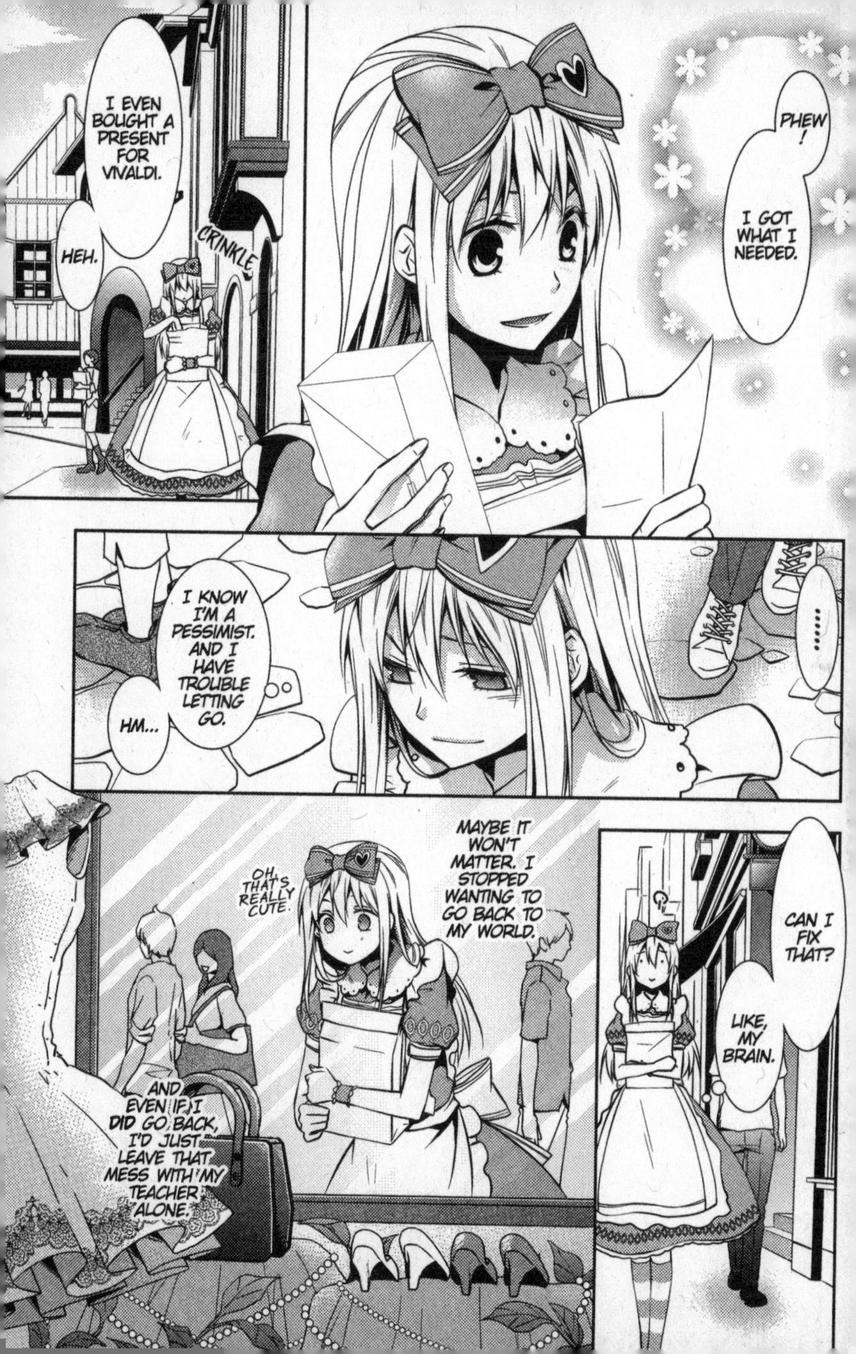
PHEW!
I GOT WHAT I NEEDED.
I EVEN BOUGHT A PRESENT FOR VIVALDI.
HEH.
CRINKLE
......
I KNOW I'M A PESSIMIST. AND I HAVE TROUBLE LETTING GO.
HM...
CAN I FIX THAT?
LIKE, MY BRAIN.
MAYBE IT WON'T MATTER. I STOPPED WANTING TO GO BACK TO MY WORLD.
OH, THAT'S REALLY CUTE.
AND EVEN IF I DID GO BACK, I'D JUST LEAVE THAT MESS WITH MY TEACHER ALONE.

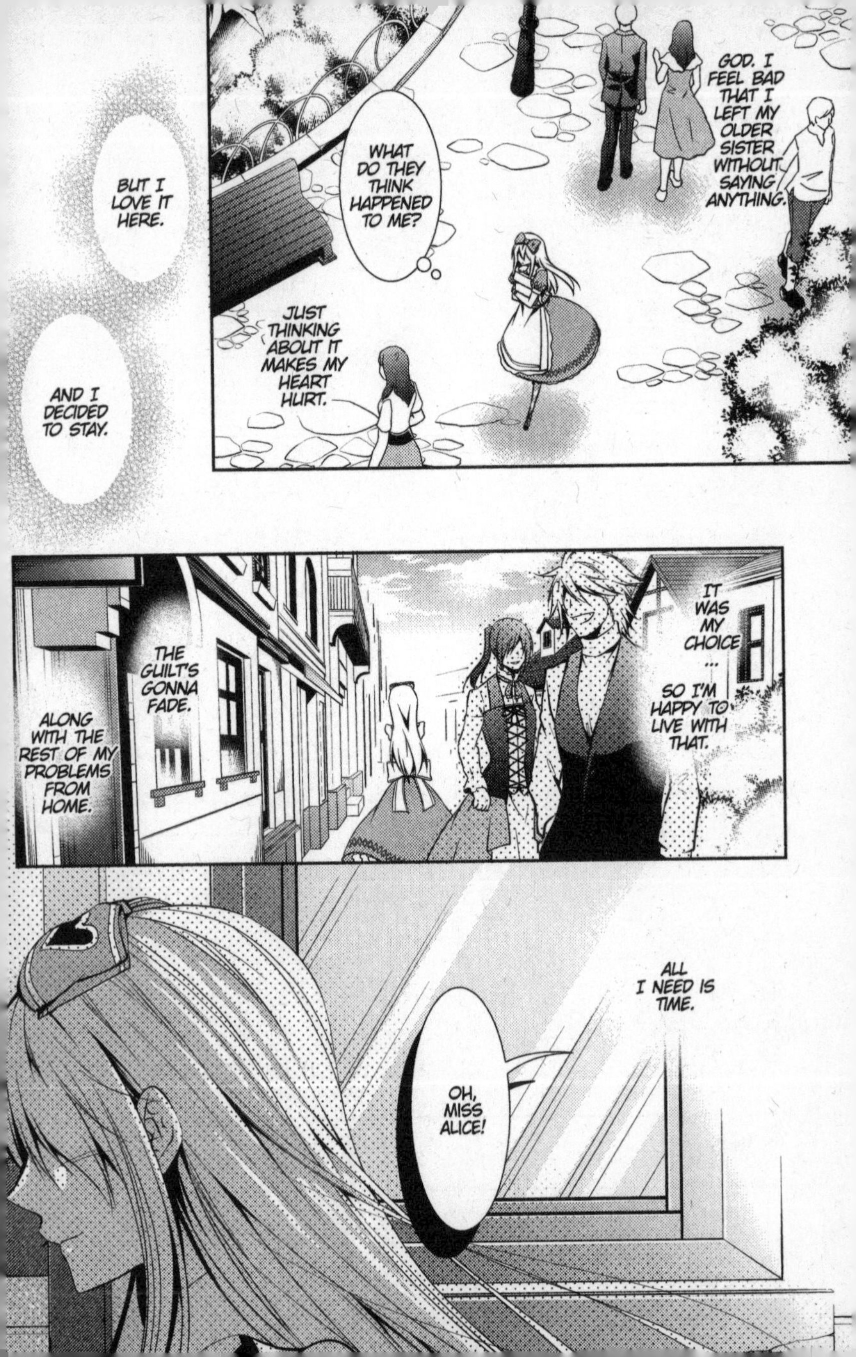
GOD. I FEEL BAD THAT I LEFT MY OLDER SISTER WITHOUT SAYING ANYTHING.
WHAT DO THEY THINK HAPPENED TO ME?
JUST THINKING ABOUT IT MAKES MY HEART HURT.
BUT I LOVE IT HERE.
AND I DECIDED TO STAY.
IT WAS MY CHOICE...
SO I'M HAPPY TO LIVE WITH THAT.
THE GUILT'S GONNA FADE.
ALONG WITH THE REST OF MY PROBLEMS FROM HOME.
ALL I NEED IS TIME.
OH, MISS ALICE!

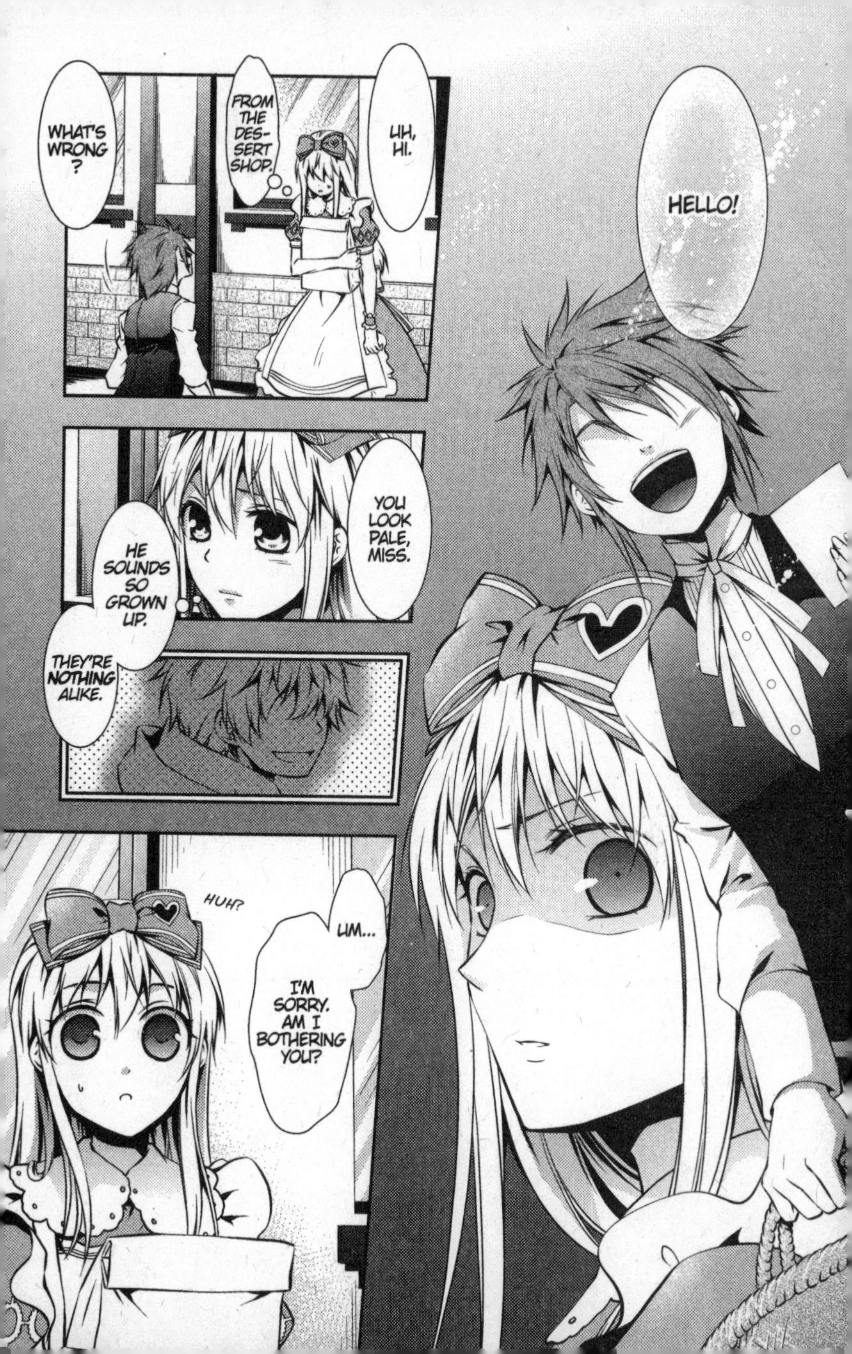
HELLO!
UH, HI.
FROM THE DESSERT SHOP.
WHAT'S WRONG?
YOU LOOK PALE, MISS.
HE SOUNDS SO GROWN UP.
THEY'RE NOTHING ALIKE.
UM... I'M SORRY. AM I BOTHERING YOU?
HUH?

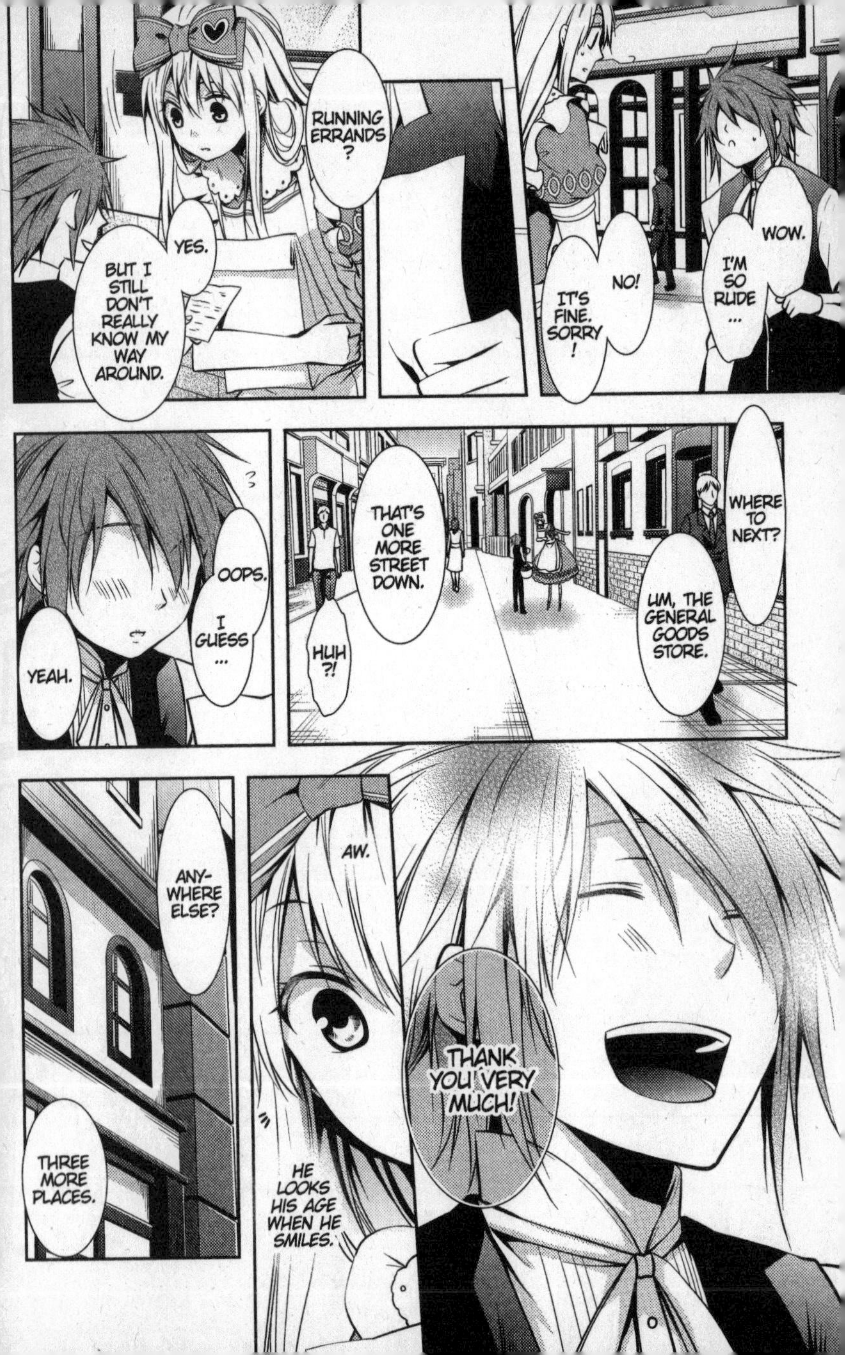
WOW.
I'M SO RUDE...
NO!
IT'S FINE. SORRY!
RUNNING ERRANDS?
YES.
BUT I STILL DON'T REALLY KNOW MY WAY AROUND.
WHERE TO NEXT?
UM, THE GENERAL GOODS STORE.
THAT'S ONE MORE STREET DOWN.
HUH?!
OOPS.
I GUESS...
YEAH.
AW.
THANK YOU VERY MUCH!
HE LOOKS HIS AGE WHEN HE SMILES.
ANY-WHERE ELSE?
THREE MORE PLACES.

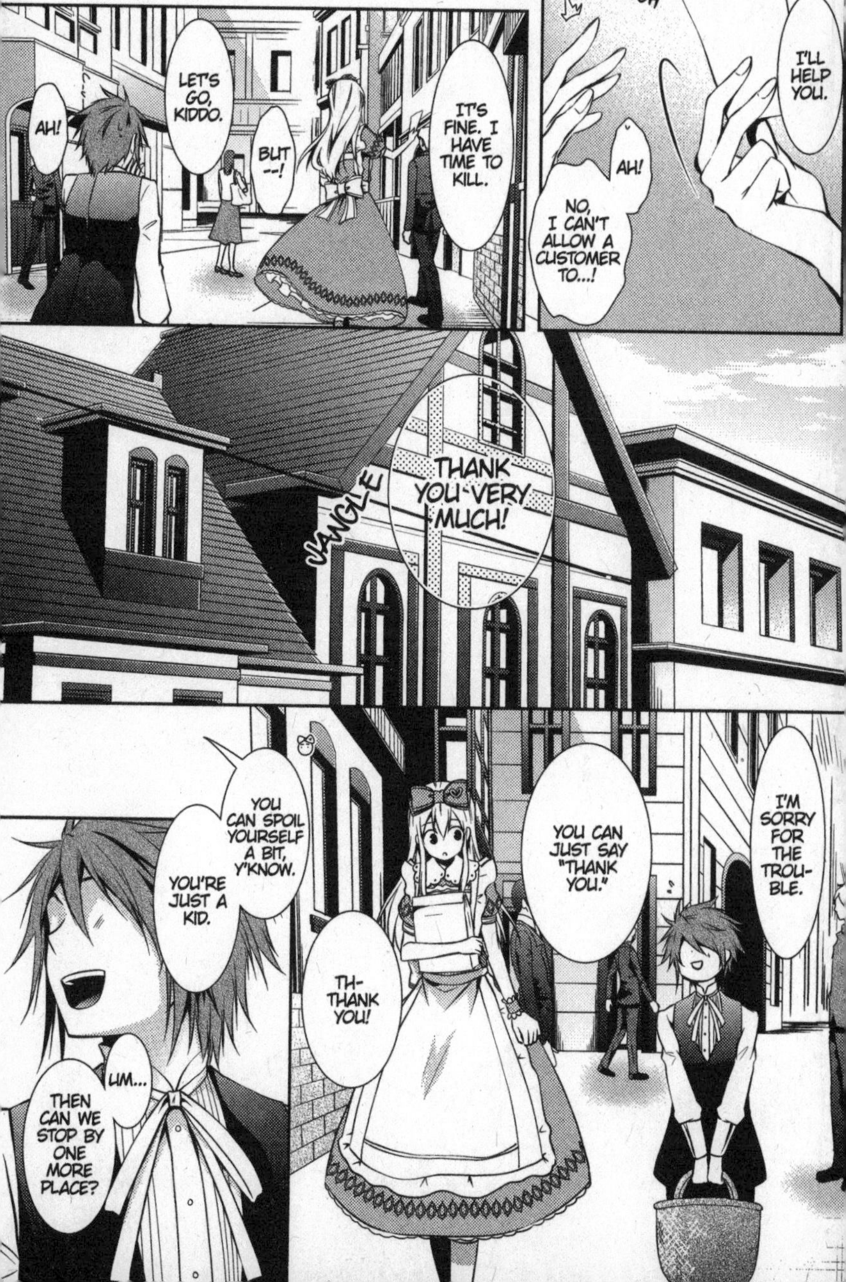
SNATCH
I'LL HELP YOU.
AH!
NO, I CAN'T ALLOW A CUSTOMER TO...!
IT'S FINE. I HAVE TIME TO KILL.
BUT --!
LET'S GO, KIDDO.
AH!
JANGLE
THANK YOU VERY MUCH!
I'M SORRY FOR THE TROUBLE.
YOU CAN JUST SAY "THANK YOU."
TH-THANK YOU!
YOU CAN SPOIL YOURSELF A BIT, Y'KNOW.
YOU'RE JUST A KID.
UM...
THEN CAN WE STOP BY ONE MORE PLACE?

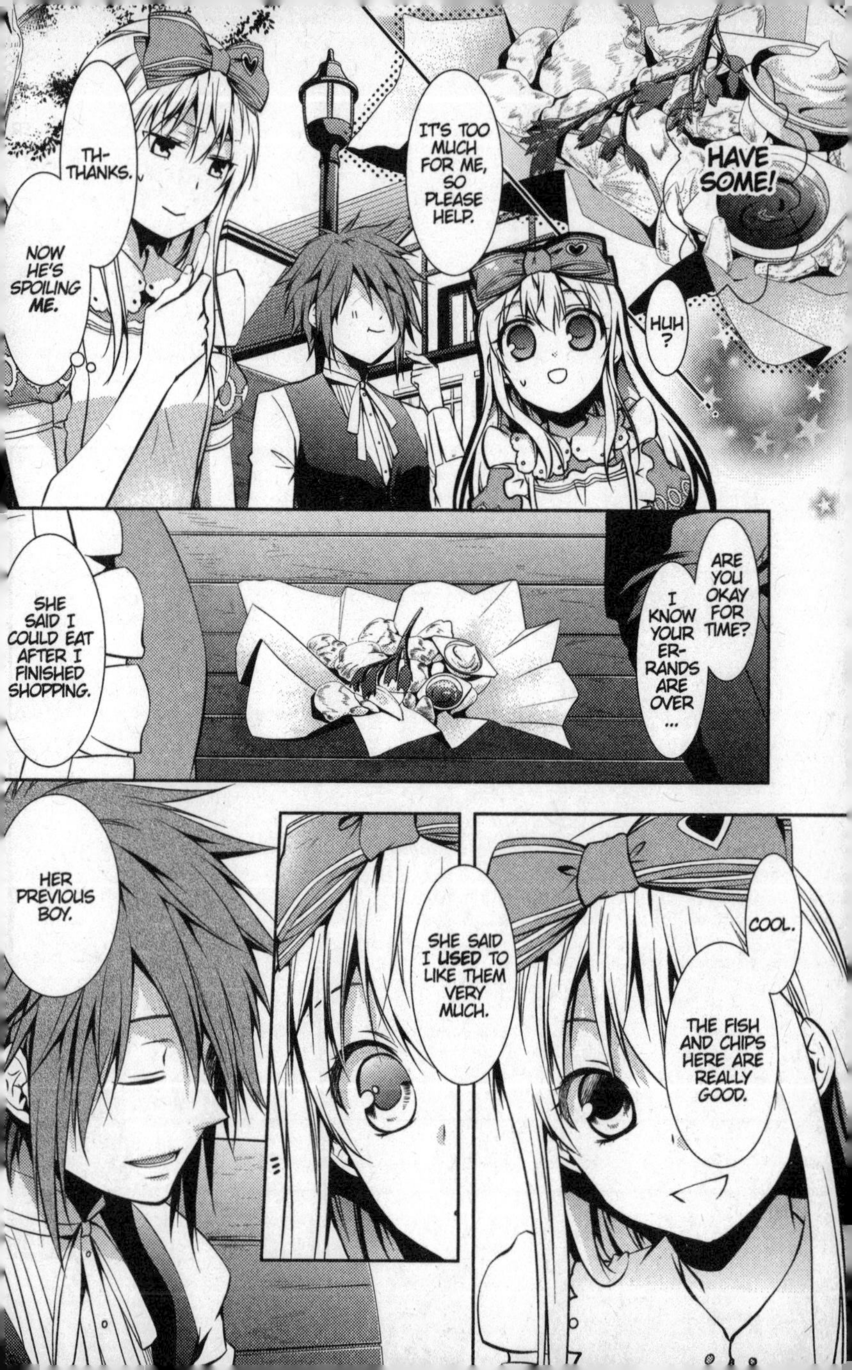
HAVE SOME!
HUH?
IT'S TOO MUCH FOR ME, SO PLEASE HELP.
TH-THANKS.
NOW HE'S SPOILING ME.
ARE YOU OKAY FOR TIME?
I KNOW YOUR ER-RANDS ARE OVER...
SHE SAID I COULD EAT AFTER I FINISHED SHOPPING.
COOL.
THE FISH AND CHIPS HERE ARE REALLY GOOD.
SHE SAID I USED TO LIKE THEM VERY MUCH.
HER PREVIOUS BOY.

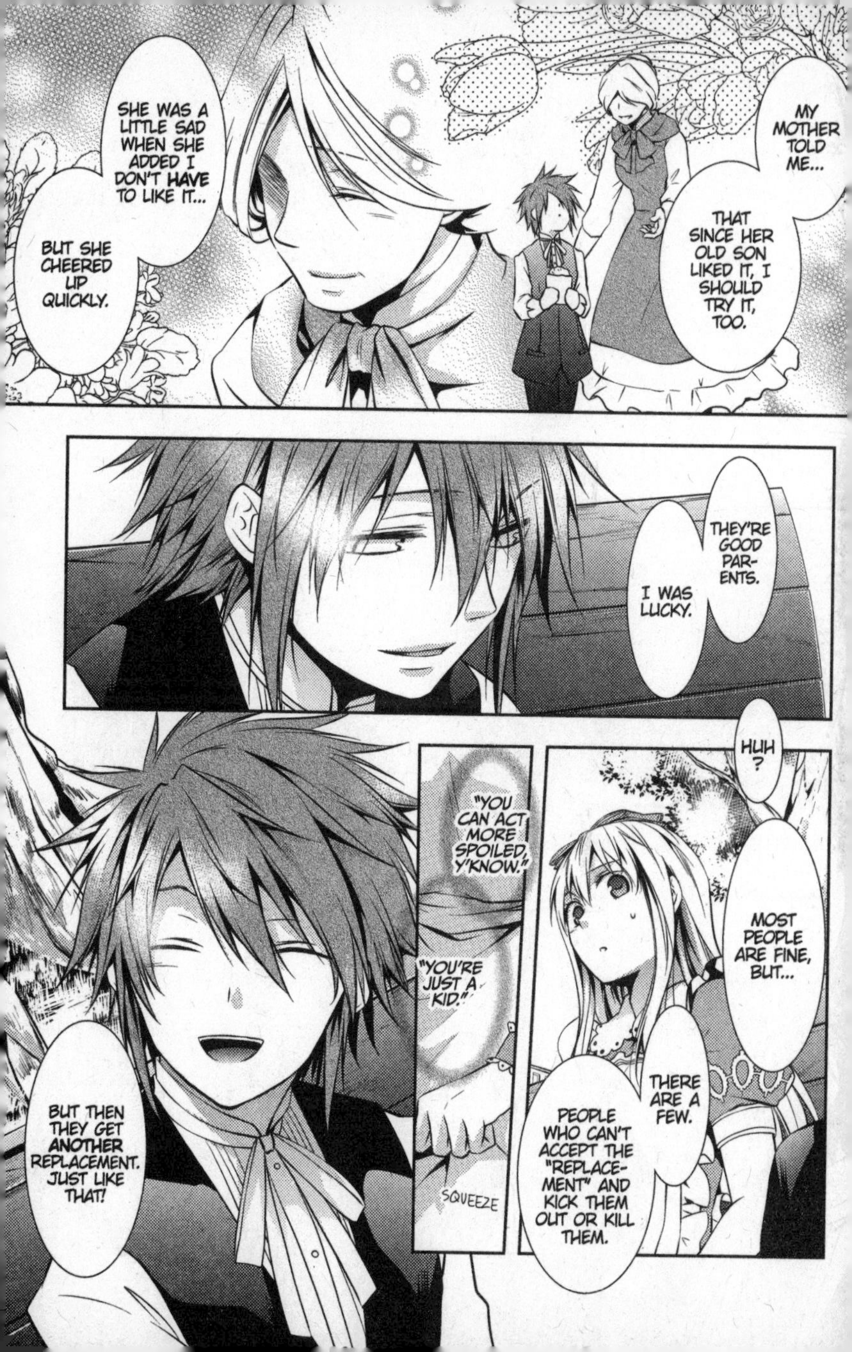
MY MOTHER TOLD ME...
THAT SINCE HER OLD SON LIKED IT, I SHOULD TRY IT, TOO.
SHE WAS A LITTLE SAD WHEN SHE ADDED I DON'T HAVE TO LIKE IT...
BUT SHE CHEERED UP QUICKLY.
THEY'RE GOOD PAR-ENTS.
I WAS LUCKY.
HUH?
MOST PEOPLE ARE FINE, BUT...
THERE ARE A FEW.
PEOPLE WHO CAN'T ACCEPT THE "REPLACE-MENT" AND KICK THEM OUT OR KILL THEM.
"YOU CAN ACT MORE SPOILED, Y'KNOW."
"YOU'RE JUST A KID."
SQUEEZE
BUT THEN THEY GET ANOTHER REPLACEMENT. JUST LIKE THAT!

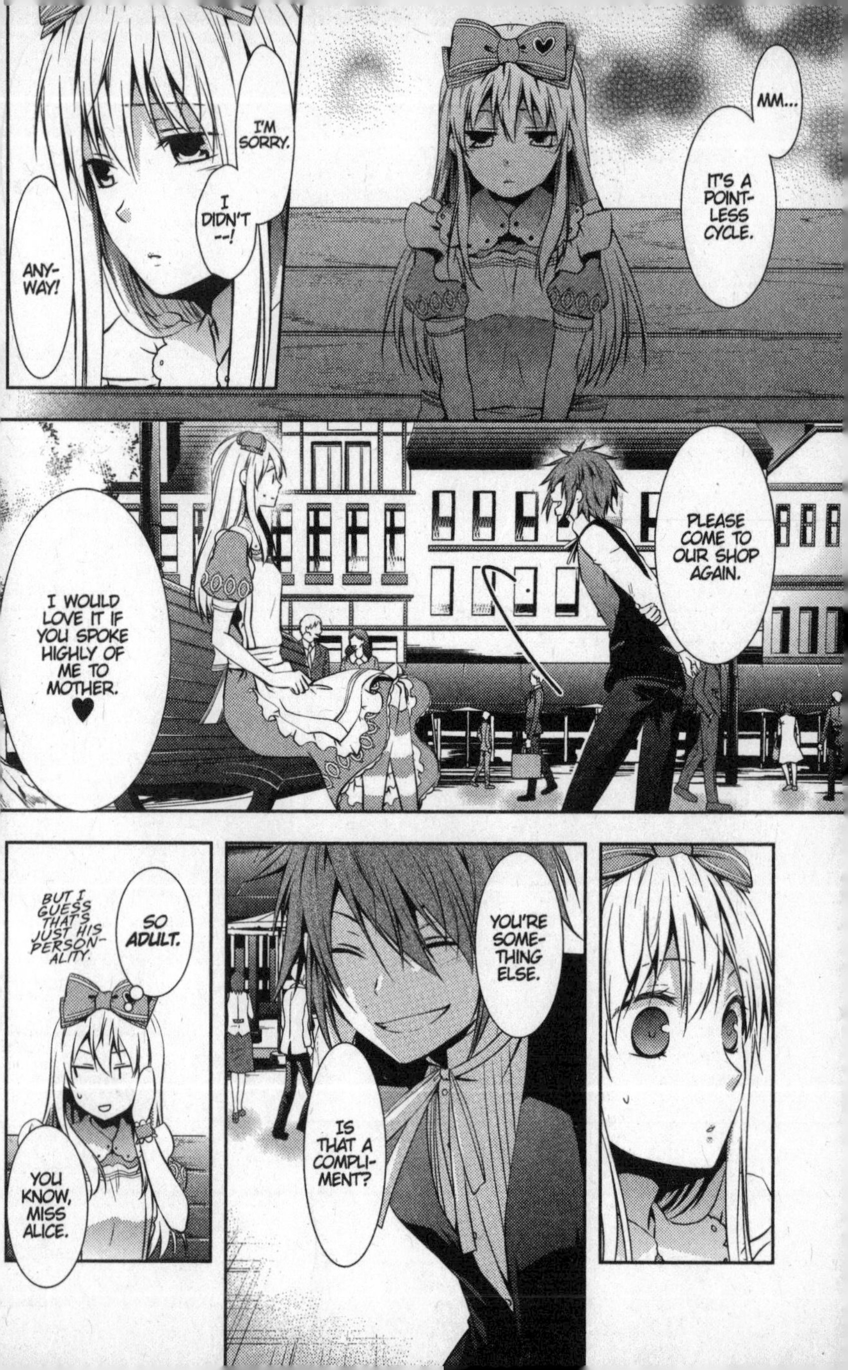
MM...
IT'S A POINTLESS CYCLE.
I'M SORRY.
I DIDN'T --!
ANYWAY!
PLEASE COME TO OUR SHOP AGAIN.
I WOULD LOVE IT IF YOU SPOKE HIGHLY OF ME TO MOTHER. ♥
YOU'RE SOMETHING ELSE.
IS THAT A COMPLIMENT?
SO ADULT.
BUT I GUESS THAT'S JUST HIS PERSONALITY.
YOU KNOW, MISS ALICE.

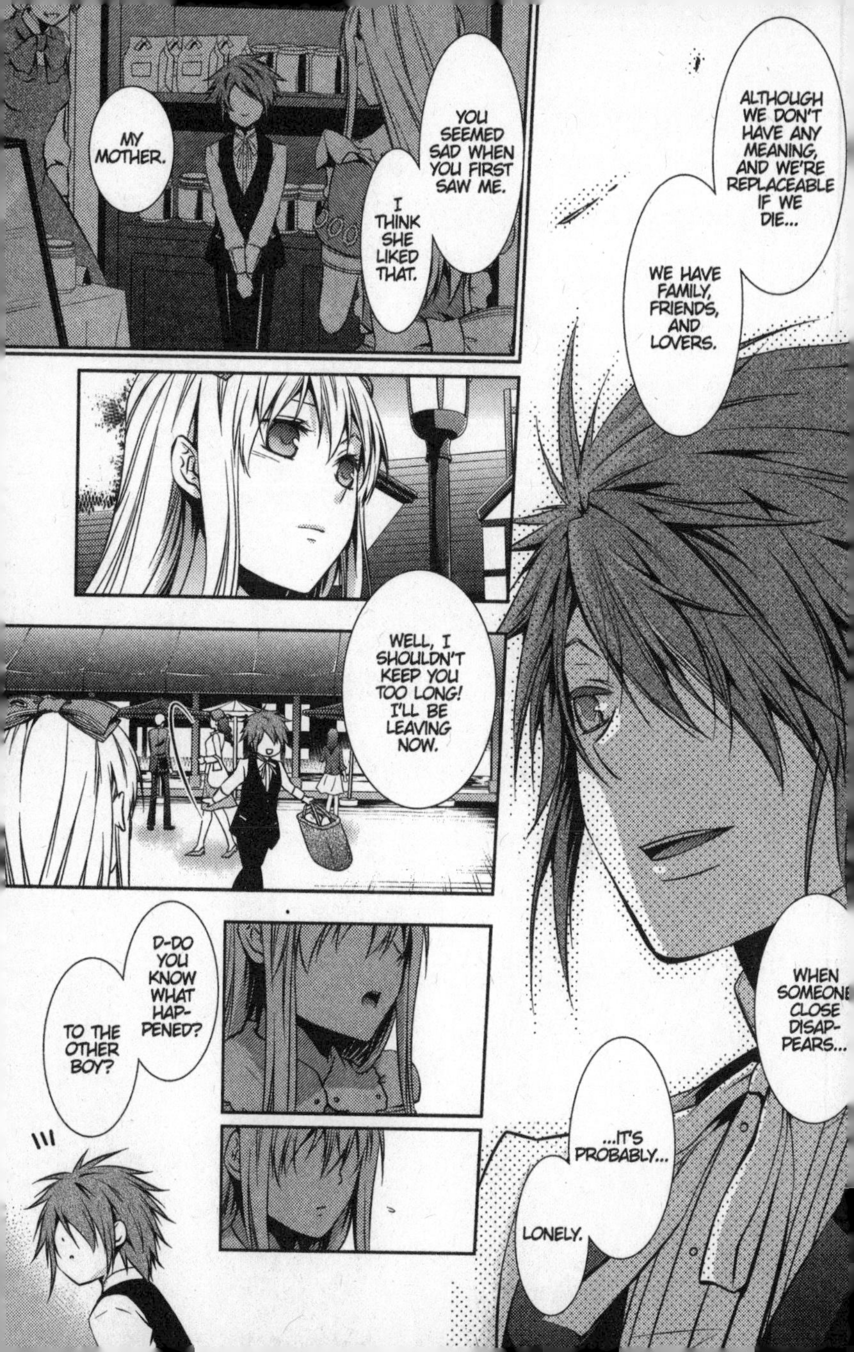
ALTHOUGH WE DON'T HAVE ANY MEANING, AND WE'RE REPLACEABLE IF WE DIE...
WE HAVE FAMILY, FRIENDS, AND LOVERS.
WHEN SOMEONE CLOSE DISAPPEARS...
...IT'S PROBABLY...
LONELY.
YOU SEEMED SAD WHEN YOU FIRST SAW ME.
I THINK SHE LIKED THAT.
MY MOTHER.
WELL, I SHOULDN'T KEEP YOU TOO LONG! I'LL BE LEAVING NOW.
D-DO YOU KNOW WHAT HAP-PENED?
TO THE OTHER BOY?

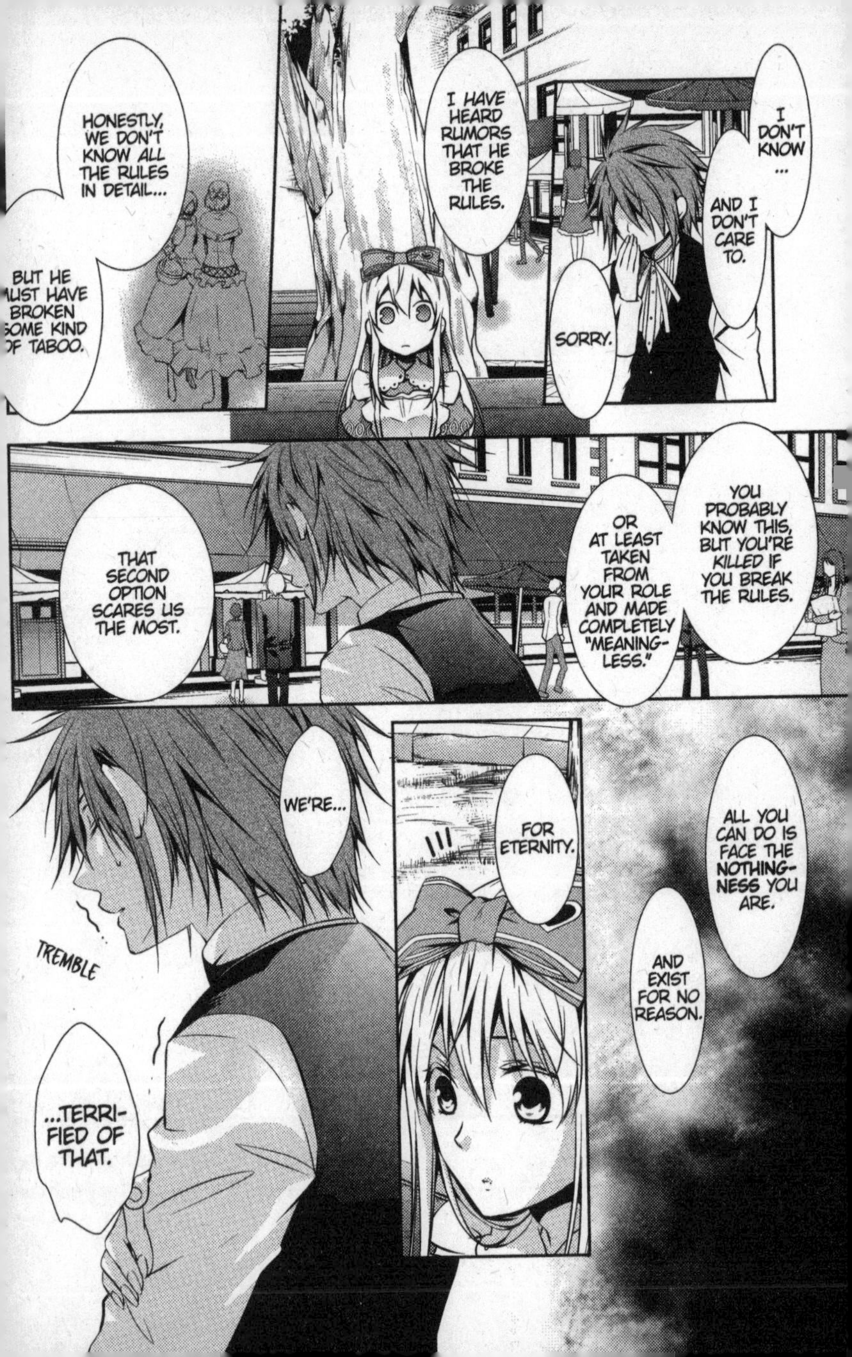

I DON'T KNOW ...
AND I DON'T CARE TO.
SORRY.
I HAVE HEARD RUMORS THAT HE BROKE THE RULES.
HONESTLY, WE DON'T KNOW ALL THE RULES IN DETAIL...
BUT HE MUST HAVE BROKEN SOME KIND OF TABOO.
YOU PROBABLY KNOW THIS, BUT YOU'RE KILLED IF YOU BREAK THE RULES.
OR AT LEAST TAKEN FROM YOUR ROLE AND MADE COMPLETELY "MEANING-LESS."
THAT SECOND OPTION SCARES US THE MOST.
ALL YOU CAN DO IS FACE THE NOTHING-NESS YOU ARE.
AND EXIST FOR NO REASON.
FOR ETERNITY.
WE'RE...
TREMBLE
...TERRI-FIED OF THAT.

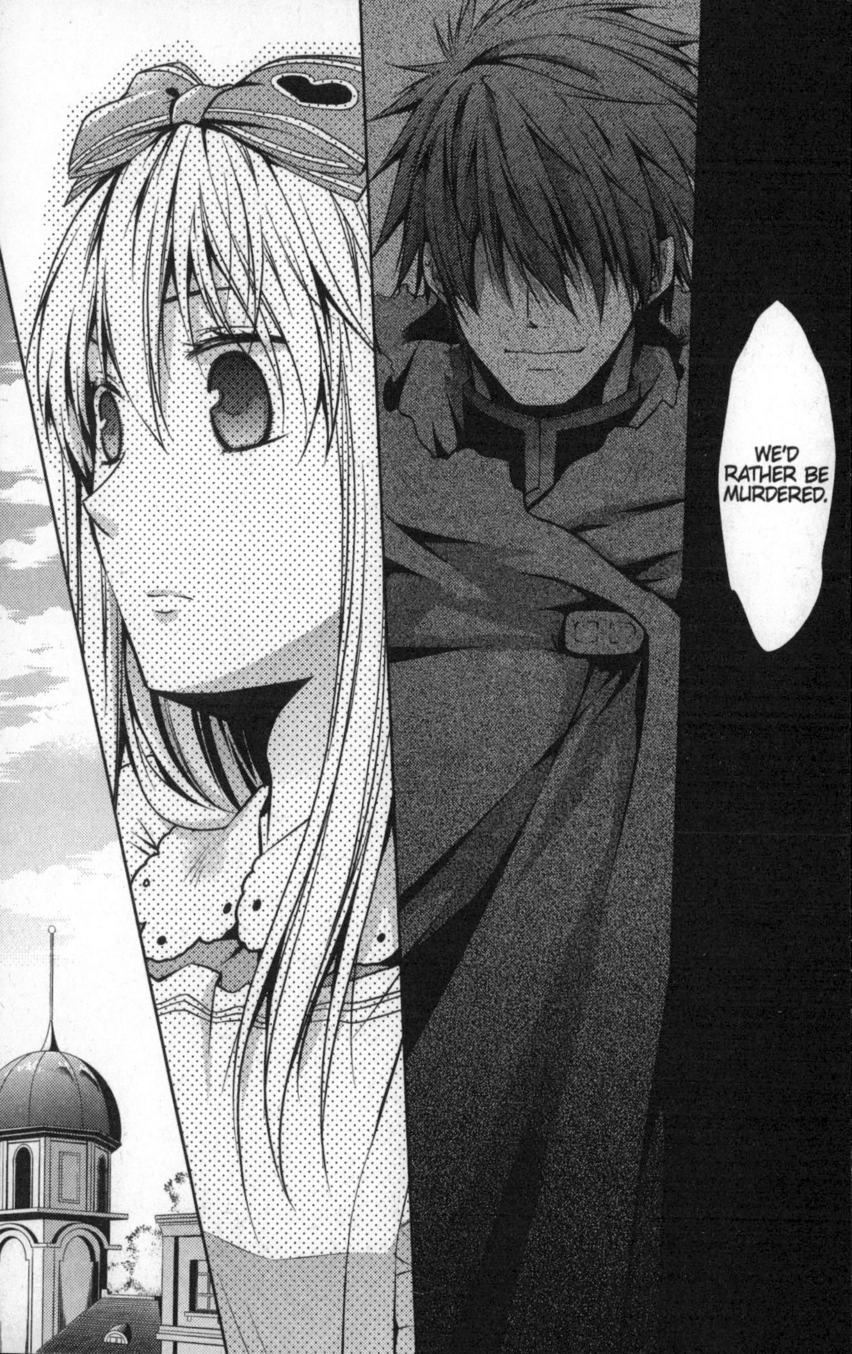
WE'D RATHER BE MURDERED.

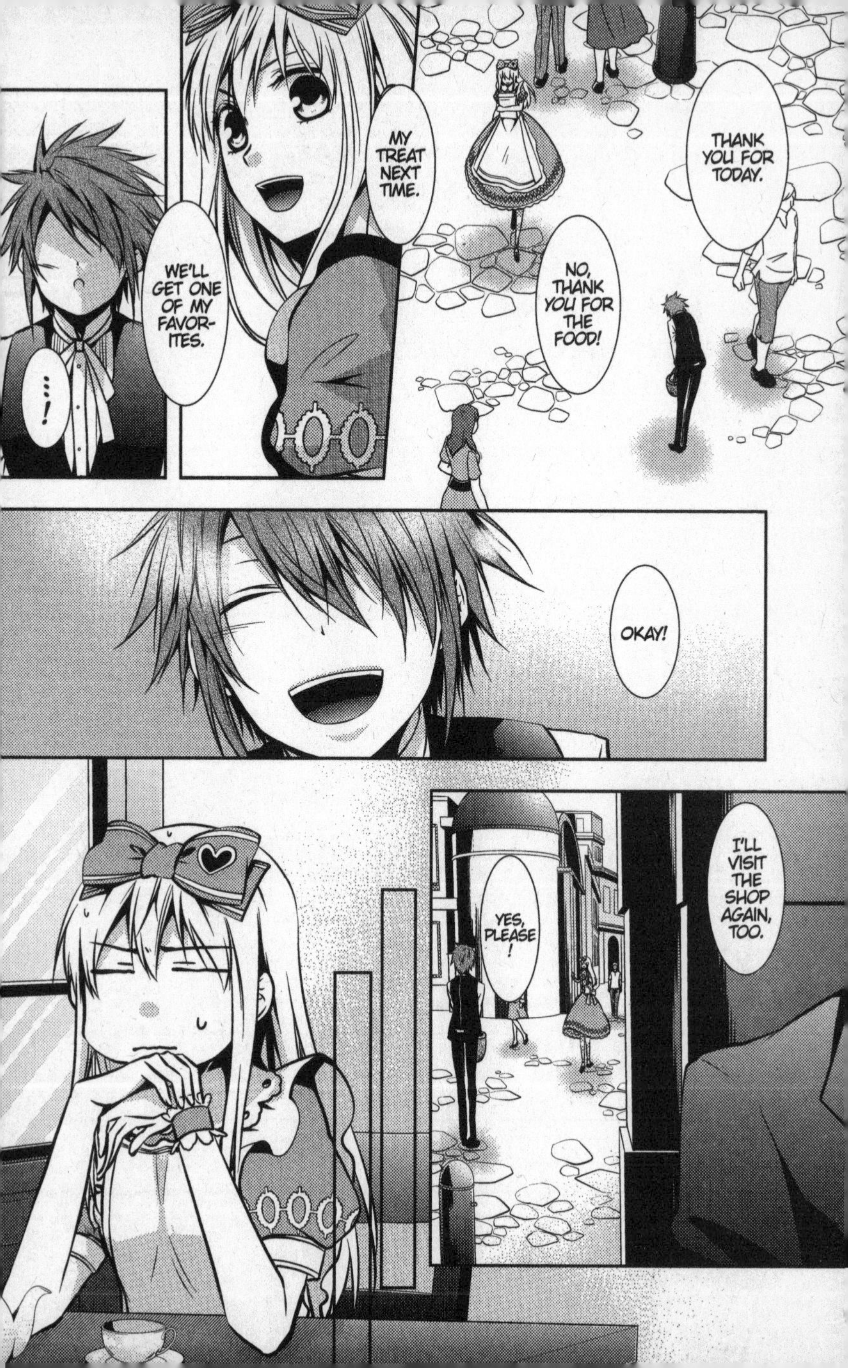
THANK YOU FOR TODAY.
NO, THANK YOU FOR THE FOOD!
MY TREAT NEXT TIME.
WE'LL GET ONE OF MY FAVORITES.
...!
OKAY!
I'LL VISIT THE SHOP AGAIN, TOO.
YES, PLEASE!

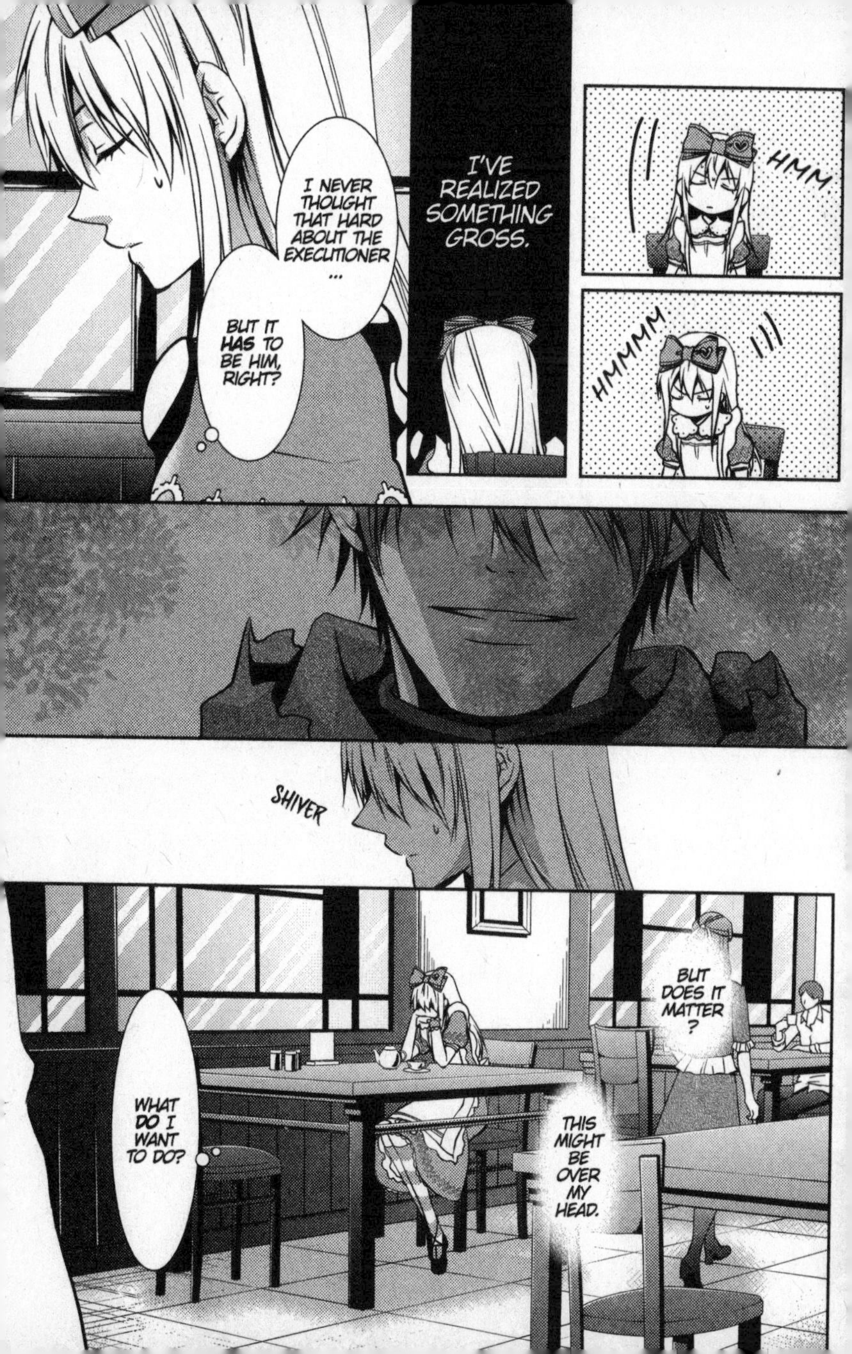
HMM
HMMMM
I'VE REALIZED SOMETHING GROSS.
I NEVER THOUGHT THAT HARD ABOUT THE EXECUTIONER ...
BUT IT HAS TO BE HIM, RIGHT?
SHIVER
BUT DOES IT MATTER?
THIS MIGHT BE OVER MY HEAD.
WHAT DO I WANT TO DO?

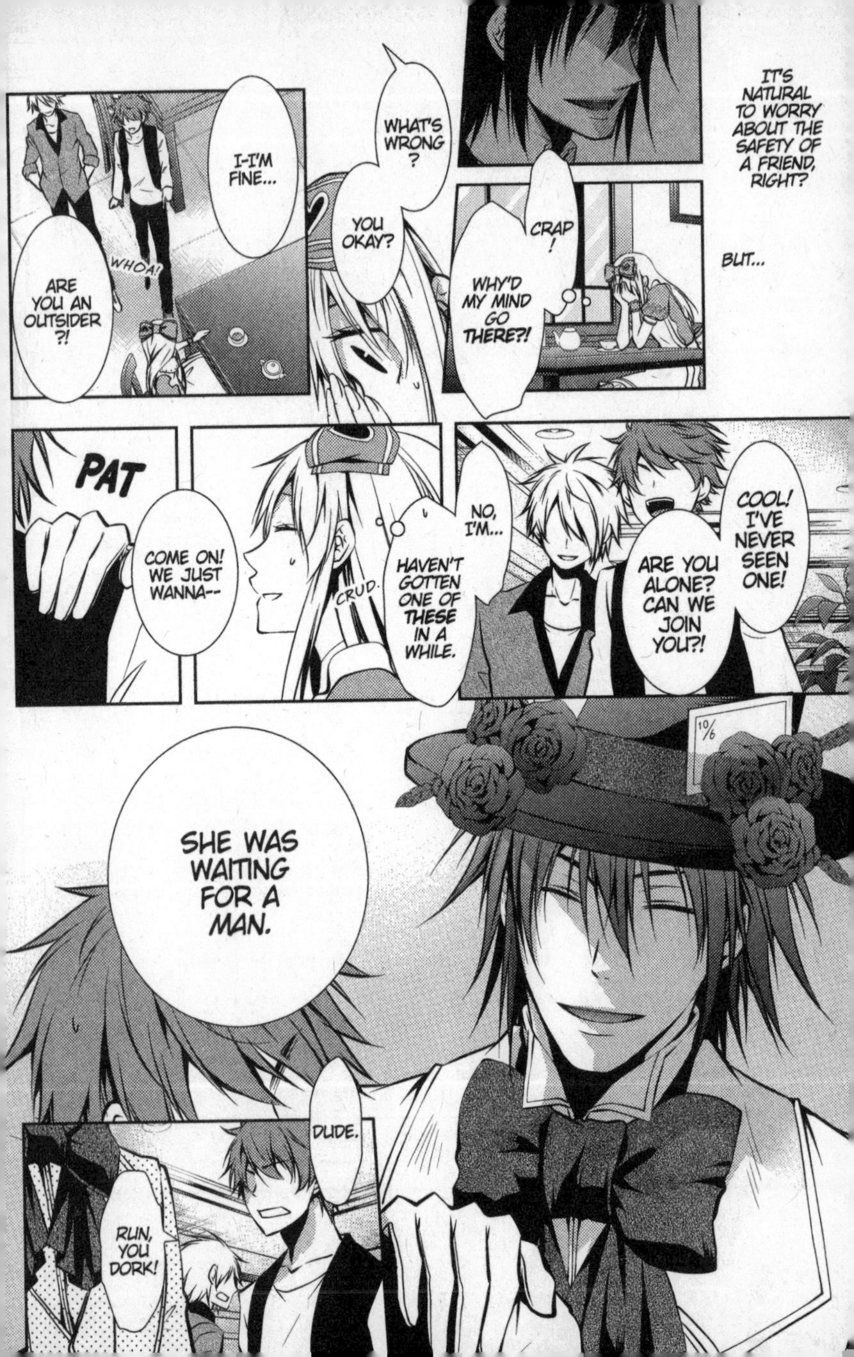
IT'S NATURAL TO WORRY ABOUT THE SAFETY OF A FRIEND, RIGHT?
BUT...
CRAP!
WHY'D MY MIND GO THERE?!
WHAT'S WRONG?
YOU OKAY?
I-I'M FINE...
WHOA!
ARE YOU AN OUTSIDER?!
COOL! I'VE NEVER SEEN ONE!
ARE YOU ALONE? CAN WE JOIN YOU?!
NO, I'M...
HAVEN'T GOTTEN ONE OF THESE IN A WHILE.
CRUD.
COME ON! WE JUST WANNA--
PAT
SHE WAS WAITING FOR A MAN.
DUDE.
RUN, YOU DORK!

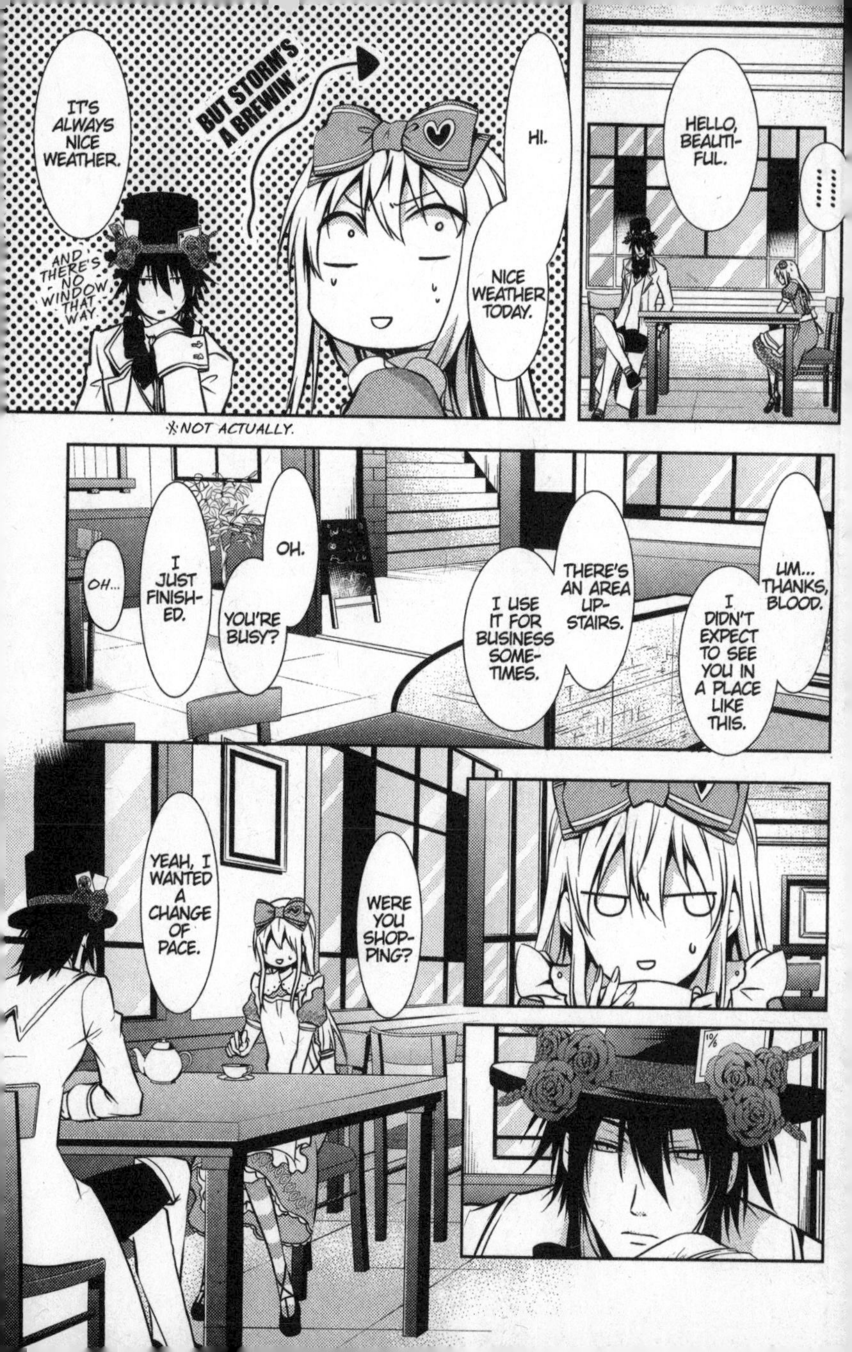

HELLO, BEAUTIFUL.
......
HI.
NICE WEATHER TODAY.
BUT STORM'S A BREWIN'...
IT'S ALWAYS NICE WEATHER.
AND THERE'S NO WINDOW THAT WAY
※NOT ACTUALLY.
UM... THANKS, BLOOD.
I DIDN'T EXPECT TO SEE YOU IN A PLACE LIKE THIS.
THERE'S AN AREA UPSTAIRS.
I USE IT FOR BUSINESS SOMETIMES.
OH.
YOU'RE BUSY?
I JUST FINISHED.
OH...
WERE YOU SHOPPING?
YEAH, I WANTED A CHANGE OF PACE.

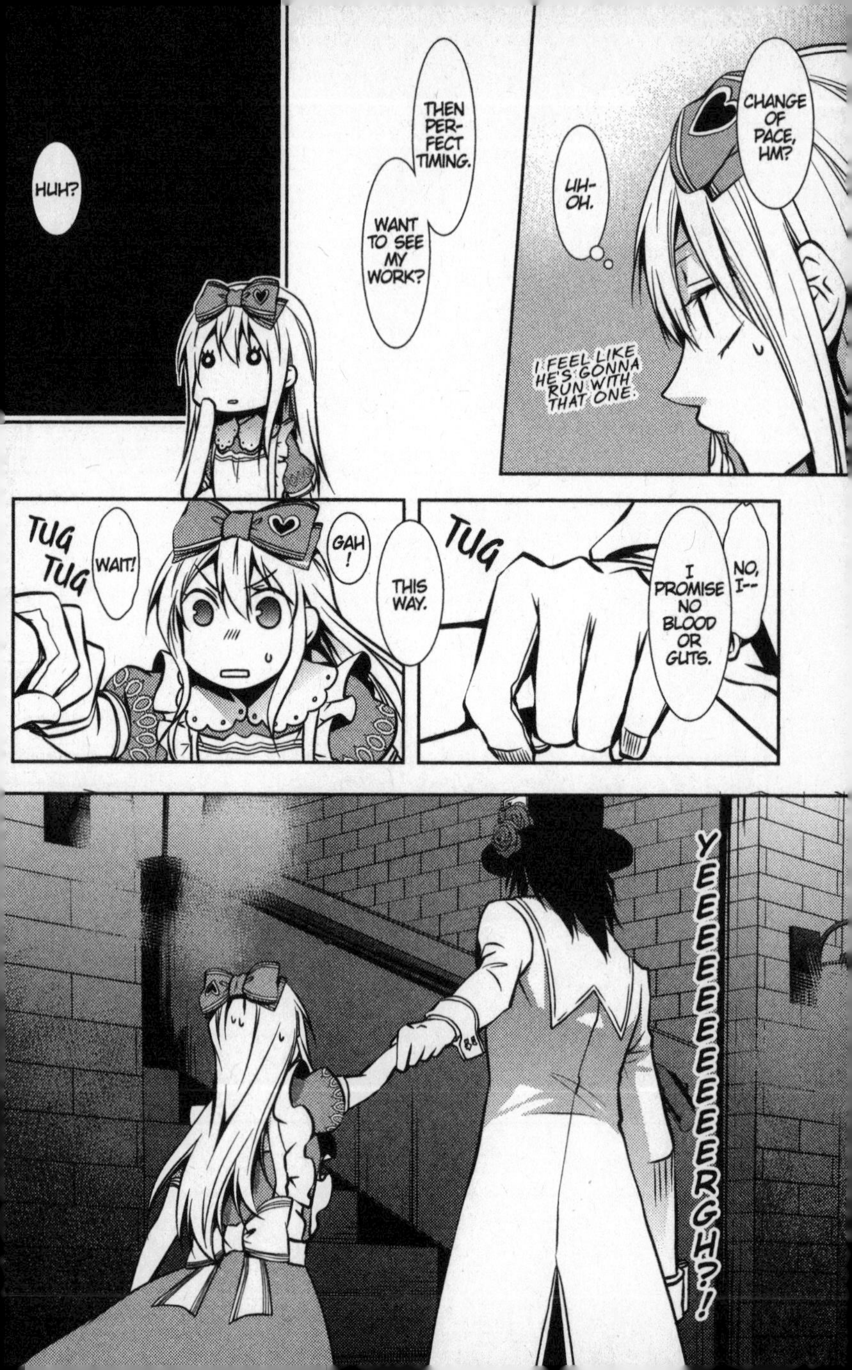
CHANGE OF PACE, HM?
UH-OH.
I FEEL LIKE HE'S GONNA RUN WITH THAT ONE.
THEN PERFECT TIMING.
WANT TO SEE MY WORK?
HUH?
TUG
NO, I--
I PROMISE NO BLOOD OR GUTS.
THIS WAY.
GAH!
TUG TUG
WAIT!
YEEEEEEEEEEERGH?!

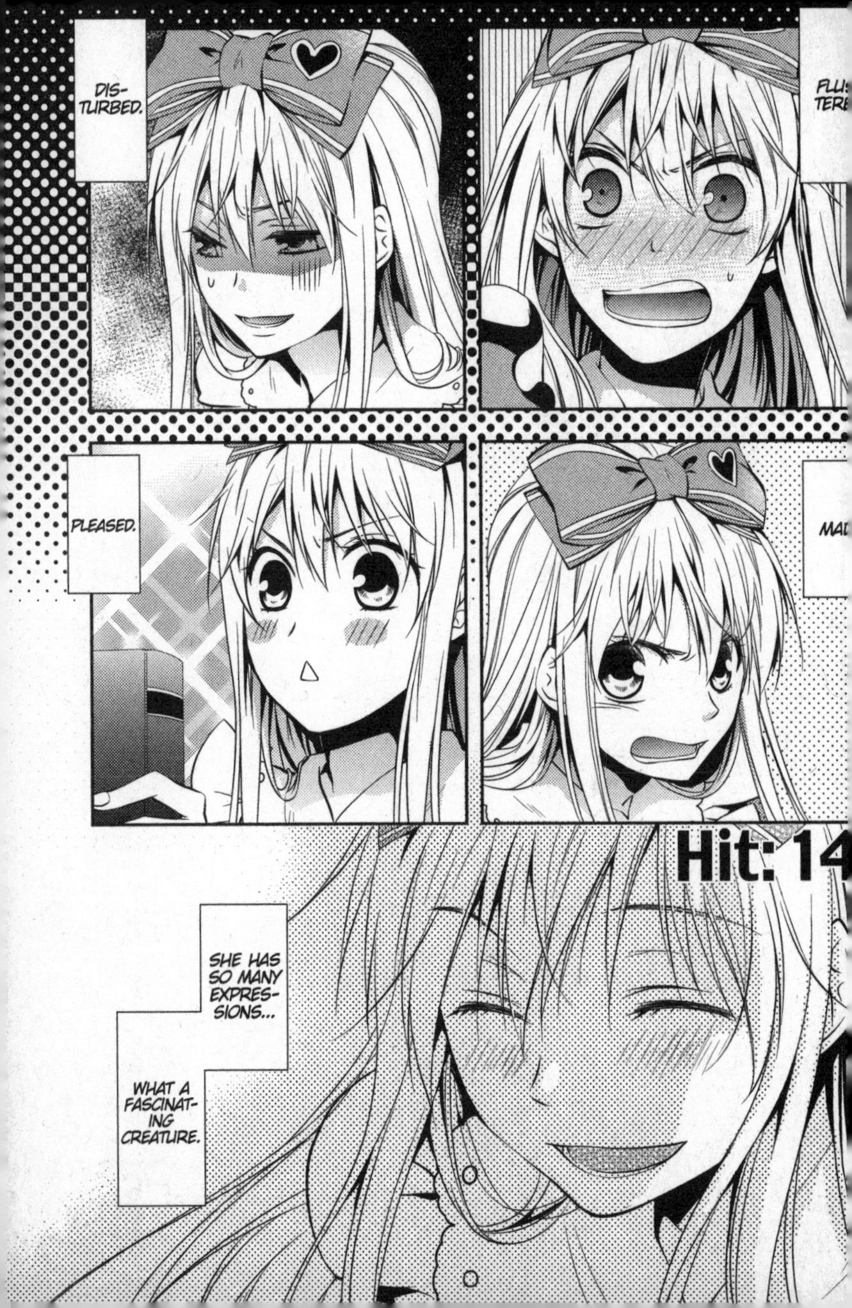
FLUS TERE
DIS- TURBED.
MA
PLEASED.
Hit: 14
SHE HAS SO MANY EXPRES- SIONS...
WHAT A FASCINAT- ING CREATURE.

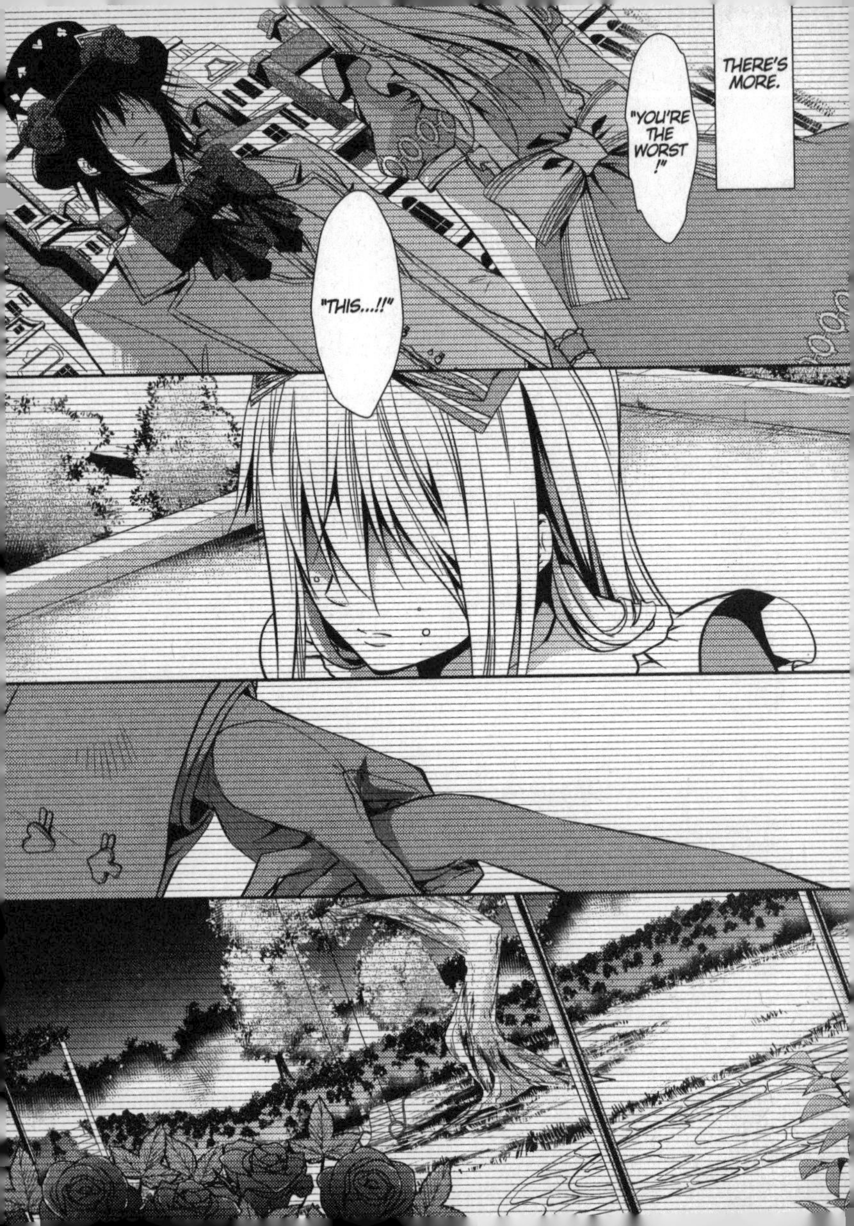
THERE'S MORE.
"YOU'RE THE WORST!"
"THIS...!!"

Hit: 14

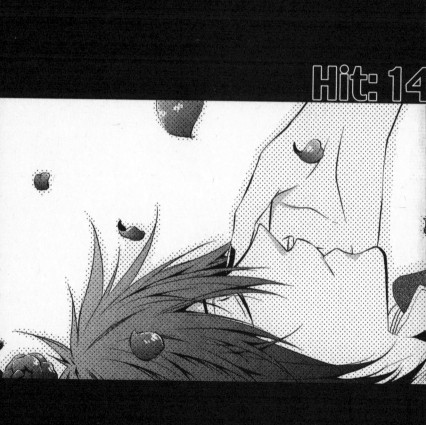

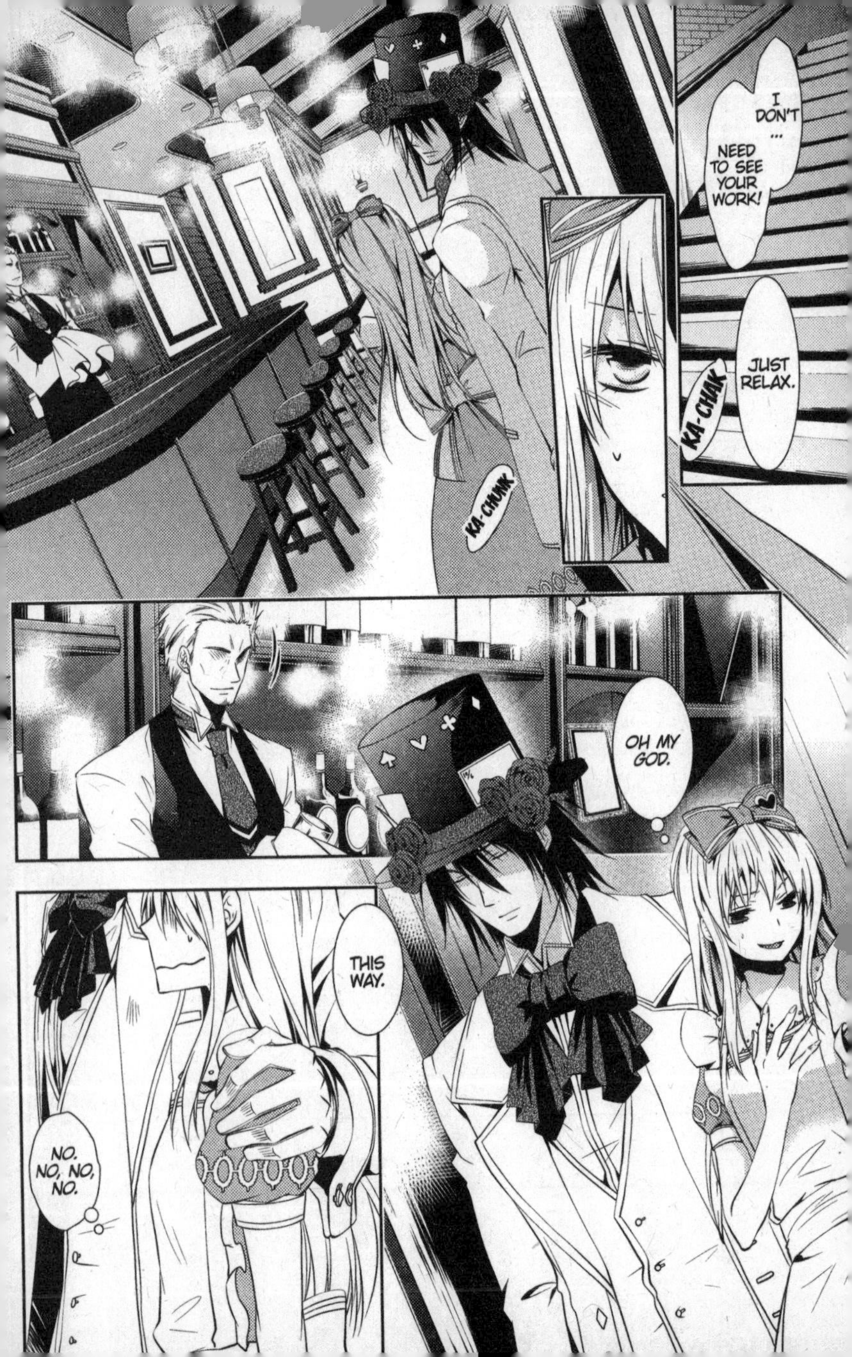

I DON'T ... NEED TO SEE YOUR WORK!
JUST RELAX.
KA-CHAK
KA-CHUNK
OH MY GOD.
THIS WAY.
NO. NO, NO, NO.

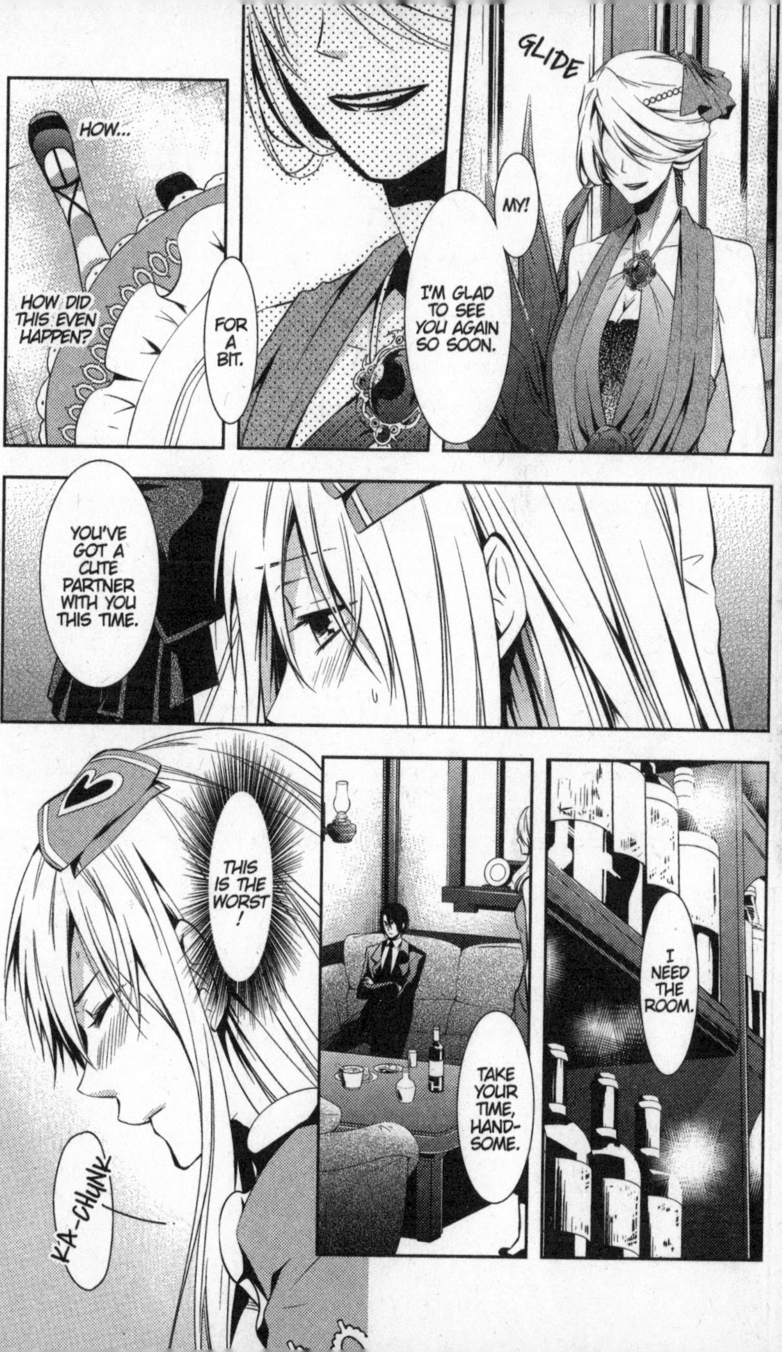
GLIDE
MY!
I'M GLAD TO SEE YOU AGAIN SO SOON.
FOR A BIT.
HOW...
HOW DID THIS EVEN HAPPEN?
YOU'VE GOT A CUTE PARTNER WITH YOU THIS TIME.
I NEED THE ROOM.
TAKE YOUR TIME, HAND-SOME.
THIS IS THE WORST!
KA-CHUNK

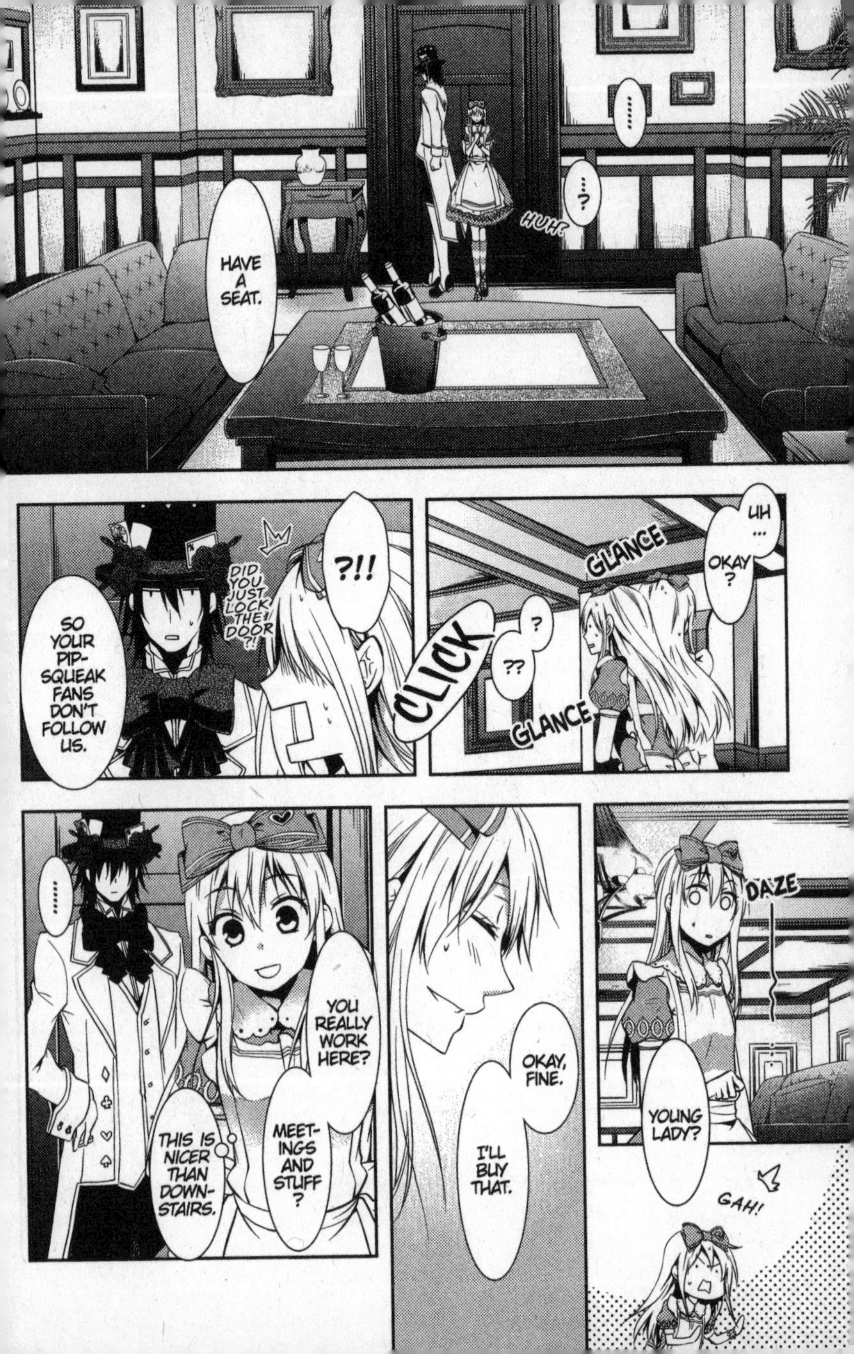
……
…?
HUH?
HAVE A SEAT.
UH … OKAY?
GLANCE
?
??
GLANCE
?!!
CLICK
DID YOU JUST LOCK THE DOOR?!
SO YOUR PIP-SQUEAK FANS DON'T FOLLOW US.
DAZE
YOUNG LADY?
GAH!
OKAY, FINE.
I'LL BUY THAT.
YOU REALLY WORK HERE?
MEET-INGS AND STUFF?
THIS IS NICER THAN DOWN-STAIRS.
……

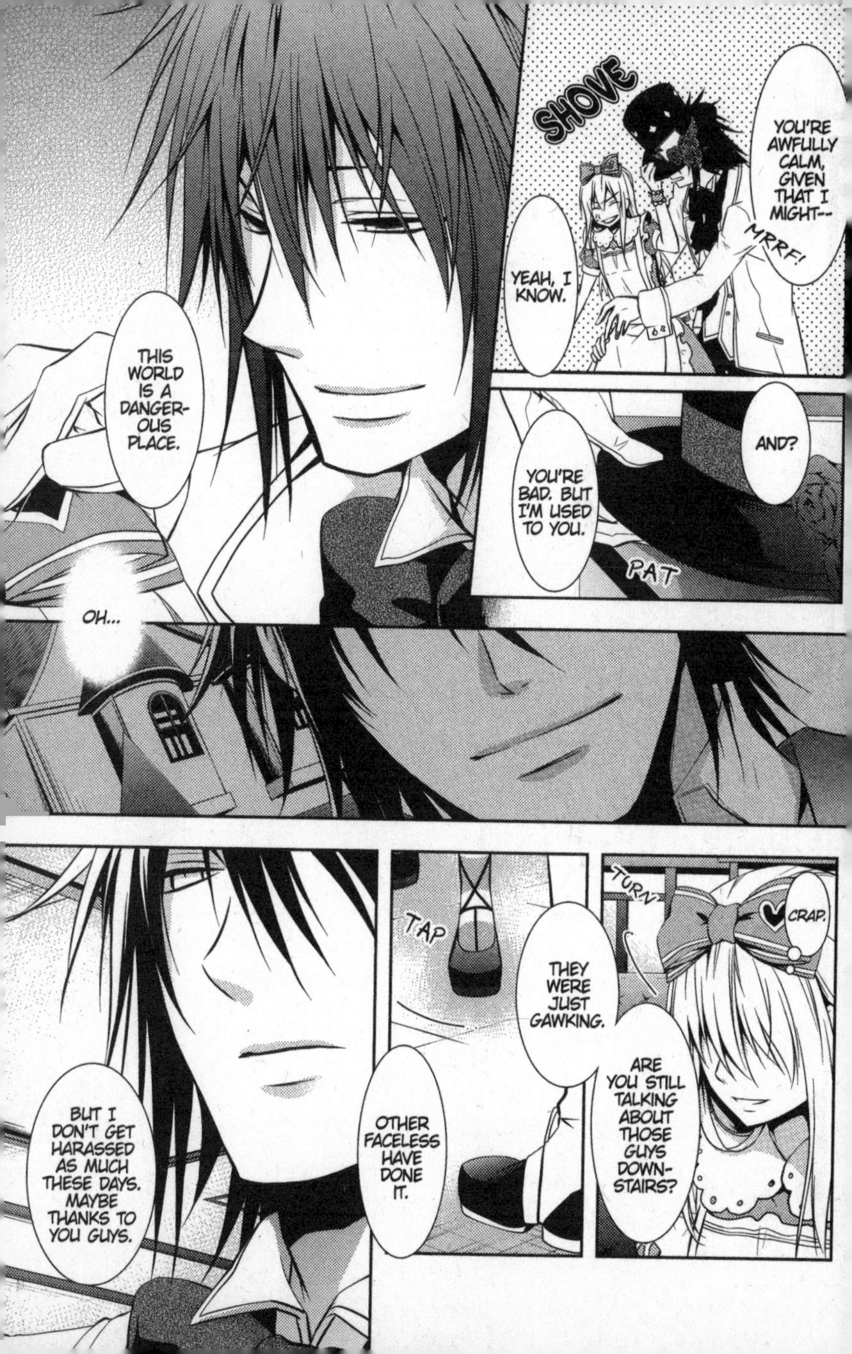
SHOVE
YOU'RE AWFULLY CALM, GIVEN THAT I MIGHT--
MRRF!
YEAH, I KNOW.
AND?
YOU'RE BAD. BUT I'M USED TO YOU.
PAT
THIS WORLD IS A DANGER-OUS PLACE.
OH...
CRAP.
TURN
ARE YOU STILL TALKING ABOUT THOSE GUYS DOWN-STAIRS?
THEY WERE JUST GAWKING.
TAP
OTHER FACELESS HAVE DONE IT.
BUT I DON'T GET HARASSED AS MUCH THESE DAYS. MAYBE THANKS TO YOU GUYS.

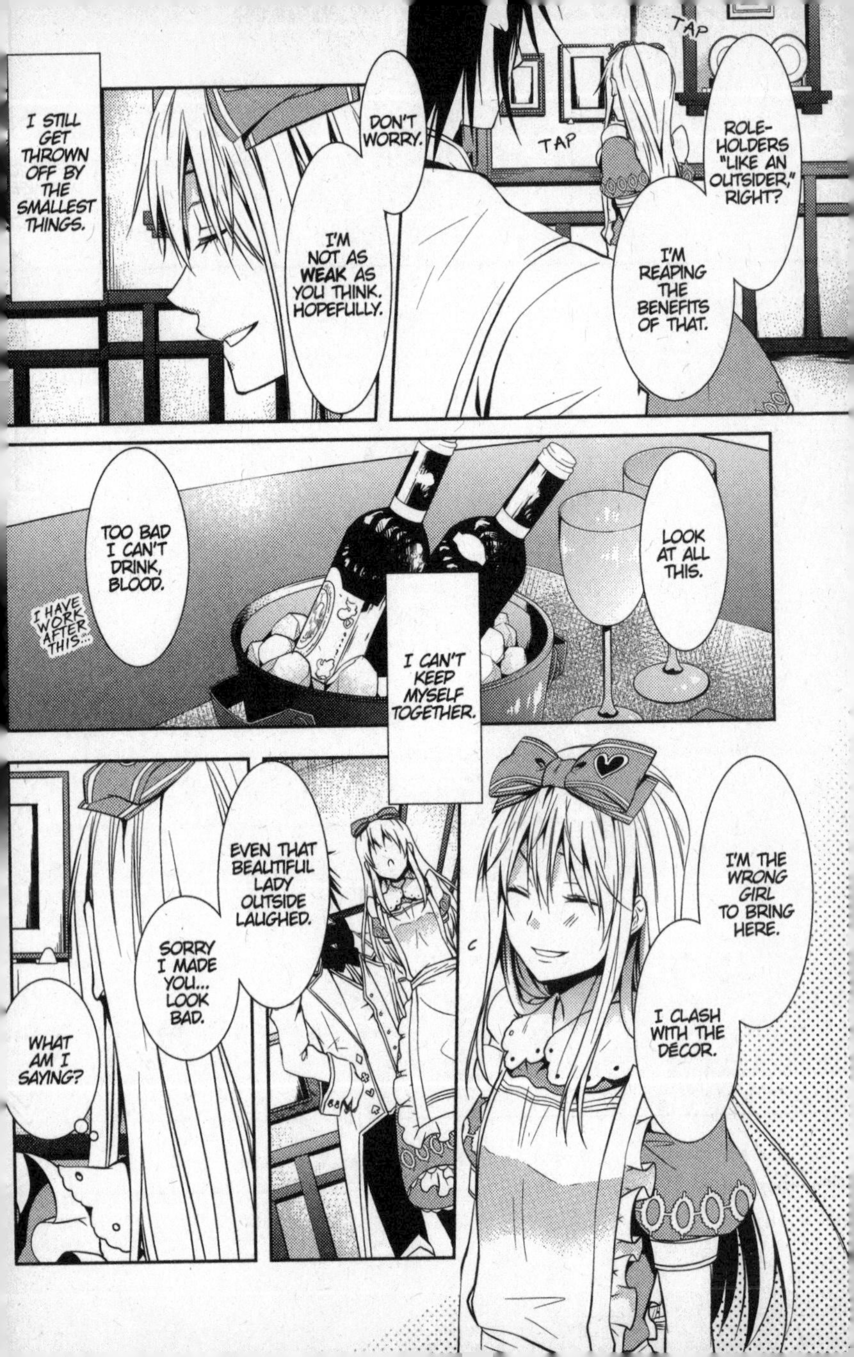
TAP
TAP
ROLE-HOLDERS "LIKE AN OUTSIDER," RIGHT?
I'M REAPING THE BENEFITS OF THAT.
DON'T WORRY.
I'M NOT AS WEAK AS YOU THINK. HOPEFULLY.
I STILL GET THROWN OFF BY THE SMALLEST THINGS.
LOOK AT ALL THIS.
TOO BAD I CAN'T DRINK, BLOOD.
I HAVE WORK AFTER THIS...
I CAN'T KEEP MYSELF TOGETHER.
I'M THE WRONG GIRL TO BRING HERE.
I CLASH WITH THE DÉCOR.
EVEN THAT BEAUTIFUL LADY OUTSIDE LAUGHED.
SORRY I MADE YOU... LOOK BAD.
WHAT AM I SAYING?

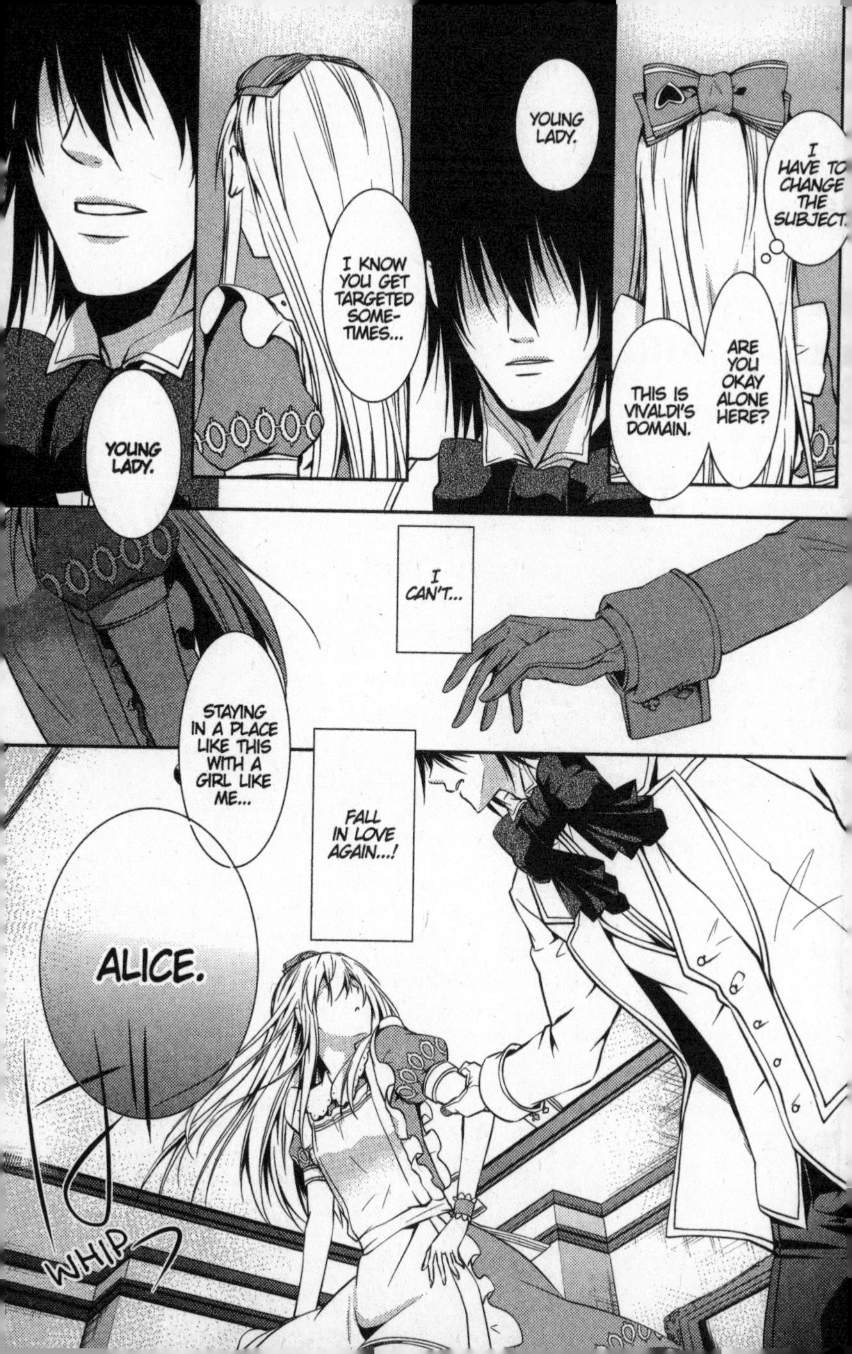

I HAVE TO CHANGE THE SUBJECT.
ARE YOU OKAY ALONE HERE?
THIS IS VIVALDI'S DOMAIN.
YOUNG LADY.
I KNOW YOU GET TARGETED SOME-TIMES...
YOUNG LADY.
I CAN'T...
STAYING IN A PLACE LIKE THIS WITH A GIRL LIKE ME...
FALL IN LOVE AGAIN...!
ALICE.
WHIP

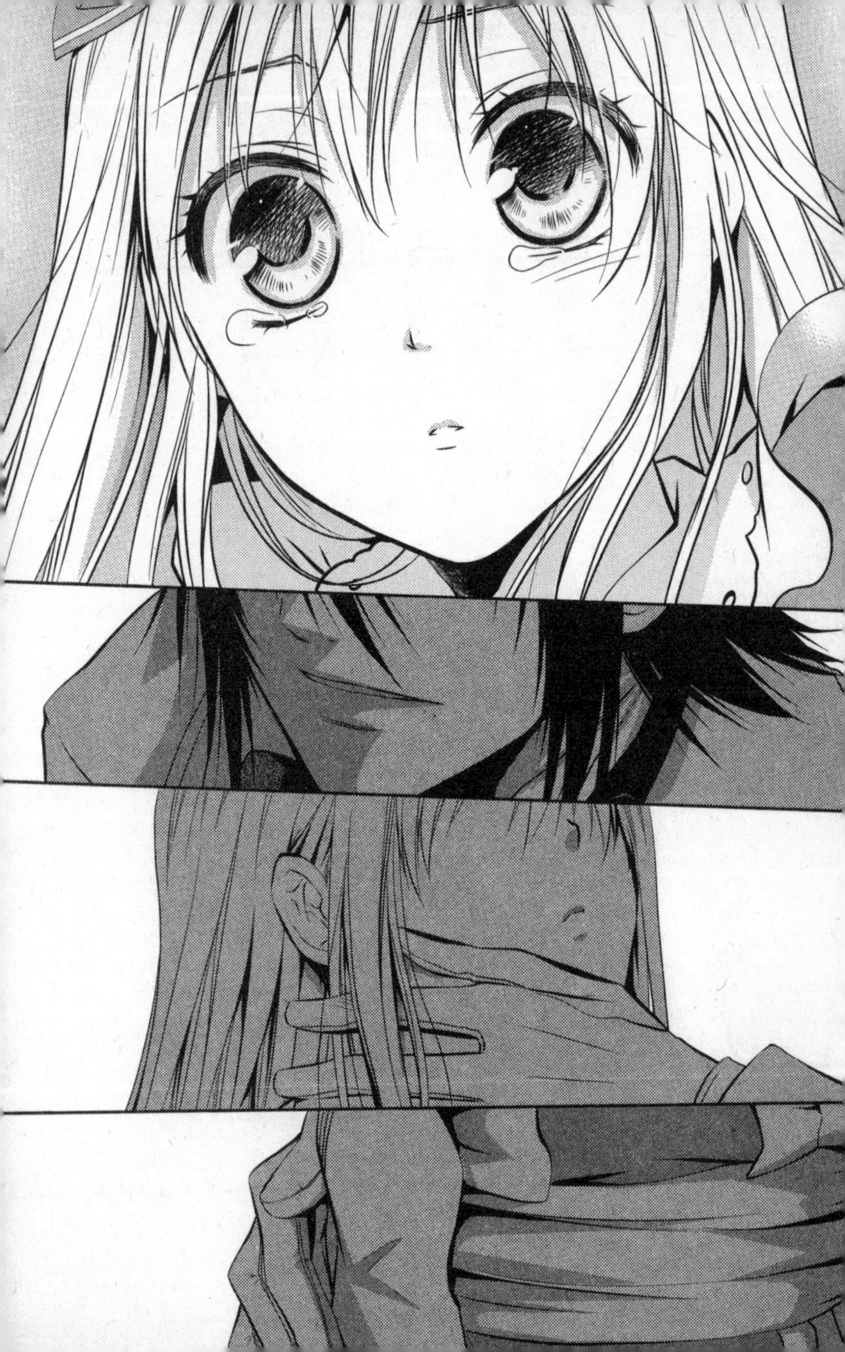

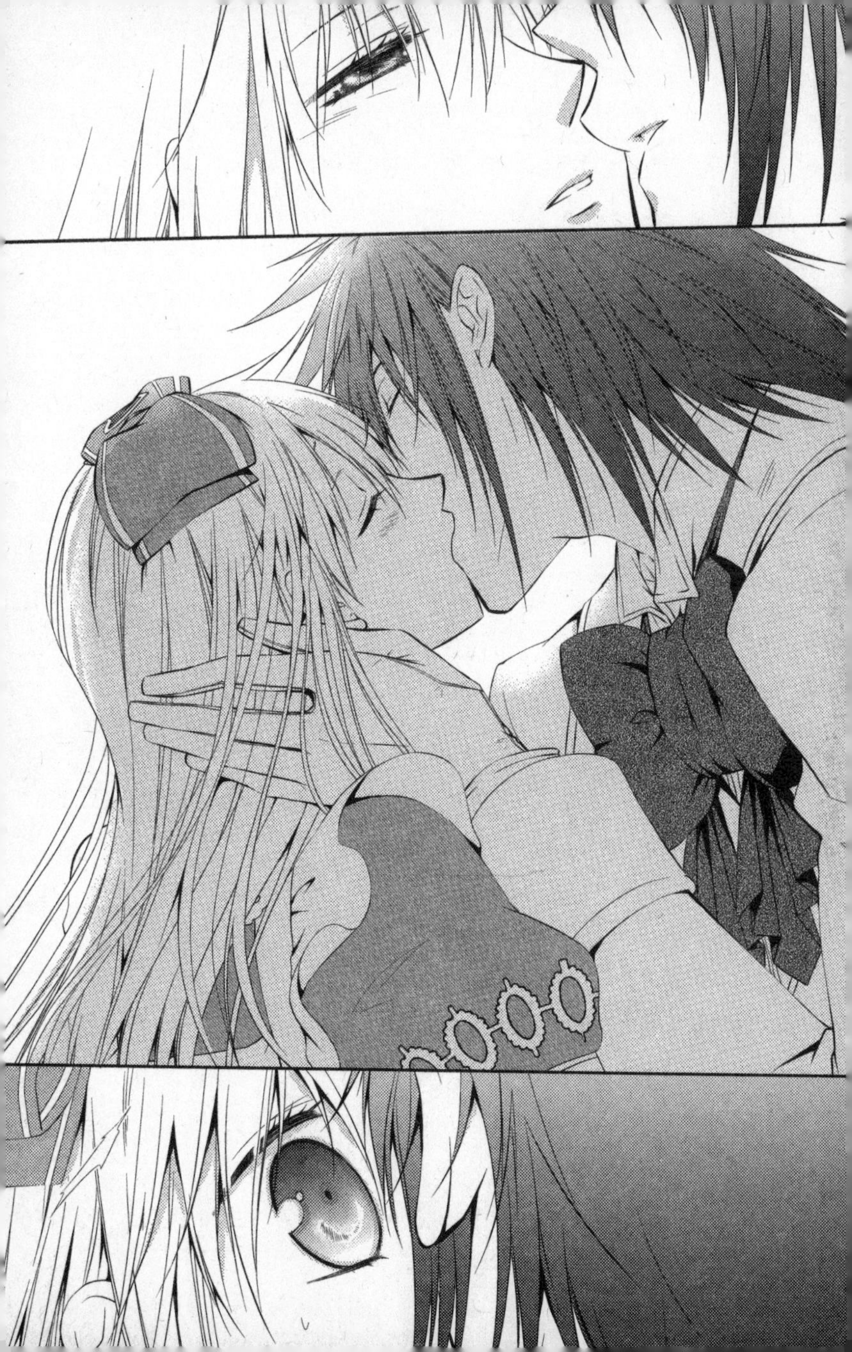

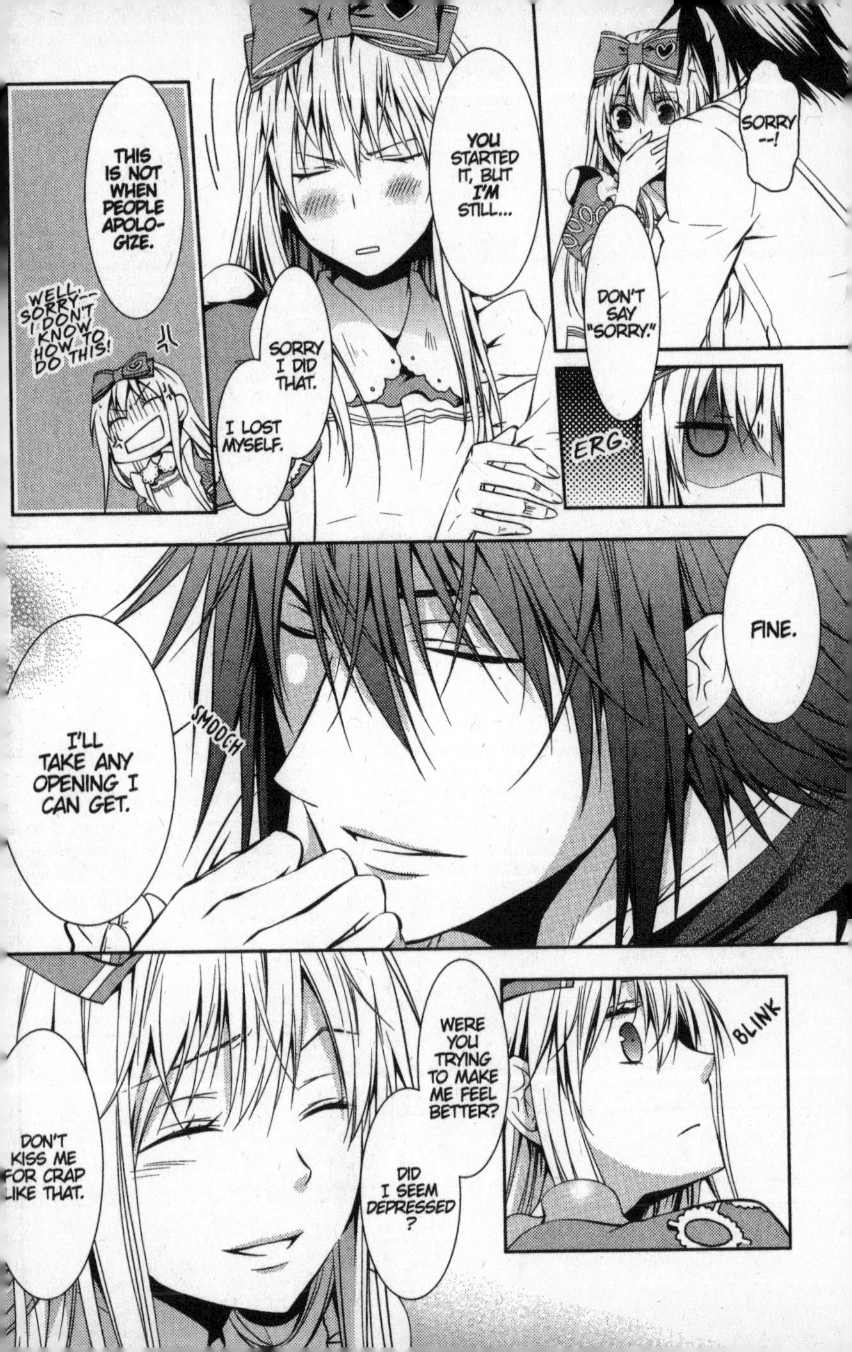
SORRY--!
DON'T SAY "SORRY."
ERG.
YOU STARTED IT, BUT I'M STILL...
SORRY I DID THAT.
I LOST MYSELF.
THIS IS NOT WHEN PEOPLE APOLO-GIZE.
WELL-- SORRY I DON'T KNOW HOW TO DO THIS!
FINE.
SMOOCH
I'LL TAKE ANY OPENING I CAN GET.
BLINK
WERE YOU TRYING TO MAKE ME FEEL BETTER?
DID I SEEM DEPRESSED?
DON'T KISS ME FOR CRAP LIKE THAT.

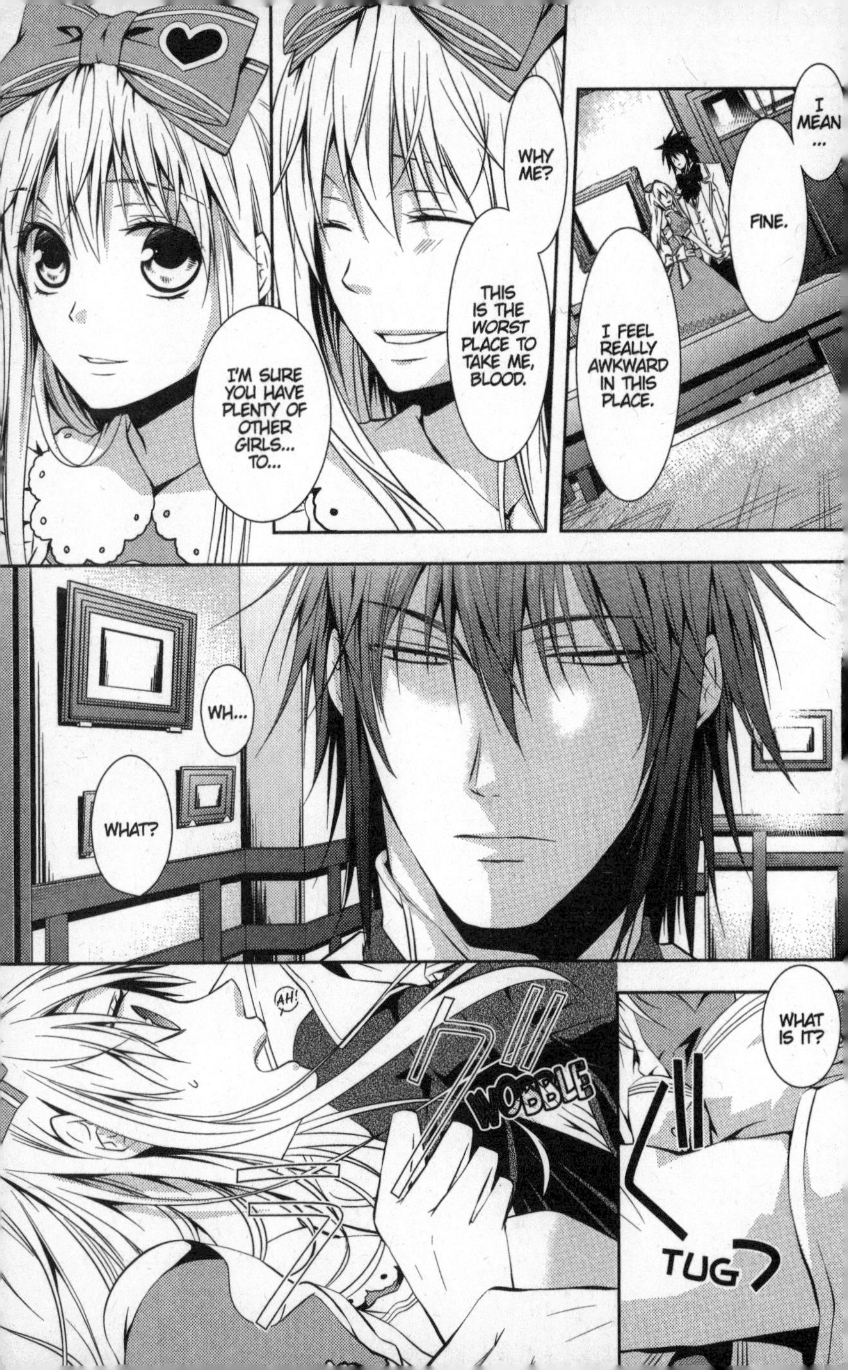
I MEAN ...
FINE.
I FEEL REALLY AWKWARD IN THIS PLACE.
WHY ME?
THIS IS THE WORST PLACE TO TAKE ME, BLOOD.
I'M SURE YOU HAVE PLENTY OF OTHER GIRLS... TO...
WH...
WHAT?
WHAT IS IT?
TUG
AH!
WOBBLE

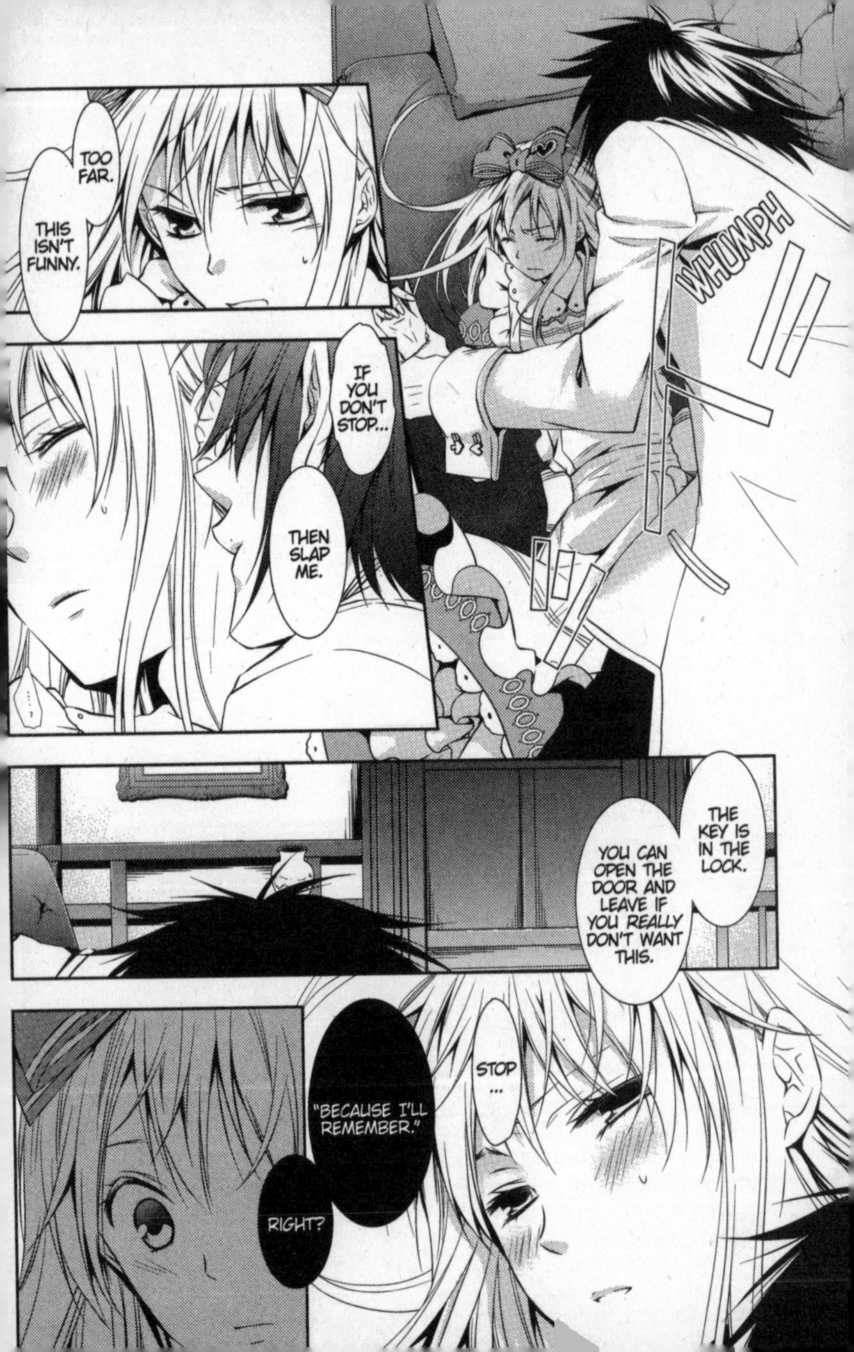
WHUMPH
TOO FAR.
THIS ISN'T FUNNY.
IF YOU DON'T STOP...
THEN SLAP ME.
THE KEY IS IN THE LOCK.
YOU CAN OPEN THE DOOR AND LEAVE IF YOU REALLY DON'T WANT THIS.
STOP ...
"BECAUSE I'LL REMEMBER."
RIGHT?

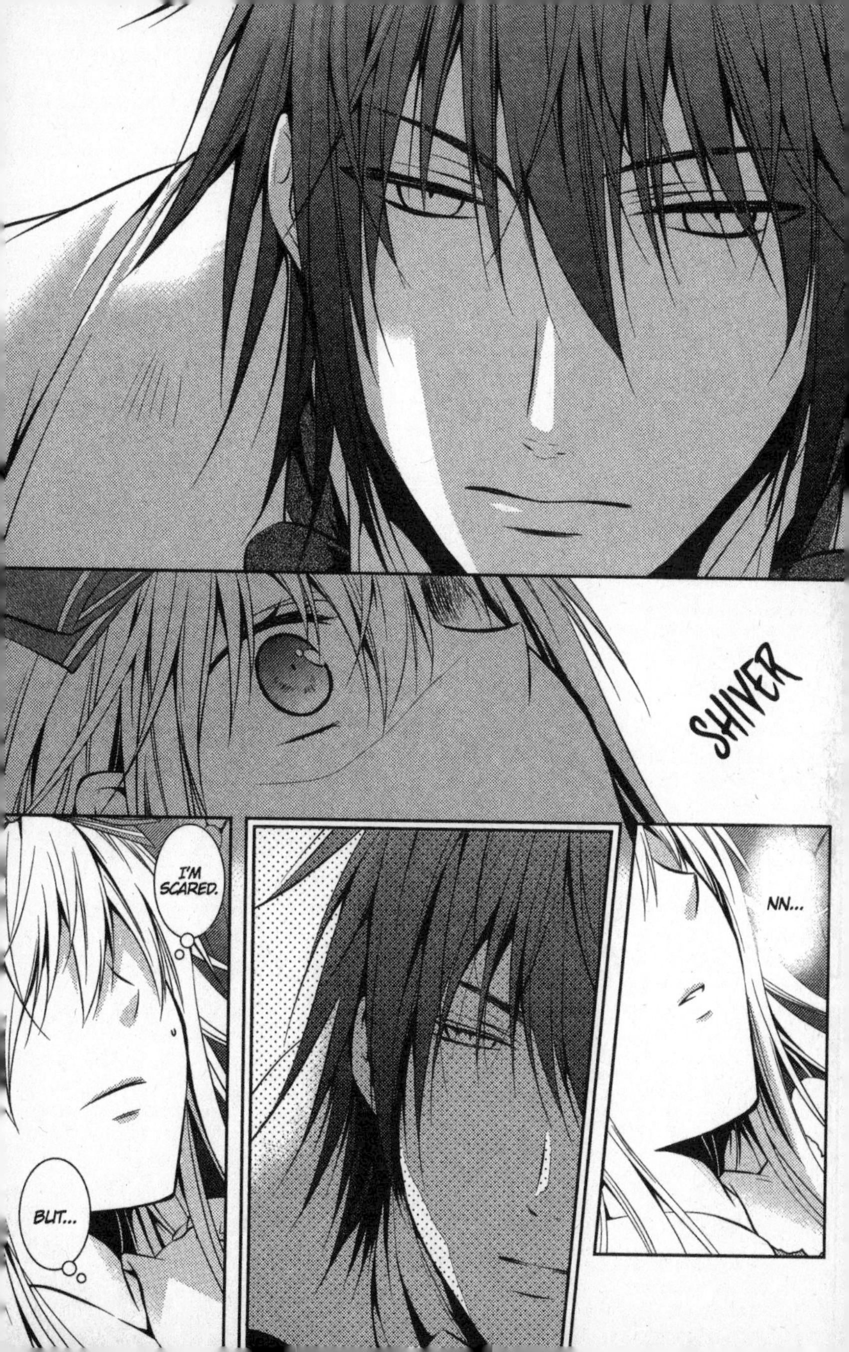
SHIVER
NN...
I'M SCARED.
BUT...

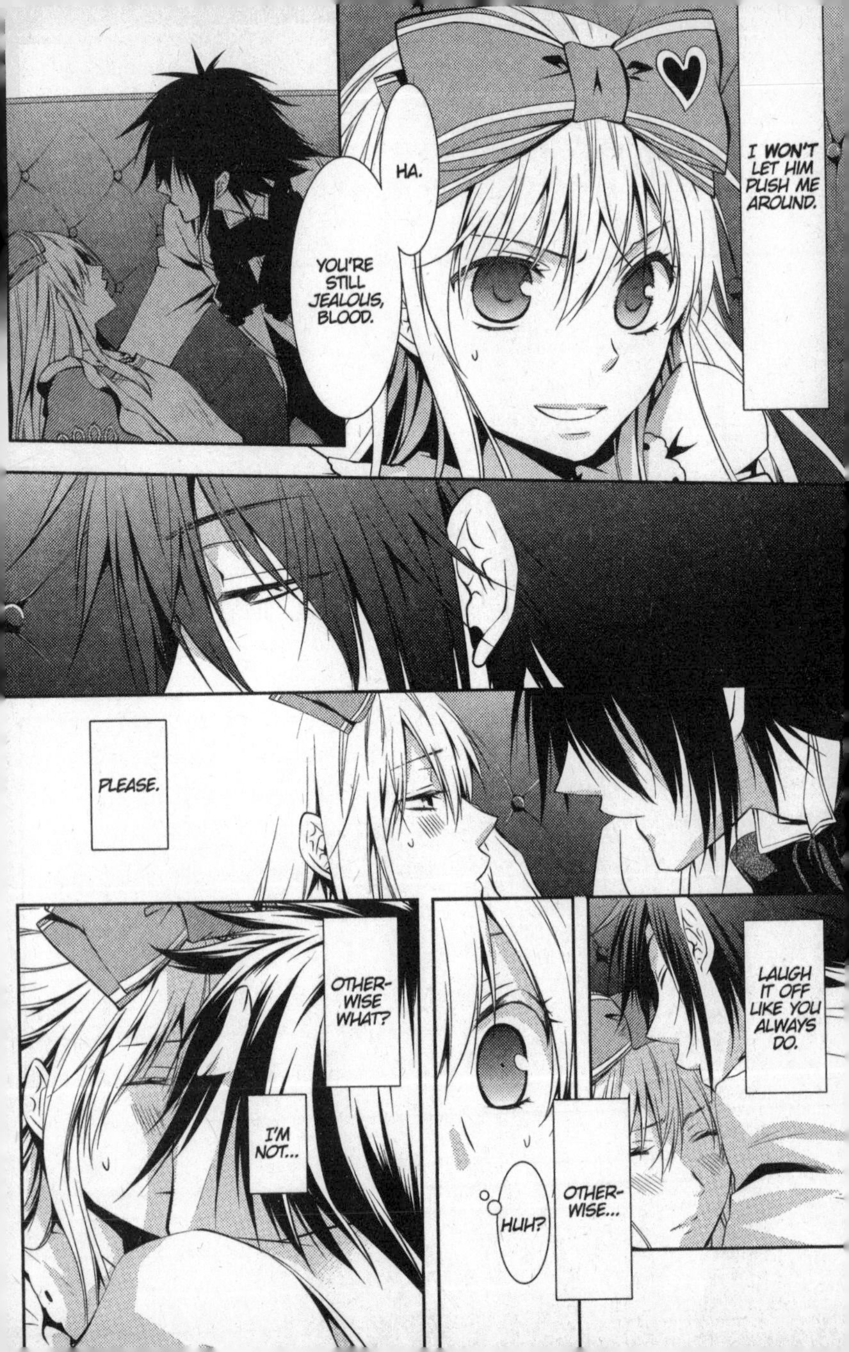
I WON'T LET HIM PUSH ME AROUND.
HA.
YOU'RE STILL JEALOUS, BLOOD.
PLEASE.
LAUGH IT OFF LIKE YOU ALWAYS DO.
OTHER-WISE...
HUH?
OTHER-WISE WHAT?
I'M NOT...

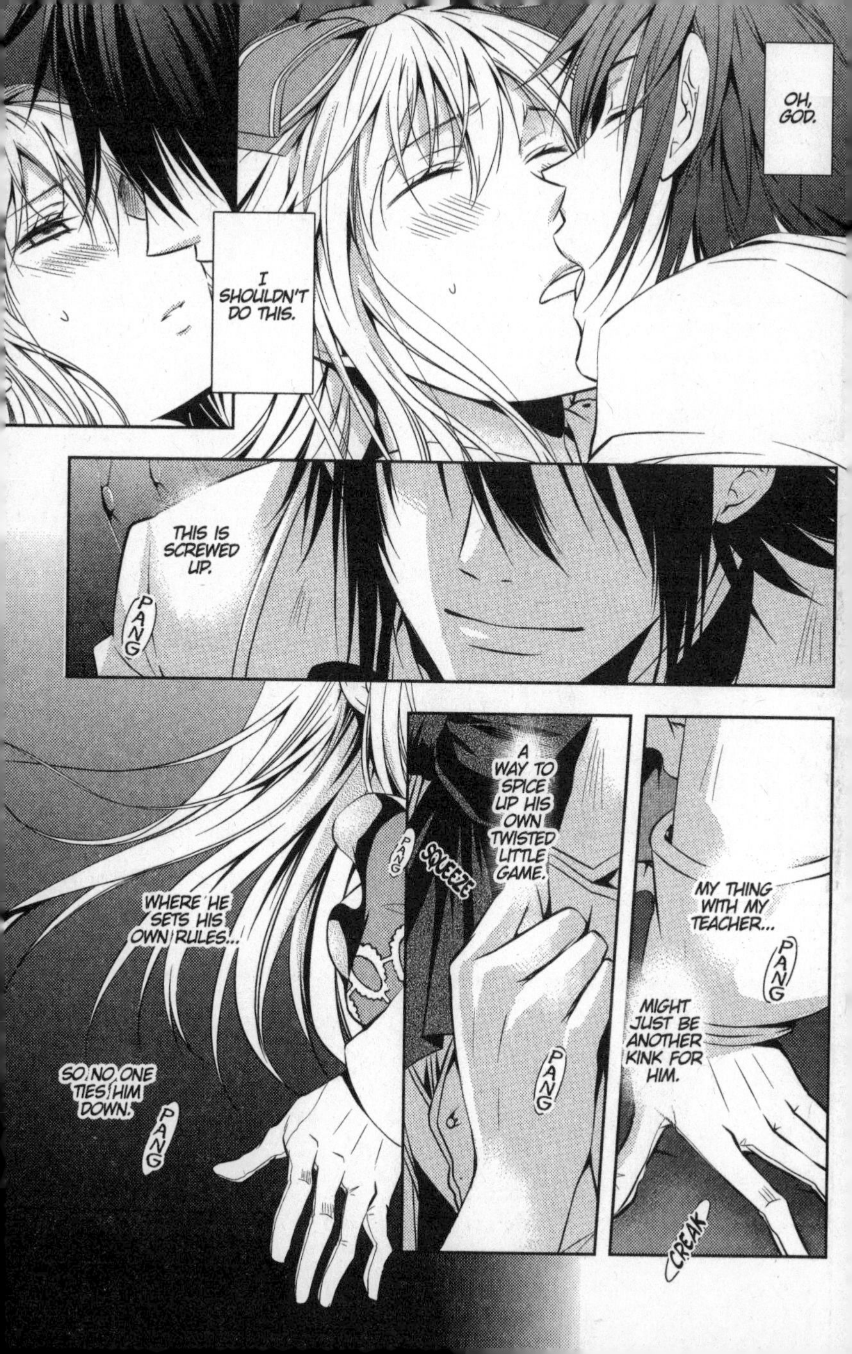
OH, GOD.
I SHOULDN'T DO THIS.
THIS IS SCREWED UP.
PANG
MY THING WITH MY TEACHER...
PANG
MIGHT JUST BE ANOTHER KINK FOR HIM.
CREAK
A WAY TO SPICE UP HIS OWN TWISTED LITTLE GAME.
PANG
SQUEEZE
PANG
WHERE HE SETS HIS OWN RULES...
SO NO ONE TIES HIM DOWN.
PANG

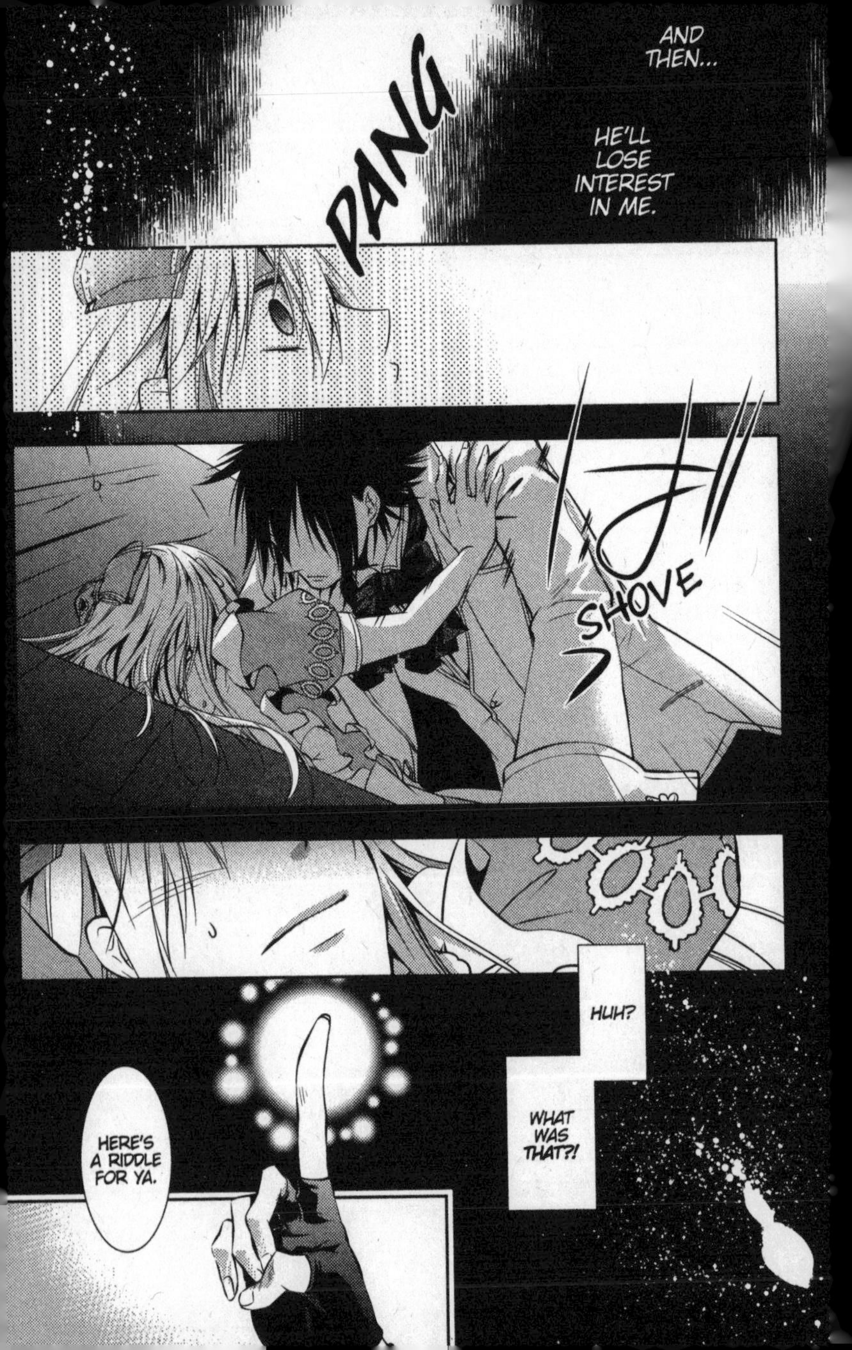
AND THEN...
HE'LL LOSE INTEREST IN ME.
PANG
SHOVE
HUH?
WHAT WAS THAT?!
HERE'S A RIDDLE FOR YA.

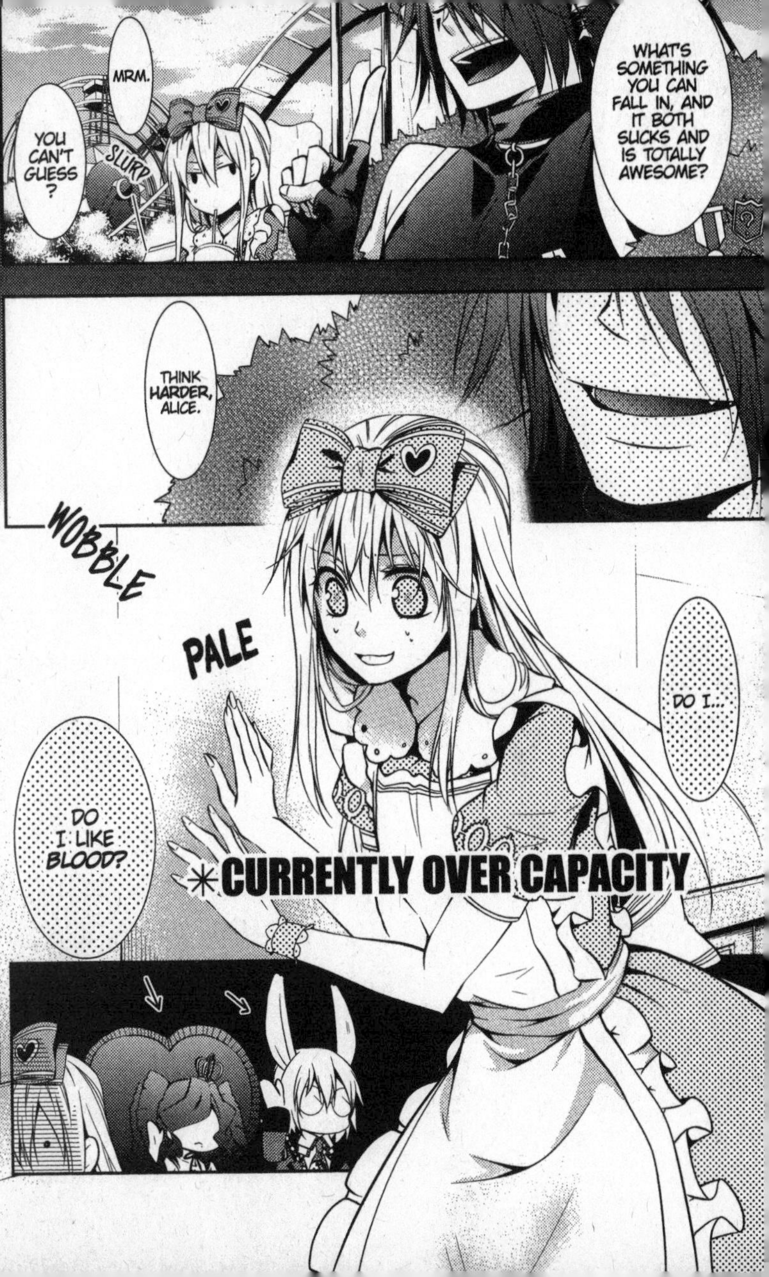
WHAT'S SOMETHING YOU CAN FALL IN, AND IT BOTH SUCKS AND IS TOTALLY AWESOME?
MRM.
SLURP
YOU CAN'T GUESS ?
THINK HARDER, ALICE.
WOBBLE
PALE
DO I...
DO I LIKE BLOOD?
*CURRENTLY OVER CAPACITY

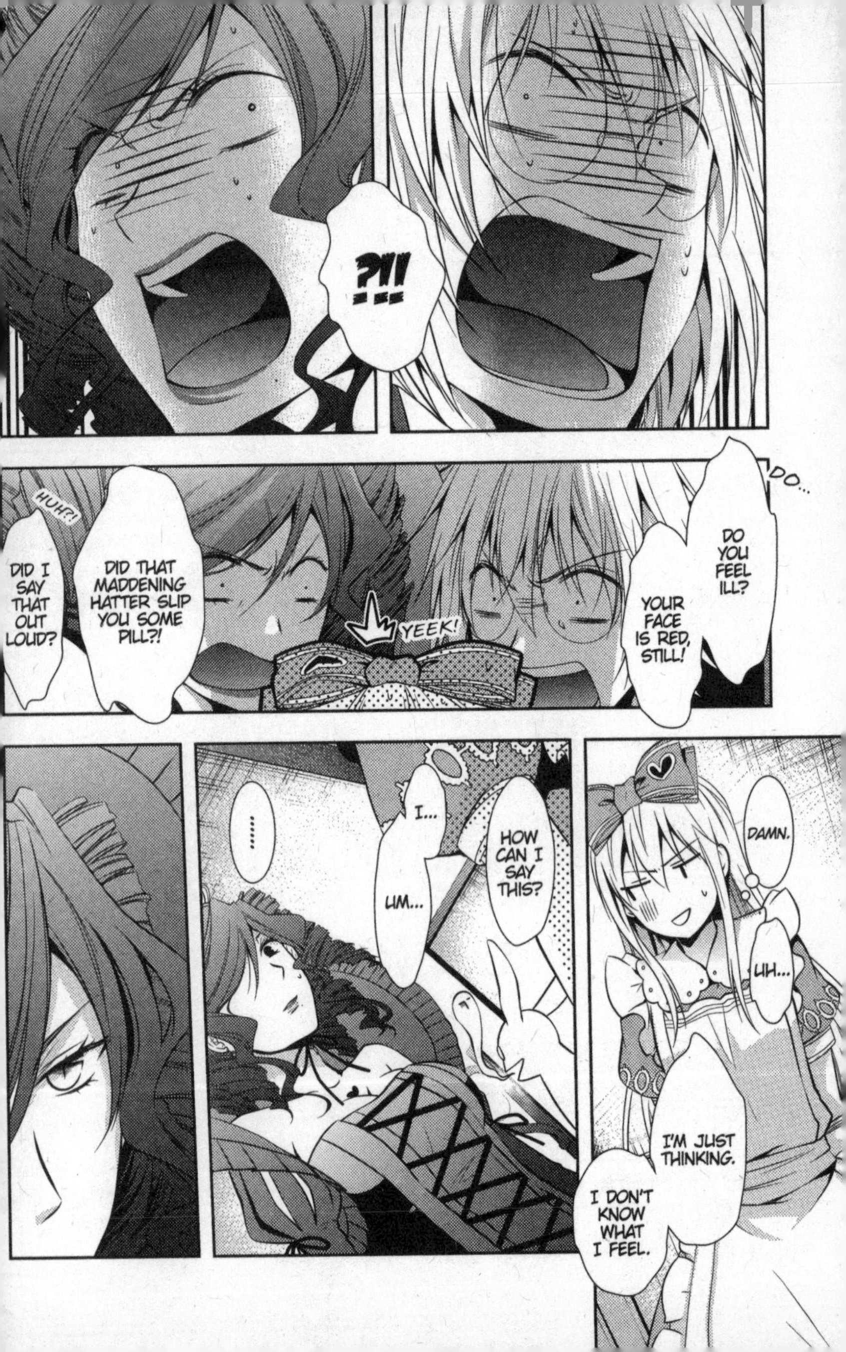
?!!
DO...
DO YOU FEEL ILL?
YOUR FACE IS RED, STILL!
YEEK!
DID THAT MADDENING HATTER SLIP YOU SOME PILL?!
HUH?!
DID I SAY THAT OUT LOUD?
DAMN.
UH...
I'M JUST THINKING.
I DON'T KNOW WHAT I FEEL.
HOW CAN I SAY THIS?
I...
UM...
......

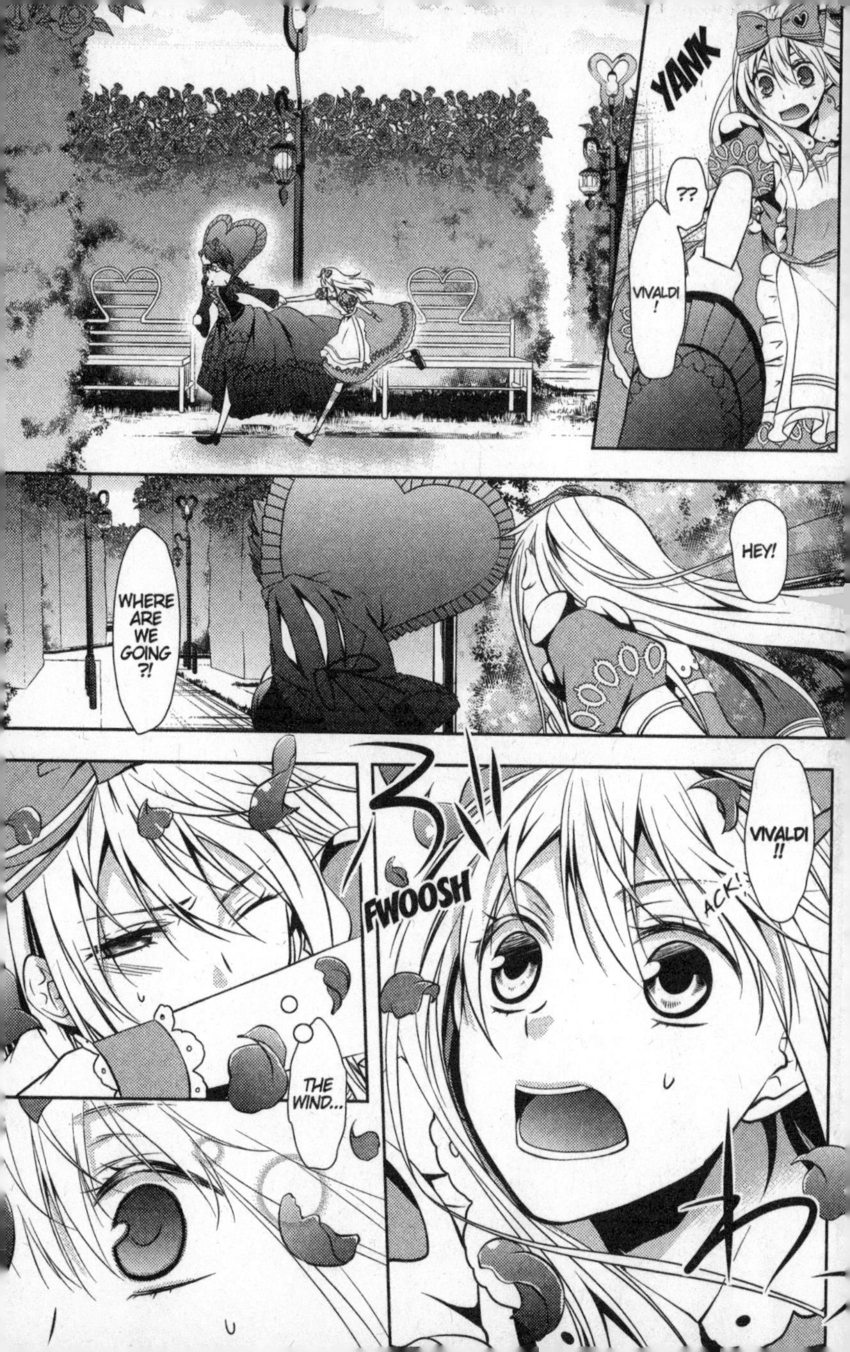
YANK
??
VIVALDI!
HEY!
WHERE ARE WE GOING?!
VIVALDI!!
ACK!
FWOOSH
THE WIND...

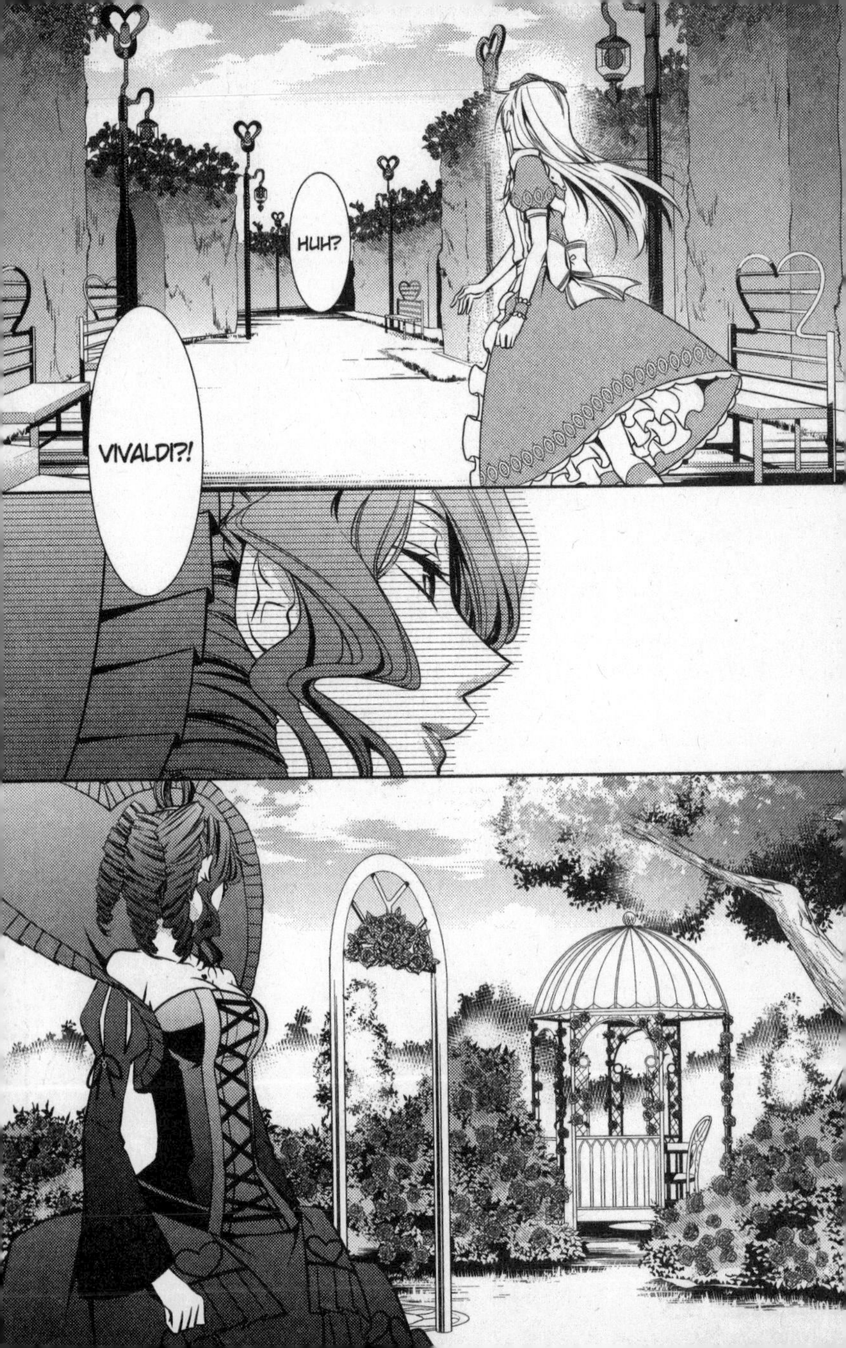
HUH?
VIVALDI?!

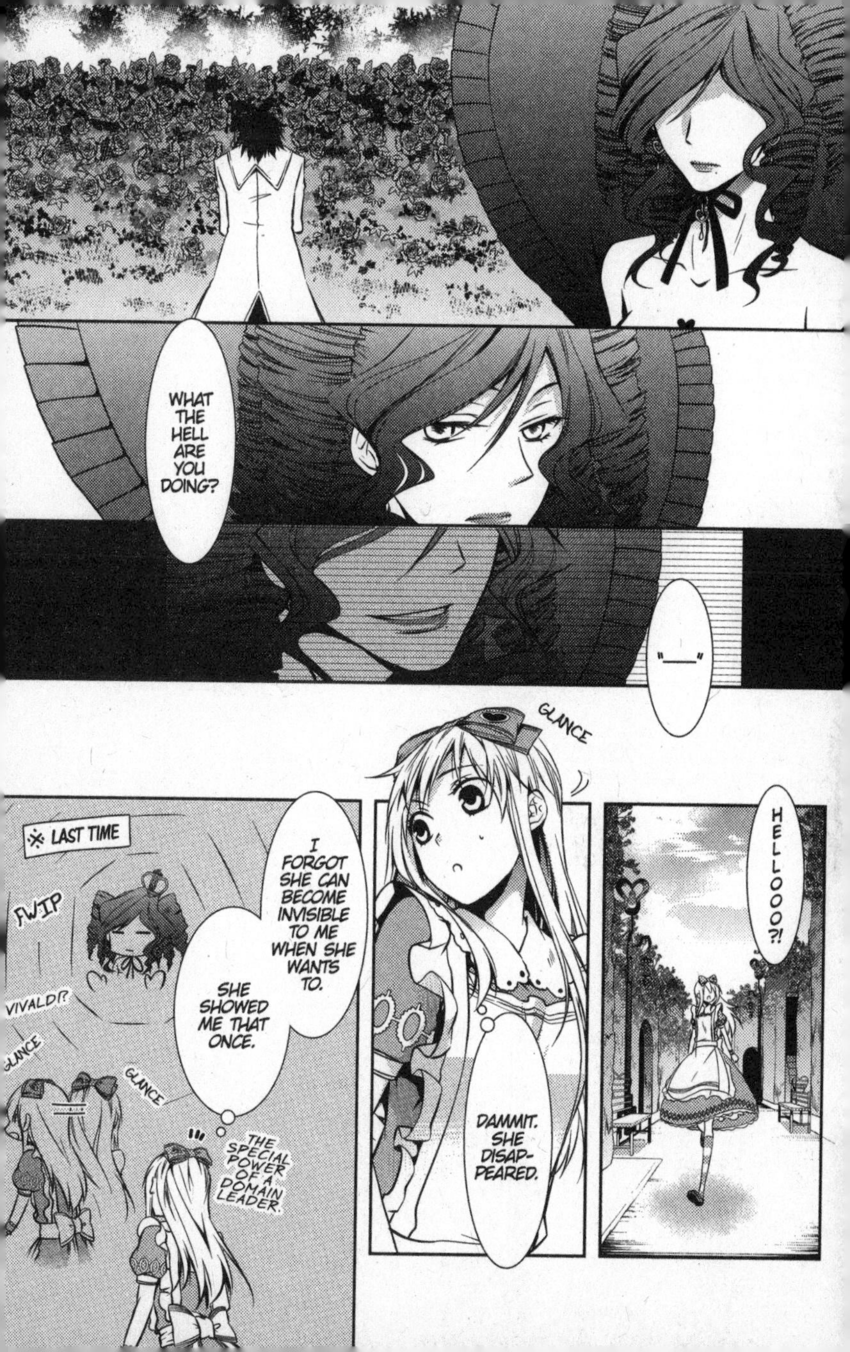
WHAT THE HELL ARE YOU DOING?
"——"
HELLOOOO?!
GLANCE
DAMMIT. SHE DISAP-PEARED.
I FORGOT SHE CAN BECOME INVISIBLE TO ME WHEN SHE WANTS TO.
SHE SHOWED ME THAT ONCE.
※ LAST TIME
FWIP
VIVALDI?
GLANCE
GLANCE
THE SPECIAL POWER OF A DOMAIN LEADER.

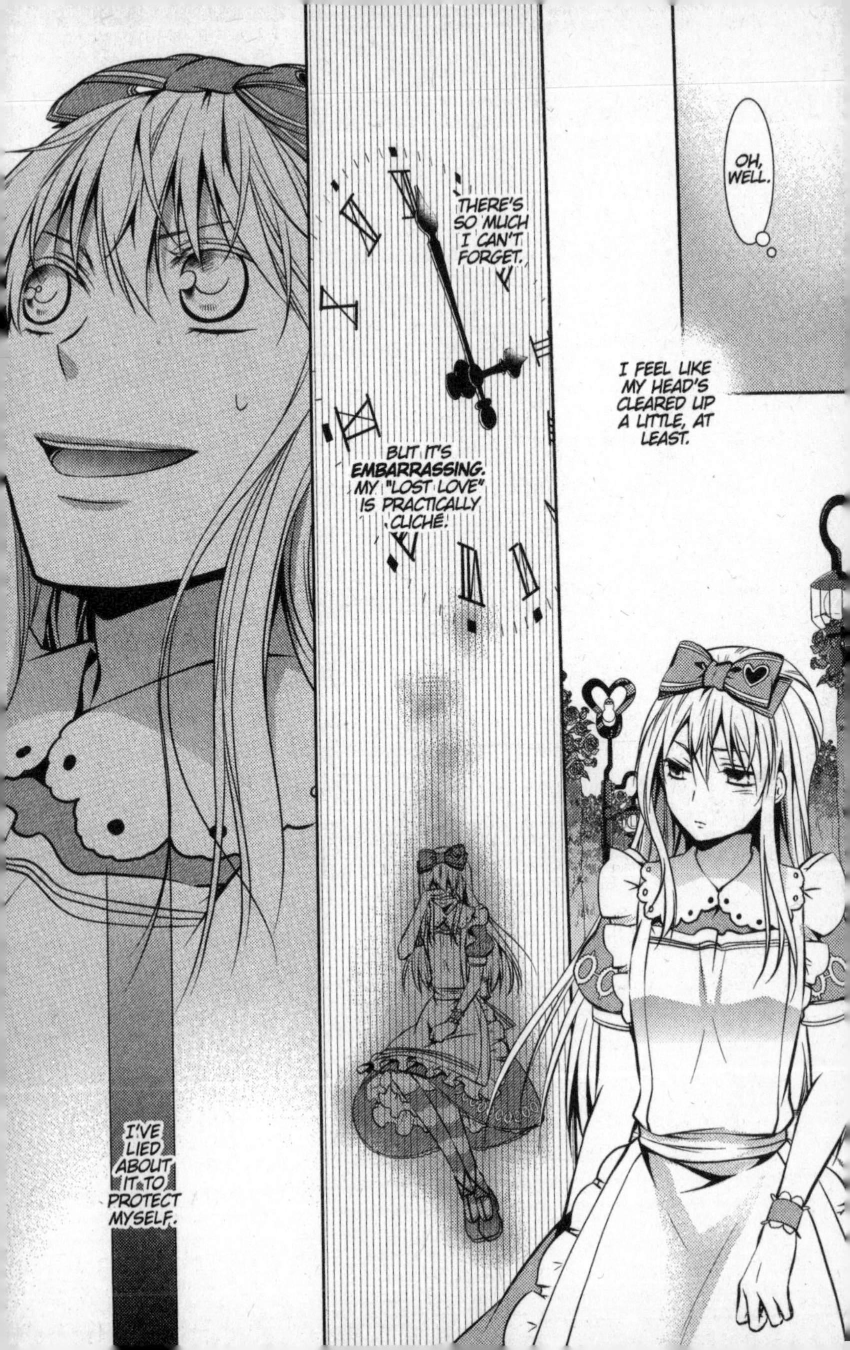
OH, WELL.
I FEEL LIKE MY HEAD'S CLEARED UP A LITTLE, AT LEAST.
THERE'S SO MUCH I CAN'T FORGET.
BUT IT'S EMBARRASSING. MY "LOST LOVE" IS PRACTICALLY CLICHE.
I'VE LIED ABOUT IT TO PROTECT MYSELF.

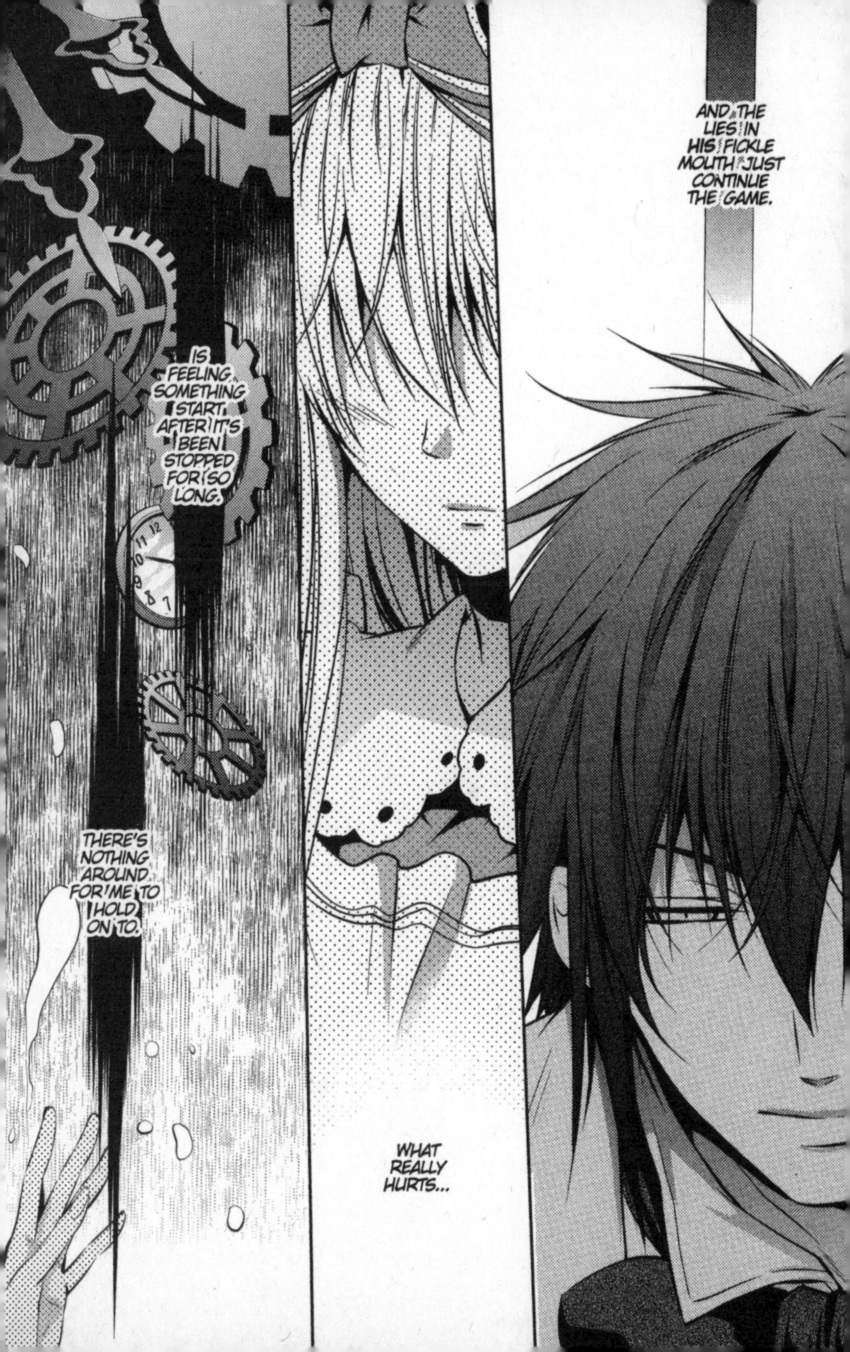
AND THE LIES IN HIS FICKLE MOUTH JUST CONTINUE THE GAME.
WHAT REALLY HURTS...
IS FEELING SOMETHING START AFTER IT'S BEEN STOPPED FOR SO LONG.
THERE'S NOTHING AROUND FOR ME TO HOLD ON TO.

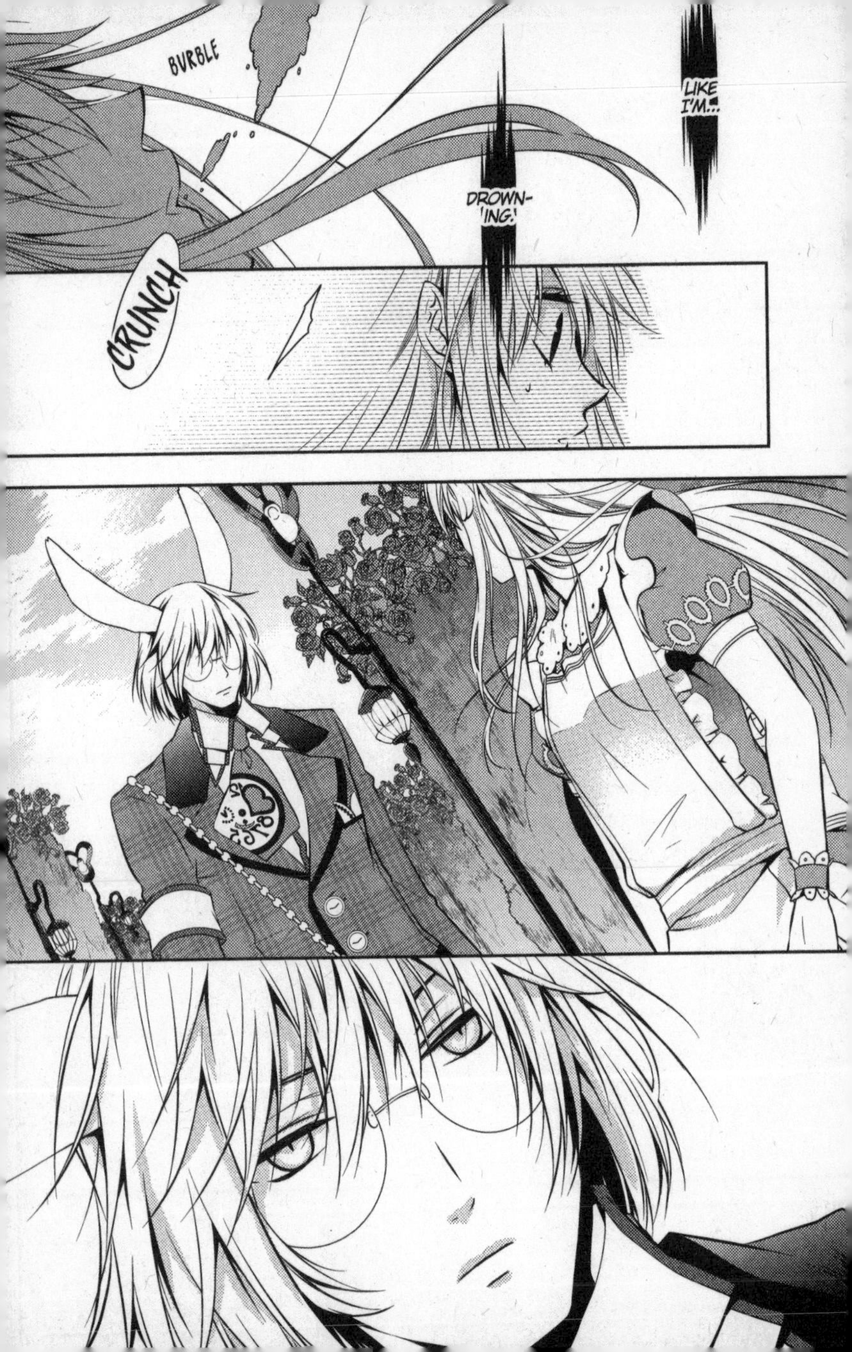
LIKE I'M...
DROWN-ING!
BURBLE
CRUNCH

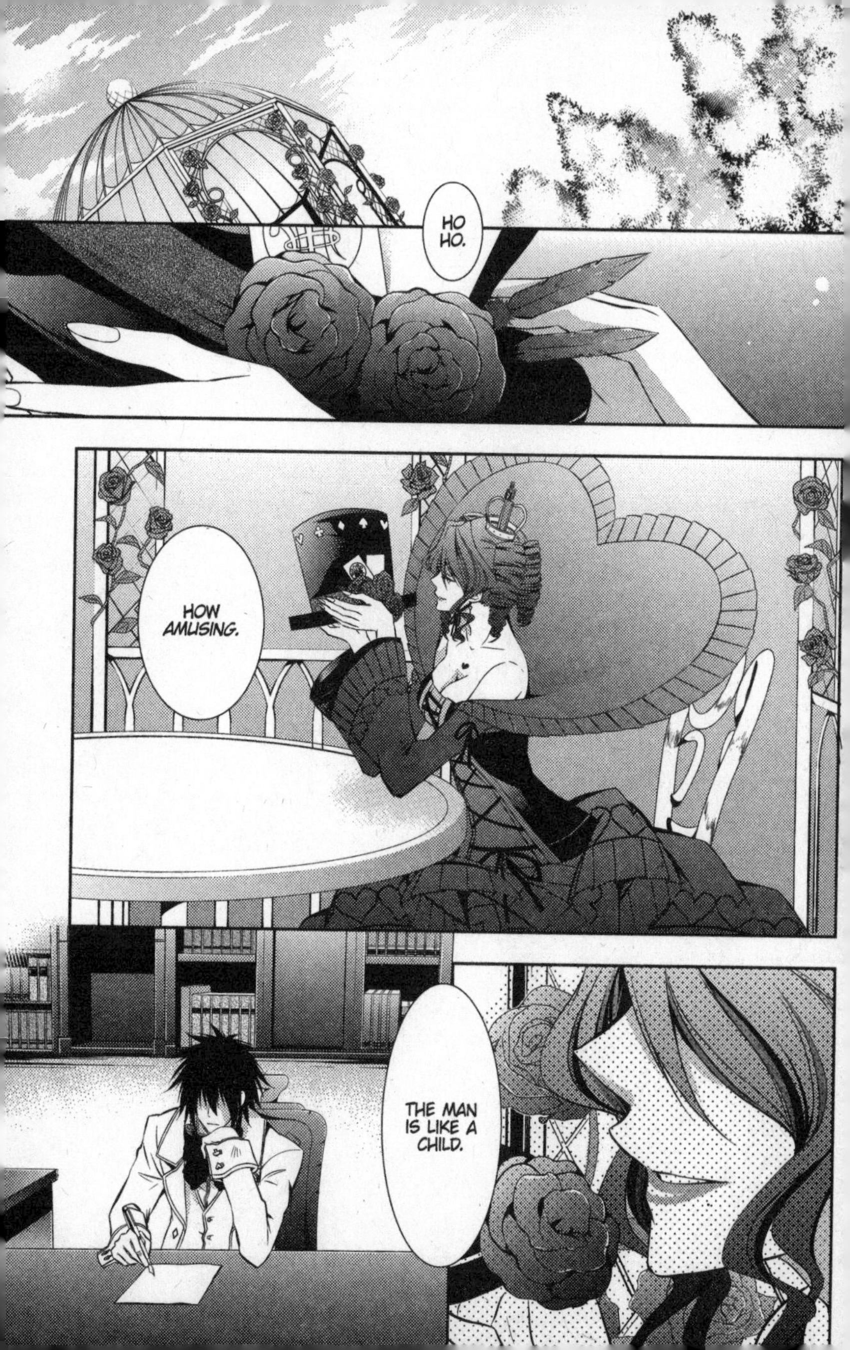
HO HO.
HOW AMUSING.
THE MAN IS LIKE A CHILD.

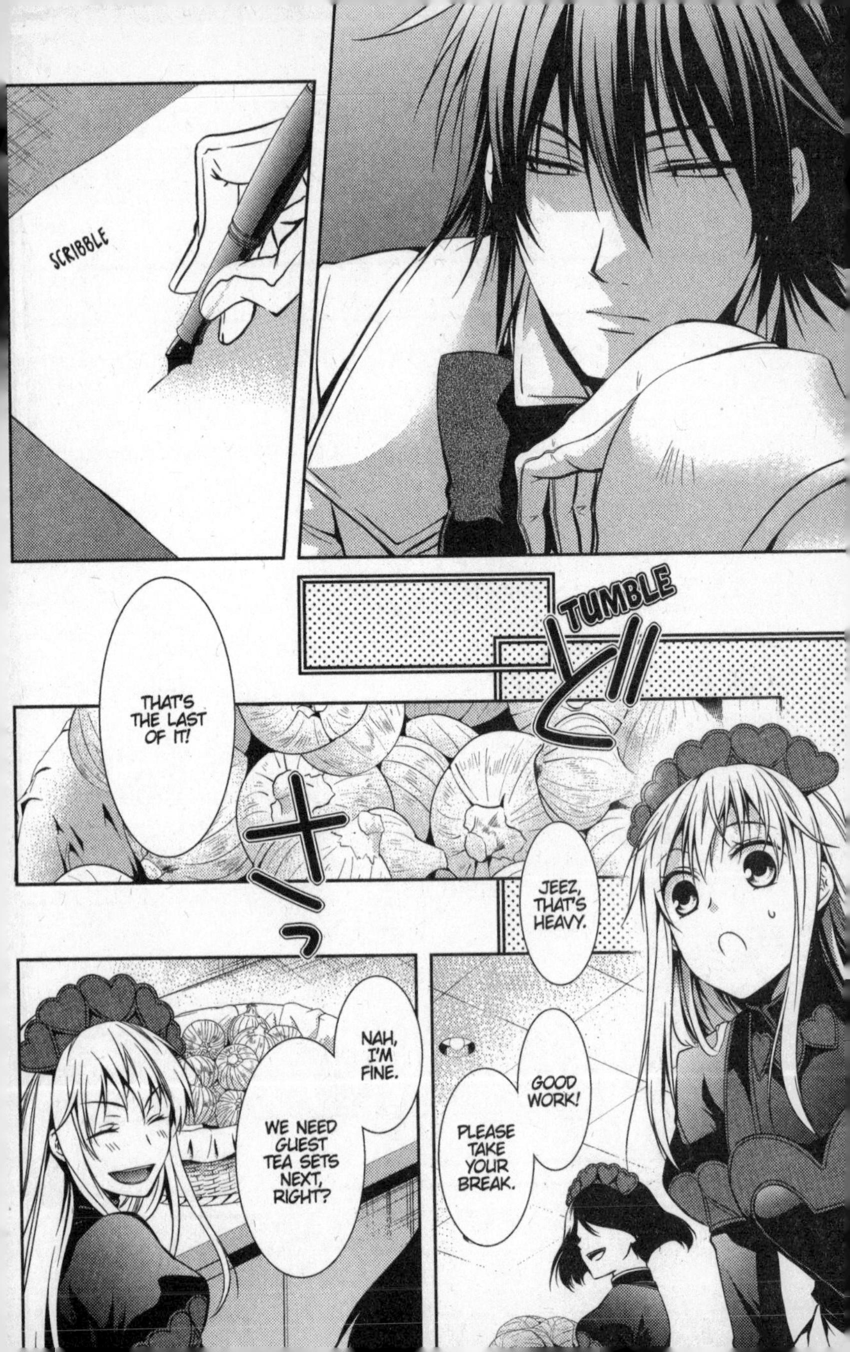
SCRIBBLE
TUMBLE
THAT'S THE LAST OF IT!
JEEZ, THAT'S HEAVY.
GOOD WORK!
PLEASE TAKE YOUR BREAK.
NAH, I'M FINE.
WE NEED GUEST TEA SETS NEXT, RIGHT?

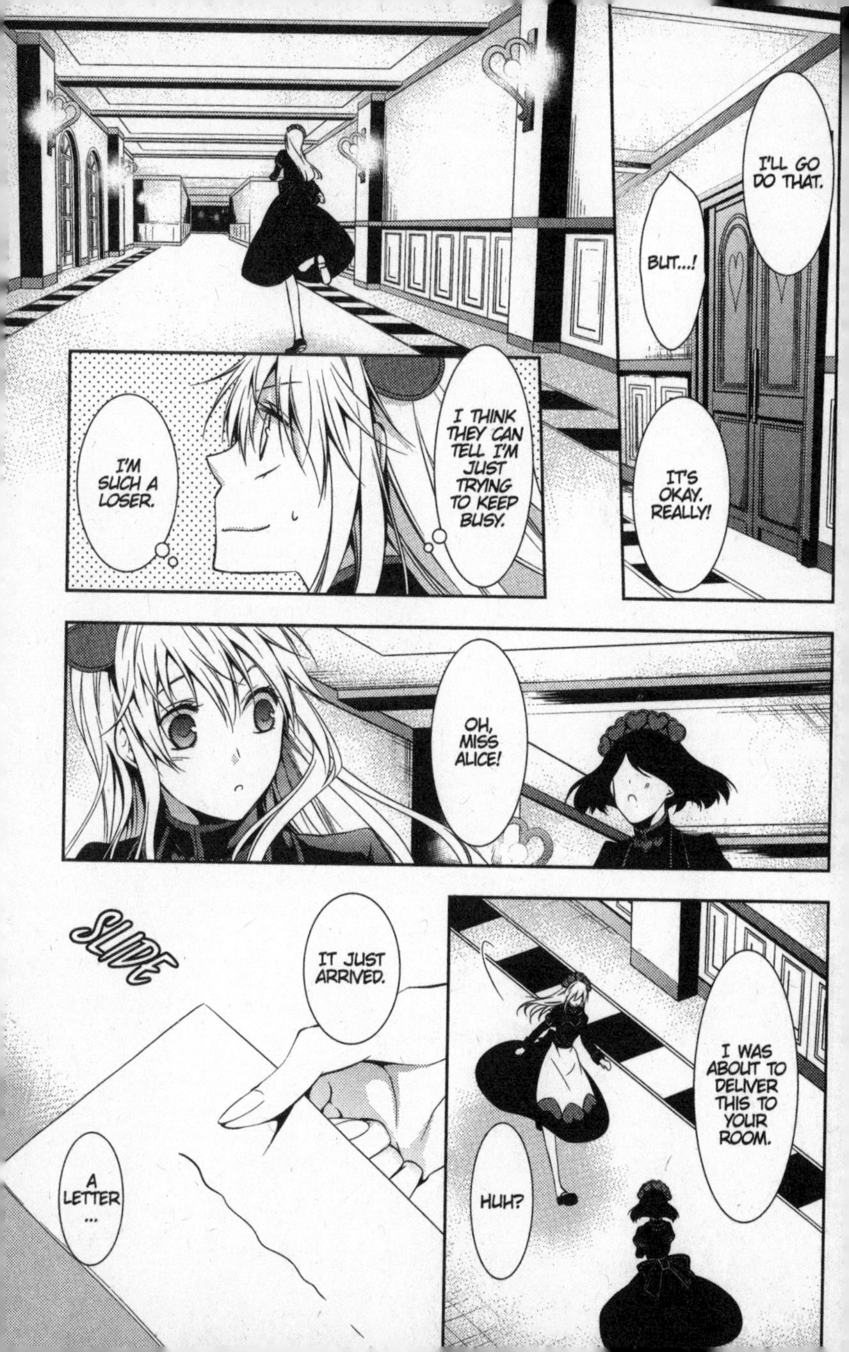
I'LL GO DO THAT.
BUT...!
IT'S OKAY. REALLY!
I THINK THEY CAN TELL I'M JUST TRYING TO KEEP BUSY.
I'M SUCH A LOSER.
OH, MISS ALICE!
I WAS ABOUT TO DELIVER THIS TO YOUR ROOM.
HUH?
IT JUST ARRIVED.
SLIDE
A LETTER ...

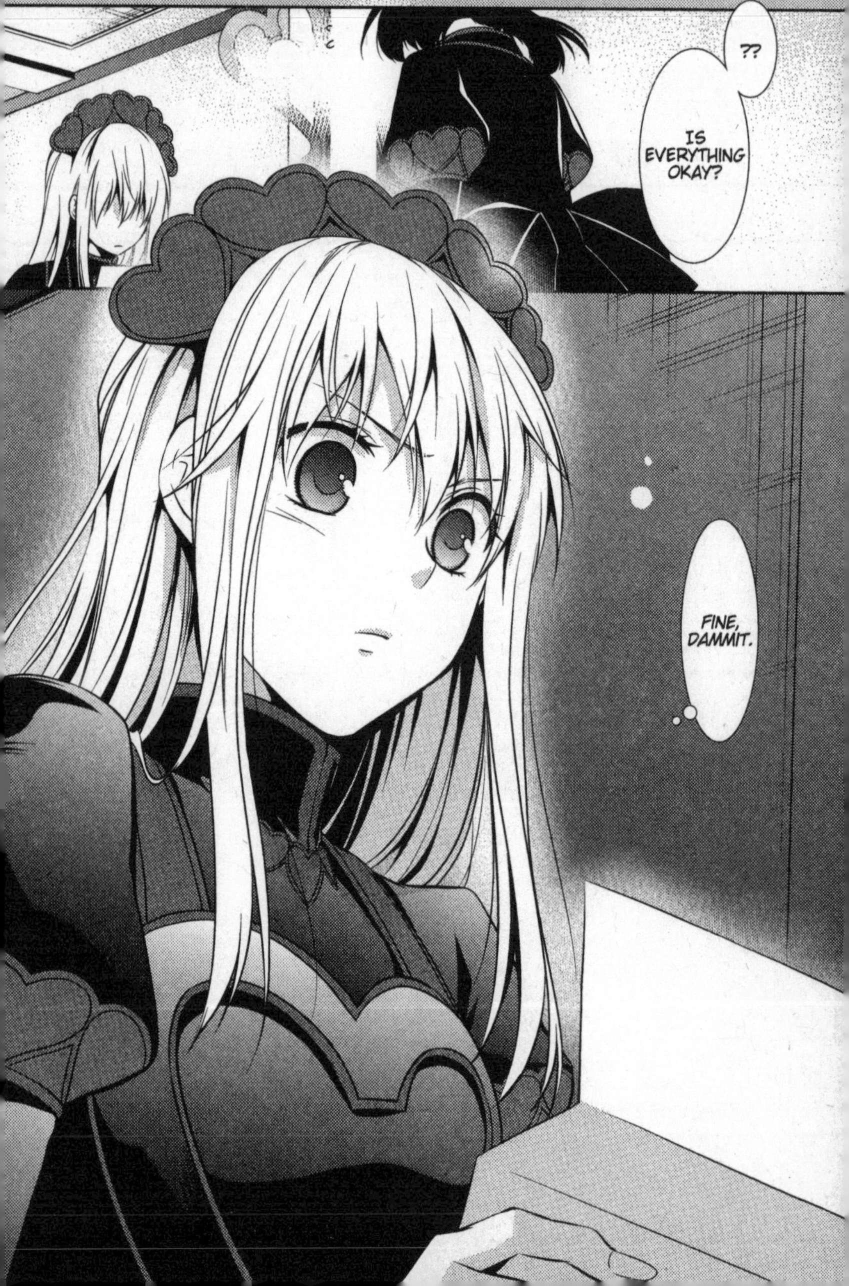
??
IS EVERYTHING OKAY?
FINE, DAMMIT.

Hit: 15

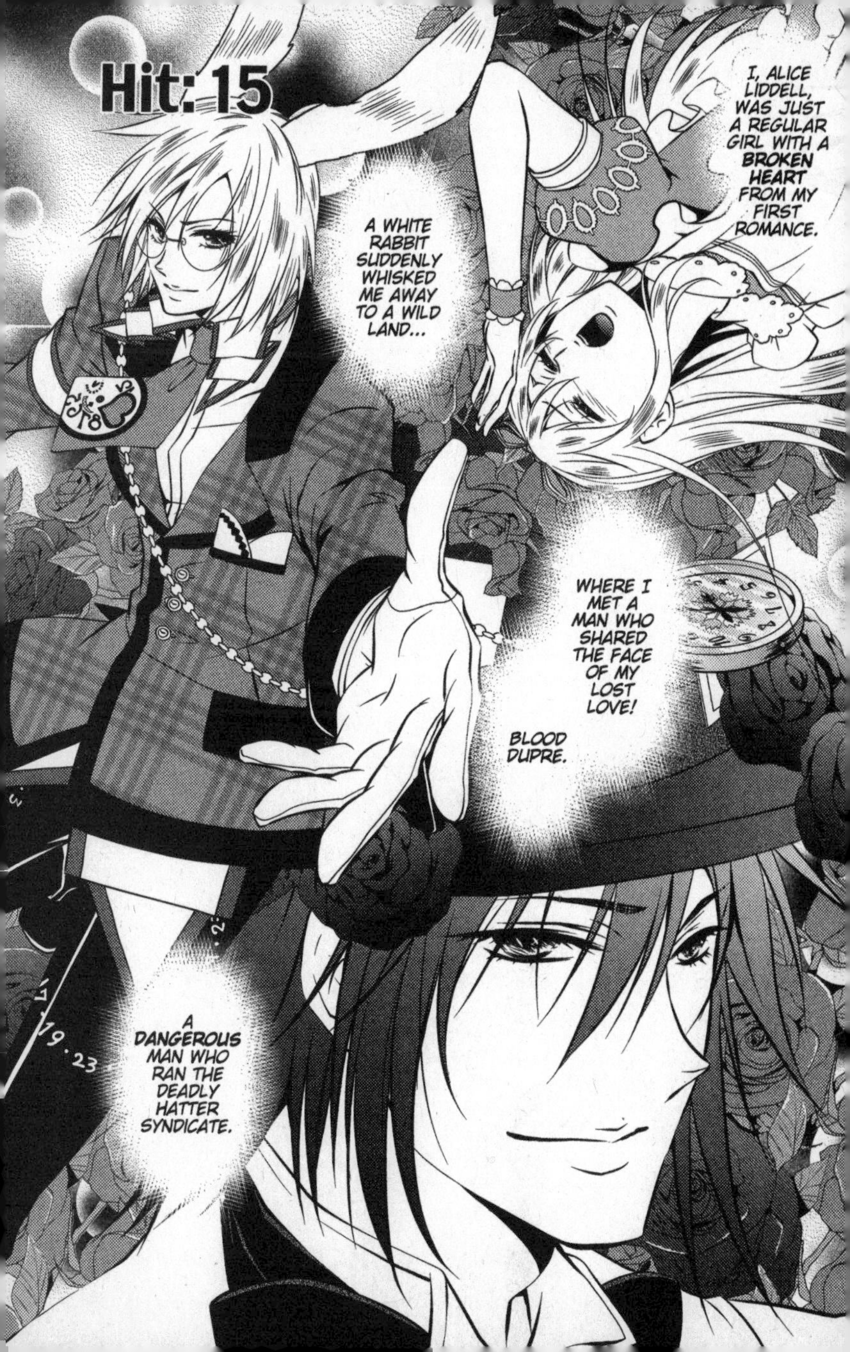
I, ALICE LIDDELL, WAS JUST A REGULAR GIRL WITH A **BROKEN HEART** FROM MY FIRST ROMANCE.
A WHITE RABBIT SUDDENLY WHISKED ME AWAY TO A WILD LAND...
WHERE I MET A MAN WHO SHARED THE FACE OF MY LOST LOVE!
BLOOD DUPRE.
A **DANGEROUS** MAN WHO RAN THE DEADLY HATTER SYNDICATE.

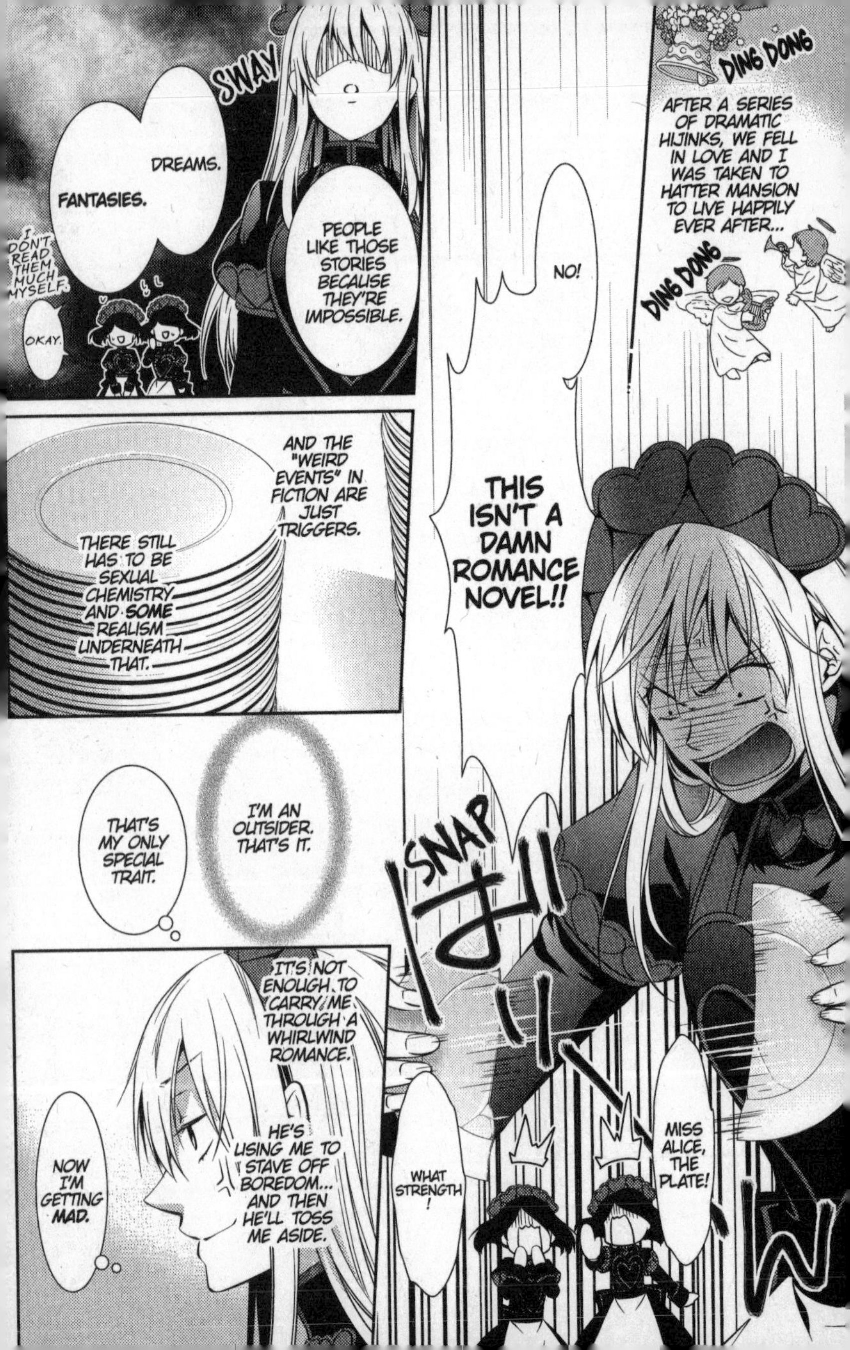
DING DONG
AFTER A SERIES OF DRAMATIC HIJINKS, WE FELL IN LOVE AND I WAS TAKEN TO HATTER MANSION TO LIVE HAPPILY EVER AFTER...
DING DONG
NO!
THIS ISN'T A DAMN ROMANCE NOVEL!!
SNAP
MISS ALICE, THE PLATE!
WHAT STRENGTH!
SWAY
DREAMS.
FANTASIES.
PEOPLE LIKE THOSE STORIES BECAUSE THEY'RE IMPOSSIBLE.
I DON'T READ THEM MUCH MYSELF.
OKAY.
AND THE "WEIRD EVENTS" IN FICTION ARE JUST TRIGGERS.
THERE STILL HAS TO BE SEXUAL CHEMISTRY AND SOME REALISM UNDERNEATH THAT.
I'M AN OUTSIDER. THAT'S IT.
THAT'S MY ONLY SPECIAL TRAIT.
IT'S NOT ENOUGH TO CARRY ME THROUGH A WHIRLWIND ROMANCE.
HE'S USING ME TO STAVE OFF BOREDOM... AND THEN HE'LL TOSS ME ASIDE.
NOW I'M GETTING MAD.

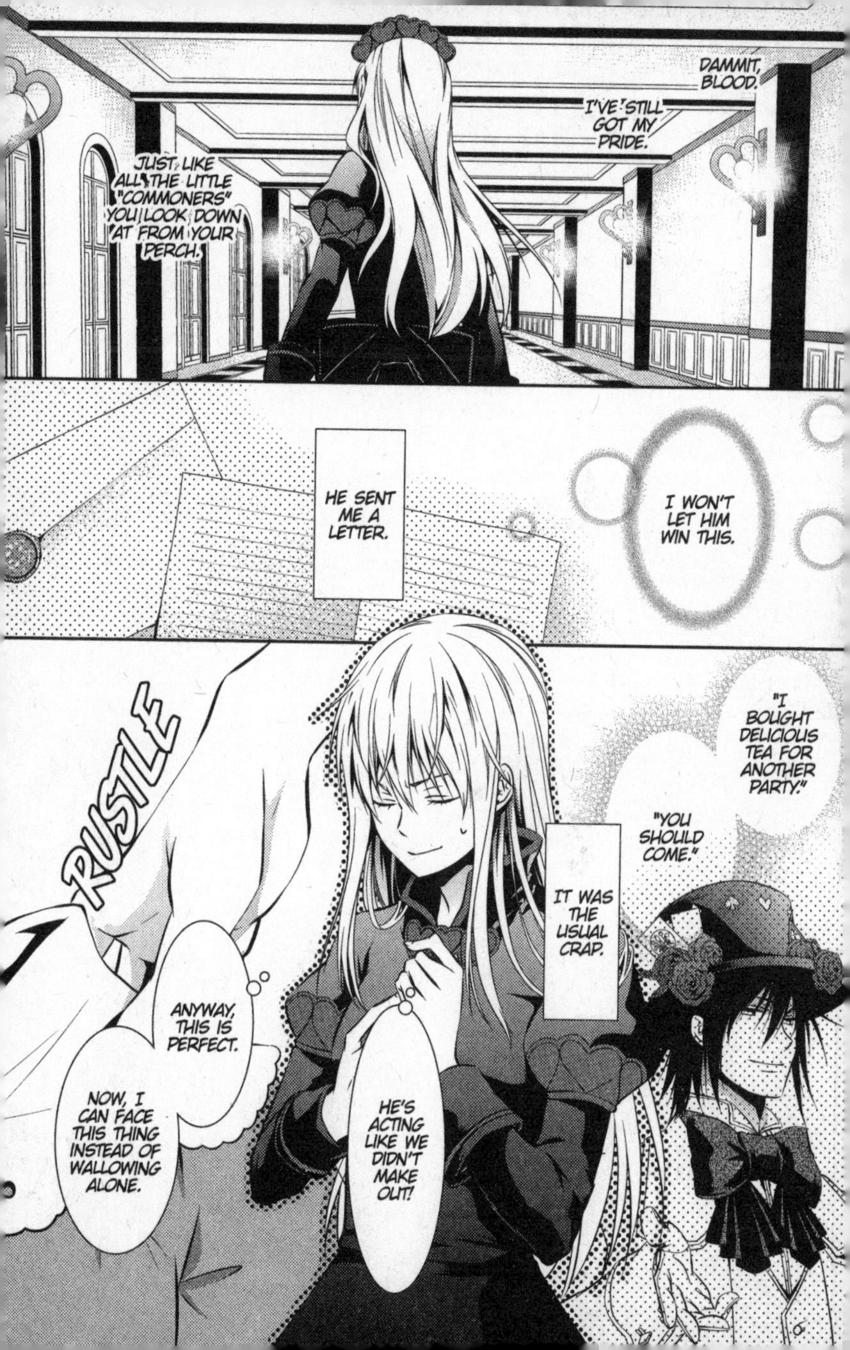
DAMMIT, BLOOD.
I'VE STILL GOT MY PRIDE.
JUST LIKE ALL THE LITTLE "COMMONERS" YOU LOOK DOWN AT FROM YOUR PERCH.
I WON'T LET HIM WIN THIS.
HE SENT ME A LETTER.
"I BOUGHT DELICIOUS TEA FOR ANOTHER PARTY."
"YOU SHOULD COME."
IT WAS THE USUAL CRAP.
HE'S ACTING LIKE WE DIDN'T MAKE OUT!
ANYWAY, THIS IS PERFECT.
NOW, I CAN FACE THIS THING INSTEAD OF WALLOWING ALONE.
RUSTLE

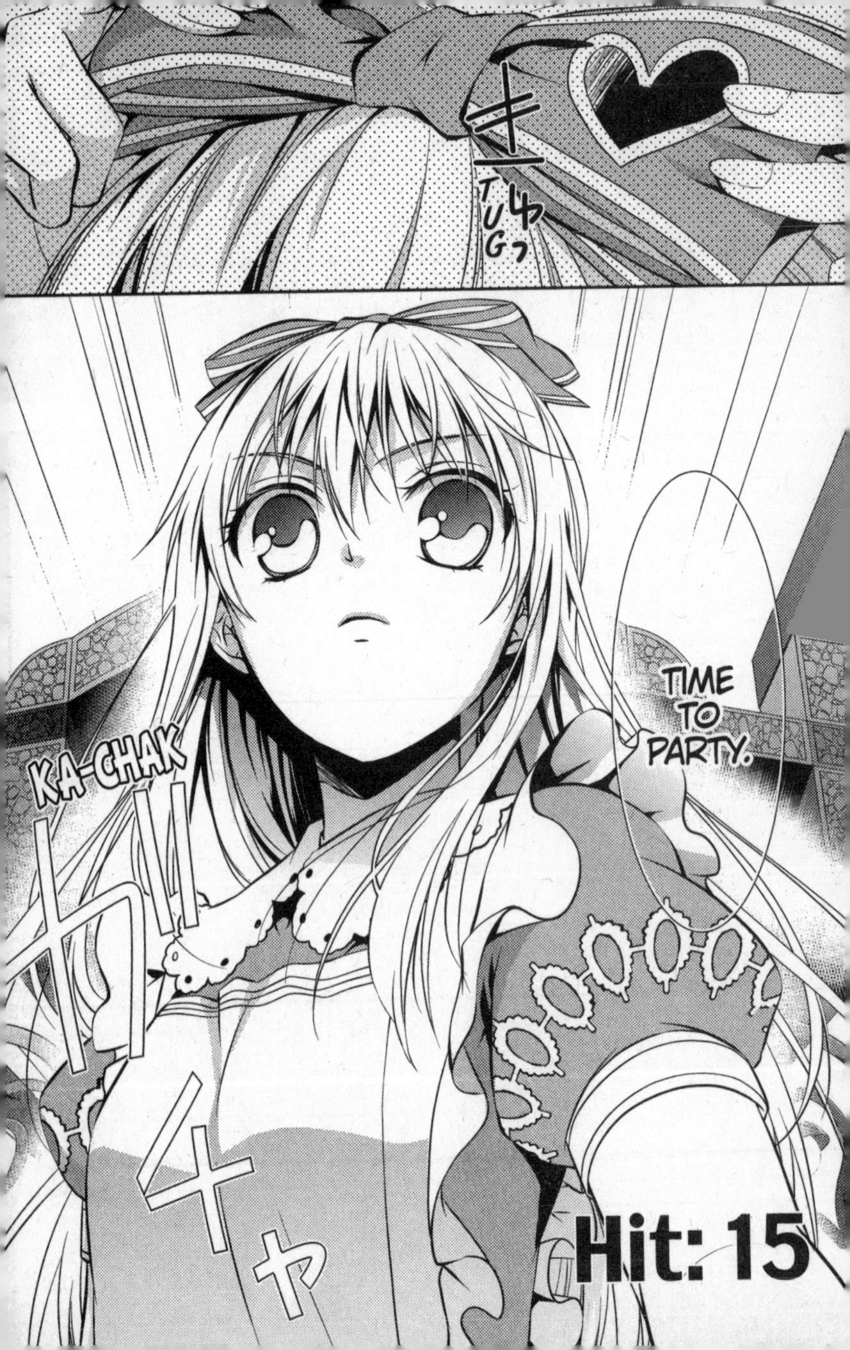
TUG
TIME TO PARTY.
KA-CHAK
Hit: 15

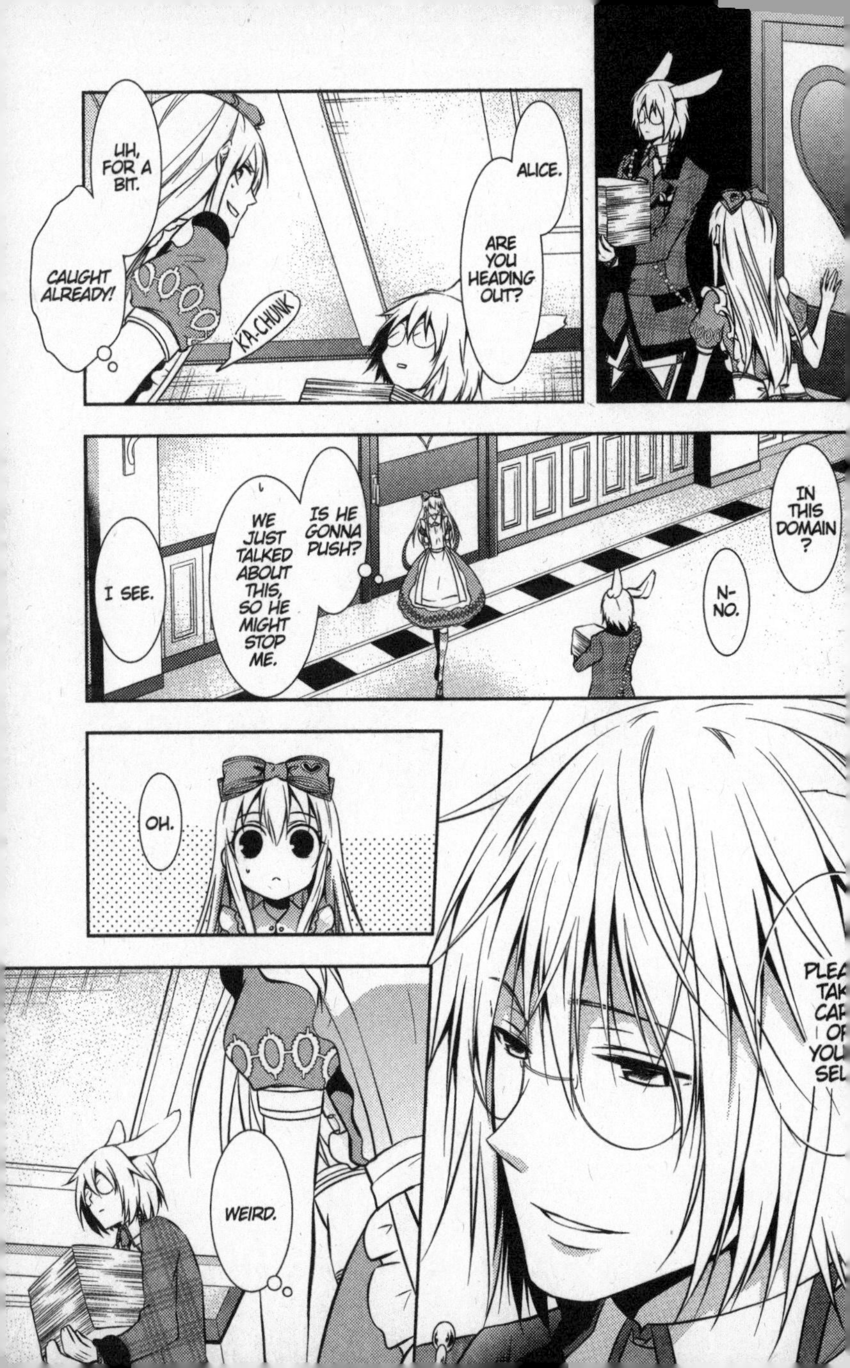
ALICE.
ARE YOU HEADING OUT?
UH, FOR A BIT.
KA-CHUNK
CAUGHT ALREADY!
IN THIS DOMAIN?
N-NO.
IS HE GONNA PUSH?
WE JUST TALKED ABOUT THIS, SO HE MIGHT STOP ME.
I SEE.
PLEA TAK CAR OF YOU SEL
OH.
WEIRD.

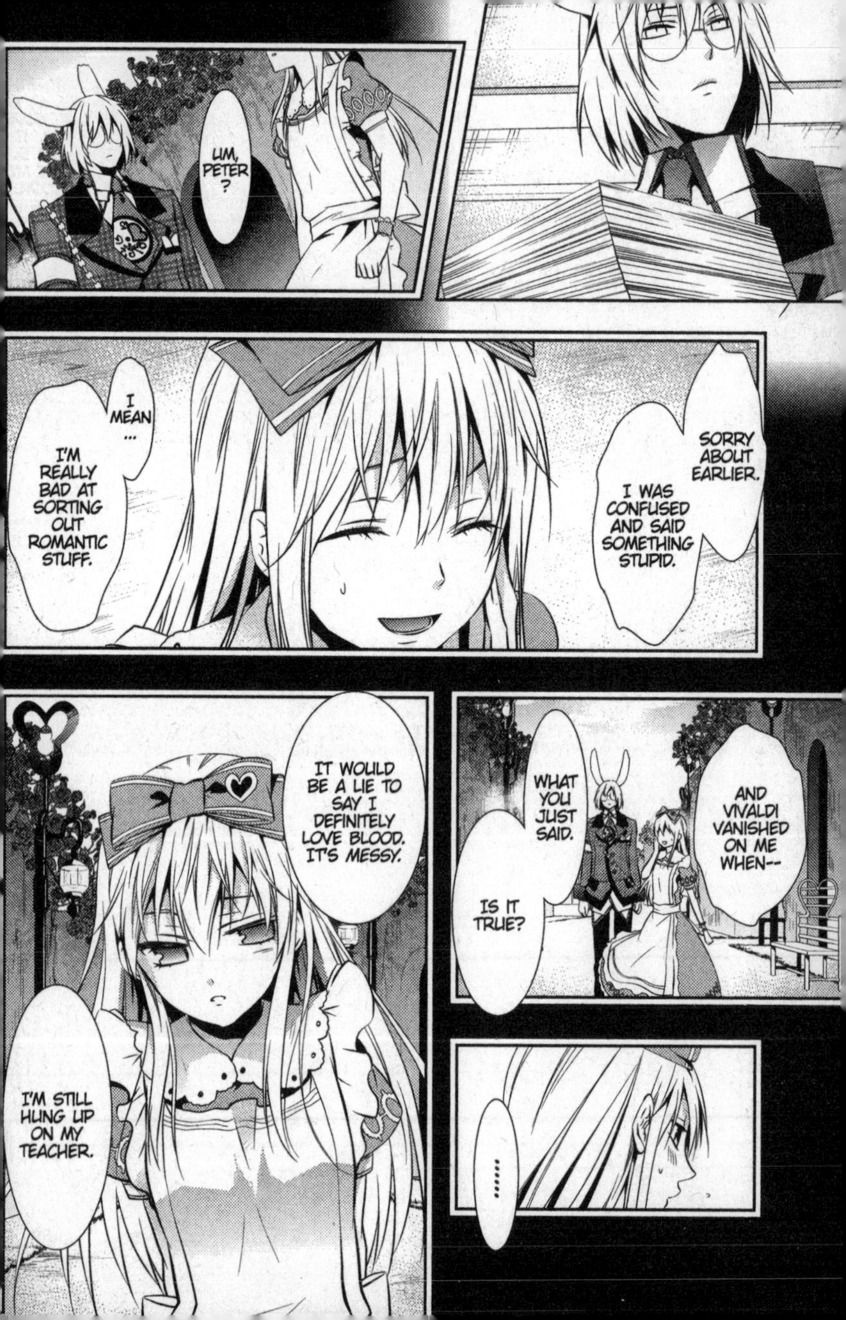
UM, PETER ?
SORRY ABOUT EARLIER.
I WAS CONFUSED AND SAID SOMETHING STUPID.
I MEAN ...
I'M REALLY BAD AT SORTING OUT ROMANTIC STUFF.
AND VIVALDI VANISHED ON ME WHEN--
WHAT YOU JUST SAID.
IS IT TRUE?
......
IT WOULD BE A LIE TO SAY I DEFINITELY LOVE BLOOD. IT'S MESSY.
I'M STILL HUNG UP ON MY TEACHER.

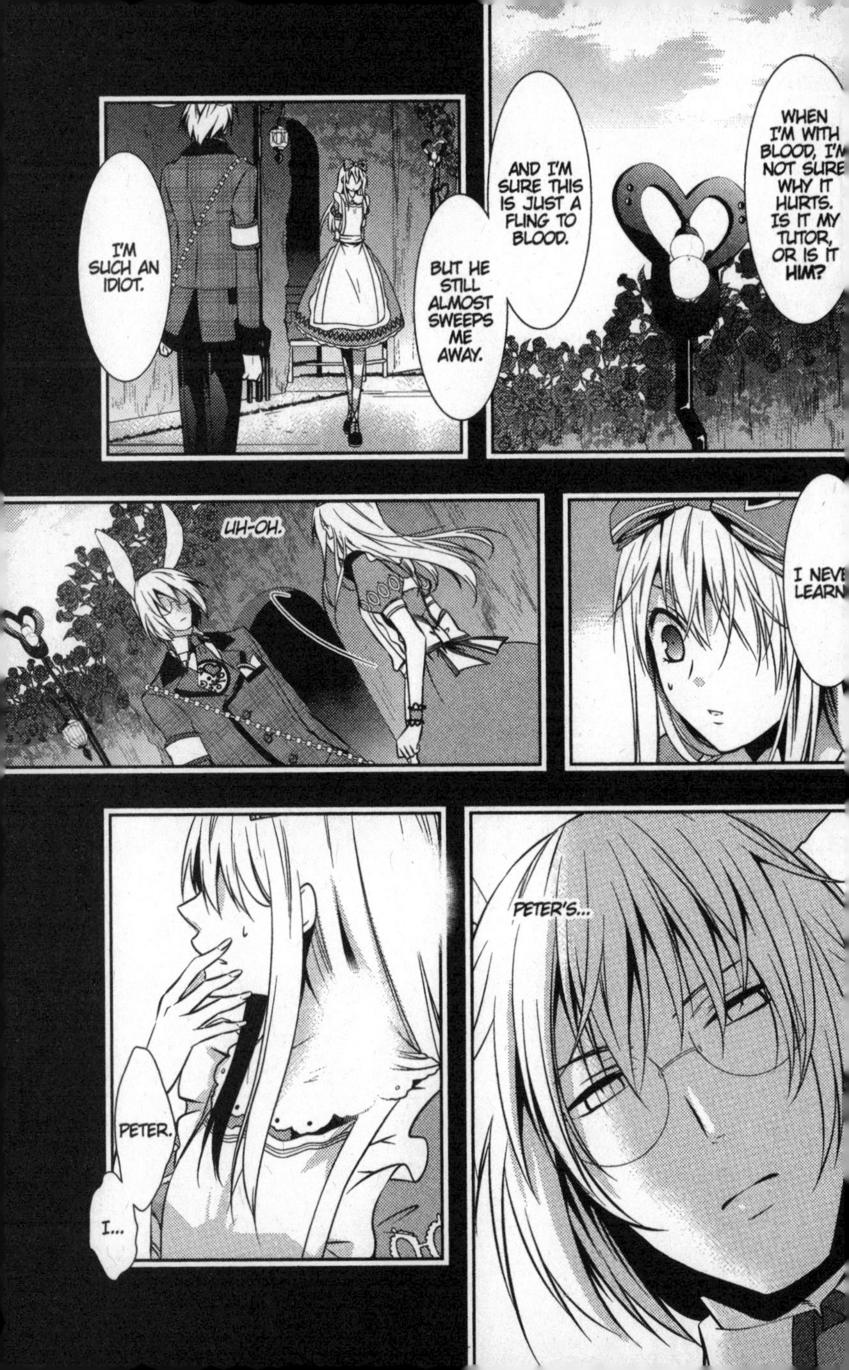
WHEN I'M WITH BLOOD, I'M NOT SURE WHY IT HURTS. IS IT MY TUTOR, OR IS IT HIM?
AND I'M SURE THIS IS JUST A FLING TO BLOOD.
BUT HE STILL ALMOST SWEEPS ME AWAY.
I'M SUCH AN IDIOT.
I NEVE LEARN
UH-OH.
PETER'S...
PETER.
I...

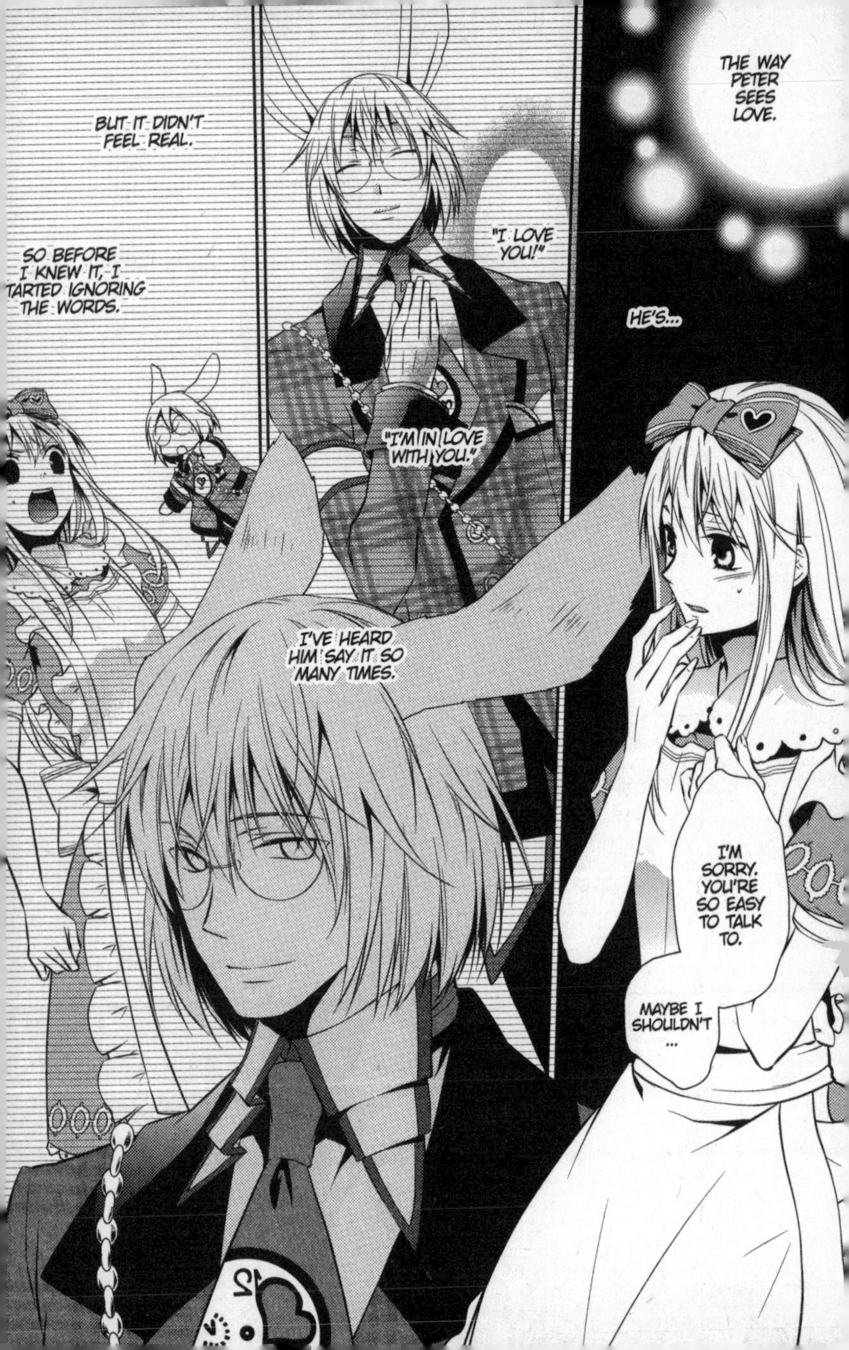
THE WAY PETER SEES LOVE.
HE'S...
"I LOVE YOU!"
"I'M IN LOVE WITH YOU."
I'VE HEARD HIM SAY IT SO MANY TIMES.
BUT IT DIDN'T FEEL REAL.
SO BEFORE I KNEW IT, I TARTED IGNORING THE WORDS.
I'M SORRY. YOU'RE SO EASY TO TALK TO.
MAYBE I SHOULDN'T ...

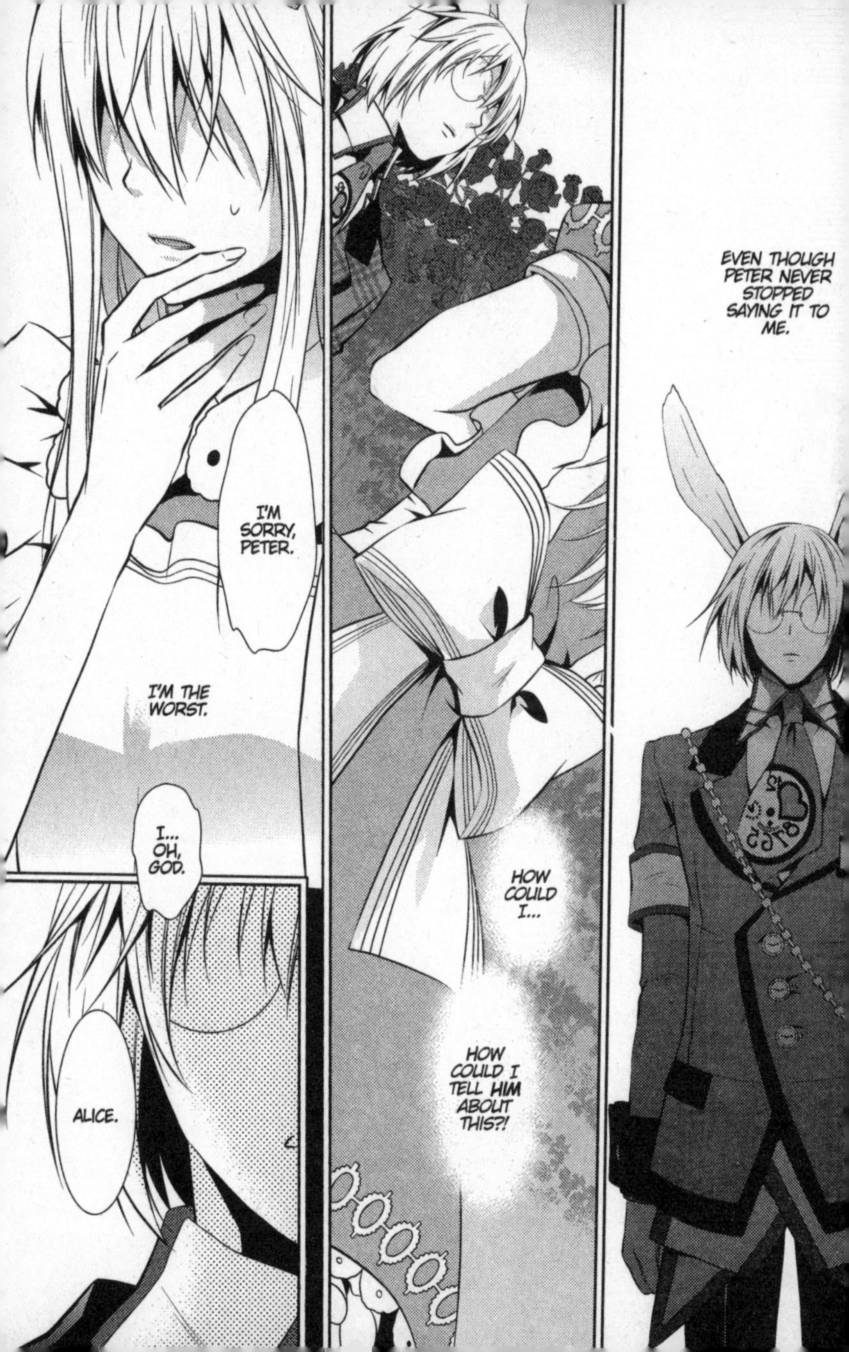
EVEN THOUGH PETER NEVER STOPPED SAYING IT TO ME.
HOW COULD I...
HOW COULD I TELL HIM ABOUT THIS?!
I'M SORRY, PETER.
I'M THE WORST.
I... OH, GOD.
ALICE.

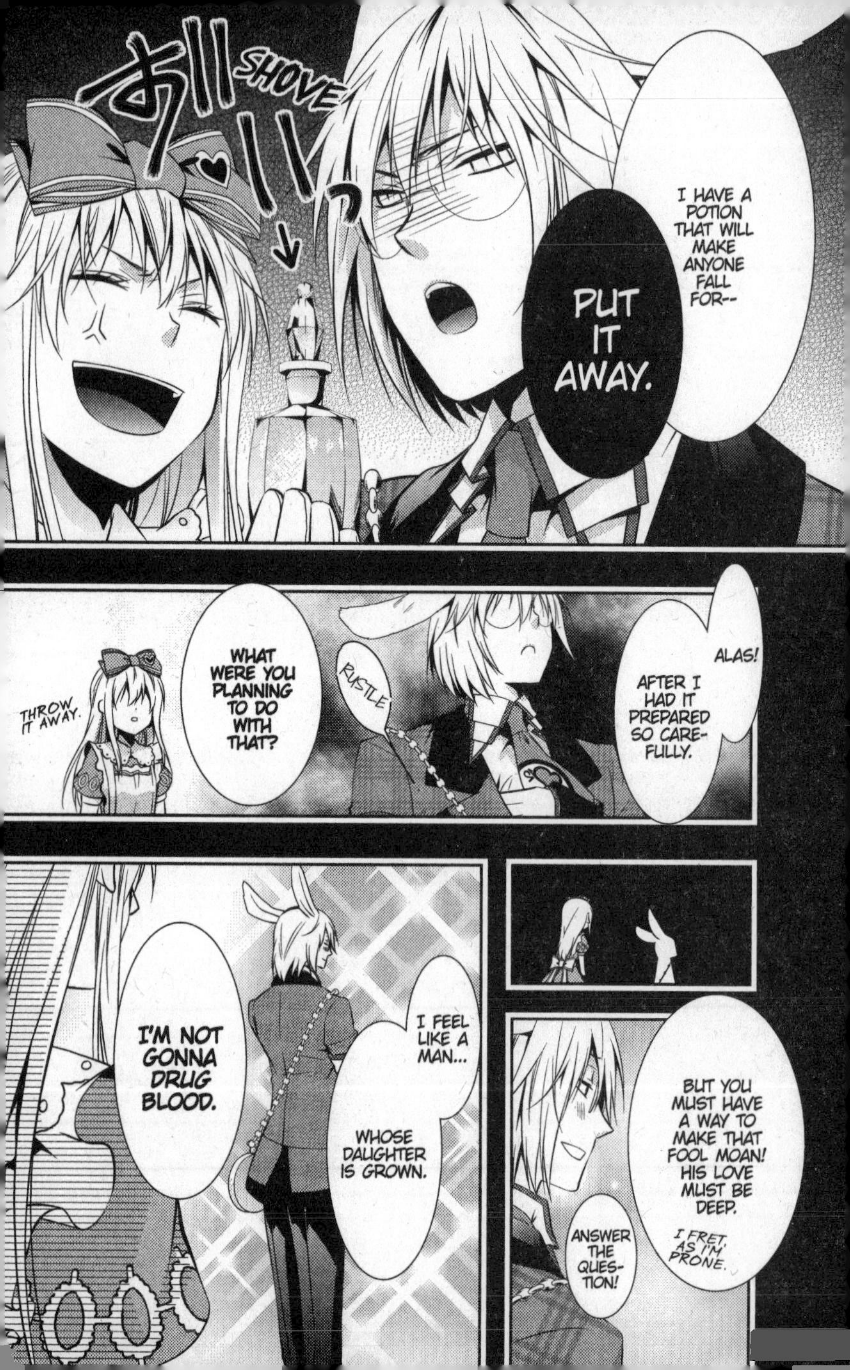
I HAVE A POTION THAT WILL MAKE ANYONE FALL FOR--
PUT IT AWAY.
SHOVE
ALAS!
AFTER I HAD IT PREPARED SO CARE-FULLY.
RUSTLE
WHAT WERE YOU PLANNING TO DO WITH THAT?
THROW IT AWAY.
BUT YOU MUST HAVE A WAY TO MAKE THAT FOOL MOAN! HIS LOVE MUST BE DEEP.
I FRET, AS I'M PRONE.
ANSWER THE QUES-TION!
I FEEL LIKE A MAN...
WHOSE DAUGHTER IS GROWN.
I'M NOT GONNA DRUG BLOOD.

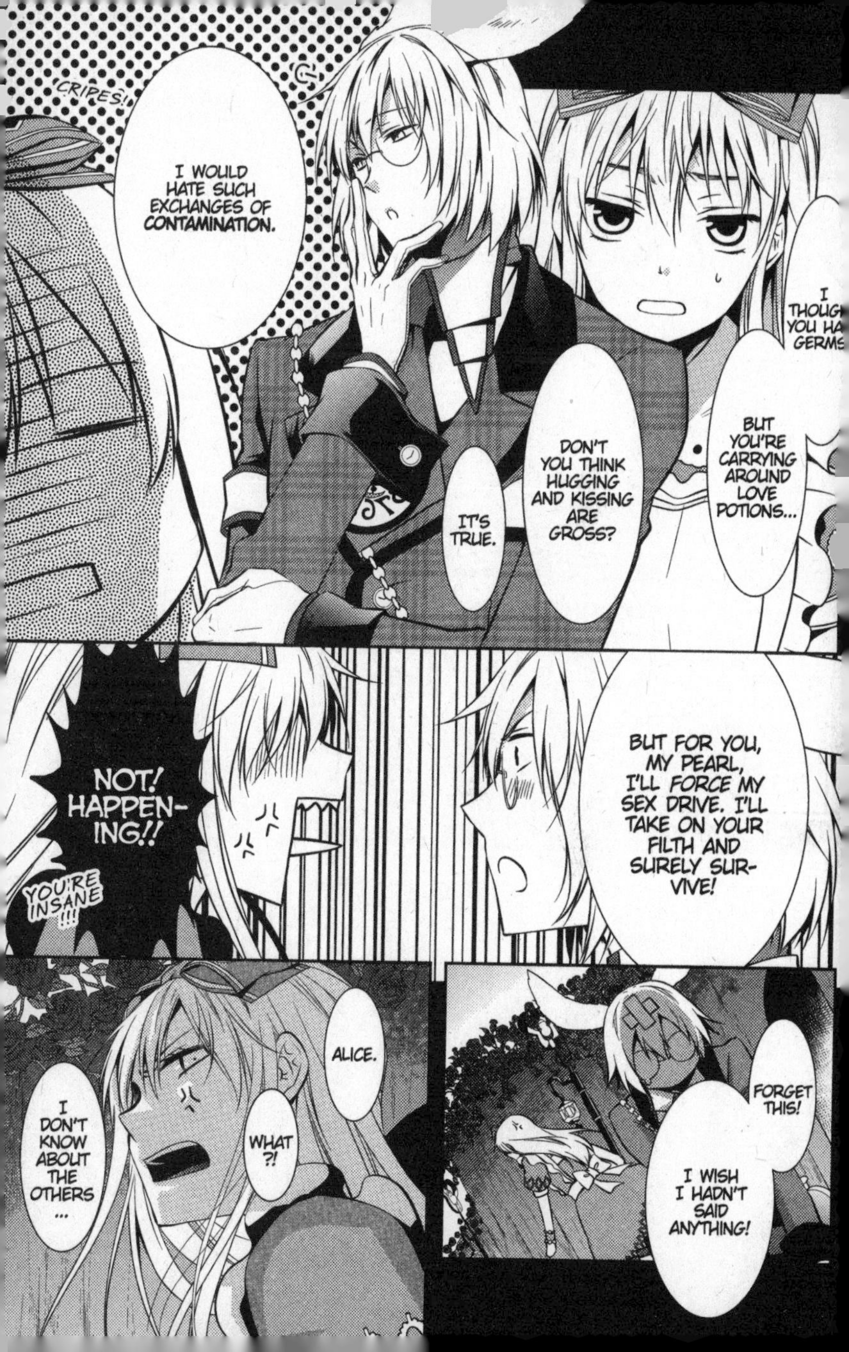
I THOUGH YOU HA GERMS
BUT YOU'RE CARRYING AROUND LOVE POTIONS...
DON'T YOU THINK HUGGING AND KISSING ARE GROSS?
IT'S TRUE.
I WOULD HATE SUCH EXCHANGES OF CONTAMINATION.
CRIPES!
BUT FOR YOU, MY PEARL, I'LL FORCE MY SEX DRIVE. I'LL TAKE ON YOUR FILTH AND SURELY SUR-VIVE!
NOT! HAPPEN-ING!!
YOU'RE INSANE!!!
FORGET THIS!
I WISH I HADN'T SAID ANYTHING!
ALICE.
WHAT?!
I DON'T KNOW ABOUT THE OTHERS...

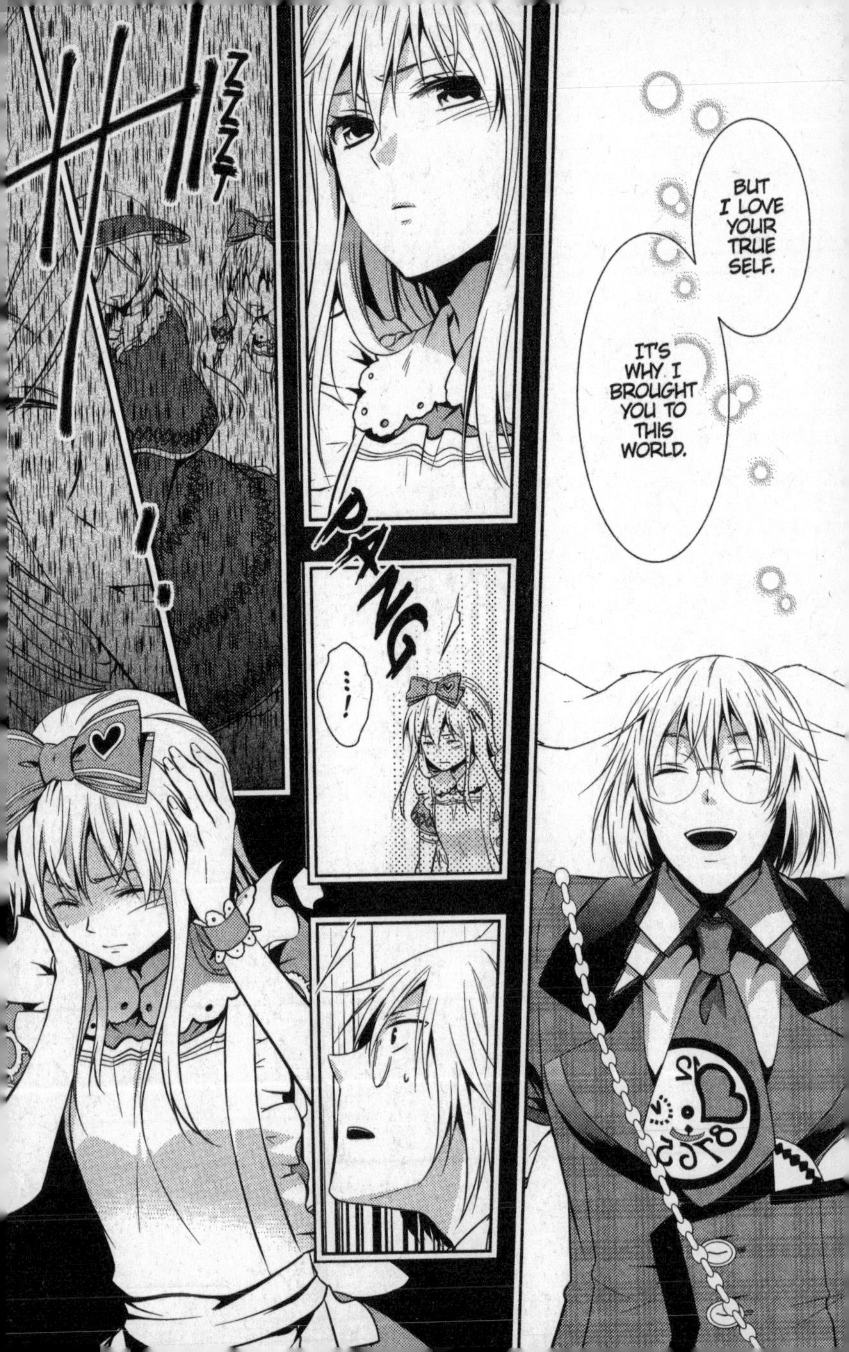
BUT I LOVE YOUR TRUE SELF.
IT'S WHY I BROUGHT YOU TO THIS WORLD.
PANG
...!
ZZZZT

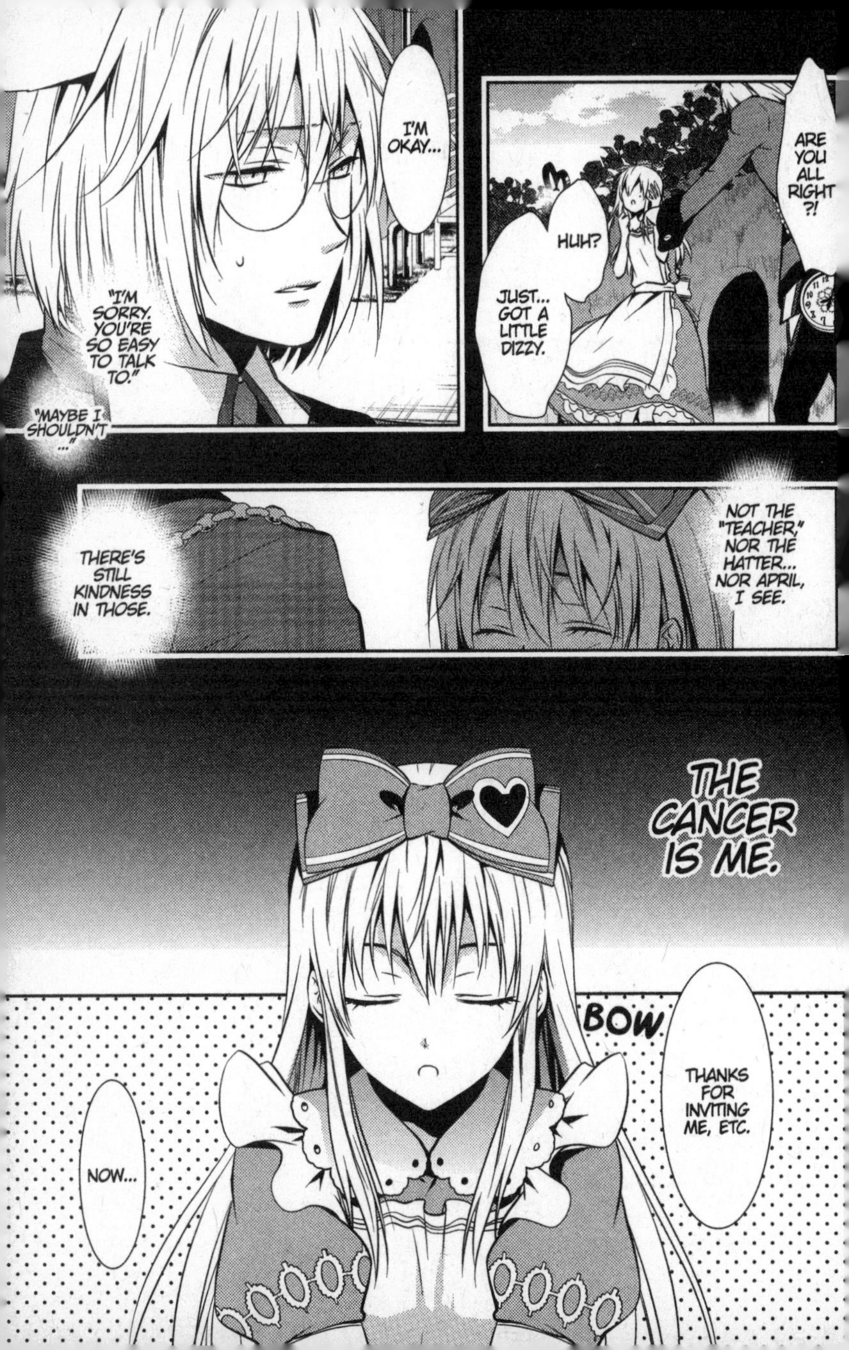
ARE YOU ALL RIGHT ?!
HUH?
JUST... GOT A LITTLE DIZZY.
I'M OKAY...
"I'M SORRY. YOU'RE SO EASY TO TALK TO."
"MAYBE I SHOULDN'T ..."
NOT THE "TEACHER," NOR THE HATTER... NOR APRIL, I SEE.
THERE'S STILL KINDNESS IN THOSE.
THE CANCER IS ME.
BOW
THANKS FOR INVITING ME, ETC.
NOW...

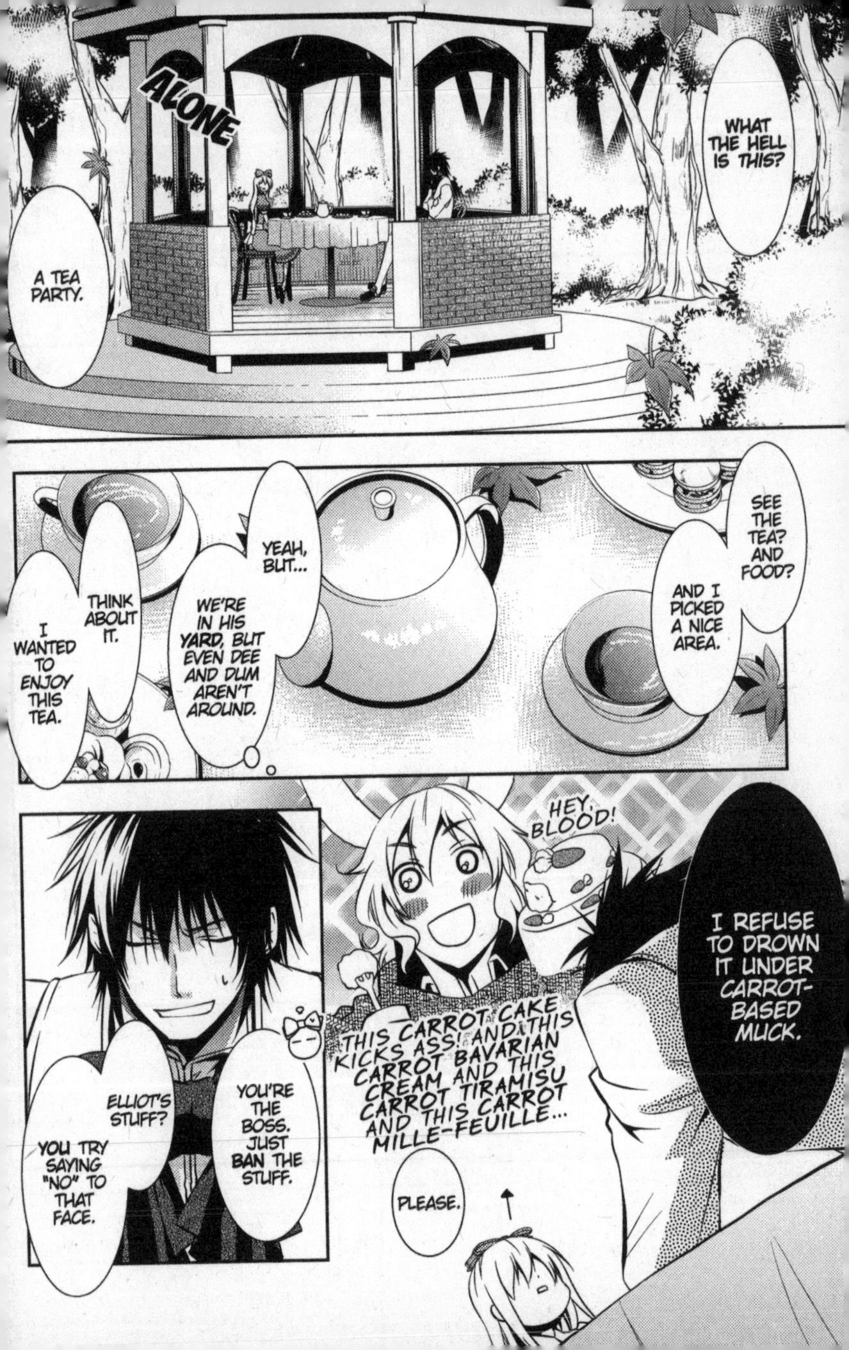
WHAT THE HELL IS THIS?
ALONE
A TEA PARTY.
SEE THE TEA? AND FOOD?
AND I PICKED A NICE AREA.
YEAH, BUT...
WE'RE IN HIS YARD, BUT EVEN DEE AND DUM AREN'T AROUND.
THINK ABOUT IT.
I WANTED TO ENJOY THIS TEA.
I REFUSE TO DROWN IT UNDER CARROT-BASED MUCK.
HEY, BLOOD!
THIS CARROT CAKE KICKS ASS! AND THIS CARROT BAVARIAN CREAM AND THIS CARROT TIRAMISU AND THIS CARROT MILLE-FEUILLE...
PLEASE.
YOU'RE THE BOSS. JUST BAN THE STUFF.
ELLIOT'S STUFF?
YOU TRY SAYING "NO" TO THAT FACE.

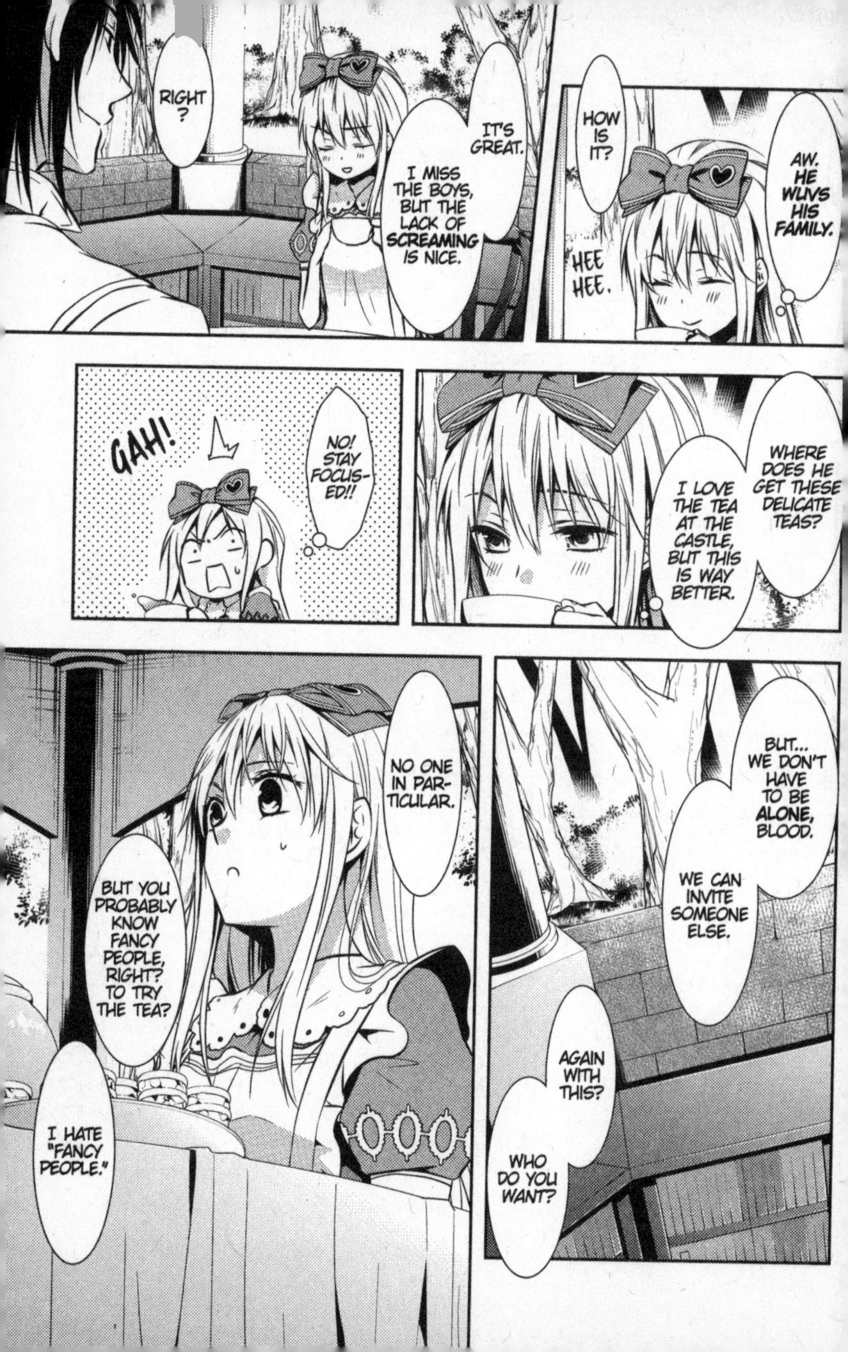
HOW IS IT?
AW. HE WUVS HIS FAMILY.
HEE HEE.
IT'S GREAT.
I MISS THE BOYS, BUT THE LACK OF SCREAMING IS NICE.
RIGHT?
WHERE DOES HE GET THESE DELICATE TEAS?
I LOVE THE TEA AT THE CASTLE, BUT THIS IS WAY BETTER.
NO! STAY FOCUS-ED!!
GAH!
BUT... WE DON'T HAVE TO BE ALONE, BLOOD.
WE CAN INVITE SOMEONE ELSE.
AGAIN WITH THIS?
WHO DO YOU WANT?
NO ONE IN PAR-TICULAR.
BUT YOU PROBABLY KNOW FANCY PEOPLE, RIGHT? TO TRY THE TEA?
I HATE "FANCY PEOPLE."

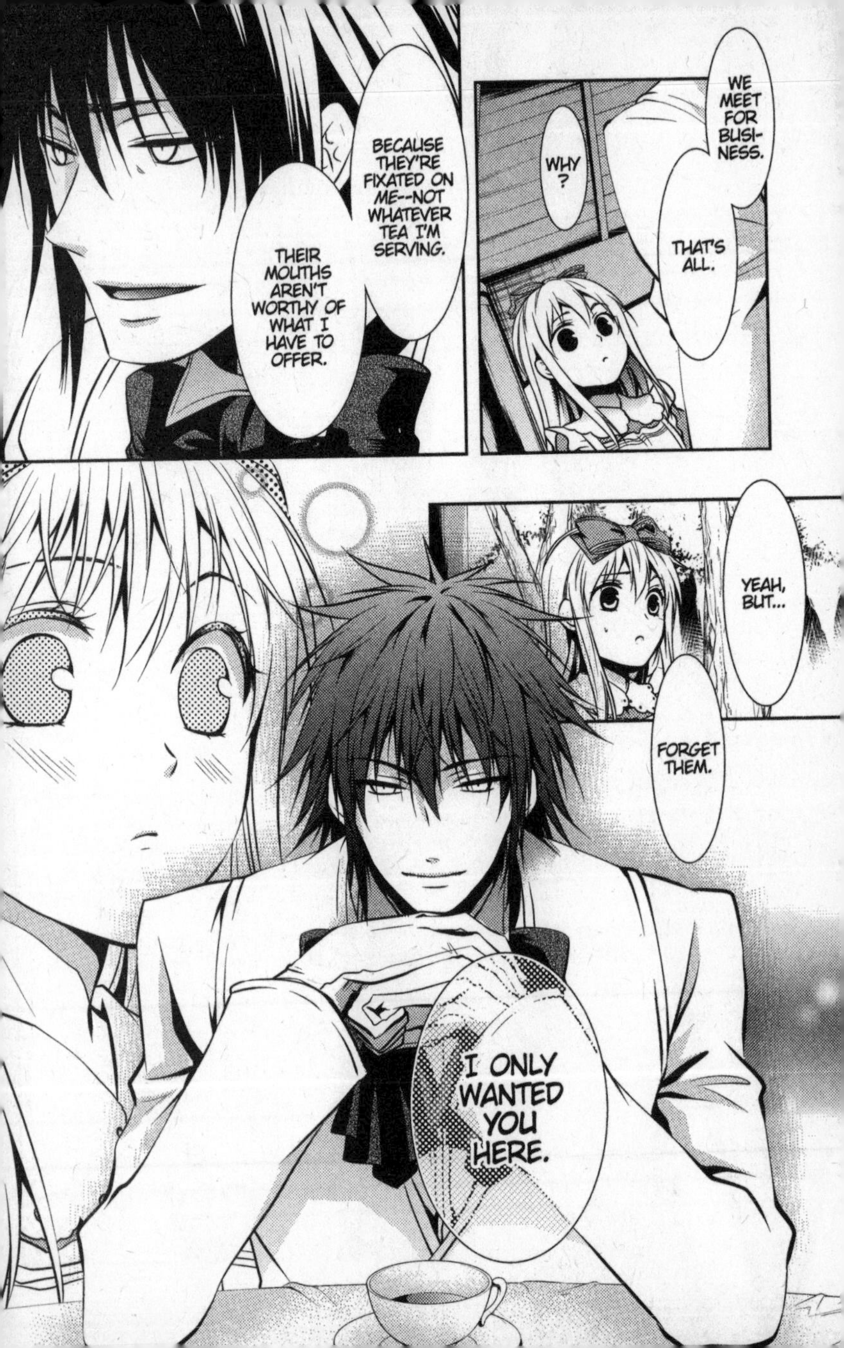
WE MEET FOR BUSINESS.
THAT'S ALL.
WHY?
BECAUSE THEY'RE FIXATED ON ME--NOT WHATEVER TEA I'M SERVING.
THEIR MOUTHS AREN'T WORTHY OF WHAT I HAVE TO OFFER.
YEAH, BUT...
FORGET THEM.
I ONLY WANTED YOU HERE.

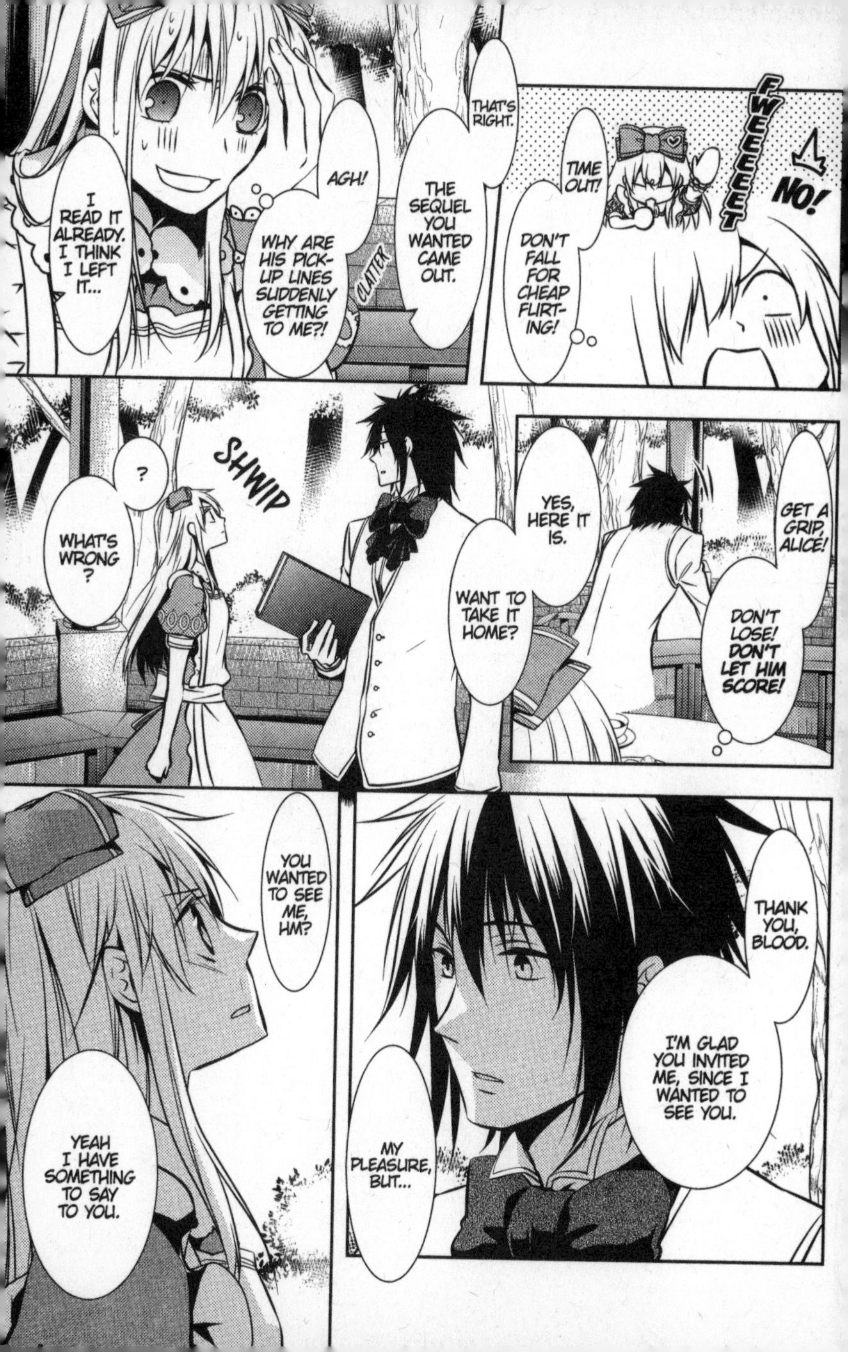
NO!
FWEEEEET
TIME OUT!
DON'T FALL FOR CHEAP FLIRTING!
THAT'S RIGHT.
THE SEQUEL YOU WANTED CAME OUT.
AGH!
WHY ARE HIS PICK-UP LINES SUDDENLY GETTING TO ME?!
CLATTER
I READ IT ALREADY. I THINK I LEFT IT...
GET A GRIP, ALICE!
DON'T LOSE! DON'T LET HIM SCORE!
YES, HERE IT IS.
WANT TO TAKE IT HOME?
SHWIP
?
WHAT'S WRONG?
THANK YOU, BLOOD.
I'M GLAD YOU INVITED ME, SINCE I WANTED TO SEE YOU.
MY PLEASURE, BUT...
YOU WANTED TO SEE ME, HM?
YEAH I HAVE SOMETHING TO SAY TO YOU.

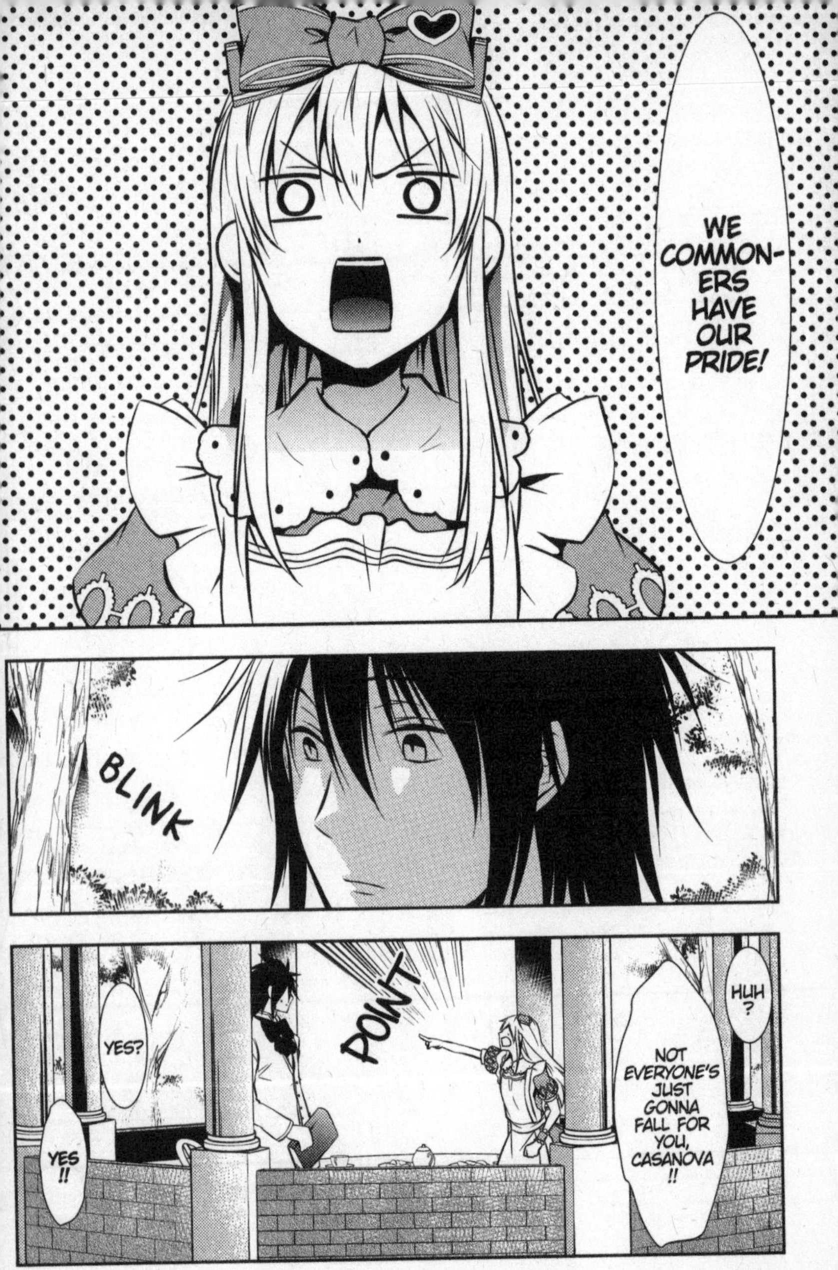
WE COMMONERS HAVE OUR PRIDE!
BLINK
HUH?
NOT EVERYONE'S JUST GONNA FALL FOR YOU, CASANOVA!!
POINT
YES?
YES!!

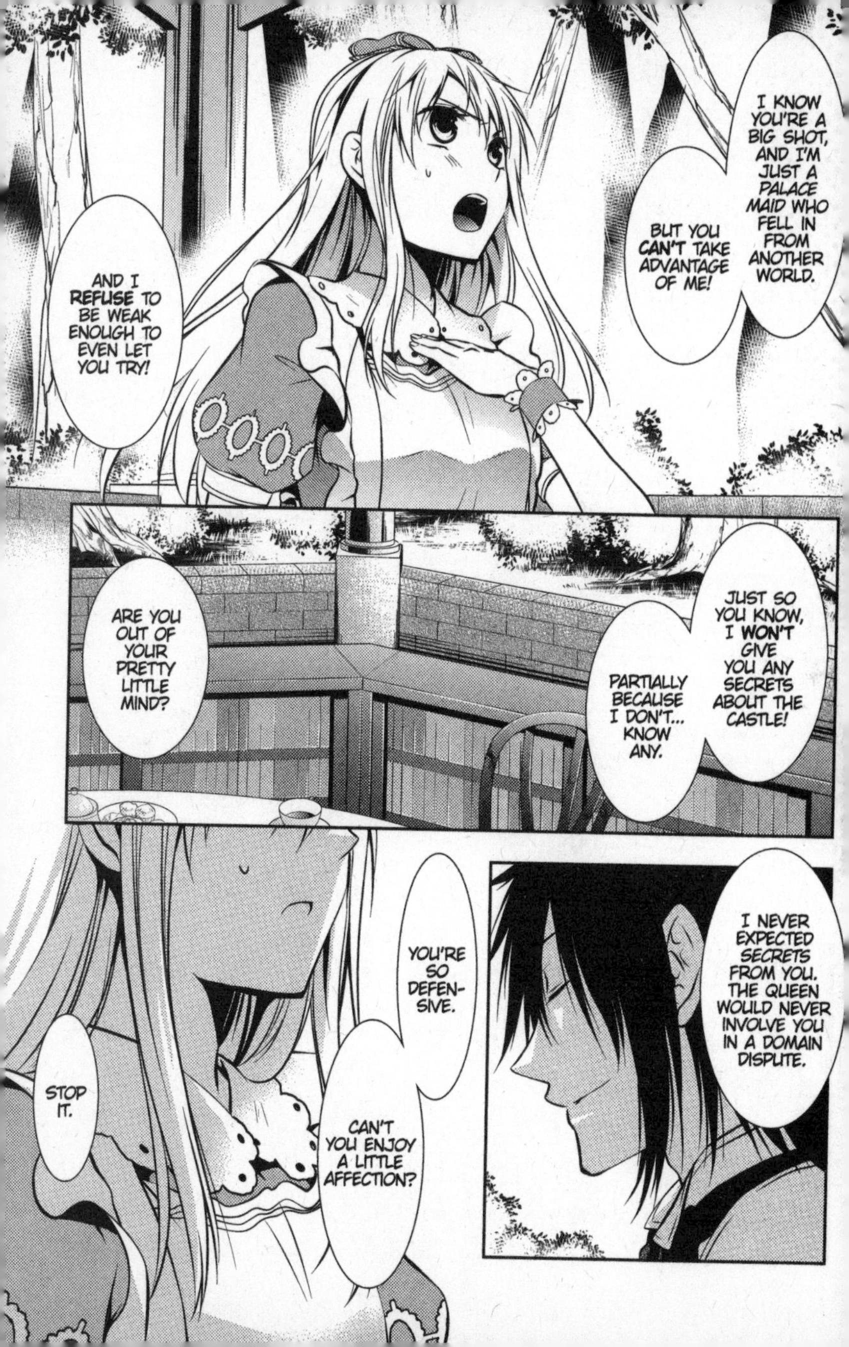
I KNOW YOU'RE A BIG SHOT, AND I'M JUST A PALACE MAID WHO FELL IN FROM ANOTHER WORLD.
BUT YOU CAN'T TAKE ADVANTAGE OF ME!
AND I REFUSE TO BE WEAK ENOUGH TO EVEN LET YOU TRY!
JUST SO YOU KNOW, I WON'T GIVE YOU ANY SECRETS ABOUT THE CASTLE!
PARTIALLY BECAUSE I DON'T... KNOW ANY.
ARE YOU OUT OF YOUR PRETTY LITTLE MIND?
I NEVER EXPECTED SECRETS FROM YOU. THE QUEEN WOULD NEVER INVOLVE YOU IN A DOMAIN DISPUTE.
YOU'RE SO DEFEN-SIVE.
CAN'T YOU ENJOY A LITTLE AFFECTION?
STOP IT.

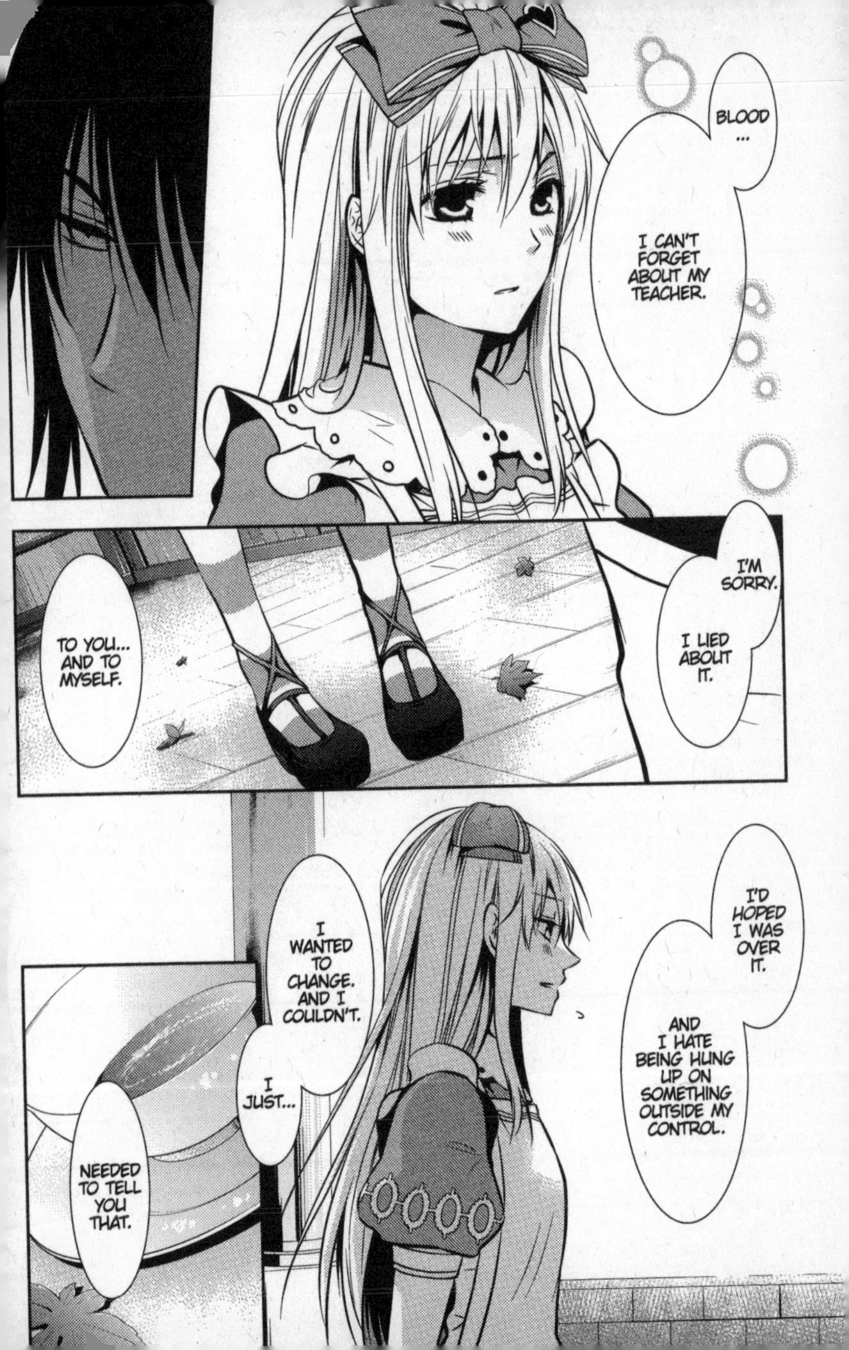
BLOOD...
I CAN'T FORGET ABOUT MY TEACHER.
I'M SORRY.
I LIED ABOUT IT.
TO YOU... AND TO MYSELF.
I'D HOPED I WAS OVER IT.
AND I HATE BEING HUNG UP ON SOMETHING OUTSIDE MY CONTROL.
I WANTED TO CHANGE. AND I COULDN'T.
I JUST...
NEEDED TO TELL YOU THAT.

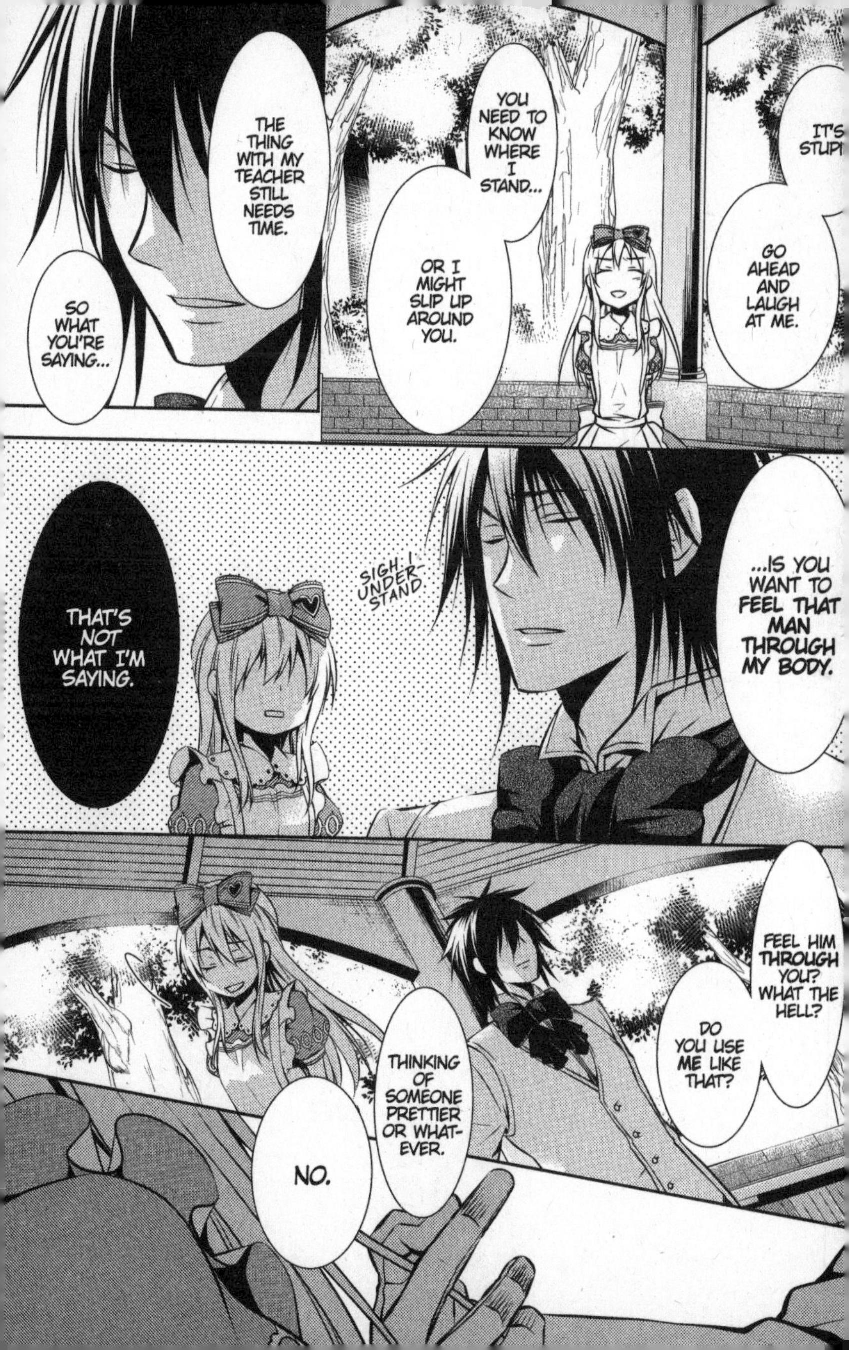
IT'S STUPI
GO AHEAD AND LAUGH AT ME.
YOU NEED TO KNOW WHERE I STAND...
OR I MIGHT SLIP UP AROUND YOU.
THE THING WITH MY TEACHER STILL NEEDS TIME.
SO WHAT YOU'RE SAYING...
...IS YOU WANT TO FEEL THAT MAN THROUGH MY BODY.
SIGH I UNDERSTAND.
THAT'S NOT WHAT I'M SAYING.
FEEL HIM THROUGH YOU? WHAT THE HELL?
DO YOU USE ME LIKE THAT?
THINKING OF SOMEONE PRETTIER OR WHATEVER.
NO.

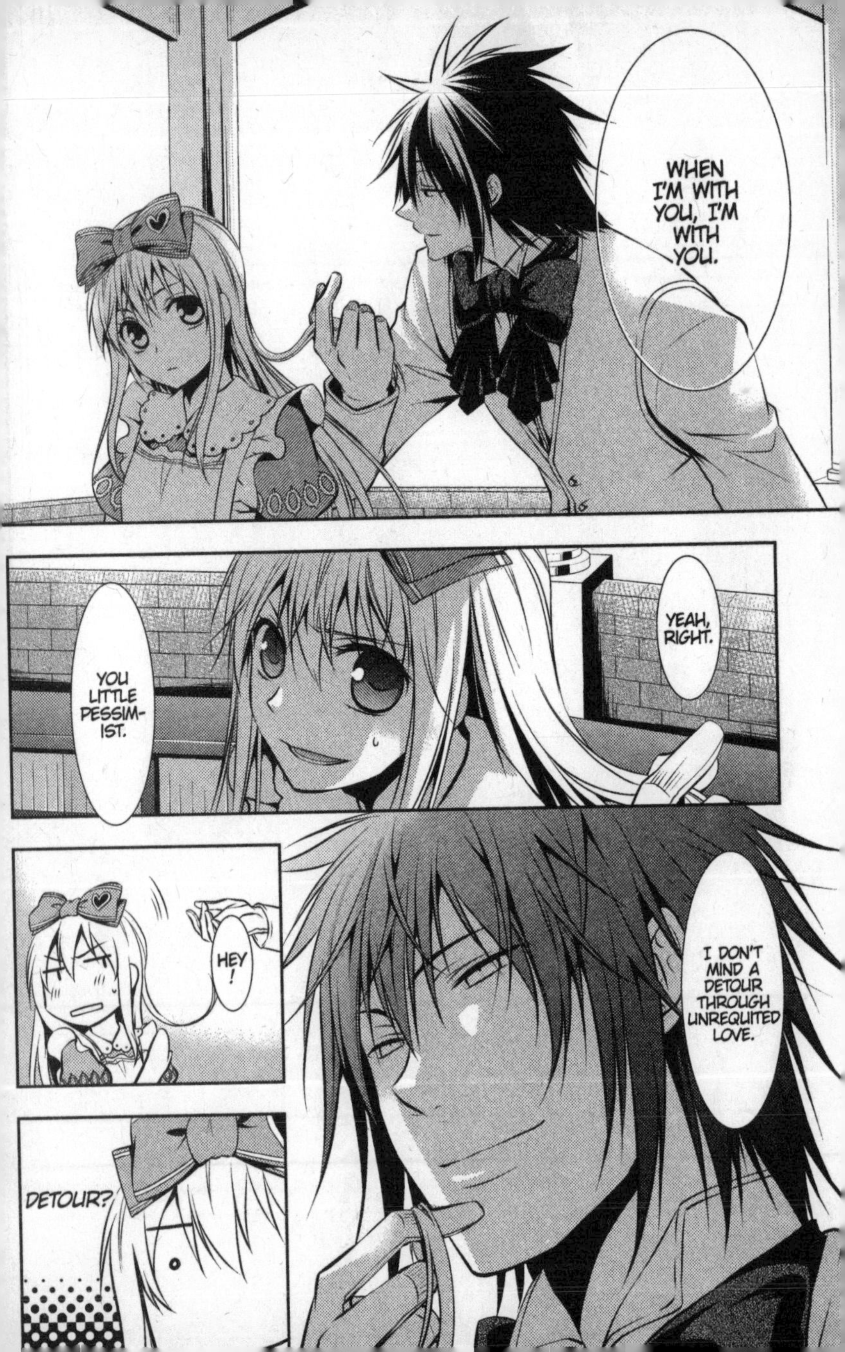
WHEN I'M WITH YOU, I'M WITH YOU.
YEAH, RIGHT.
YOU LITTLE PESSIM-IST.
I DON'T MIND A DETOUR THROUGH UNREQUITED LOVE.
HEY!
DETOUR?

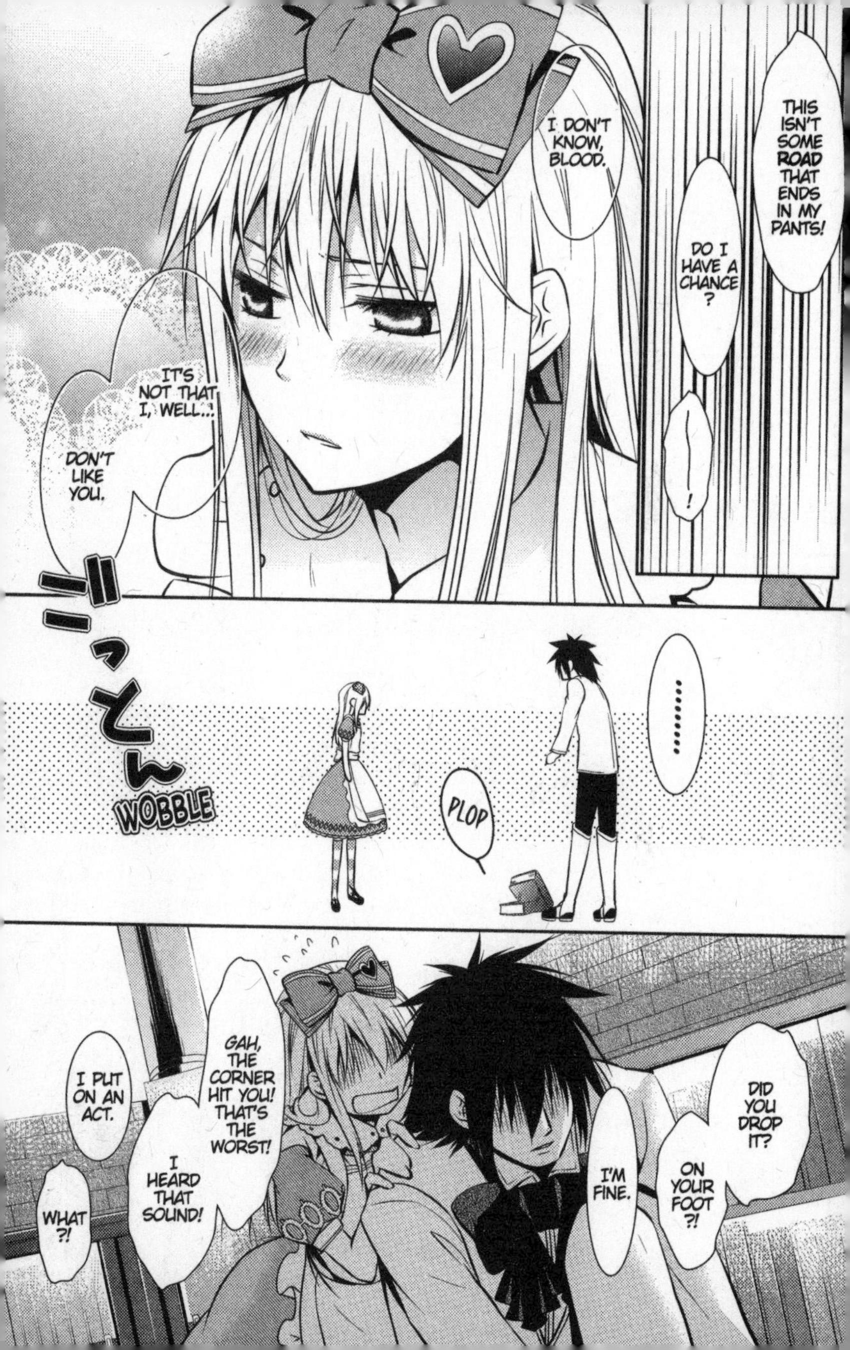
THIS ISN'T SOME ROAD THAT ENDS IN MY PANTS!
DO I HAVE A CHANCE?
!
I DON'T KNOW, BLOOD.
IT'S NOT THAT I, WELL...
DON'T LIKE YOU.
......
PLOP
ごっとん
WOBBLE
DID YOU DROP IT?
ON YOUR FOOT?!
I'M FINE.
GAH, THE CORNER HIT YOU! THAT'S THE WORST!
I HEARD THAT SOUND!
I PUT ON AN ACT.
WHAT?!

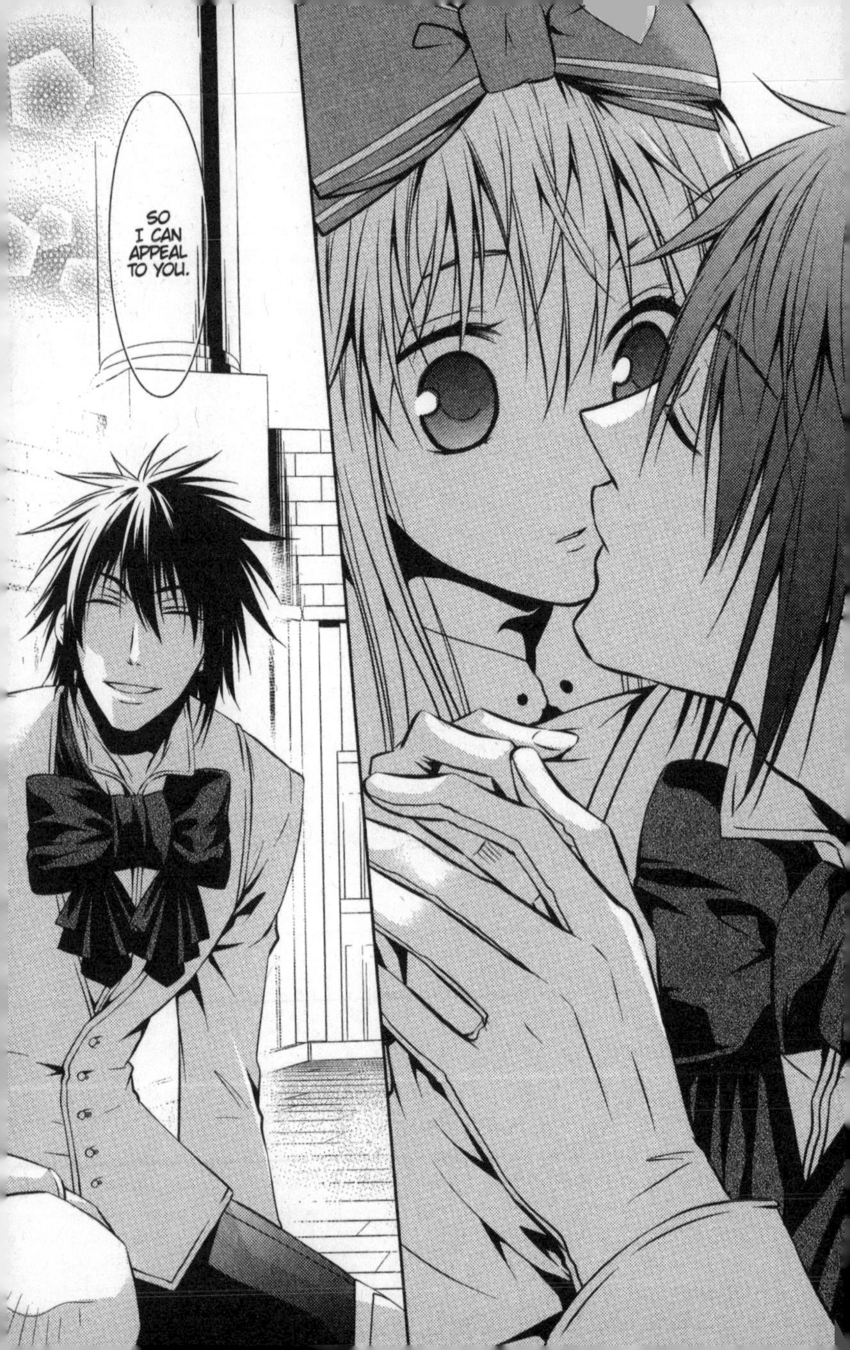
SO I CAN APPEAL TO YOU.

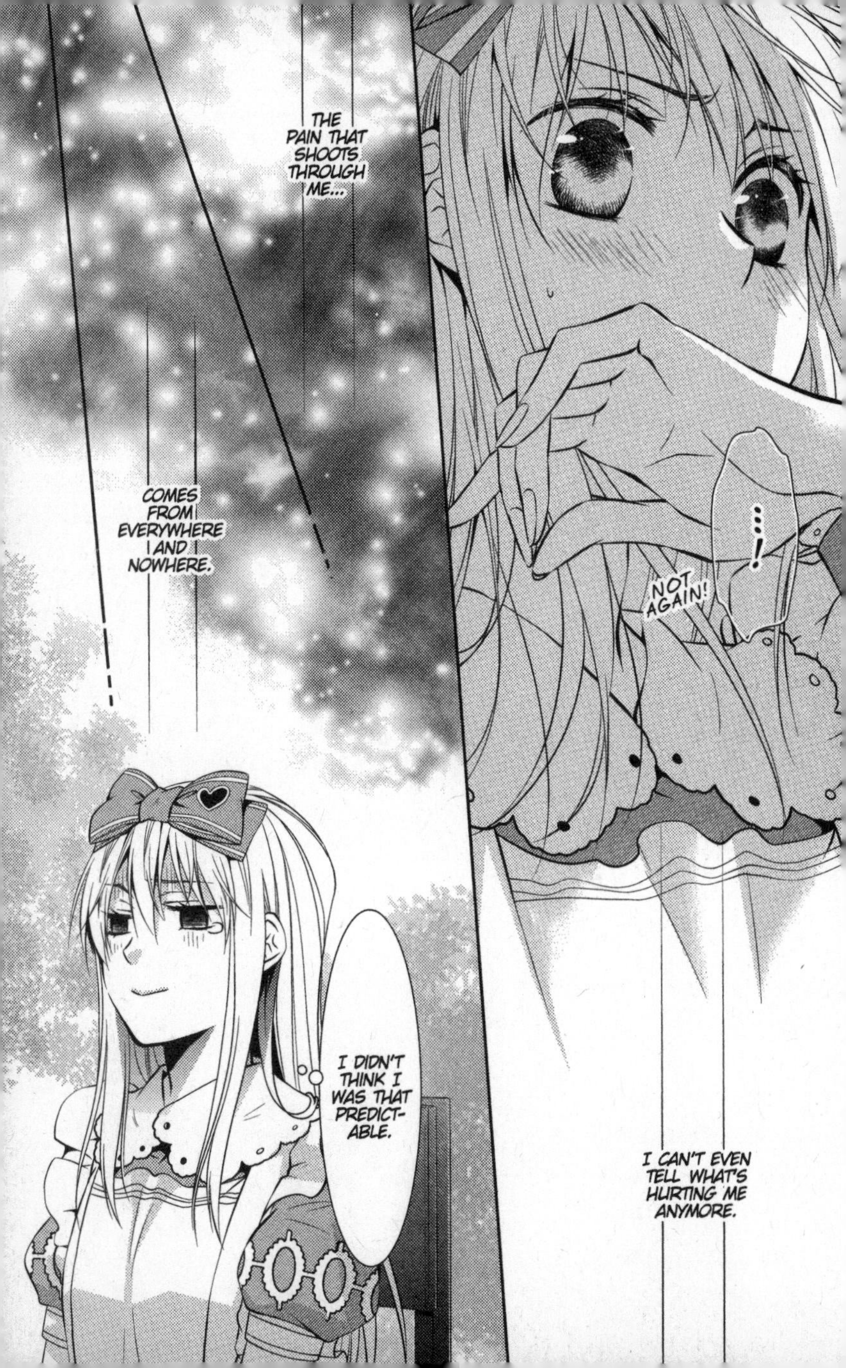
...!
NOT AGAIN!
I CAN'T EVEN TELL WHAT'S HURTING ME ANYMORE.
THE PAIN THAT SHOOTS THROUGH ME...
COMES FROM EVERYWHERE AND NOWHERE.
I DIDN'T THINK I WAS THAT PREDICT-ABLE.

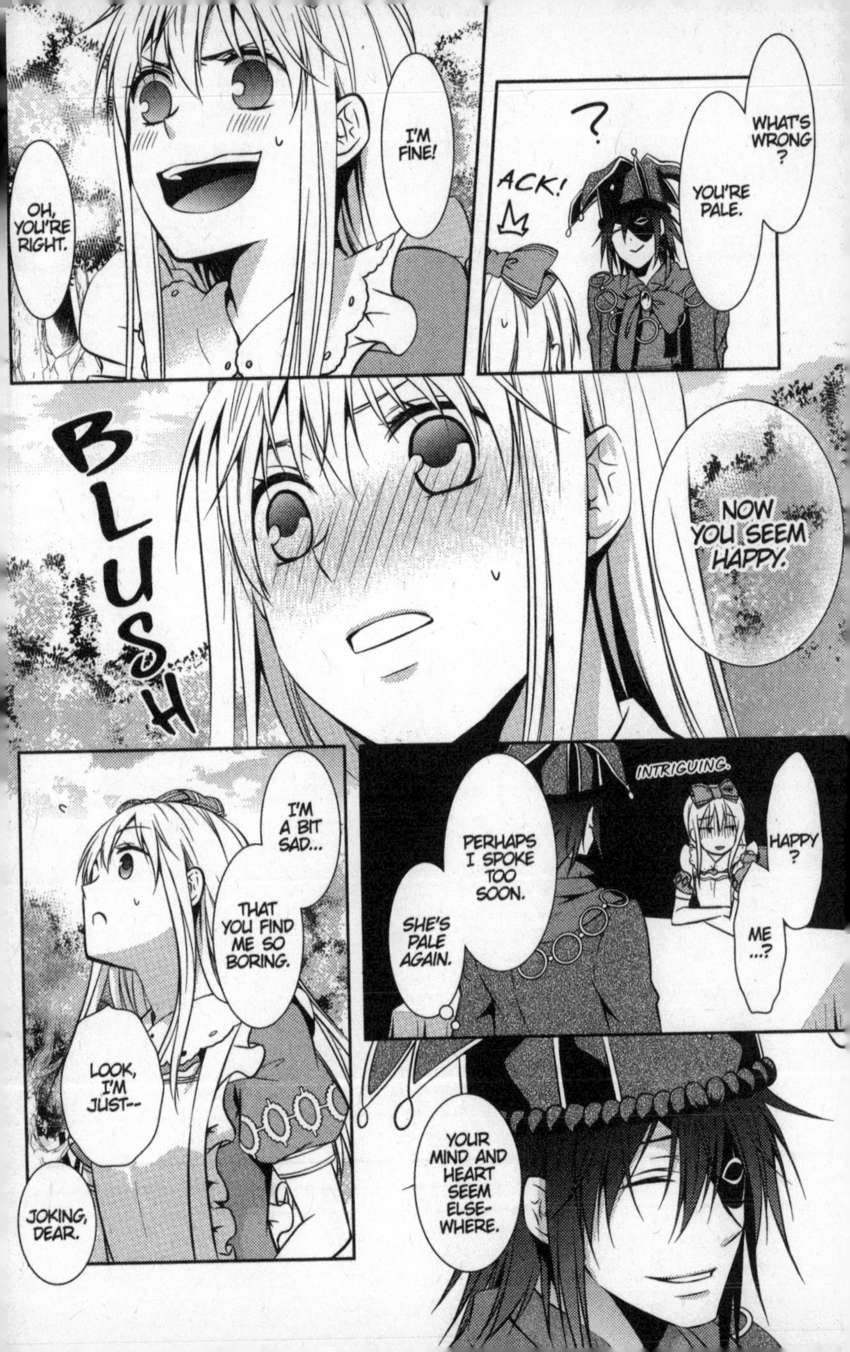
WHAT'S WRONG?
YOU'RE PALE.
?
ACK!
I'M FINE!
OH, YOU'RE RIGHT.
NOW YOU SEEM HAPPY.
BLUSH
HAPPY?
ME...?
INTRIGUING.
PERHAPS I SPOKE TOO SOON.
SHE'S PALE AGAIN.
YOUR MIND AND HEART SEEM ELSE-WHERE.
I'M A BIT SAD...
THAT YOU FIND ME SO BORING.
LOOK, I'M JUST--
JOKING, DEAR.

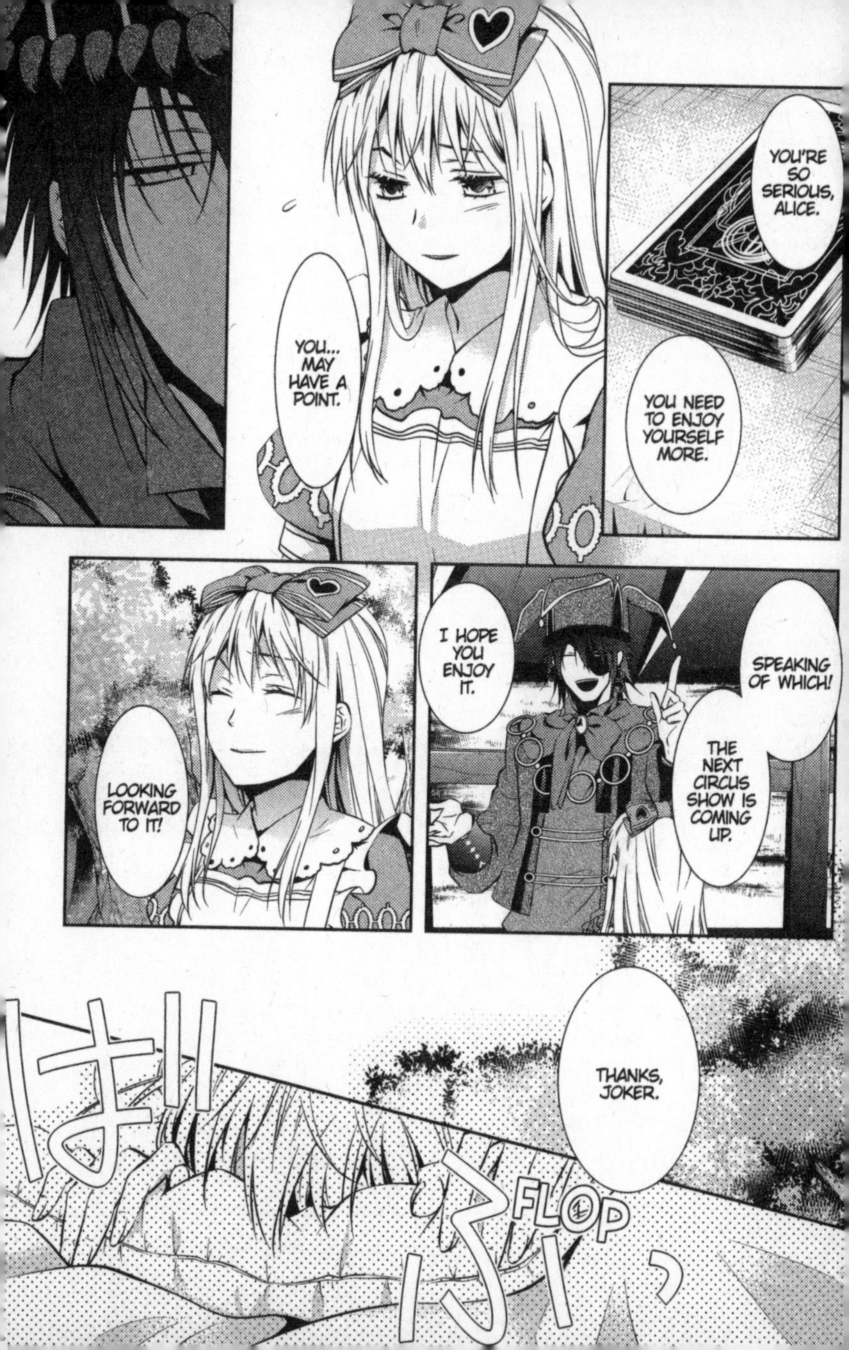
YOU'RE SO SERIOUS, ALICE.
YOU NEED TO ENJOY YOURSELF MORE.
YOU... MAY HAVE A POINT.
SPEAKING OF WHICH!
THE NEXT CIRCUS SHOW IS COMING UP.
I HOPE YOU ENJOY IT.
LOOKING FORWARD TO IT!
THANKS, JOKER.
FLOP

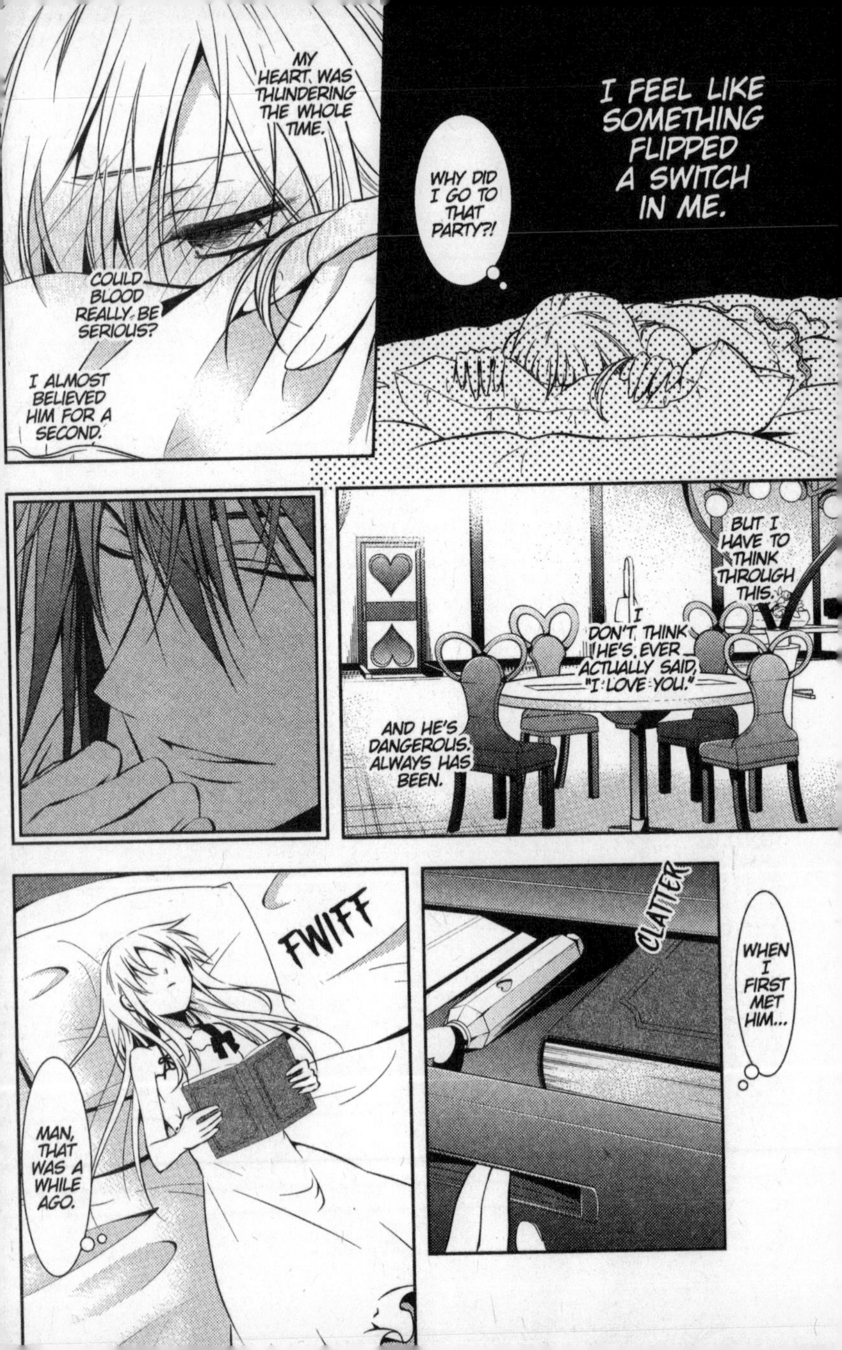
I FEEL LIKE SOMETHING FLIPPED A SWITCH IN ME.
WHY DID I GO TO THAT PARTY?!
MY HEART WAS THUNDERING THE WHOLE TIME.
COULD BLOOD REALLY BE SERIOUS?
I ALMOST BELIEVED HIM FOR A SECOND.
BUT I HAVE TO THINK THROUGH THIS.
I DON'T THINK HE'S EVER ACTUALLY SAID, "I LOVE YOU."
AND HE'S DANGEROUS. ALWAYS HAS BEEN.
CLATTER
WHEN I FIRST MET HIM...
FWIFF
MAN, THAT WAS A WHILE AGO.

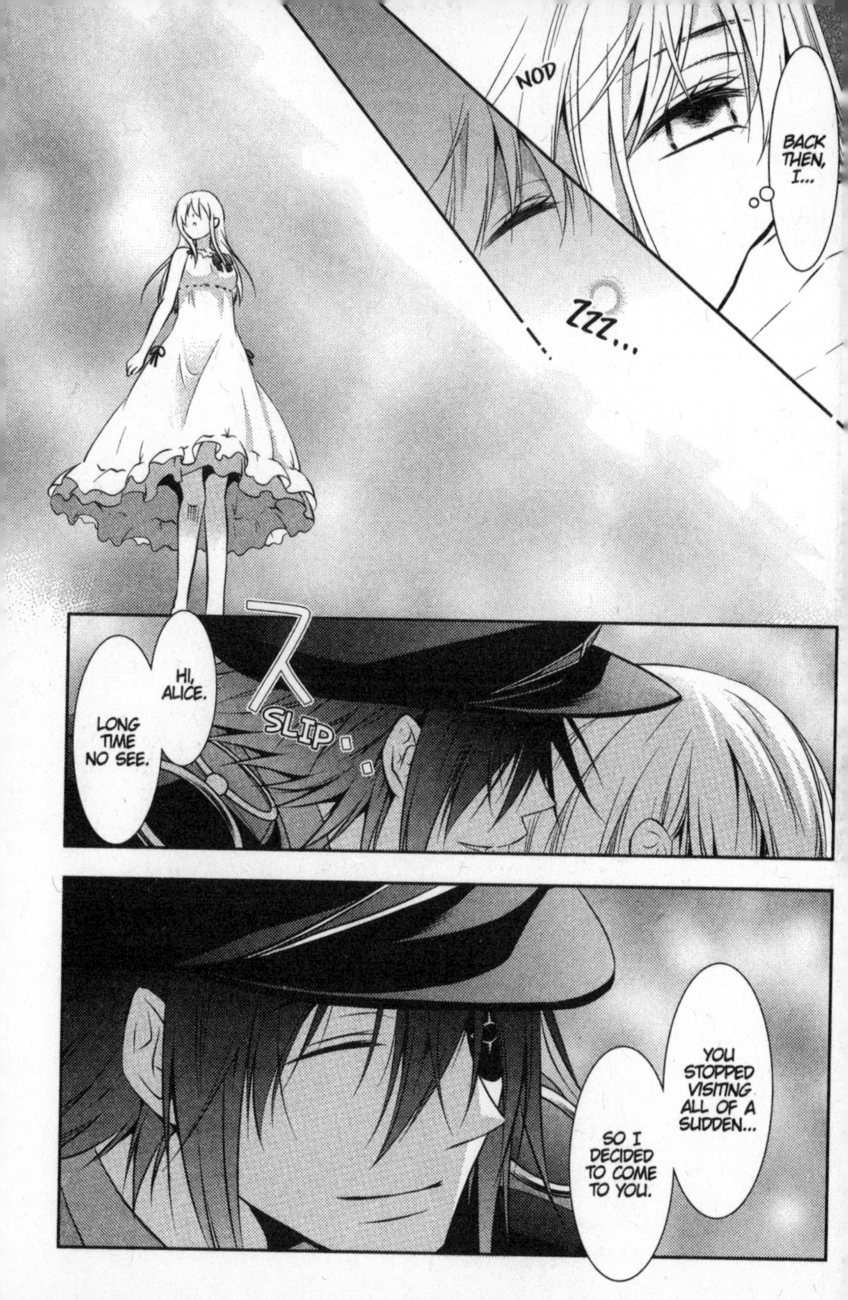
NOD
BACK THEN, I...
ZZZ...
ス
SLIP
HI, ALICE.
LONG TIME NO SEE.
YOU STOPPED VISITING ALL OF A SUDDEN...
SO I DECIDED TO COME TO YOU.

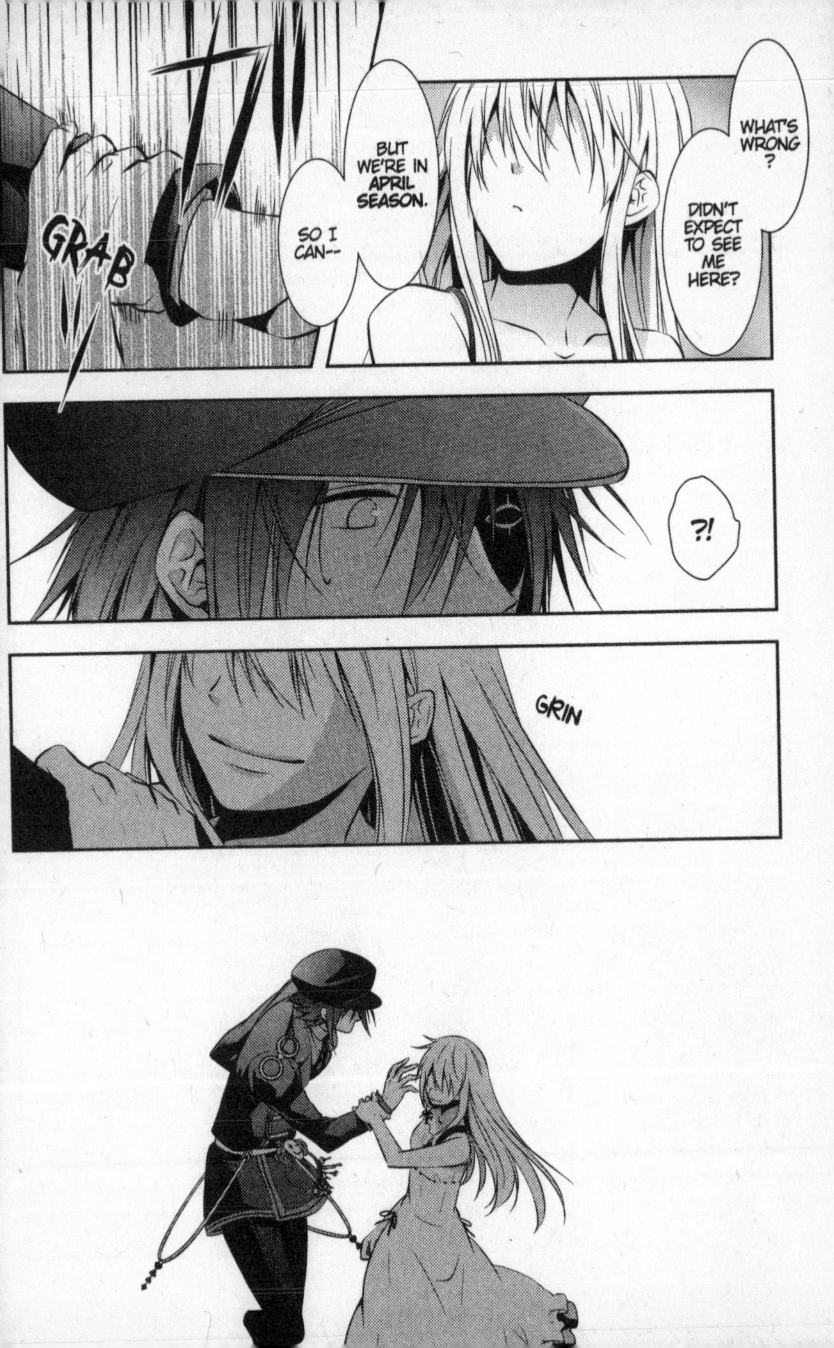
WHAT'S WRONG?
DIDN'T EXPECT TO SEE ME HERE?
BUT WE'RE IN APRIL SEASON.
SO I CAN--
GRAB
?!
GRIN

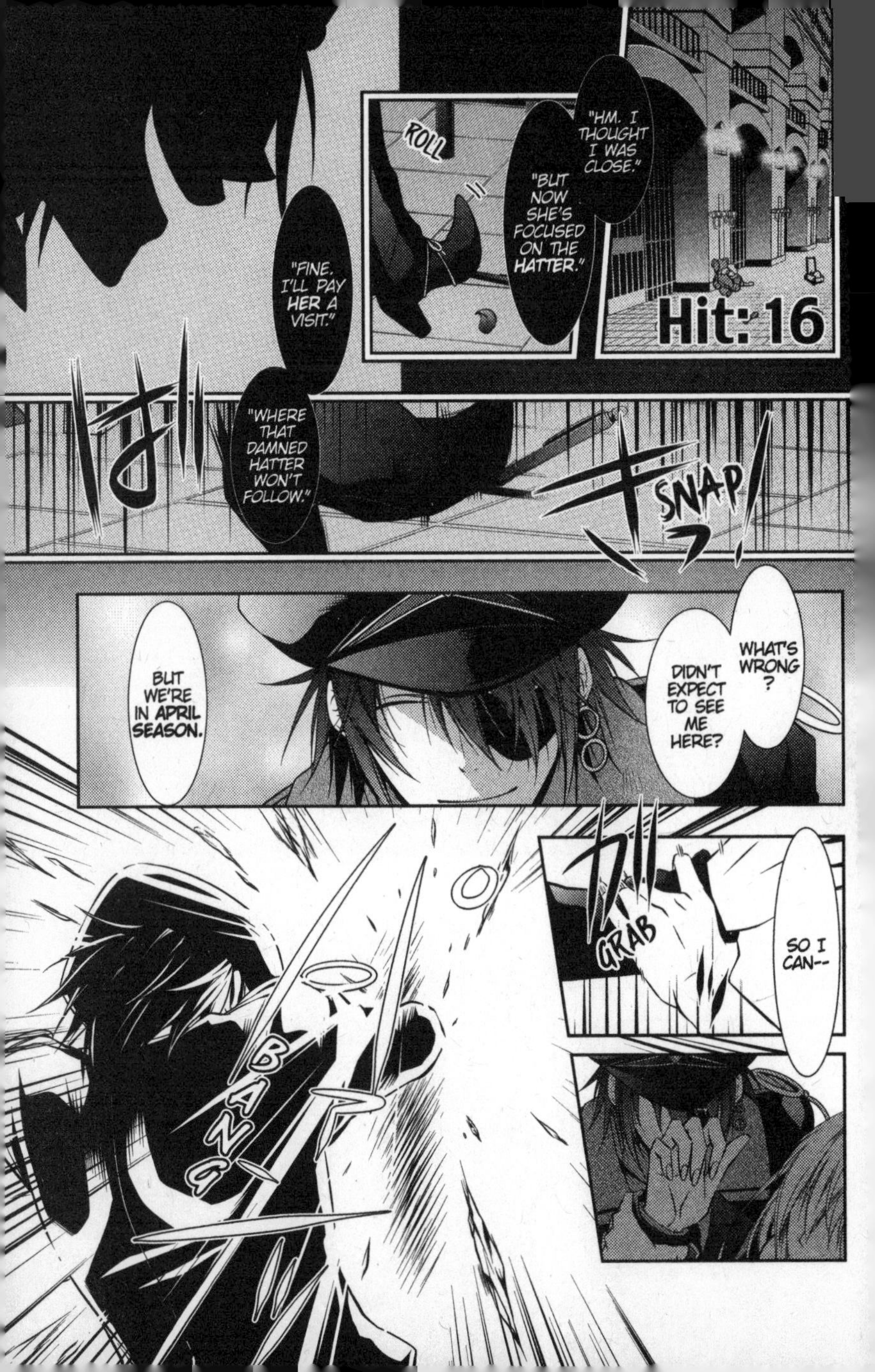
Hit: 16
"HM. I THOUGHT I WAS CLOSE."
ROLL
"BUT NOW SHE'S FOCUSED ON THE HATTER."
"FINE. I'LL PAY HER A VISIT."
"WHERE THAT DAMNED HATTER WON'T FOLLOW."
SNAP
WHAT'S WRONG?
DIDN'T EXPECT TO SEE ME HERE?
BUT WE'RE IN APRIL SEASON.
GRAB
SO I CAN--
BANG

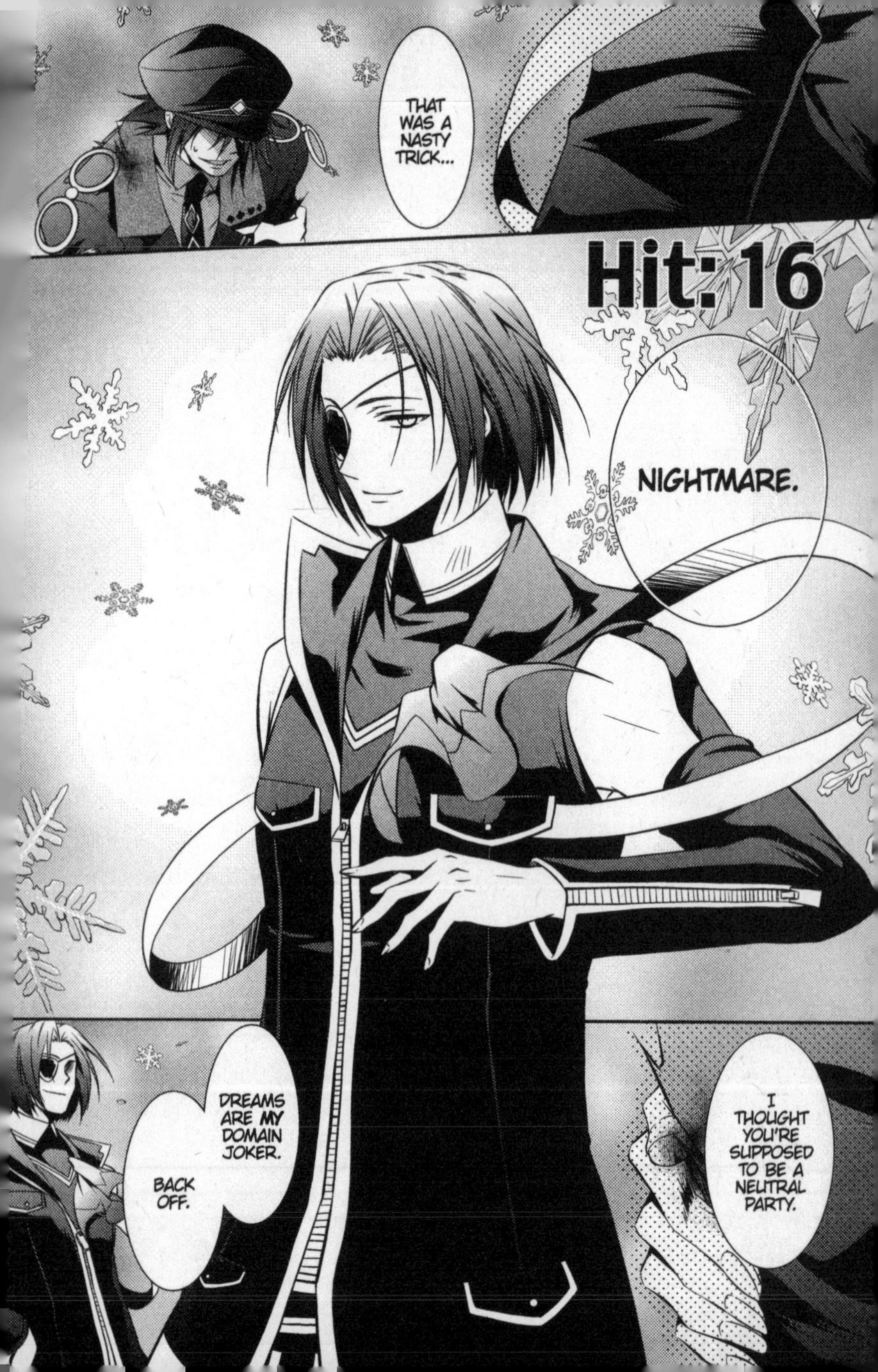
THAT WAS A NASTY TRICK...
Hit: 16
NIGHTMARE.
I THOUGHT YOU'RE SUPPOSED TO BE A NEUTRAL PARTY.
DREAMS ARE MY DOMAIN JOKER.
BACK OFF.

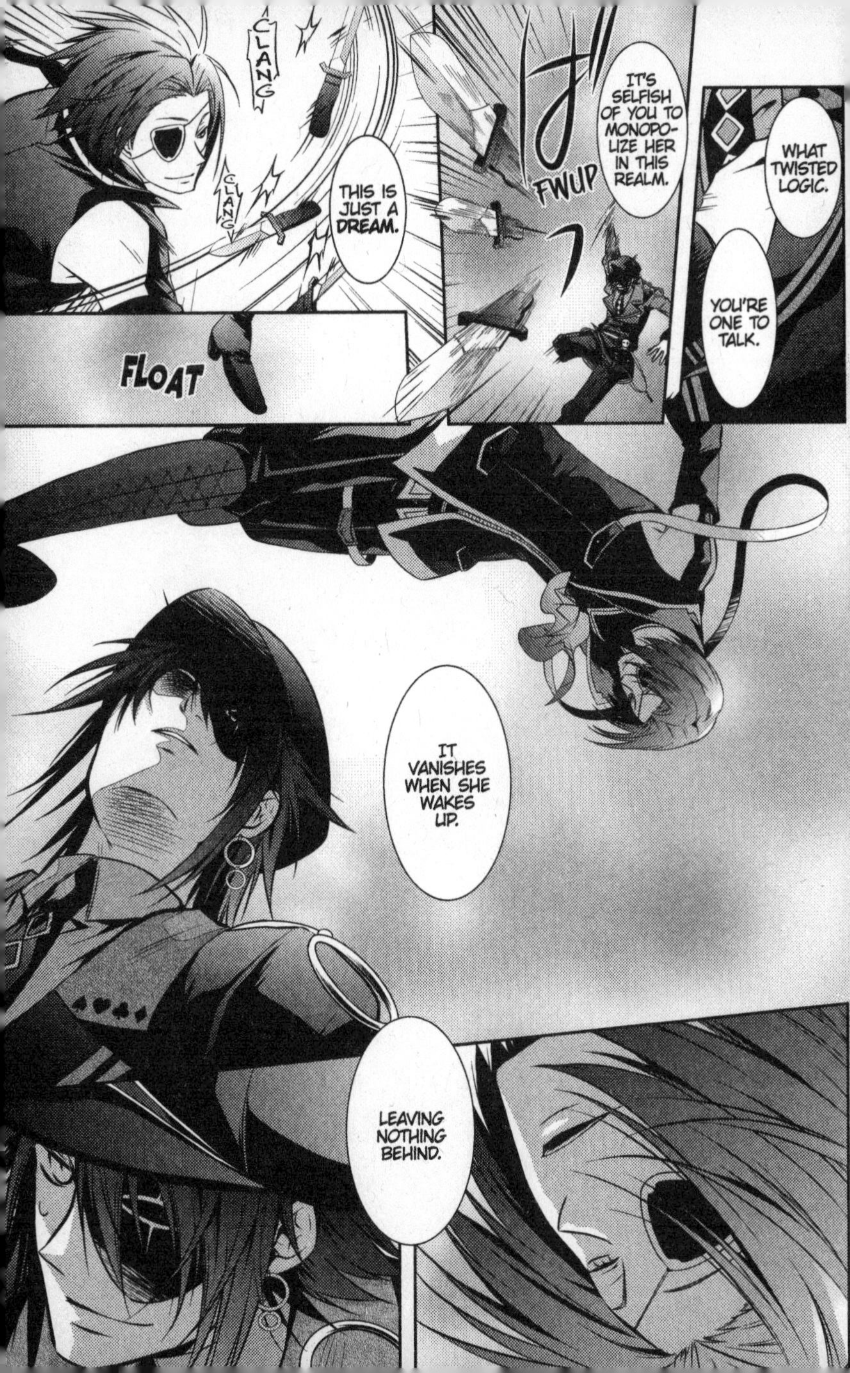
WHAT TWISTED LOGIC.
YOU'RE ONE TO TALK.
IT'S SELFISH OF YOU TO MONOPOLIZE HER IN THIS REALM.
FWUP
THIS IS JUST A DREAM.
CLANG
CLANG
FLOAT
IT VANISHES WHEN SHE WAKES UP.
LEAVING NOTHING BEHIND.

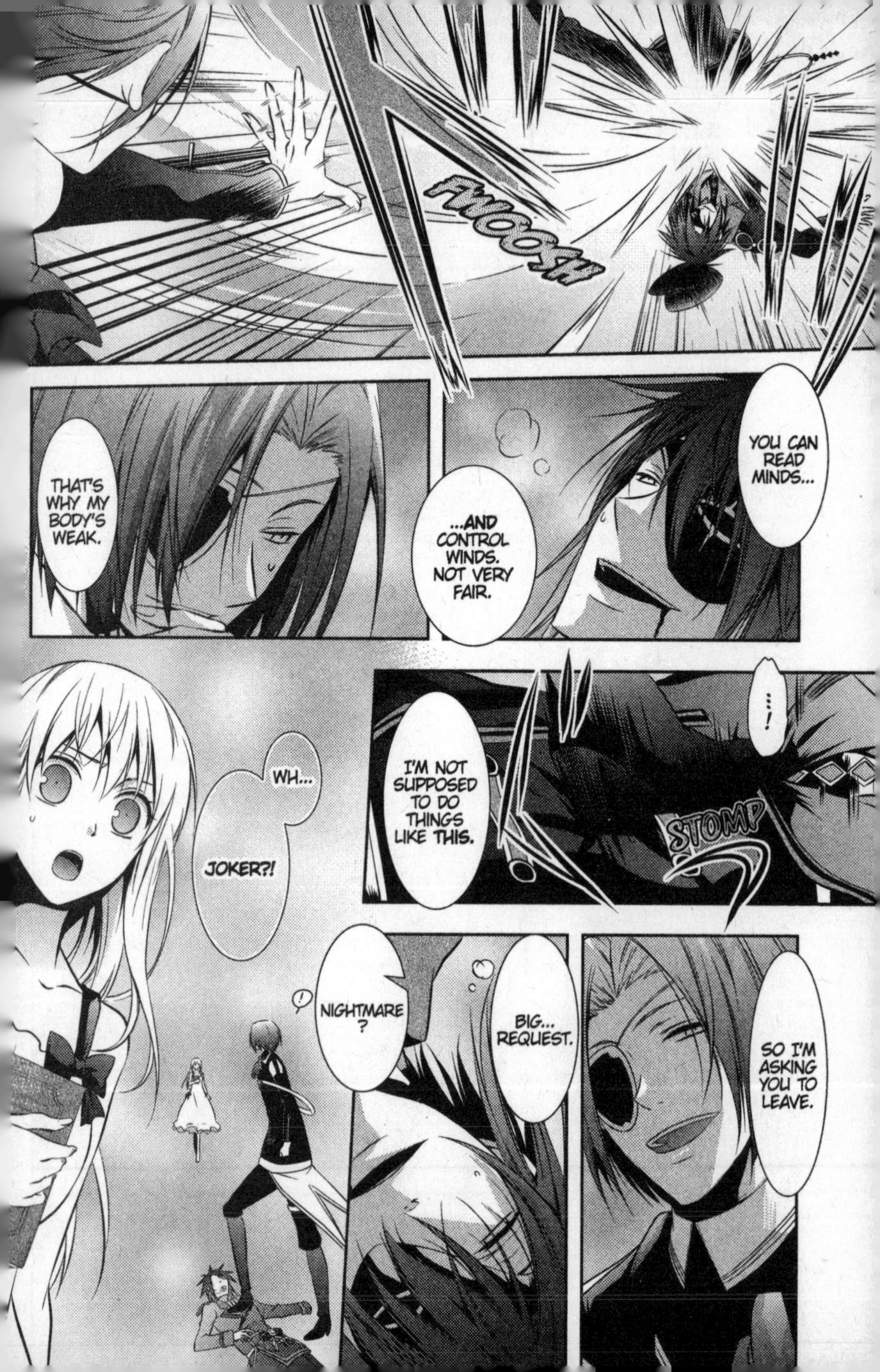
FWOOSH!!
YOU CAN READ MINDS...
...AND CONTROL WINDS. NOT VERY FAIR.
THAT'S WHY MY BODY'S WEAK.
...!
I'M NOT SUPPOSED TO DO THINGS LIKE THIS.
STOMP
SO I'M ASKING YOU TO LEAVE.
BIG... REQUEST.
!
NIGHTMARE?
WH...
JOKER?!

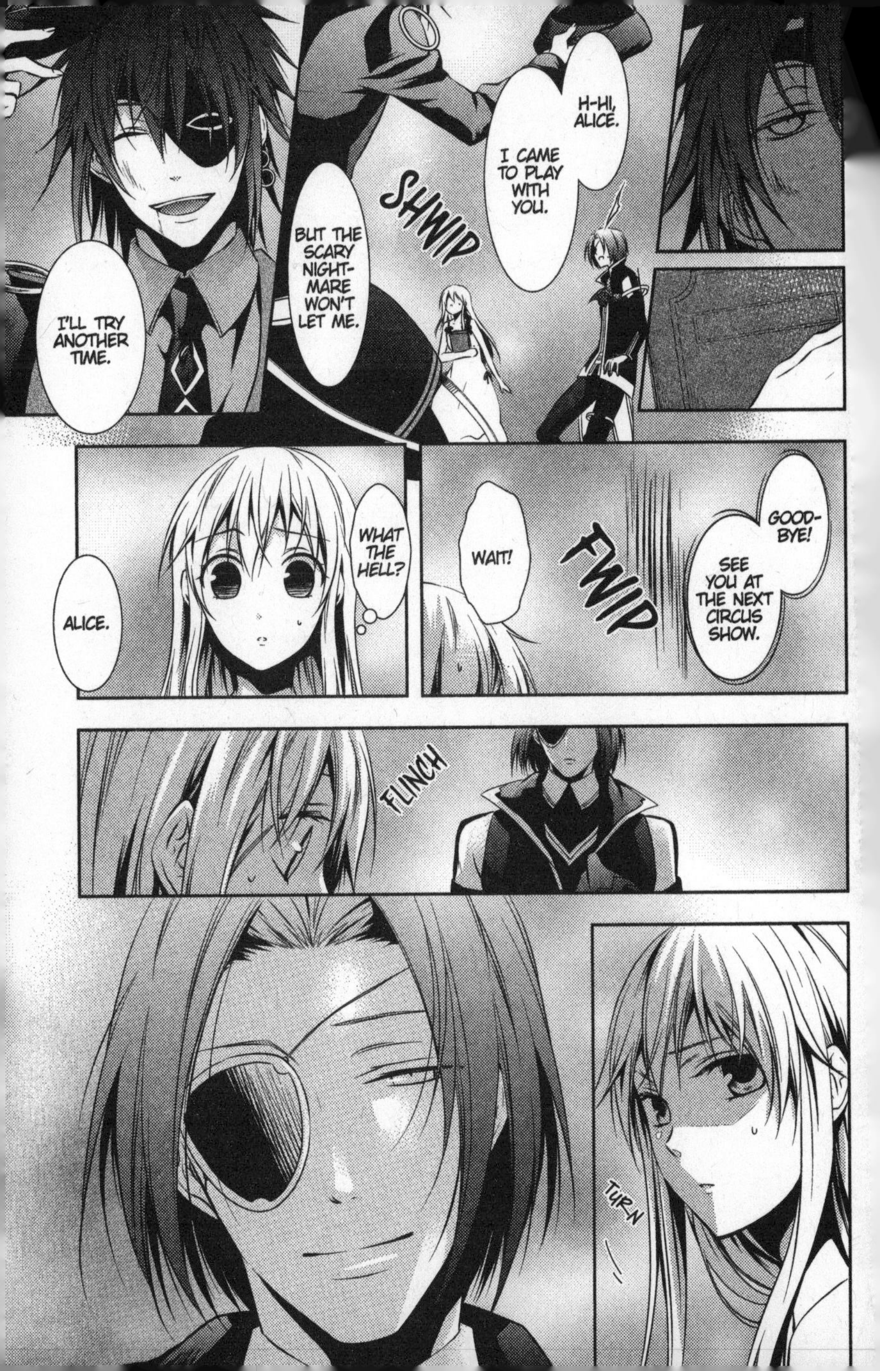
H-HI, ALICE.
I CAME TO PLAY WITH YOU.
SHWIP
BUT THE SCARY NIGHT-MARE WON'T LET ME.
I'LL TRY ANOTHER TIME.
GOOD-BYE!
SEE YOU AT THE NEXT CIRCUS SHOW.
FWIP
WAIT!
WHAT THE HELL?
ALICE.
FLINCH
TURN

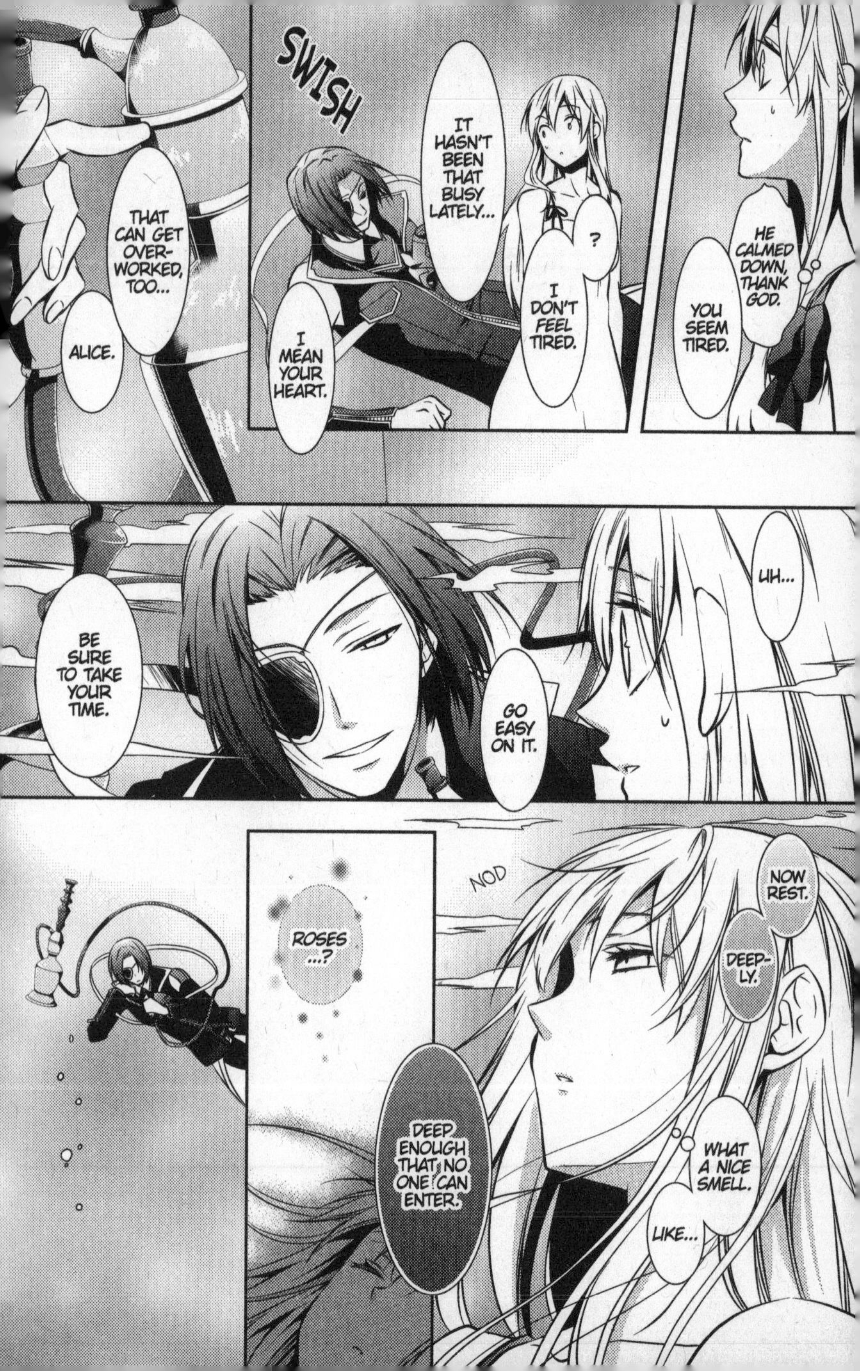
HE CALMED DOWN, THANK GOD.
YOU SEEM TIRED.
?
I DON'T FEEL TIRED.
SWISH
IT HASN'T BEEN THAT BUSY LATELY...
I MEAN YOUR HEART.
THAT CAN GET OVER-WORKED, TOO...
ALICE.
UH...
GO EASY ON IT.
BE SURE TO TAKE YOUR TIME.
NOW REST.
DEEP-LY.
NOD
WHAT A NICE SMELL.
LIKE...
DEEP ENOUGH THAT NO ONE CAN ENTER.
ROSES ...?

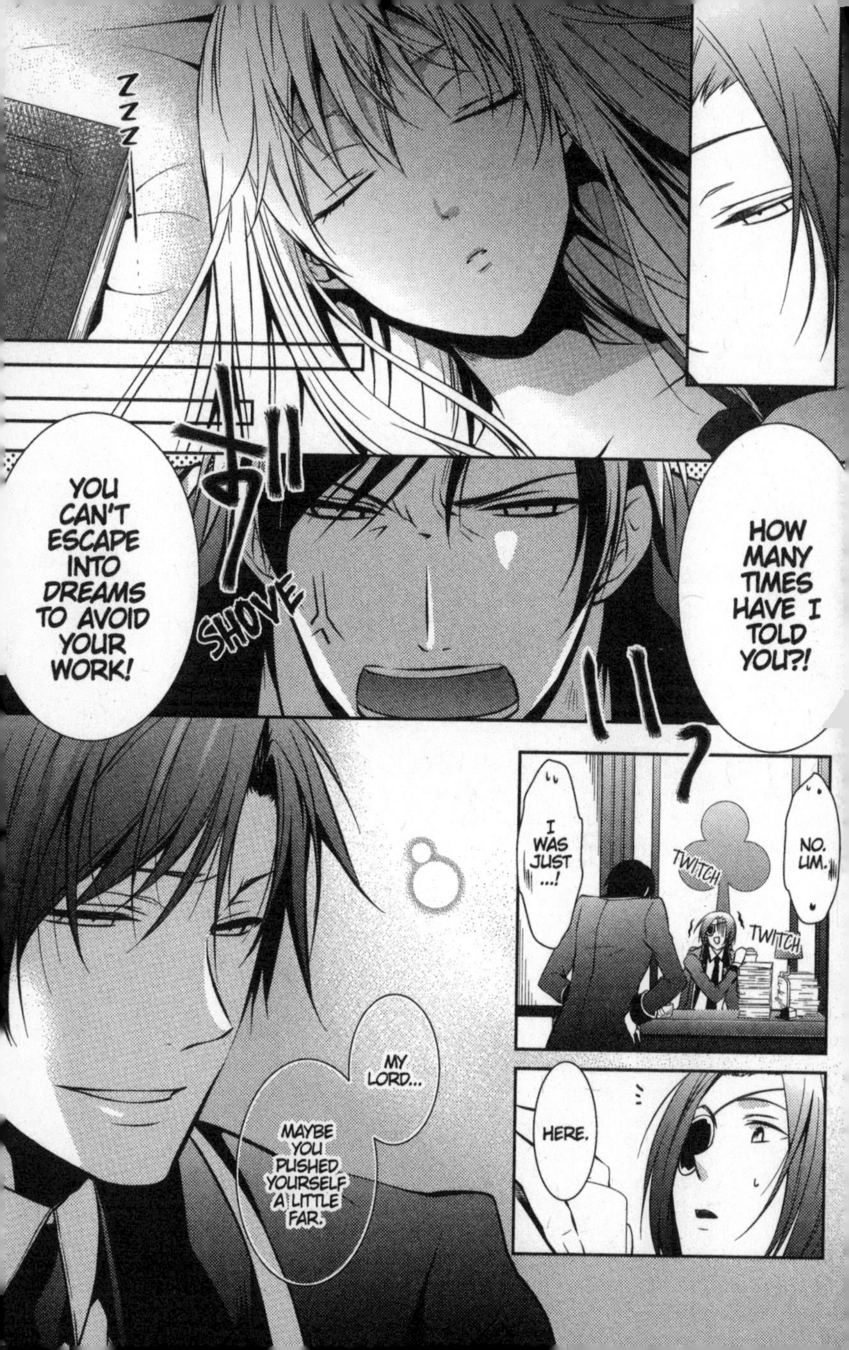
ZZZ
...
HOW MANY TIMES HAVE I TOLD YOU?!
SHOVE
YOU CAN'T ESCAPE INTO DREAMS TO AVOID YOUR WORK!
NO. UM.
TWITCH
TWITCH
I WAS JUST ...!
HERE.
MY LORD...
MAYBE YOU PUSHED YOURSELF A LITTLE FAR.

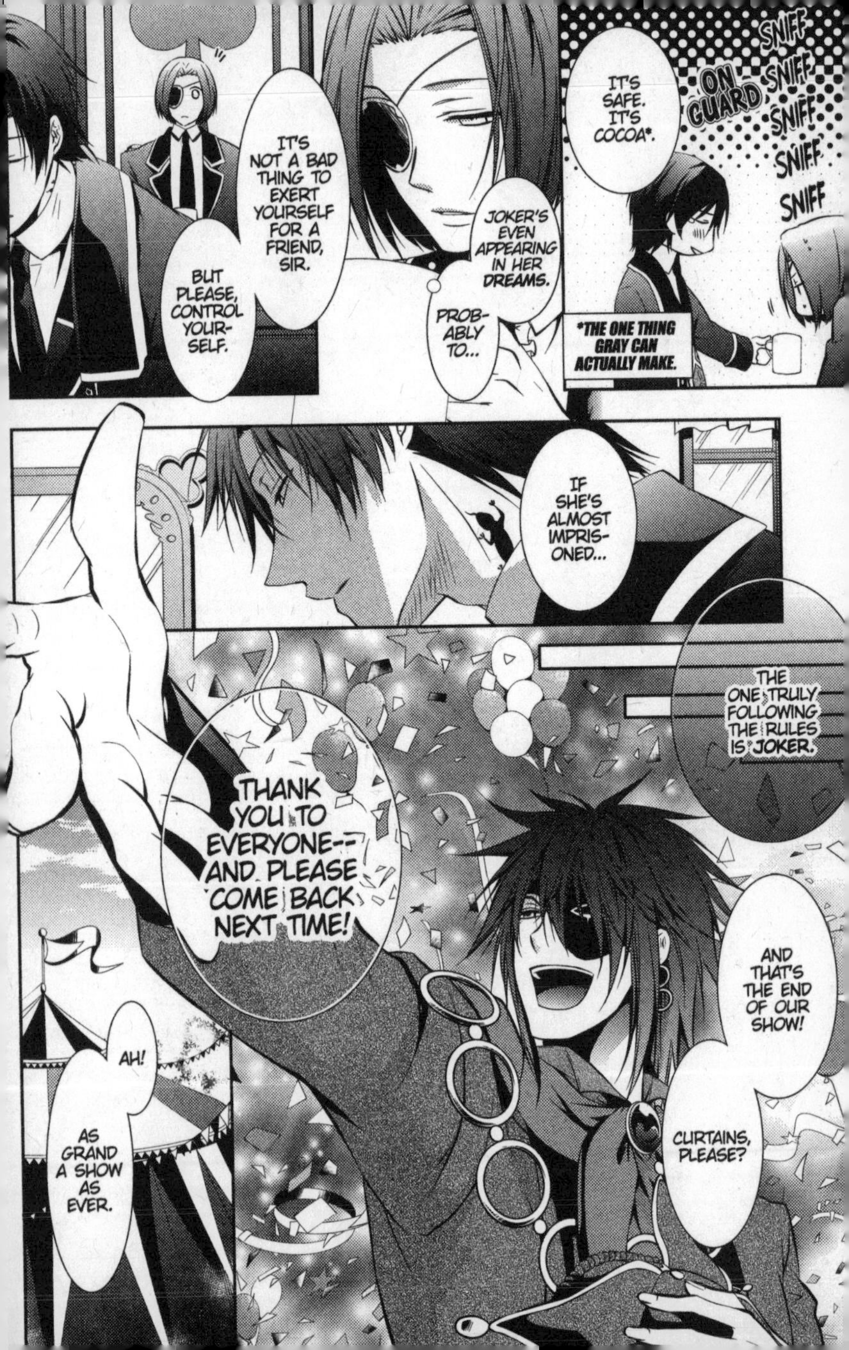

SNIFF
SNIFF
SNIFF
SNIFF
SNIFF
ON GUARD
IT'S SAFE. IT'S COCOA*.
*THE ONE THING GRAY CAN ACTUALLY MAKE.
JOKER'S EVEN APPEARING IN HER DREAMS.
PROBABLY TO...
IT'S NOT A BAD THING TO EXERT YOURSELF FOR A FRIEND, SIR.
BUT PLEASE, CONTROL YOURSELF.
IF SHE'S ALMOST IMPRISONED...
THE ONE TRULY FOLLOWING THE RULES IS JOKER.
AND THAT'S THE END OF OUR SHOW!
CURTAINS, PLEASE?
THANK YOU TO EVERYONE-- AND PLEASE COME BACK NEXT TIME!
AH!
AS GRAND A SHOW AS EVER.

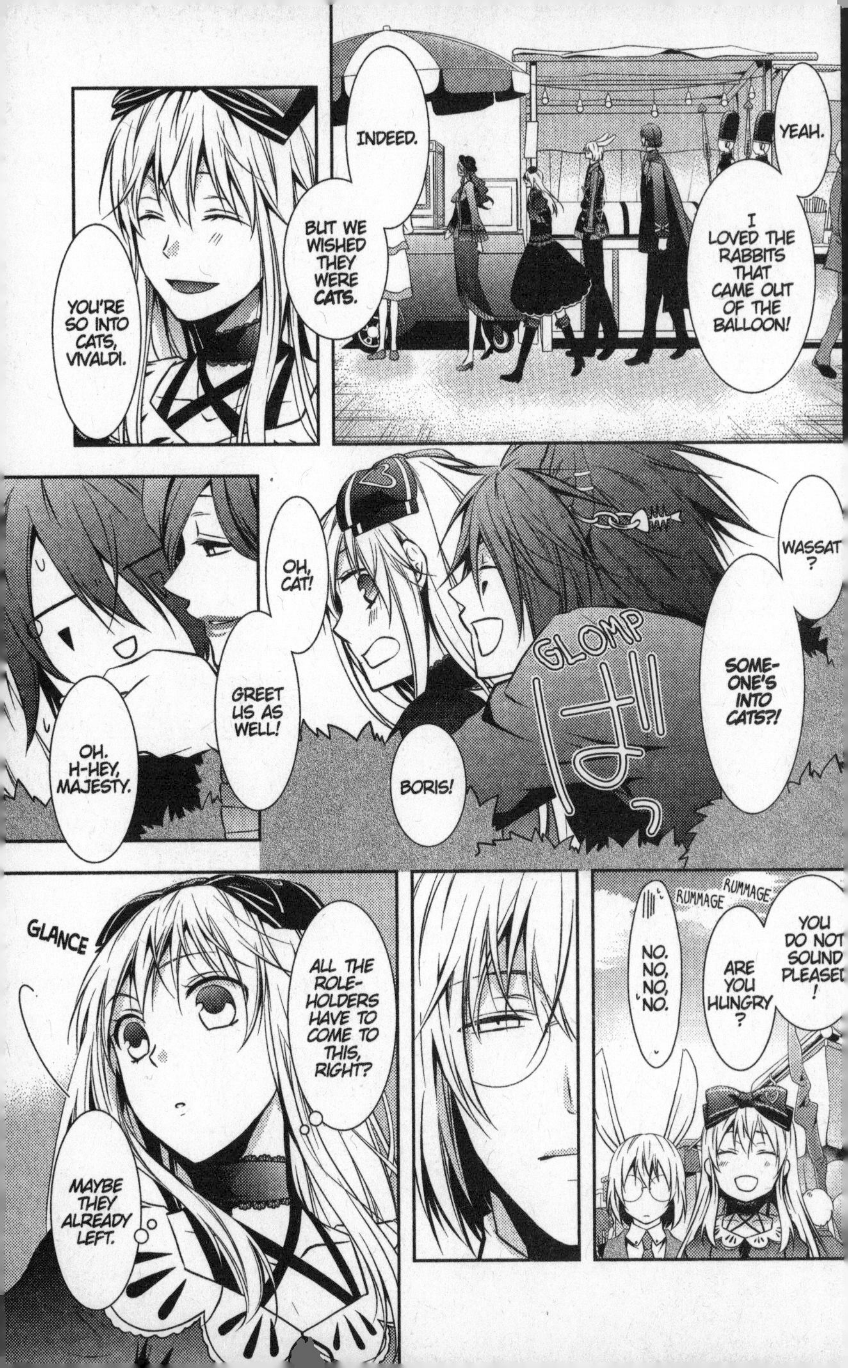
YEAH.
I LOVED THE RABBITS THAT CAME OUT OF THE BALLOON!
INDEED.
BUT WE WISHED THEY WERE CATS.
YOU'RE SO INTO CATS, VIVALDI.
WASSAT?
SOME-ONE'S INTO CATS?!
GLOMP
BORIS!
OH, CAT!
GREET US AS WELL!
OH. H-HEY, MAJESTY.
RUMMAGE RUMMAGE
YOU DO NOT SOUND PLEASED!
ARE YOU HUNGRY?
NO. NO, NO, NO.
GLANCE
ALL THE ROLE-HOLDERS HAVE TO COME TO THIS, RIGHT?
MAYBE THEY ALREADY LEFT.

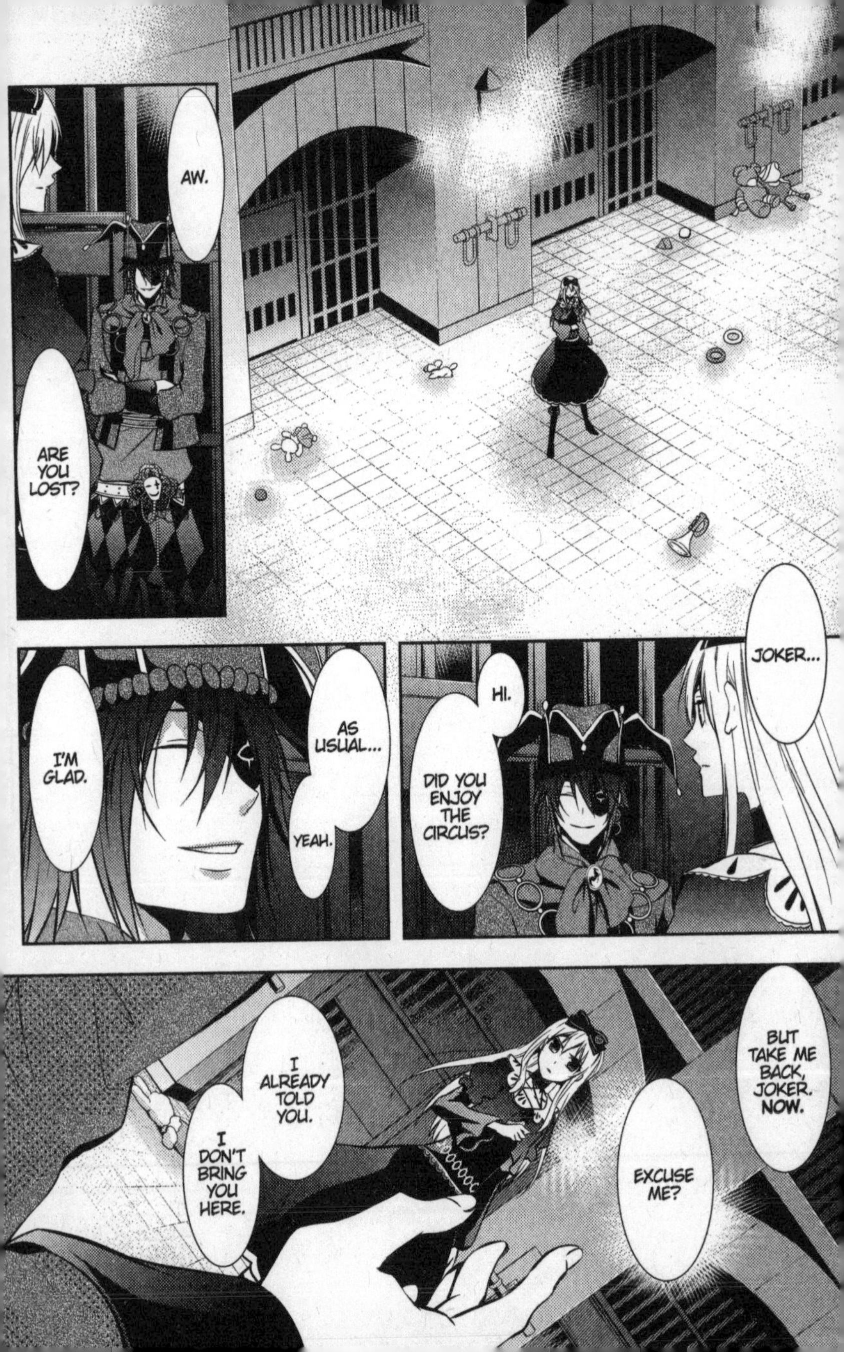
AW.
ARE YOU LOST?
JOKER...
HI.
DID YOU ENJOY THE CIRCUS?
AS USUAL...
YEAH.
I'M GLAD.
BUT TAKE ME BACK, JOKER. NOW.
EXCUSE ME?
I ALREADY TOLD YOU.
I DON'T BRING YOU HERE.

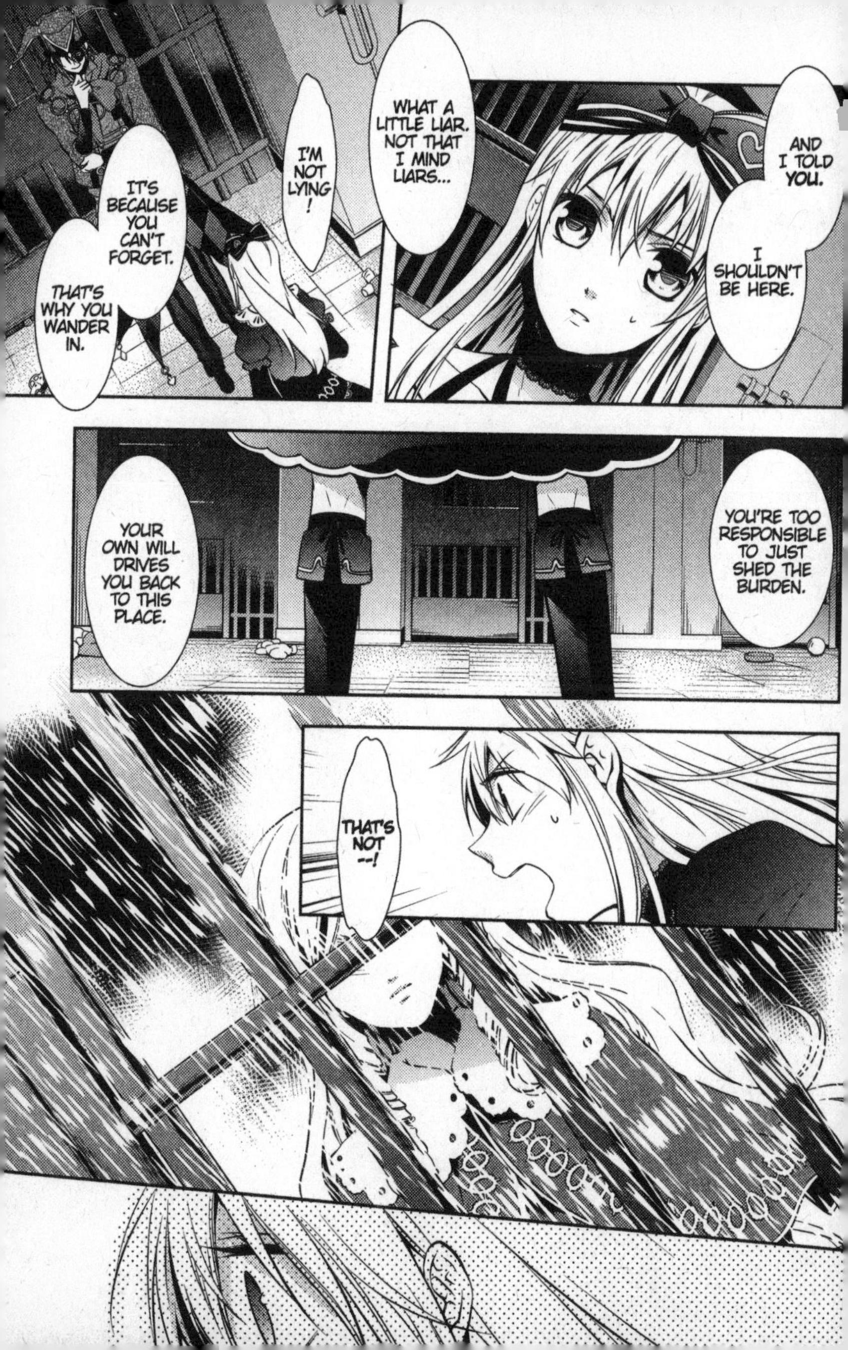
AND I TOLD YOU.
I SHOULDN'T BE HERE.
WHAT A LITTLE LIAR. NOT THAT I MIND LIARS...
I'M NOT LYING!
IT'S BECAUSE YOU CAN'T FORGET.
THAT'S WHY YOU WANDER IN.
YOU'RE TOO RESPONSIBLE TO JUST SHED THE BURDEN.
YOUR OWN WILL DRIVES YOU BACK TO THIS PLACE.
THAT'S NOT --!

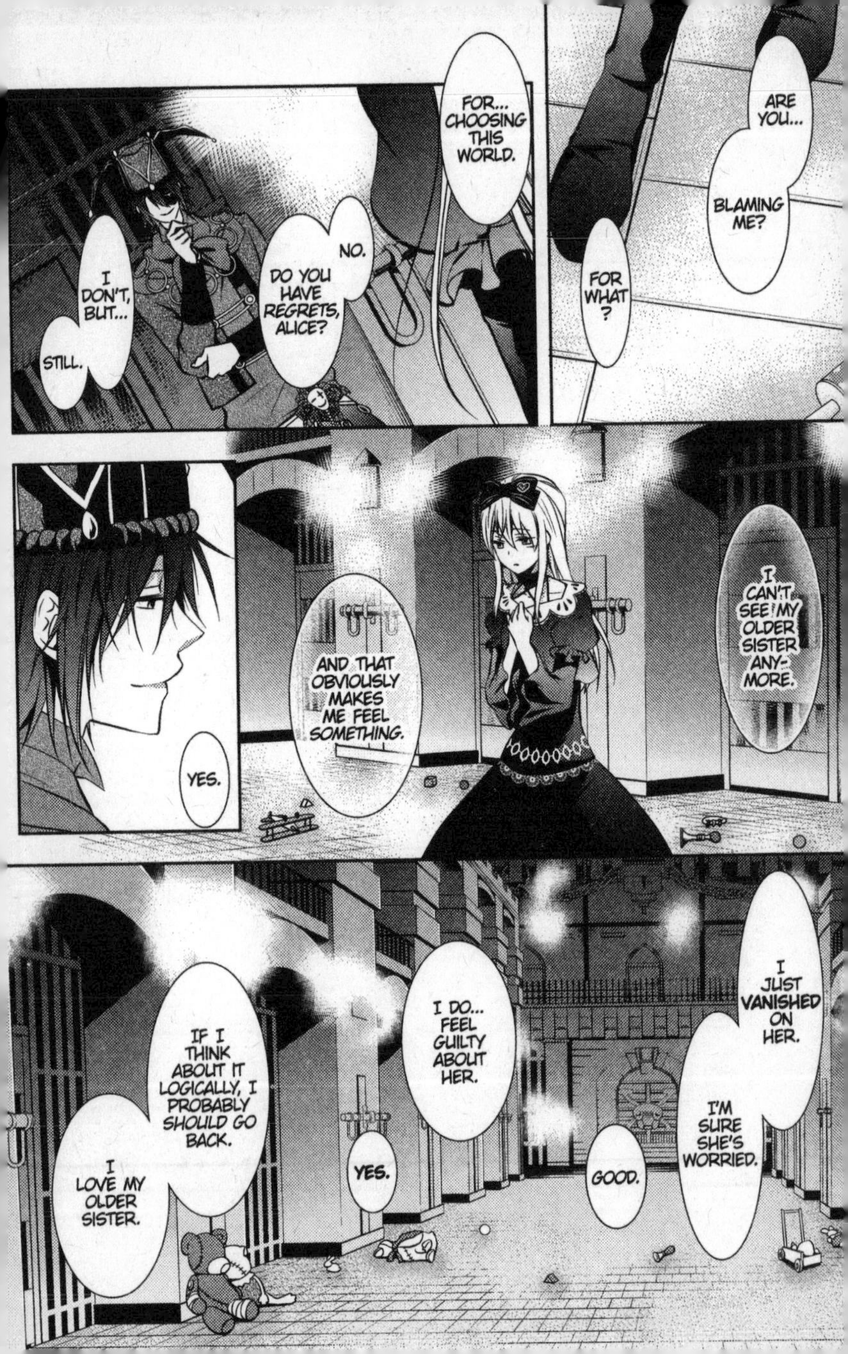
ARE YOU...
BLAMING ME?
FOR WHAT?
FOR... CHOOSING THIS WORLD.
NO.
DO YOU HAVE REGRETS, ALICE?
I DON'T, BUT...
STILL.
I CAN'T SEE MY OLDER SISTER ANY-MORE.
AND THAT OBVIOUSLY MAKES ME FEEL SOMETHING.
YES.
I JUST VANISHED ON HER.
I'M SURE SHE'S WORRIED.
GOOD.
I DO... FEEL GUILTY ABOUT HER.
YES.
IF I THINK ABOUT IT LOGICALLY, I PROBABLY SHOULD GO BACK.
I LOVE MY OLDER SISTER.

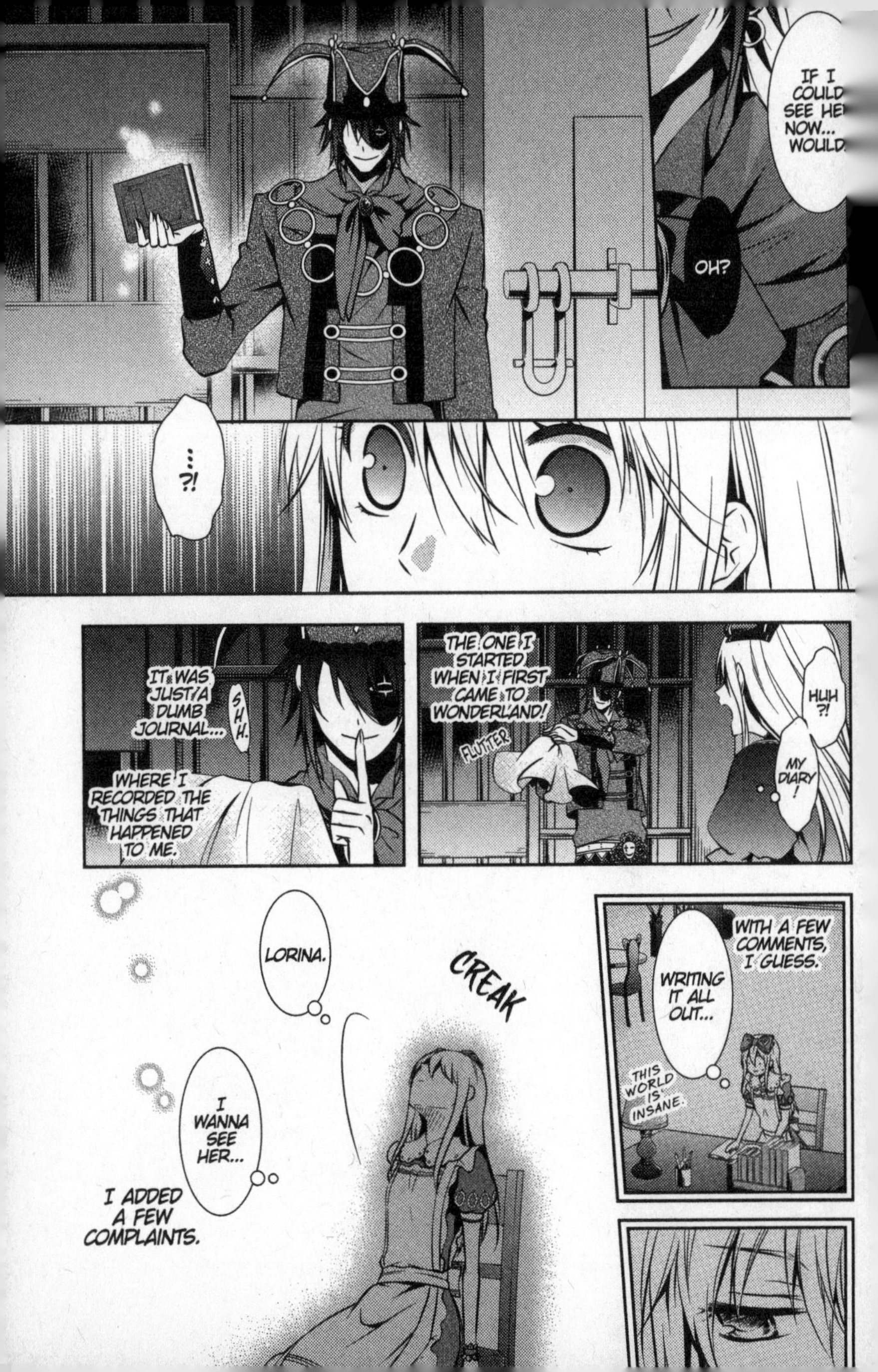
IF I COULD SEE HE NOW... WOULD
OH?
...?!
HUH ?!
MY DIARY!
THE ONE I STARTED WHEN I FIRST CAME TO WONDERLAND!
FLUTTER
SHH.
IT WAS JUST A DUMB JOURNAL...
WHERE I RECORDED THE THINGS THAT HAPPENED TO ME.
WITH A FEW COMMENTS, I GUESS.
WRITING IT ALL OUT...
THIS WORLD IS INSANE.
CREAK
LORINA.
I WANNA SEE HER...
I ADDED A FEW COMPLAINTS.

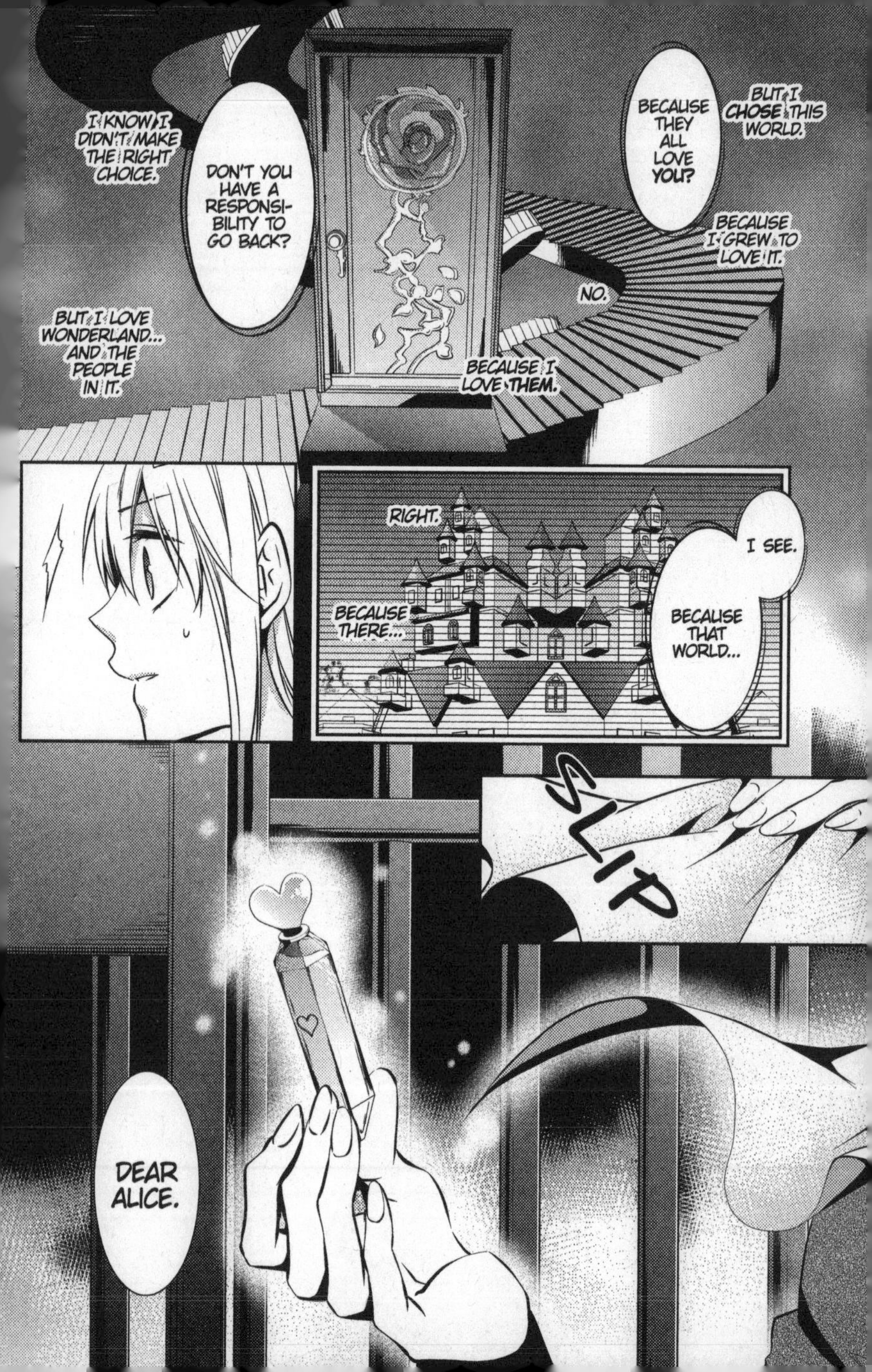
BUT I CHOSE THIS WORLD.
BECAUSE THEY ALL LOVE YOU?
BECAUSE I GREW TO LOVE IT.
NO.
BECAUSE I LOVE THEM.
DON'T YOU HAVE A RESPONSIBILITY TO GO BACK?
I KNOW I DIDN'T MAKE THE RIGHT CHOICE.
BUT I LOVE WONDERLAND... AND THE PEOPLE IN IT.
I SEE.
BECAUSE THAT WORLD...
RIGHT.
BECAUSE THERE...
SLIP
DEAR ALICE.

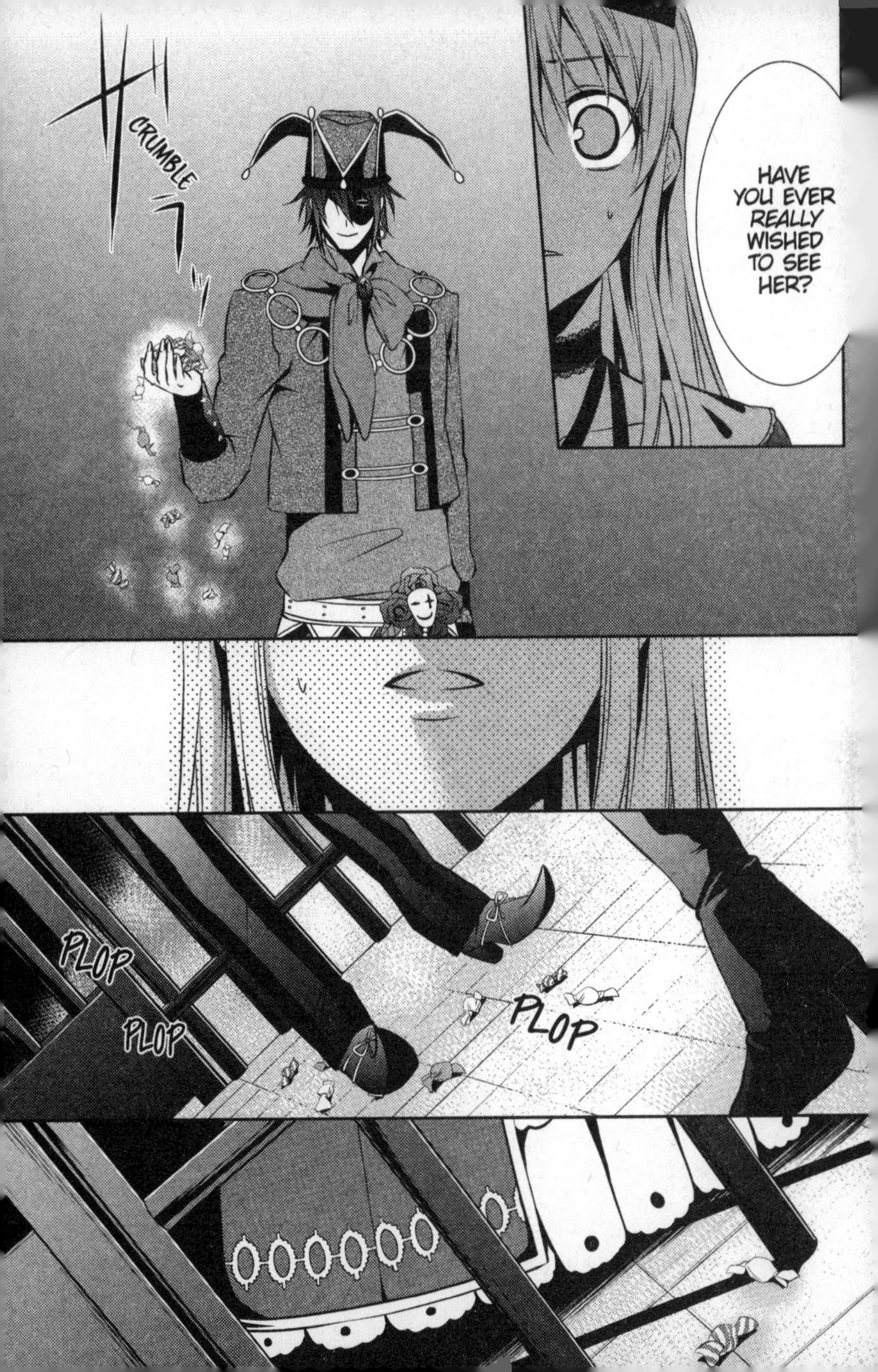
HAVE YOU EVER REALLY WISHED TO SEE HER?
CRUMBLE
PLOP
PLOP
PLOP

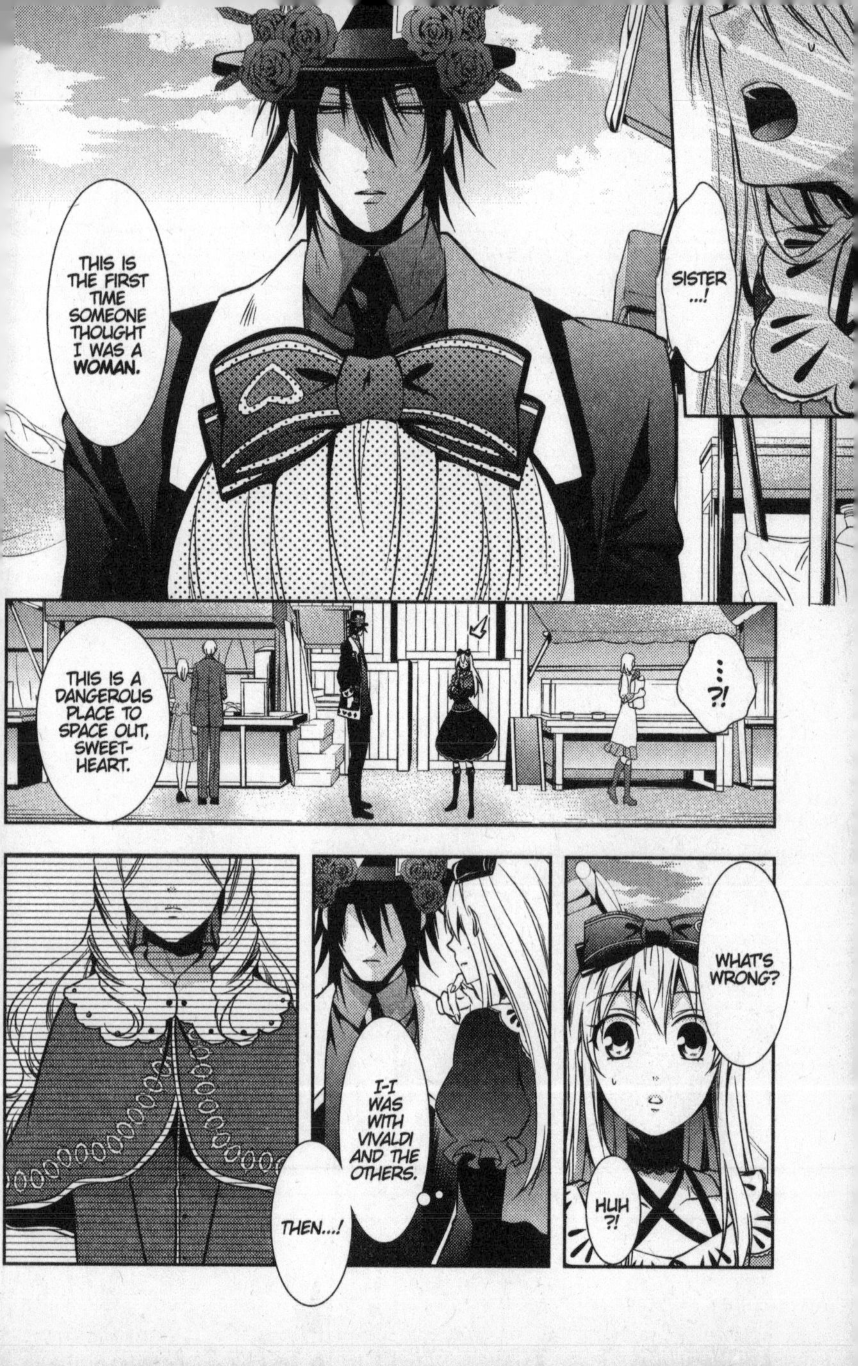
SISTER ...!
THIS IS THE FIRST TIME SOMEONE THOUGHT I WAS A WOMAN.
...?!
THIS IS A DANGEROUS PLACE TO SPACE OUT, SWEET-HEART.
WHAT'S WRONG?
HUH ?!
I-I WAS WITH VIVALDI AND THE OTHERS.
THEN...!

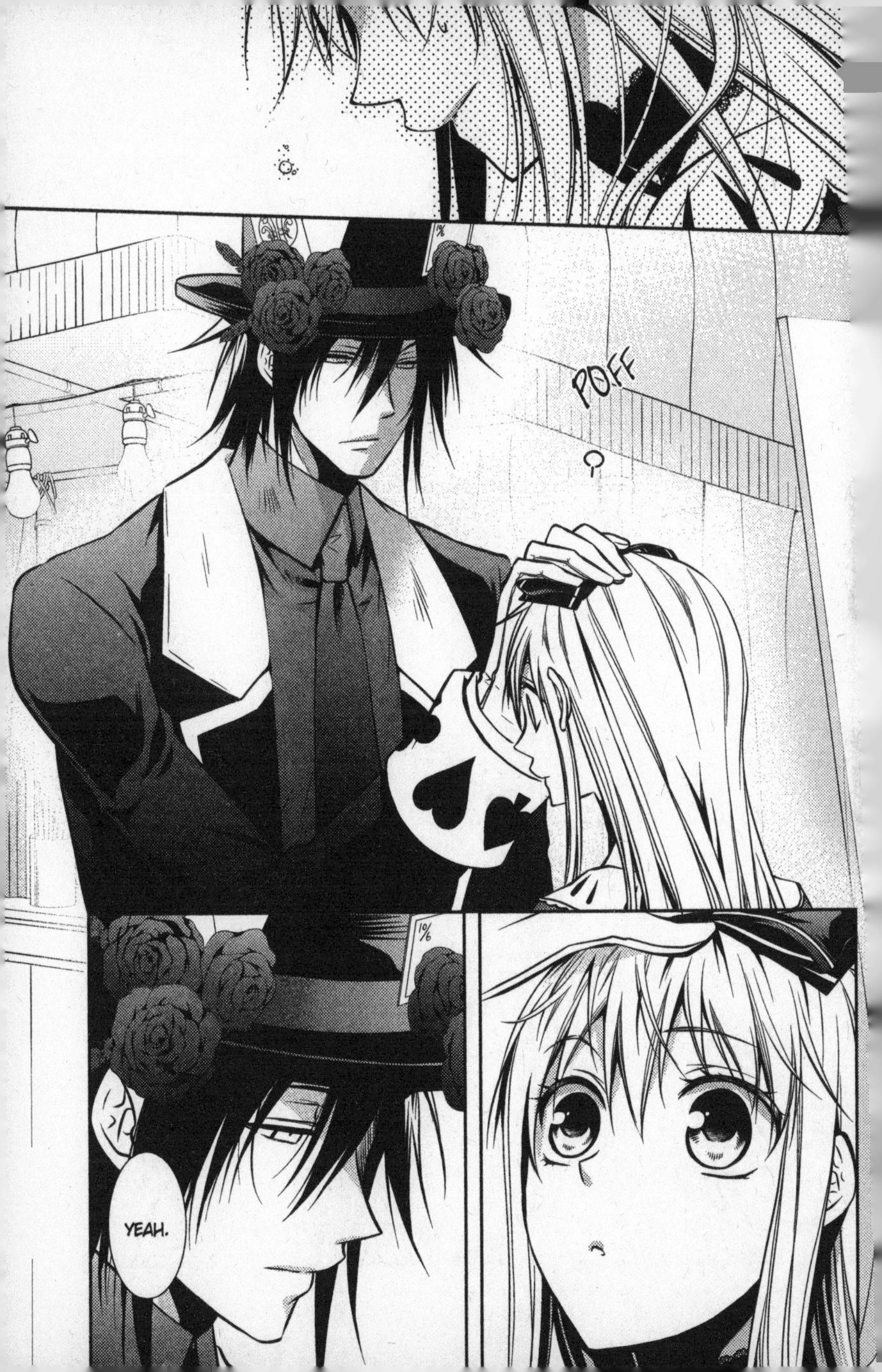
POFF
YEAH.

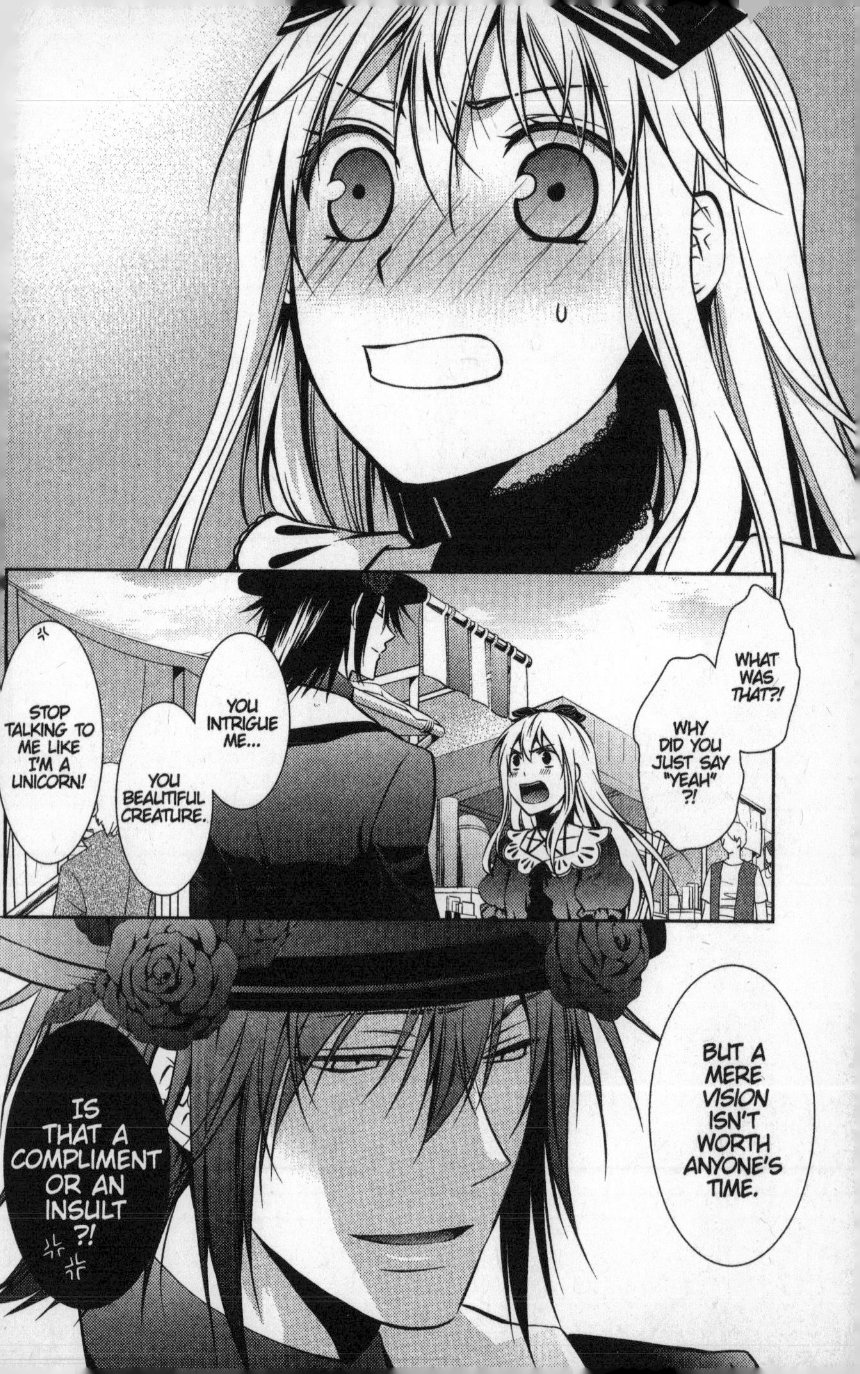
WHAT WAS THAT?!
WHY DID YOU JUST SAY "YEAH"?!
YOU INTRIGUE ME...
YOU BEAUTIFUL CREATURE.
STOP TALKING TO ME LIKE I'M A UNICORN!
BUT A MERE VISION ISN'T WORTH ANYONE'S TIME.
IS THAT A COMPLIMENT OR AN INSULT?!

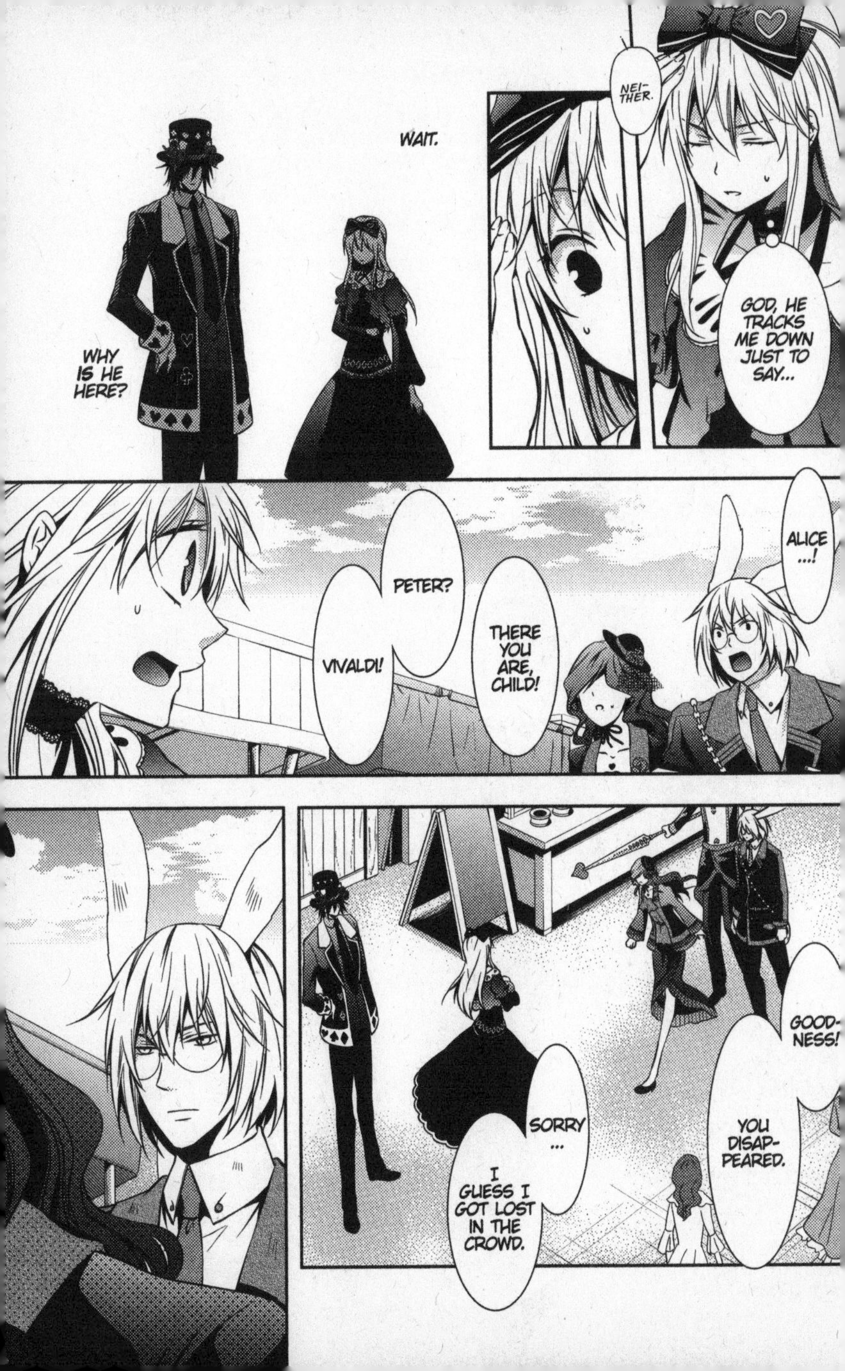
NEI-THER.
GOD, HE TRACKS ME DOWN JUST TO SAY...
WAIT.
WHY IS HE HERE?
ALICE ...!
THERE YOU ARE, CHILD!
PETER?
VIVALDI!
GOOD-NESS!
YOU DISAP-PEARED.
SORRY ...
I GUESS I GOT LOST IN THE CROWD.

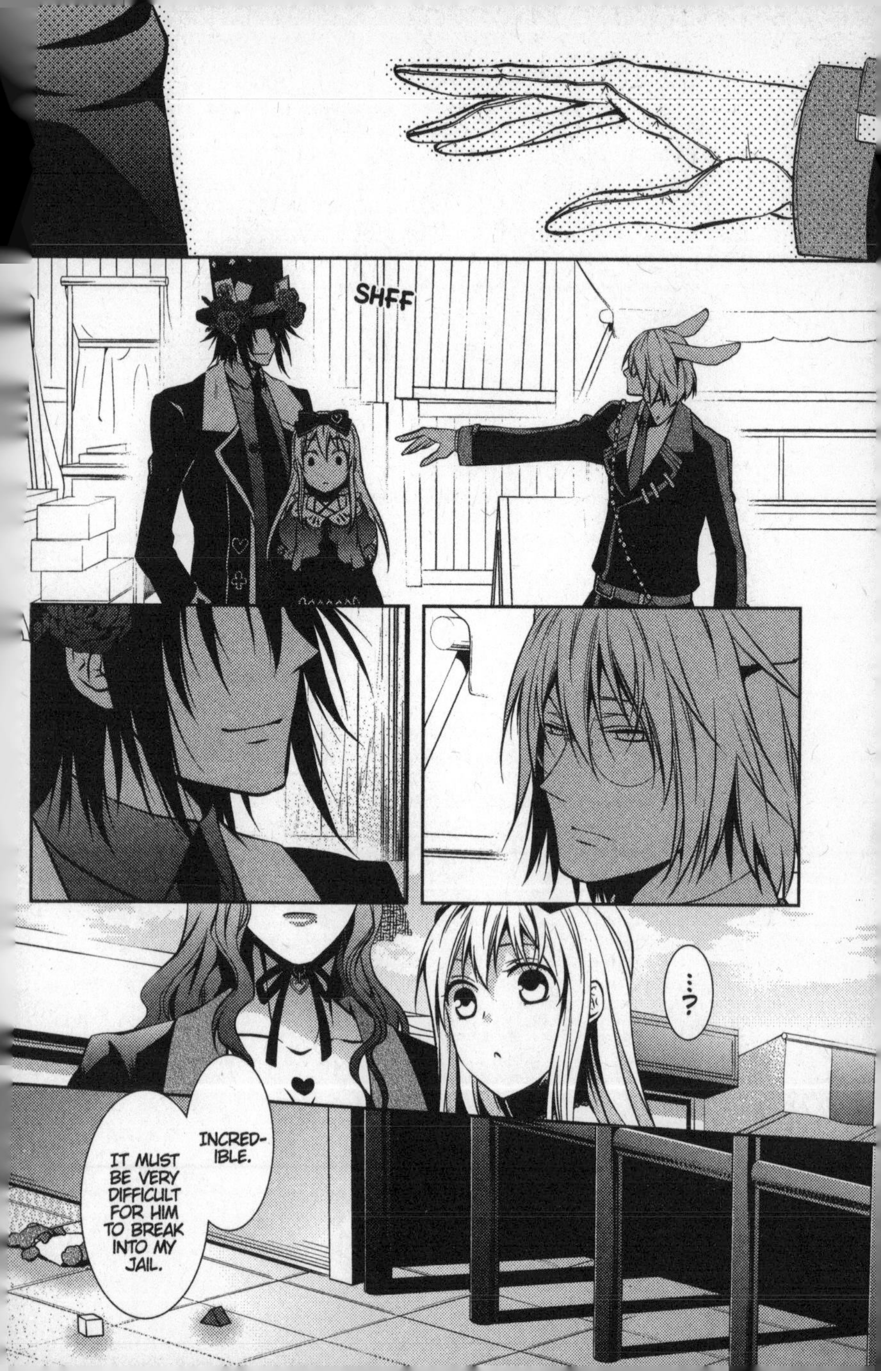
SHFF
っ…
INCRED-IBLE.
IT MUST BE VERY DIFFICULT FOR HIM TO BREAK INTO MY JAIL.

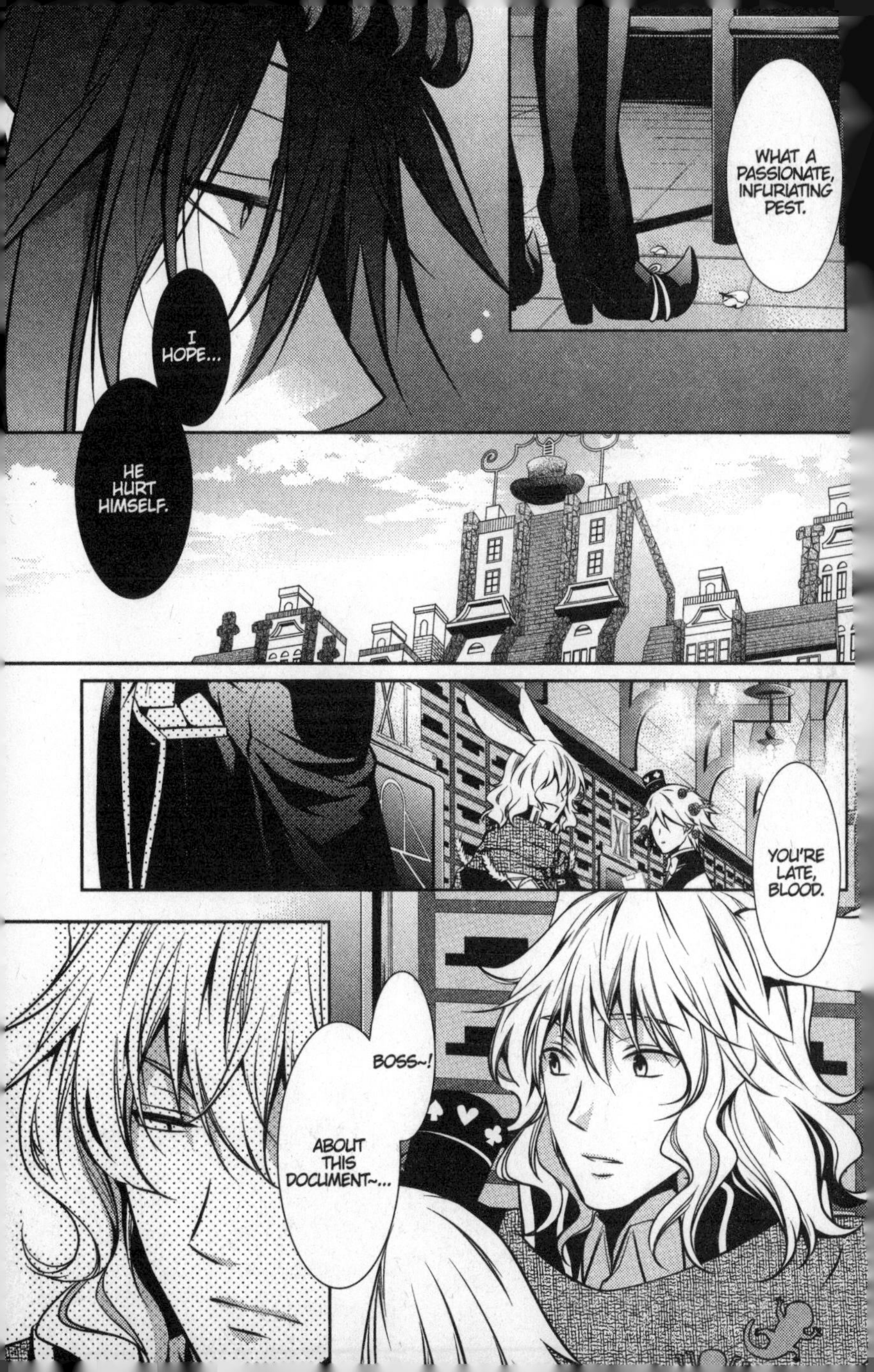
WHAT A PASSIONATE, INFURIATING PEST.
I HOPE...
HE HURT HIMSELF.
YOU'RE LATE, BLOOD.
BOSS~! ABOUT THIS DOCUMENT~...

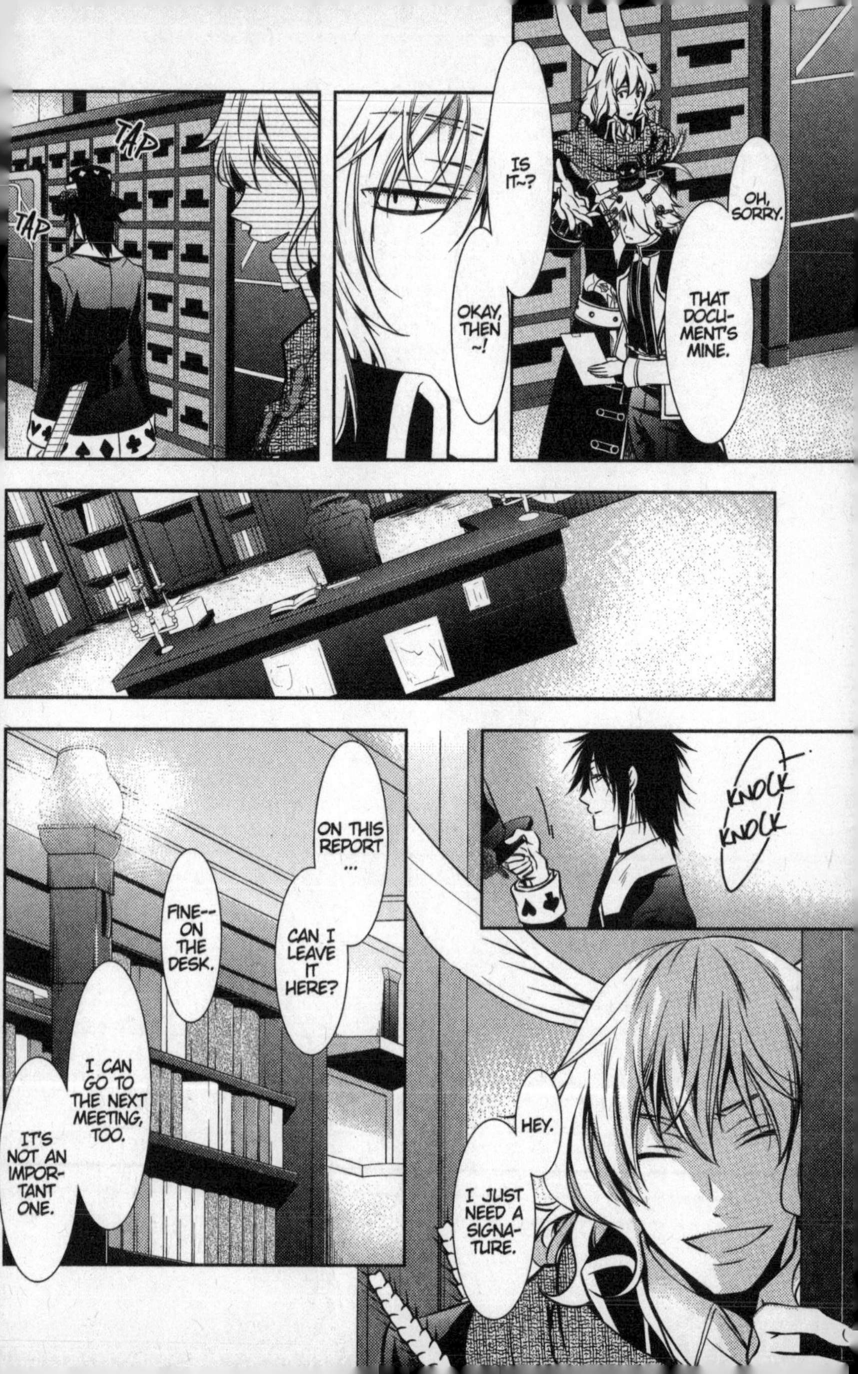
OH, SORRY.
THAT DOCUMENT'S MINE.
IS IT~?
OKAY, THEN ~!
TAP
TAP
KNOCK KNOCK
HEY.
I JUST NEED A SIGNATURE.
ON THIS REPORT ...
CAN I LEAVE IT HERE?
FINE--ON THE DESK.
I CAN GO TO THE NEXT MEETING, TOO.
IT'S NOT AN IMPORTANT ONE.

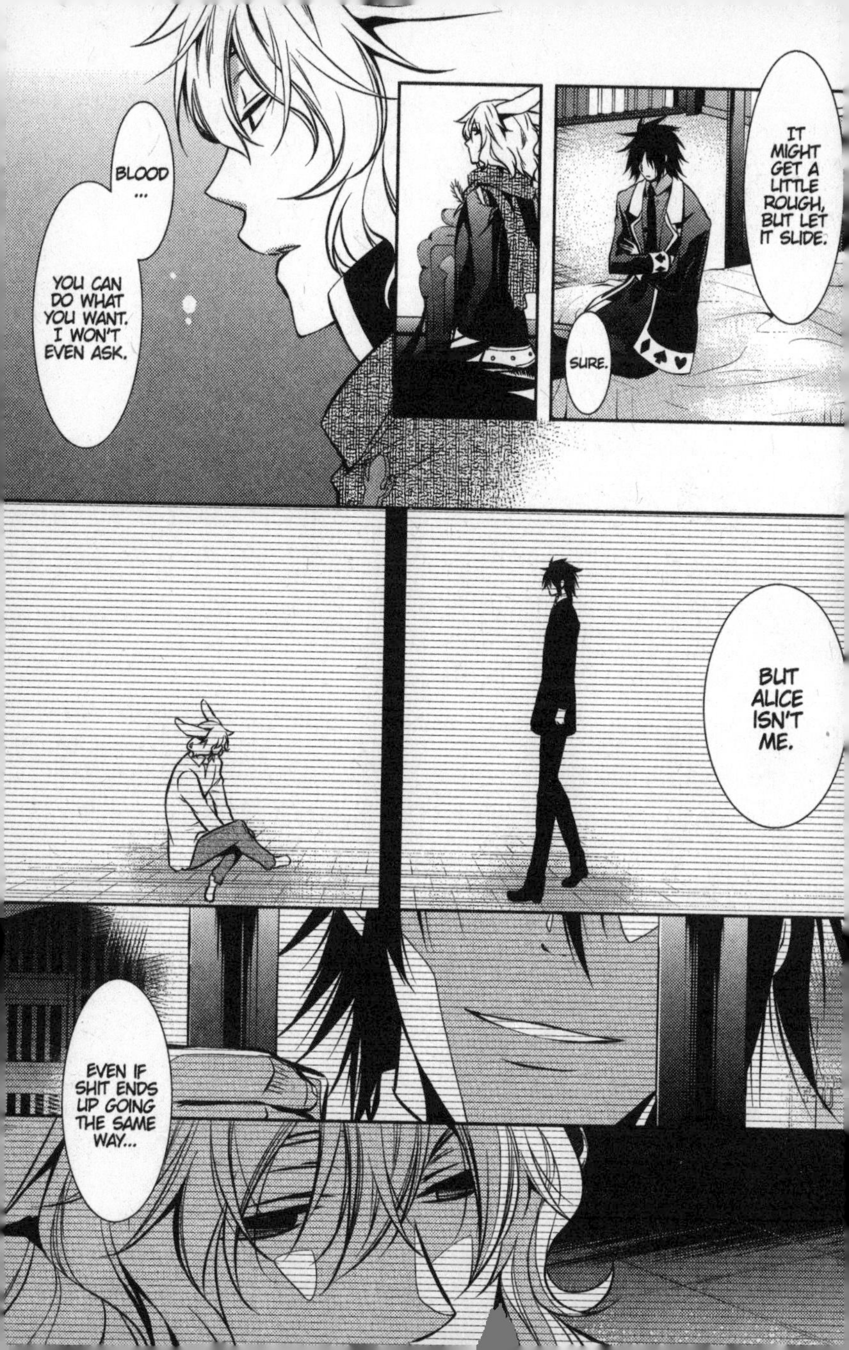
IT MIGHT GET A LITTLE ROUGH, BUT LET IT SLIDE.
SURE.
BLOOD...
YOU CAN DO WHAT YOU WANT. I WON'T EVEN ASK.
BUT ALICE ISN'T ME.
EVEN IF SHIT ENDS UP GOING THE SAME WAY...

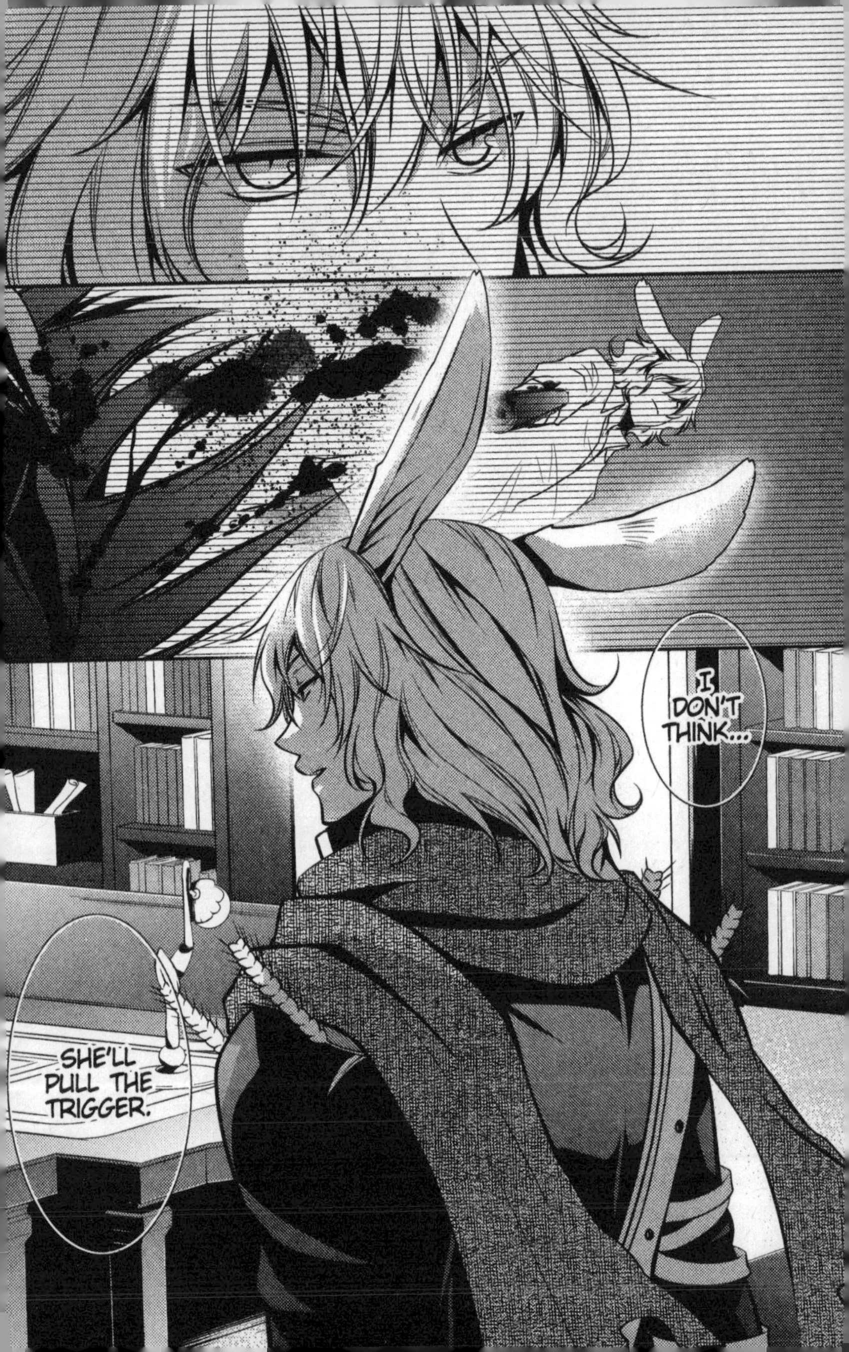

I DON'T THINK...
SHE'LL PULL THE TRIGGER.

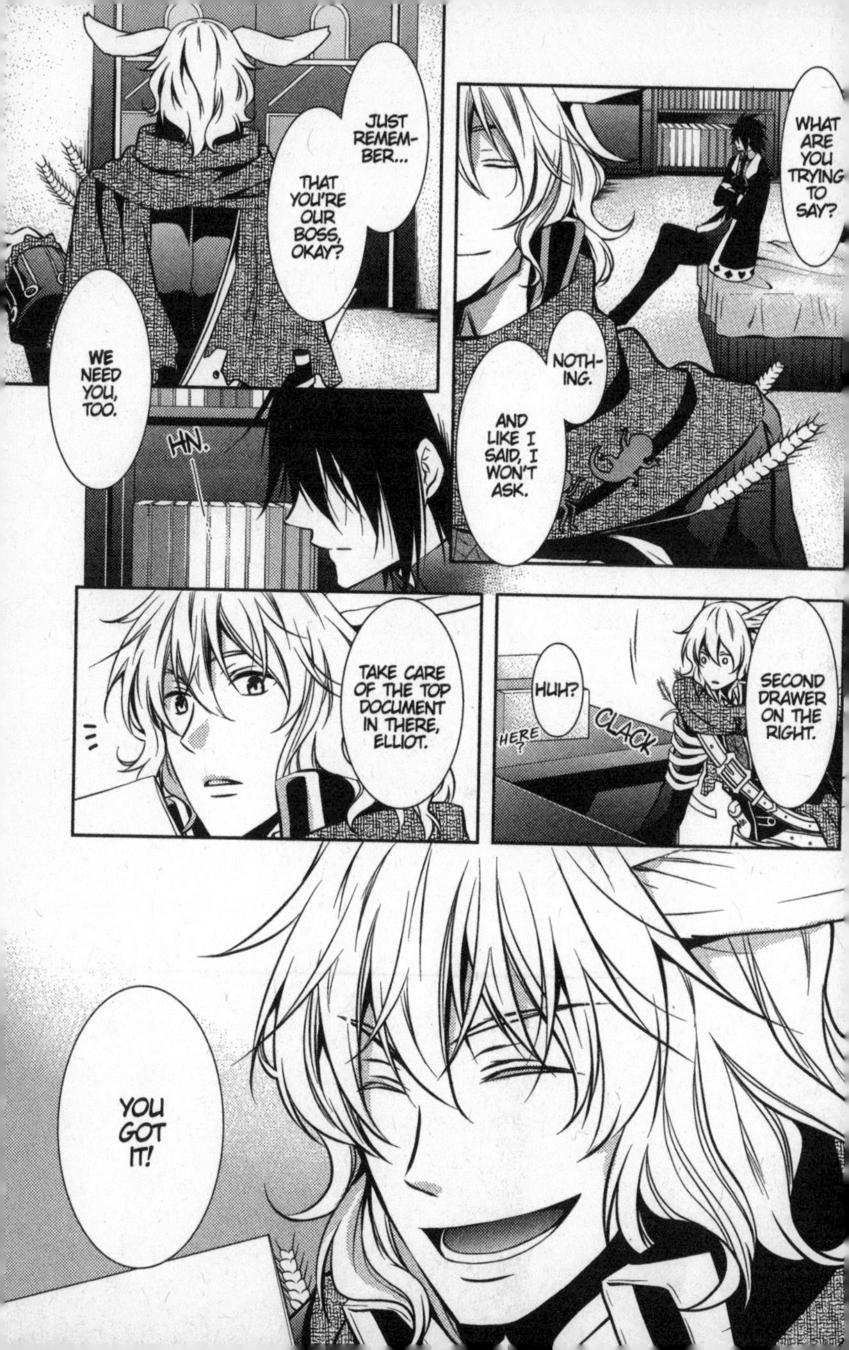
WHAT ARE YOU TRYING TO SAY?
NOTHING.
AND LIKE I SAID, I WON'T ASK.
JUST REMEMBER...
THAT YOU'RE OUR BOSS, OKAY?
WE NEED YOU, TOO.
HN.
SECOND DRAWER ON THE RIGHT.
HUH?
CLACK
HERE?
TAKE CARE OF THE TOP DOCUMENT IN THERE, ELLIOT.
YOU GOT IT!

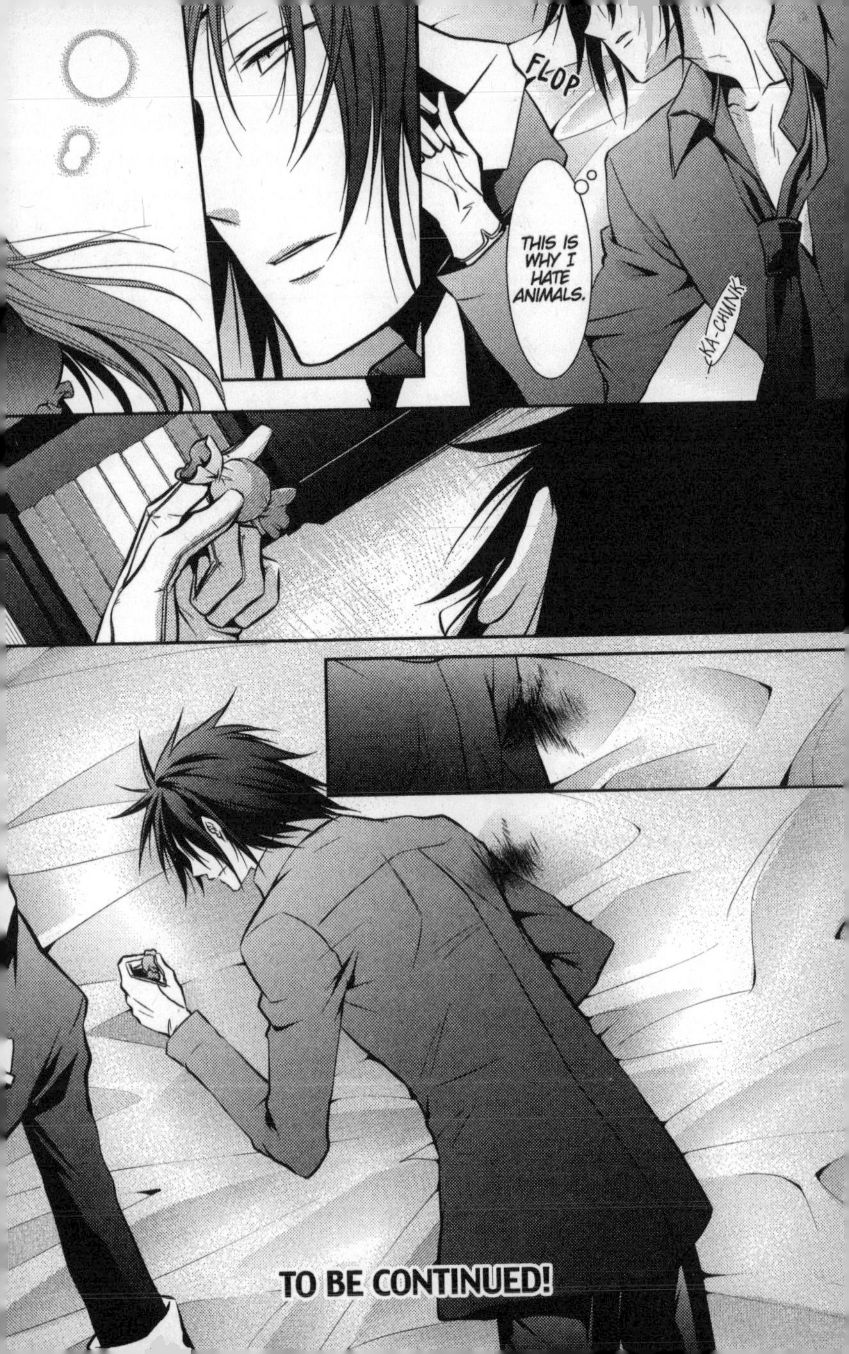
FLOP
THIS IS WHY I HATE ANIMALS.
KA-CHUNK
TO BE CONTINUED!

I FIGURED I'D INTRODUCE **ALICE IN THE COUNTRY OF DIAMONDS** USING "SMALL ALICE" HERE.

DIAMONDS CONTINUES AFTER **ALICE IN THE COUNTRY OF JOKER** ENDS.

THIS TIME, ALICE WAS KICKED OUT DURING THE MOVE.

NONE OF THE PEOPLE IN THE COUNTRY OF DIAMONDS EVEN KNOW HER.

ONLY NIGHT-MARE CAN TALK TO HER EVERY ONCE IN A WHILE.
HIS ROLE IS TO EXPLAIN THE SITUATION AND SEND HER OFF.
BON VOYAGE!
FLAP
FLAP
BAM
BAM
BAM
HM?
KA-CHAK
PACKED
KA-CHUNK
IT'S THE BEGINNING OF A NEW ADVENTURE FOR ALICE.

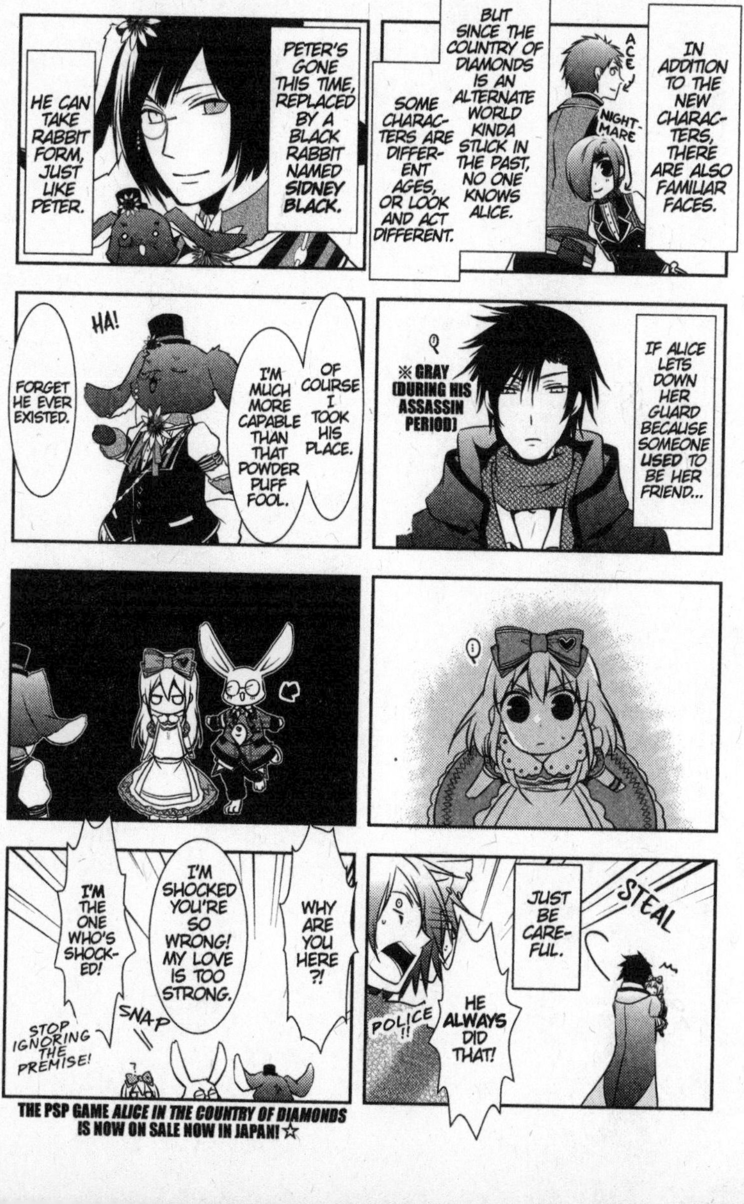
IN ADDITION TO THE NEW CHARACTERS, THERE ARE ALSO FAMILIAR FACES.
ACE
NIGHTMARE
BUT SINCE THE COUNTRY OF DIAMONDS IS AN ALTERNATE WORLD KINDA STUCK IN THE PAST, NO ONE KNOWS ALICE.
SOME CHARACTERS ARE DIFFERENT AGES, OR LOOK AND ACT DIFFERENT.
PETER'S GONE THIS TIME, REPLACED BY A BLACK RABBIT NAMED SIDNEY BLACK.
HE CAN TAKE RABBIT FORM, JUST LIKE PETER.
IF ALICE LETS DOWN HER GUARD BECAUSE SOMEONE USED TO BE HER FRIEND...
※GRAY (DURING HIS ASSASSIN PERIOD)
OF COURSE I TOOK HIS PLACE.
I'M MUCH MORE CAPABLE THAN THAT POWDER PUFF FOOL.
HA!
FORGET HE EVER EXISTED.
STEAL
JUST BE CAREFUL.
HE ALWAYS DID THAT!
POLICE!!
WHY ARE YOU HERE?!
I'M SHOCKED YOU'RE SO WRONG! MY LOVE IS TOO STRONG.
I'M THE ONE WHO'S SHOCKED!
SNAP
STOP IGNORING THE PREMISE!

THE PSP GAME *ALICE IN THE COUNTRY OF DIAMONDS* IS NOW ON SALE NOW IN JAPAN! ☆

COMING SOON

MARCH 2014
Alice in the Country of Clover:
March's Hare

APRIL 2014
Alice in the Country of Clover:
Nightmare

MAY 2014
Alice in the Country of Hearts:
Love Labyrinth of Thorns

JUNE 2014
Alice in the Country of Joker:
Cirus and Liar's Game Vol. 5